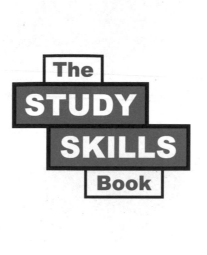

The
**STUDY
SKILLS**
Book

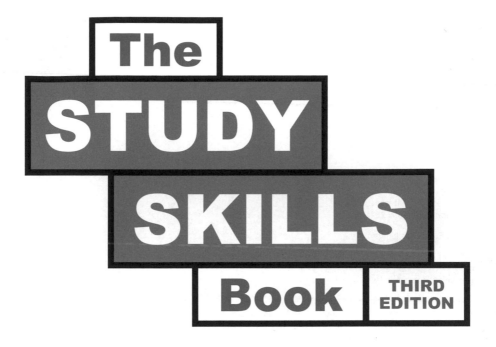

The STUDY SKILLS Book

THIRD EDITION

KATHLEEN McMILLAN and JONATHAN WEYERS

PEARSON

Harlow, England • London • New York • Boston • San Francisco • Toronto • Sydney
Auckland • Singapore • Hong Kong • Tokyo • Seoul • Taipei • New Delhi
Cape Town • São Paulo • Mexico City • Madrid • Amsterdam • Munich • Paris • Milan

Pearson Education Limited
Edinburgh Gate
Harlow
Essex CM20 2JE
England

and Associated Companies throughout the world

Visit us on the World Wide Web at:
www.pearson.com/uk

First published as The Smarter Student 2006
Second edition published as The Smarter Study Skills Companion 2009
Rejacketed edition published 2011
Third edition published 2012

© Pearson Education Limited 2012

ISBN: 978-0-273-77331-3

British Library Cataloguing-in-Publication Data
A catalogue record for this book is available from the British Library

Library of Congress Cataloging-in-Publication Data
McMillan, Kathleen.
   The study skills book / Kathleen McMillan and Jonathan Weyers. -- 3rd ed.
      p. cm.
   Includes bibliographical references and index.
   ISBN 978-0-273-77331-3 (pbk.)
   1. Study skills.   2. Students, Foreign--Great Britain.   3. College student orientation--Great Britain.
I. Weyers, Jonathan D. B.   II. Title.
   LB2395.M4443 2012
   371.30281--dc23
                                                         2012015643

10 9 8 7 6 5 4 3 2 1
16 15 14 13 12

Typeset in 9/12pt Helvetica Neue Roman by 35
Printed by Ashford Colour Press Ltd., Gosport

CONTENTS

IMPROVING YOUR ACADEMIC WRITING

PERFORMING WELL IN COURSE ASSESSMENTS

ABOUT THE AUTHORS

Dr. Kathleen McMillan was formerly Academic Skills Advisor and Senior Lecturer, University of Dundee.

Dr. Jonathan Weyers was formerly Director of Quality Assurance, University of Dundee and is now a freelance author specialising in books on learning and writing in Higher Education.

This book represents a synthesis based on nearly 60 years of combined teaching experience. Between us, we've taught at all levels – including middle school, upper school, further education, undergraduate, postgraduate and within academic staff development. We've supported students in a wide range of topics – from biology to dentistry; architecture to orthopaedic surgery; history to social work, information and communication technology to English as a foreign language.

Over the years, we've presented hundreds of tutorials and lectures and run many workshops and practicals using different techniques including team-teaching alongside colleagues and one-to-one tuition. Above all, we've spoken to countless students, both individually and in focus groups, consulted with fellow academics about core skills that underpin a wide range of disciplines and have observed at close quarters our own children going through the university system. We have read widely and tested many ideas. This book is a distillation of all the best tips and techniques we've come across or have developed ourselves.

We're delighted that you've chosen *The Study Skills Book* and we'd like to think it's because this book promises insight into the university experience and gives you plenty of useful tips to help you settle into the new rhythms of university life and learning.

Whatever your age and experience, learning at university marks an exciting new phase in your life – a time of anticipation and of new challenges. Very quickly you'll be faced with sorting out your life as a student, attending your first lectures, getting logged on to the university computer system, email and e-learning tools. There will be a lot of information to gather, filter and make into some sort of sense. All the while you'll be meeting new people of different ages and outlooks who are in exactly the same position. All in all, it's a stimulating but demanding time. Learning at university builds on one basic notion: that is that students, regardless of age or experience, are good at organising themselves and so will quickly conform to the standards that the university community expects. As experienced academics, we know that this is not achieved quite as quickly as everyone – staff, students (and their families) – might wish, partly because there is so much to learn how to do.

This book is about helping new (and not so new) students gain and develop the skills, attributes and knowledge that universities require of them. Of course, you will already have some of these skills – from school, from college, from employment and even just from life in general – but this book takes you further. In 'Understanding what university involves' and 'Managing yourself', we begin with some tips and insights about what university involves and then take you through the very first days when you're coming to terms with your new environment and deciding how you're going to organise your life.

Then we move into the kinds of things that you'll need to be able to do as your course gets underway. This all comes into 'Developing your learning skills' – useful tips on practical things such as taking notes in lectures, using the library, engaging with e-learning and thinking critically. As your course gathers pace, you'll find that you're having to tackle all sorts of writing assignments and in 'Improving your academic writing' you'll find valuable suggestions to guide you from planning to submission, with help along the way on topics such as punctuation, spelling and grammar, so that your writing is well developed and meets academic requirements.

As you work your way through your first semester, you'll find that you encounter all sorts of different kinds of assessment – in lab practicals, in debates, in tests and other written submissions. 'Performing well in course assessments' gives you some insights as to how these assessments work and how you can gain the best marks possible. Then we come to Section 6: 'Succeeding in exams', which gives you tried-and-tested tips from revision technique to coping with exam nerves. Finally, in 'Planning for the future' we can peep over the edge of the university world and look to the future by considering career planning and kick-starting your career.

We had many kinds of students in mind when we decided to write this text and we hope that it will meet your personal needs – regardless of your experience and background. We've tried to remain faithful to the idea that this book is one that you can dip into in time of need. We've tried to evolve a layout that makes information easy to find.

We wish you the best of times at university and hope that the tips we have collated will help you succeed in all you do, academically and socially, tackle assignments with confidence and produce better results. Despite all the advice given here, we acknowledge that there is always an element of luck in any good performance, and we hope you get this when and if required. We'd be delighted to hear your opinion of the book, any suggestions you have for additions and improvements, and especially if you feel that it has made a positive difference to the way you study and approach university life.

Kathleen McMillan and Jonathan Weyers

ACKNOWLEDGEMENTS

We would like to offer sincere thanks to the many people who have influenced us and contributed in one way or another to the production of this book.

Countless students over the years have helped us to test our ideas. As we produced drafts of chapters, the following students made specific comments either as individuals or as members of focus groups: Scott Allardice, Mariam Azhar, Eleanor Dempsey, Sandie Ferrens, Daniel Harper, Wai Lee, Kara McAuley, Katherine McBay, Leanne Murphy and David Wallace. Our PREP resit summer school students also provided valuable feedback on the revision and exam tips.

We are grateful to the following University of Dundee colleagues and others who collaborated directly or indirectly: Margaret Adamson, Michael Allardice, John Berridge, Richard Campbell, Kate Christie, Margaret Forrest, Anne-Marie Greenhill, Jane Illés, Andy Jackson, Allan Jones, Neale Laker, Kirsty Millar, Eric Monaghan, Dave Murie, Julie Naismith, Fiona O'Donnell, Richard Parsons, Neil Paterson, Jane Prior, Mhairi Robb, Anne Scott, Dorothy Smith, Eric Smith, Gordon Spark, Karen Stulka, David Walker, Amanda Whitehead, Will Whitfield, David Wishart, Hilary-Kay Young and the late Neil Glen. We are indebted to the support and interest of the Royal Literary Fund and particularly the RLF Writing Fellows in our university, distinguished authors in their own right, who have given wise words of counsel – Bill Kirton, Brian Callison, Jonathan Falla and Gordon Meade. Also, we acknowledge those at other universities who have helped frame our thoughts, especially our good friends Rob Reed, Nicki Hedge and Esther Daborn, as well as the membership of the Scottish Effective Learning Advisors who work so energetically to help students to develop the key skills that are addressed in this book.

We owe a special debt to the senior colleagues who encouraged various projects that contributed to this book, and who allowed us the freedom to pursue this avenue of scholarship, especially Robin Adamson, Chris Carter, Alan Davidson, Ian Francis, Rod Herbert, Eric Monaghan and David Swinfen.

At Pearson Education, we have had excellent support and advice, especially from Steve Temblett, Simon Lake, Rob Cottee, Lauren Hayward and Alex Seabrook.

Finally, we would like to say thanks to our long-suffering but nevertheless enthusiastic families: Derek, Keith, Fiona and Tom; and Mary, Paul and James, all of whom helped in various capacities.

Publisher's acknowledgements

We are grateful to the following for permission to reproduce copyright material:

Figure 42.1 adapted from *The Chambers Dictionary*, Chambers Harrap Publishers (2003); Figure 42.3 adapted from *The Penguin A–Z Thesaurus*, Penguin Books (Fergusson, R. and Manser, M. 2001).

In some instances we have been unable to trace the owners of copyright material, and we would appreciate any information that would enable us to do so.

1

HOW TO USE THIS BOOK

The Study Skills Book is divided into 71 chapters, each providing you with tips for a specific set of skills. These are arranged in seven parts, covering student life from choices made at entry, through to final exams and job-seeking. The aim is to provide bite-sized discussions of each topic that allow you to find and digest relevant material as easily as possible.

At the start of each chapter there is a brief introduction to the topics covered, then the core material, divided into appropriate sections. Additional tips, definitions, examples and illustrations are provided in three different types of tip boxes, as shown on page 2. Some of these points are repeated in different chapters where this is justified on grounds of relevance, bearing in mind that the book is likely to be consulted on a chapter-by-chapter basis.

The core material in each chapter is as concise and straightforward as possible. It is laid out in numbered lists and bullet points wherever appropriate. Figures and tables are used to provide examples and to delve into 'deeper' or more detailed issues separately from the main text. Blank versions of some tables are included in the Appendix, in case you may wish to use these. Copyright on these forms is waived, so you can copy them for personal use as required.

Many cross references to other chapters (Ch) have been included to avoid duplication of material and thereby save space. At the end of each chapter there is a set of practical tips that supplements the advice presented within the text. The text references within chapters are collated on pages 449–50.

You should treat all these elements as items on a menu from which you can select suitable ideas and approaches. Our advice is to adopt those you feel will fit with your needs and personality, but at the same time we would encourage you to experiment. If you are already using some of the tips successfully, take confidence from the fact that you are probably doing the right thing. If ideas are new, please keep an open mind. Confronted with lack of success, many students simply try harder with a set of failed techniques, when a complete overhaul of their approach to learning may be required.

Practical tips relating to the specific chapters are given after the core material. These tips synthesise the content of the chapter and present the opportunity to adjust your approach or behaviour so that you do truly move forward in developing that particular skill area.

Some of the tips and ideas that you will find in *The Study Skills Book* are integrated, albeit in slightly different formats, into *The Smarter Student Planner* (see the references section for further details) which has been designed to help you to develop the key skills of problem-solving, action planning, reflection and lateral thinking by providing an easy to follow monthly planner along with week-at-a-glance space for all your appointments and assignments. It includes additional weekly and monthly tips that relate to the rhythms of the university year and supports your learning with a number of copyright-free templates for exam revision. The planner also provides information on grammar, spelling and punctuation as well as notes on basic maths and numeracy. These all provide quick access to reassuring information that you may need as you complete assessed work.

Tip boxes and practical tips

The boxes are of three types:

Smart tip boxes emphasise key advice to ensure you adopt a successful approach.

Information boxes provide additional information, such as useful definitions or examples.

Query boxes raise questions for you to consider about your personal approach to the topic.

At the end of each chapter, there's also a **Practical tips** section with additional tips. You should regard this as a menu from which to select the ideas that appeal to you and your learning personality.

2

PREPARING FOR UNIVERSITY
What you and your family need to consider

If you want to get off to a flying start at university, there are several aspects of student life that you should think about beforehand. This chapter prompts you to reflect on possible changes in your study methods, financial situation, accommodation and personal life.

Going to university is a life-changing event. It will be an experience that is exhilarating and mind-expanding, but perhaps a little daunting at first. In this book, we aim to peel away some of the myths and mysteries of academic study and help you to make the most of your university years.

Self-orientation and decision-making are themes of this chapter. The aim is to ensure that your start is as positive as possible. This reflective process is one you may wish to return to from time to time as you progress through university, both to assess your progress and reset your targets (see also **Ch 7**). The checklists presented here are designed to focus your thoughts, rather than feed you answers; your responses will depend on your own situation and personality. Like much at university, success in turning these thoughts into action will depend on *you* rather than anyone else.

GOAL SETTING AT UNIVERSITY

Your goals at university may vary according to whether you are planning your next move after school or college or whether you are returning to study after doing other things. For both types of student, a good question to ask yourself is: 'Where do I want to be in five years' time and then in ten years' time?'

To help you answer these questions, do the 'goal-setting exercise' in the Query Box on page 4. You may not have answers to all the questions right now, but they will help you to start thinking about deeper issues in your life and how you might tackle the challenges of university.

Whether you have just left school or college or are returning to study after time away from a learning environment, the challenges of university life remain broadly similar. It's your responses to them that will possibly be quite different.

ACADEMIC ASPECTS

A large portion of this book deals with the skills required for study at university level, many of which will be quite different from those required at school or college. Before embarking on your course, you may benefit from carrying out a mental 'audit' of your current abilities to allow you to focus on areas where you can gain maximum benefit from improvement.

You might start this process by considering the questions below. If you find the final question rather open-ended, a scan through the list of chapters in this book (pages v–vii) will provide a sense of the range of skills you will be expected to have mastered by the time you graduate. Also **Ch 6** provides further information on this topic.

There is much you can do personally to improve your academic skills levels:

- sign up for appropriate skills-related courses and workshops (for example, those for IT skills, effective writing);
- read textbooks, including this one, that provide relevant guidance and advice;
- search for web-based resources that fit your needs;
- seek help from tutors and support staff – they will provide an impartial, confidential and free service;
- absorb and act upon the feedback you receive on your assessed work.

FINANCIAL MATTERS

For many people, the decision to enter university has important financial implications. No matter what your personal circumstances, it is probably helpful to work out, in broad terms, how much your university education will cost. Figure 2.1 gives some broad categories of expenditure for a typical student and shows what proportion of the total costs each is estimated to take up, and Table 2.1 provides a listing of potential costs to take into account, some of which may be unexpected. The questions on page 7 will also help you define your responses to the financial challenges of university life. **Ch 9** covers other issues that will help you to create a working budget to manage your finances.

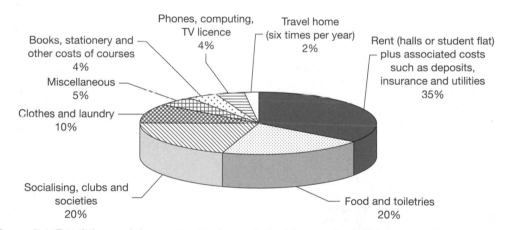

Figure 2.1 Breakdown of the costs of being a student (per annum). These proportions are approximate and assume that the student is living in self-catering accommodation. Depending on location, the total costs may amount to £6250–10000 (2011–12 figures, *excluding* fees) and in some cities the proportional cost of accommodation may be greater. A student living at home might have reduced accommodation costs, but possibly higher travel spending. Mature students may have a different pattern of spending related to pre-existing responsibilities.

Questions to ask yourself about financing your university studies

■ Have I got a good idea of what my university education will cost me?

■ How much will my partner or family be helping me?

■ How much debt am I prepared to take on?

■ How will I control my expenditure?

■ Will I need to take on part-time work to finance myself?

■ Will I need to get a summer job to help finance myself?

■ How will I balance the time and energy needed to work with the time and energy required for study, especially close to exams?

Table 2.1 Expected and unexpected costs of being at university. This list is not exhaustive, but is designed to help you anticipate your main categories of expenditure (see also Figure 2.1). Table Z.1 (page 446) is a spreadsheet to help you manage your budget as a student (see also **Ch 9**).

Category of expenditure	Examples	Comments
Fees	● Tuition fees	These vary according to where you come from and where you are studying (see text)
Accommodation costs	● Hall fees ● Rent/mortgage ● Insurance ● Utilities (gas, electricity, phone)	At the present time, students do not have to pay council tax. Insurance and utility costs are inclusive in some types of accommodation
Living and social costs	● Food ● Drink ● Entertainment ● Clubs and societies	Even if living in catered accommodation, you will incur additional food costs, e.g. at lunchtime or in the evening. Entertainment costs will depend on what sort of 'social animal' you intend to be
Travel costs	● Fares or season tickets ● Car maintenance and fuel ● Parking ● Tolls ● Visits home	These are greatly dependent on the distance between your accommodation and the campus site(s) you need to visit. Student discounts can apply to some forms of transport
Study costs	● Books, stationery ● Equipment ● Lab deposits ● Field trips ● Computing ● Photocopying and printing	Equipment costs, lab deposits and costs of field trips will only apply in certain subjects
Personal costs	● Mobile phone ● Laundry ● Toiletries ● Haircuts ● Clothing ● Presents	These are dependent on lifestyle and how fashion conscious you may be
Other	● Childminding/babysitting ● Holidays ● TV licence	A TV licence is required for all persons in shared accommodation unless it is a group let

The university fee system is complex because the fee and loan amounts and terminologies depend on your nationality and where in the UK you are studying. Precise amounts of fees and loan arrangements may vary year on year. Consult the Universities UK website (**www.universitiesuk.ac.uk/UKHESector/Pages/StudentFinance.aspx**) for up-to-date and detailed information. UK students with low household income may have part or all of their fees paid for them. Visit **www.direct.gov.uk** for further information on Higher Education student finance. Links are provided for relevant agencies in Northern Ireland, Scotland and Wales.

Many institutions have advisory staff who offer advice and information on money matters. Often there is a student hardship fund, which can be used in cases of extreme financial difficulty. Note that, as a student, you may be entitled to preferential treatment, such as exemptions from payment of taxes such as council tax, cheap travel and concession pricing in stores and entertainment venues.

ACCOMMODATION CHOICES

Student accommodation is a real concern – you will need to live somewhere that is relatively comfortable, warm and secure. To help focus your thoughts on the choices available, Table 2.2 summarises the pros and cons of different types of accommodation. The main options available to you are:

- **Living away from home.** This can be a big step for some, but most students settle in within a few weeks. You can live in university accommodation, or rent within the private sector. Accommodation in university halls is a safe option and may be guaranteed for first-year students unless they enter through UCAS 'clearing'. While the quality of privately rented rooms is more variable, some universities will have inspected and graded such accommodation. For rented accommodation, you will have to sign a lease or contract for a fixed period. You may have to pay a deposit, for example, the equivalent of one month's rent, which will be refundable on departure. Any charges for damages would be deducted from this deposit.

Legal aspects of accommodation ✔

Different legislation governs furnished and unfurnished accommodation. You can gain advice on this and other matters relating to renting property from Citizens' Advice Bureaux and also from student services in your institution.

- **Living in the family home.** This provides a familiar environment, but both the student and the family members should recognise that it involves changes for the whole family, whether you are living in the parental home or in your own home with a partner and possibly children.

Whatever your accommodation, you will need time, space and peace to study. Ideally, this zone should be for your sole use, with good facilities, such as a network connection and storage for your books and files.

Whether you live at home or not, going to university often involves new or altered relationships. The questions in the Query Box on page 9 will help you reflect on the adjustments you and your friends and family may need to make.

Table 2.2 Factors to consider when selecting accommodation for university

	Living in university accommodation (student halls and flats)	Living in rented accommodation (private sector)	Living at home with your family
Potential advantages and benefits	• Costs reasonable • Facilities clean, warm and safe • Ready-made social network • Halls may have a good social calendar • Meals provided (at a cost) • Rent inclusive of some services* • Facilities like kitchen and laundry on hand • Support of hall warden(s) • Good complaints procedures	• Wide range of choice • More privacy • Less disturbance and noise (but not always) • Freedom to select those you live with • Your choice of food and meal times • Fewer restrictions	• Familiar environment • Support of family members • Potentially cheaper option • Easy to keep up existing social contacts • Home cooking • Help with services* and laundry • No contracts and no deposits
Potential disadvantages and problems	• Facilities possibly basic • Lengthy contract period • Can be noisy and lacking in privacy • No or little choice of neighbours or flatmates • You might not like the food • Restricted opening/curfews • Financial penalties for damage caused by others • You may have to share a room • Less easy to escape from campus confines	• Can be a costly option • Need to pay a refundable deposit • Additional costs of services* • Potential to be isolated and lonely • Conditions and furnishing may not be ideal • May need to sign up for a lengthy period • Shopping, cooking and cleaning required • Extra travel costs and loss of time commuting	• May be difficult to focus on studies • IT connections may be required • Travel costs and loss of time commuting • Lack of university-based social life • Your desire for personal freedom may conflict with the wishes and lifestyle of your family • Lack of academic and social contact with peers on campus

*'Services' include cleaning, heating, lighting, electricity and/or gas, telephone, internet connection.

How well do you think you will get on with others (not your family)?

- ❑ brilliantly
- ❑ it'll be fine
- ❑ I've some reservations
- ❑ don't like the idea at all

How well do you think others (not your family) will like living with you?

- ❑ I'm easy-going
- ❑ I like my own space
- ❑ I'm not good in the mornings or late at night – I need my sleep
- ❑ I don't tolerate fools gladly

How do you think your family will adjust to you becoming a university student?

- ❑ I think they'll be very supportive
- ❑ I think they'll understand that I need some space and time to myself
- ❑ I think they'll miss me

What compromises might you need to make if you share accommodation with people:

- – in a university residence?
- – in a student flat?

If you are a student living at home, what adjustments will need to be made:

- – by you?
- – by other family members?

SELF-MAINTENANCE

Especially if you are leaving the family home for the first prolonged period, being a student can mean quite a large readjustment to your way of life. You will have to take responsibility for yourself and live with the decisions you make.

'Self-maintenance' encompasses a wide range of matters, including feeding yourself, doing your laundry, time management and companionship. Some new skills you may need to consider are:

- shopping for yourself;
- learning to cook;
- learning how to use a washing machine;
- remembering to use a washing machine;
- time management;
- meeting deadlines;
- operating on a limited budget;
- looking after your own health.

If you are living with others, there are other issues to resolve together:

- keeping shared accommodation clean;
- sharing chores fairly;
- working out an equitable way of splitting communal living costs;
- avoiding cliques and creating outcasts;
- being considerate when others need to study or work on an assignment;
- likes and dislikes regarding food and drink.

PRACTICAL TIPS TO HELP YOU PREPARE FOR UNIVERSITY

Prepare mentally for your new independence. Many new students fail to realise that no one will be telling them what to do or when to study – or even what to study. Especially in the first months, there's a risk of drifting aimlessly. You will need to set your own rules to help you achieve your goals.

Prepare mentally for the new working regime. The change from school, college or employment or unemployment can involve radical changes to your pattern and level of activity. One option is to act as if you were taking on a nine-to-five job, in that you leave home in the morning and spend your day 'working' in lectures, tutorials, practicals or private study until you return in the evening. That way you can make the most of your non-lecture time during the day. If you have work, social or sporting commitments, the need to plan your activities is even more important (see **Ch 8**).

Research your loan, grant and bursary entitlements. Check all the literature that has been sent to you and make sure you have sent off all necessary forms in good time. Look at your university's website to see whether you qualify for any grants or bursaries.

Work out a draft budget. Using the tables in this chapter and Table Z.1 on page 446, estimate as best you can what your likely costs will be and decide how to match your expected income and borrowing to these sums. This may involve making decisions about the amount of debt you are willing to incur by the end of your studies.

Research rented accommodation options thoroughly. Look especially carefully at:

- rental cost;
- room size and study facilities;
- distance from campus and lecture halls;
- whether meals are included;
- whether you might need to share a room;
- whether others of similar background to you will be housed nearby;
- whether you will have an en-suite bathroom or will have to share;
- what charges there are for an internet connection.

Decide which aspects are important to you and which are not, and select accommodation appropriately, recognising that some compromise will almost certainly be necessary.

Look into the legal situation regarding multiple occupation. If the accommodation you intend to rent has more than three unrelated people sharing, you should make sure that it has a Houses in Multiple Occupation (HMO) licence. Without this, the accommodation may not meet legal requirements and you may be at risk. Seek advice from the university support service that deals with issues related to leases and other aspects of letting contracts.

Visit the university accommodation if you can. This will help you get a feel for the options and you may be able to talk to existing students who know about specific features that you may not have thought about.

Read the small print of your accommodation contract. When choosing accommodation, read the contracts very carefully. There may be unpleasant or expensive consequences if you fail to deliver what is specified in the small print. For example, you may be penalised if you damage contents or do not clean properly (in the view of the landlord).

Act quickly to reserve accommodation. Once you have made up your mind, make contact or send back the relevant forms as quickly as possible or you may miss out because others have registered their interest first.

Check your inventory. If living in furnished rented accommodation, you should ensure that you are given (and have checked) an inventory of the equipment and furniture present at the outset. On the inventory you should note (date and sign) any broken or damaged items so that you are not charged for these when you leave.

Involve your family. Perhaps you can do this by inviting them to accompany you on a campus visit. This will give them the chance to see your new 'working' environment and it will help them to understand your university life better.

Plan to personalise your accommodation. This will help you avoid feeling homesick. Rented rooms and flats will feel very strange and impersonal at first, so arrange to bring along some favourite objects, such as posters, mascots and family photos.

3

STARTING OUT

How to get the most out of Freshers' Week

> So much goes on during Freshers' Week that it is easy to forget some of the important things you need to do. This chapter aims to help by providing a listing of important tasks.

Most universities hold a Freshers' or Welcome Week. The traditional purpose is to help new students settle in quickly. As well as a number of presentations and workshops related to effective learning at university and to your chosen course, there is usually an energetic social programme. Senior students will be around to help you to find your feet. Your university will probably send you an information pack ahead of your arrival. Do read this material, because this may be the only time that you will be given the information and when you arrive it will probably be assumed that you know it. Some universities recognise that students can suffer from 'information overload' in these first few days and weeks, so the trend now is to spread the transfer of information over a longer period and embed introductions to specific essential skills within taught modules.

ESSENTIAL, IMPORTANT AND OPTIONAL TASKS

Every new student needs to do several things during Freshers' Week:

- **Essential tasks.** These include administrative responsibilities and you *must* do these. You will find dates and times in the paperwork you will receive from the university before the academic year starts. Factor in Freshers' Week participation; you may miss essential information otherwise.

- **Important tasks.** These tasks, such as setting up a bank account, may depend on your personal situation, for example, whether you are new to the area or whether you are living locally. Banks will be vying for your custom, so check out all the deals before you make your choice of bank.

- **Optional tasks.** These will depend on your preferences and goals and might include joining a particular society.

Use Table 3.1 as a checklist to ensure you have thought of all the things you might need to do.

Table 3.1 Key tasks and activities for Freshers' Week

Type of task	Checklist of activities	Comments
Knowing what to do, when and how	▢ Review all the university documentation sent to you through the post or via website or Virtual Learning Environment to which you may have been given preliminary access. ▢ Read your Freshers' Pack – this will usually contain information from the university students' union or association ▢ Note all the appointments, events and activities that are relevant to you and plan what you will do each day	You will receive a great deal of important literature in the weeks leading up to admission to the university. You will need to sift this for information that is relevant to you. All the information from the university, the faculty and the department or school in which you will be studying will be important and you need to make sure that you read it and keep it safely.
Administration at institutional level	▢ Each student must matriculate. This is sometimes called registration, enrolment or signing up ▢ Meet your Adviser/Director of Studies. In some institutions this person might be called a Personal Tutor or a Director of Studies ▢ Collect your matriculation form and follow the instructions about signing up for your courses	The matriculation process is a fundamental procedure that confirms your admission to university, initiates your academic record, your access to facilities and the production of your student identity card. The latter provides proof of your status as a student within your institution as well as to outside agencies. You will not get your first loan cheque until you have matriculated.
Administration at college, faculty, departmental, divisional or school level	▢ Attend induction meeting ▢ Get to grips with the organisation of your university ▢ Find out your timetable, where you have to go and when ▢ You will probably have been given a map of the campus, so it is a good idea to check out ahead of time where lectures/labs/tutorials take place	The names used to describe the organisational units within a university differ from institution to institution. Most direct contact with students is made at the level at which the teaching is done, usually departmental or school level. Most units provide subject or course handbooks, which give details of timetables, locations and times of lectures. Some departments will have an induction meeting with new students when there will be an opportunity to meet the teaching staff, senior students and others from your year. You may think that you won't socialise with people from your course, but by the end of your degree they will probably be among your best friends.
Administration at local level (town or city)	▢ Arrange through the local Council Office to have your name added to the Electoral Register if you wish to vote in elections in the town or city in which you are studying	If you are a British citizen, it is possible to have a postal vote if you would prefer to vote in your home constituency in any UK-based election.

Table 3.1 (cont'd)

Type of task	Checklist of activities	Comments
Communicating with the university and beyond	Find out contact numbers and/or email addresses for: ❑ Your Adviser of Studies ❑ Your Personal Tutor (if different from above) ❑ Your subject department(s) ❑ The university library ❑ Your general practitioner (GP) – if new ❑ Your landlord (if appropriate)	Put all these details in an address book or personal organiser. Look around mobile phone providers to obtain the best deal that you can to get low cost/free email, surfing, free quota or unlimited calls and texts as well as any other offers that might be available for students. Weigh up advantages of pay-as-you-go if you feel that you need to watch your expenditure on communication.
Accommodation	❑ Book into accommodation ❑ Check that what you are signing for in terms of an inventory of equipment is actually there and in good condition ❑ Identify additional things that you may wish to purchase for your comfort or convenience ❑ If you are in private accommodation, arrange for transfer of electricity, gas or phone services to your name ❑ Make further enquiries about Council Tax Exemption as it may be that you have to apply for this explicitly	Getting to know your flatmates is important for future relationships. Everyone has particular habits and preferences, which may or may not be shared by others – this can be an exercise in 'people skills'. If you are sharing accommodation, you will need to reach an agreement with flatmates about how services are to be paid. Be aware that if your name is on the bill, then you are liable for any charges outstanding at the end of a let.
Getting to know your way around (on campus)	❑ Go on campus tour in Freshers' Week or before ❑ Apply for a student rail card/bus or tram travel permit ❑ Find on-campus facilities, e.g. library, sports hall, chaplaincy, parking zones ❑ Apply for/purchase a parking permit to park on campus if this is possible ❑ Apply for a season ticket for local parking	Finding your way around a tight-knit campus is usually quite easy, but many universities are dispersed widely and finding the cheapest and fastest method of travelling to your campus site is an important budgeting measure. Travel passes provide some help and some universities run free 'shuttle' buses between different campuses. For some people the only travel option is by private car, but to park on university property you will need to purchase a permit.
Getting to know your way around (off campus)	❑ Go on city or town tour ❑ Go on supermarket tour ❑ Find out about off-campus facilities, e.g. post office, launderette ❑ Research special student deals and loyalty card offers ❑ Find out bus, tram and train times for your journey to and from the university ❑ Find out how long it will take you to make the journey at different times of the day and week	Universities or their students' unions/associations offer tours of the local area. For some, this becomes a pub crawl, for others it is an exercise in locating key landmarks, including the local supermarkets and best places to buy food.

Type of task	Checklist of activities	Comments
Preparing to participate in the life of the university	☐ Attend Freshers' Week events; these are for everyone – not just for students living in residences or for people coming to university straight from school. ☐ Attend welcome from the Vice-chancellor/Principal ☐ Attend Societies' Fayre ☐ Join societies and clubs	There are usually two occasions in undergraduate life when you will assemble as a year group comprising all students: the welcome to the institution as you step out into uncharted territory with all the hopes and concerns that are to be expected; and graduation day, which marks the end of that journey and the fulfilment of those early hopes. In between these two dates, you have the opportunity to join societies, such as your own subject society, and many others. They contribute to the richness of university social and cultural life. Students' unions/associations usually organise some kind of 'Societies' Fayre' where you can join up. Don't miss out on all the opportunities on offer.
Getting ready for learning	☐ Purchase an academic diary ☐ Join the library and sign up for a library induction tour ☐ Participate in a library induction presentation or tour ☐ Attend IT induction and log in to your IT account ☐ If you are unsure about your IT skills, sign up for computing training sessions	Many universities and students' unions or associations publish a university diary that contains useful information about that institution, such as term/semester and vacation dates, where to go for information, sports facilities and much more.
Looking after yourself	☐ Register with a local GP practice. Representatives of local medical practices are often present at some of the Freshers' Week events and you should be able to sign up with them at that time. Note: students from some countries may be required to have a chest X-ray or courses of injections. This may also depend on your subject of study	You may need your National Health Service card in order to register with a GP. You should be able to get this from your local health board through the GP you see in your home town. You may have a choice of practices to join – ask around for recommendations. If you are an international student, you can find out how to go about registering with a doctor in the UK by visiting a practice of your choice; you also need to know that in Britain, if you are ill, the first place you need to contact is your doctor's surgery; hospitals are for emergencies only or referral by your GP.
Getting street-wise	☐ Get personal safety leaflets ☐ Buy a personal alarm – often available at discount price in students' union/association shops ☐ Make yourself aware of fire drill regulations in your accommodation	Most institutions provide information and advice on personal safety, including protecting your belongings as well as protecting yourself and your health. These are real-world issues and it is important to be aware of what you might encounter in the social scene on your campus. Many institutions or students' unions sell personal alarms and offer leaflets on drugs, sexually transmitted diseases, date-rape, theft, and other issues commonly found in the community at large. Counselling services exist in all university institutions to support all students from every background, nationality, gender orientation and creed. Counselling is free and confidential.

Table 3.1 (cont'd)

Type of task	Checklist of activities	Comments
For students with disabilities	☐ Make contact with the disability service in your institution to make them aware that you have arrived ☐ Check that facilities you have identified as being necessary for you are in place ☐ Students can choose whether they wish to disclose a condition that might be classified as a disability. It may be advantageous to disclose such information in order to obtain the most effective help. The information will be kept confidential until you authorise disclosure to others	If you have a disability, you need to consider how this might impact on your life as a student. You will probably have prepared for coming to university by contacting the disability service in your institution, but you should make contact again. Your university has a legal responsibility to provide adequate facilities, and this will be put into action if you disclose relevant information.
For international students	☐ Register for an English-language test if required ☐ Sign up for a course in English for Academic Purposes if you are a postgraduate international student who uses English as an additional language, look out for courses to help you with dissertation or thesis writing ☐ For students from some countries, there is a requirement that you register with the police. This is largely a formality, but it is something that you must do. You need to take your passport and student matriculation card with you ☐ For up-to-date information on Visa requirements, visit www.ukba.homeoffice.gov.uk	In some institutions, if you are an international student and English is not your first language, you may be obliged to take a language test as a matter of routine. If it is considered that you need to continue to develop your English language, courses will be available to you. In some cases, fees will be charged; in other cases, courses will be free of charge. Even if you have met the English language qualification for your university, remember that this is simply a benchmark requirement – your lecturers may suggest that you continue language study in addition to your discipline studies, so that you can deal competently with the reading, writing, listening and speaking required of you. All students wishing to remain in the UK for more than six months must obtain entry clearance before arriving in the UK. International students must provide evidence that they have been accepted on a full-time course of study at a UK registered centre of study, such as a university, for longer than six months. Applicants need to show that they have sufficient funds to pay fees and support themselves for the period of study. Such students may only take up part-time or vacation work but may not take up full-time employment.

PRACTICAL TIPS FOR FRESHERS

Buy a cheap filing system. You'll get lots of paperwork before you arrive and during the first few weeks of term or semester. There'll be too much to look at straight away, but some of the literature, such as course handbooks, will be very useful later on. While some handbooks may be available online, you may also be given this information in hard copy because it is considered indispensable for your studies. The temptation is to shove it all on your desk and read it later, but you'll probably lose important stuff if you do that. Spend some time sifting through all the papers you receive, put aside what you *think* you won't need (you might need it later after all) and store the rest in a logical order.

Don't spend money on impulse. During Freshers' Week there will be pressure on you to spend money: to participate in events, join clubs and societies, buy textbooks, and more. Unless you are confident in your interests and needs, save your cash until you are more certain about things. For example:

- Do you really need to join lots of clubs? There will be many demands on your time during the term/semester and you can't be an active member of them all. Select the one(s) likely to be of main interest to you. You can always join others later.

- Will you really need your own copy of all the books on your reading lists? There will usually be plenty of copies of each text in the library and if a book is peripheral you may only need to consult it a few times.

If you are living in university halls, work at getting to know your fellow students. Everyone is in the same boat, so just a little extra effort can make a difference, both for you and for them:

- Go out of your way to introduce yourself and speak to others.

- Leave your door open so you can greet those going by.

- Propose an evening event, such as a floor party or visit to a local pub.

- Look out for people who look lonely and invite them along to whatever you're doing.

- If you're a UK student, help international students particularly – they may be confused by cultural and language differences, as well as feeling homesick.

- Avoid going home at weekends in the first few weeks, or you may miss out on social events and chances to get to know people.

- Find out if people play the same sports as you and set up a match with them.

If you are living at home, try to become involved in university life. The temptation is to stick to old social and study habits, but you can gain a lot by meeting new people, getting involved in societies and clubs and studying in the university environment.

4

GENERAL EXPECTATIONS

How the university system works and how this impacts on you

Universities are large organisations, frequently with long histories and traditions that have evolved over many generations. However, it is not always so clear to students how to fit in with these traditions and what is expected of them. This chapter outlines some common requirements.

The academic community of a university consists not only of the lecturing staff who teach you, but also administrators, cleaners, janitors, secretaries, technicians, and a range of specialist staff who work behind the scenes. You will interact with many of these people as you study, maintain yourself and socialise. They will provide services for you but will expect you to do certain things to keep the system running smoothly. It's in your own best interests to understand their expectations and to try your best to meet these.

COMMUNICATING WITH THE INSTITUTION

The university machinery of administration is not really as complex as it sometimes seems. Your main role is to communicate with it effectively, for example by:

- matriculating (registering/enrolling) on the date and at the time given in your letter of acceptance;
- accessing your university email account regularly and responding to communications from staff members. Some departments only communicate on coursework and routine matters by email;

✔ Email accounts

It makes sense to transfer all your emails to the account assigned to you at university. This will make it easier for you to check for messages from staff: much of the ongoing course information will be distributed via email.

- routinely checking announcements for courses that use the university's virtual learning environment (VLE) (**Ch 28**) as well as making a habit of reading notices on college, faculty, school, departmental and course noticeboards;
- informing your college/faculty, school or course organiser of absence through illness and providing medical certificates to cover periods of absence beyond the normal period of self-certification;
- letting the university know as soon as possible if you change address, or change other personal details;
- notifying your college/faculty, school or course organiser if you find yourself having to cope with exceptional personal circumstances that mean that you will be absent for a period of time – for example, bereavement of a close relative (all such information is confidential);
- responding to written communications as required.

What if your expectations of the course aren't met?

Discuss this in the first instance with your adviser/director of studies or personal tutor. If regulations allow, you may be allowed to change modules. In some universities changes can only be made in the first few weeks.

ORGANISING YOURSELF

University is an exciting place with lots of activities beyond those your course offers. You will need to make choices about how you go about enjoying these activities while maintaining the right levels of effort for your course. To do this, you will be expected to:

- organise your activities and time effectively (**Ch 8**);
- plan your workload to meet deadlines;
- maintain your employment activities at realistic levels (no more than 15 hours a week is the usual recommendation);
- engage with all the university's codes of practice, for example, on plagiarism (**Ch 36**), IT etiquette and responsible use of the internet;
- arrange your social life around your studies;
- maintain a balance between work, study, social life and other family responsibilities.

Planning ahead

To get the most out of your course, map out the things you need to do in relation to your course programme(s) in a diary, semester/term/monthly/weekly planner such as *The Smarter Student Planner* or electronic diary:

- every day
- every week
- at other times.

LEARNING NEW SKILLS

University learning often requires you to do things in a different way from school, college or work. This means that you have to be receptive to learning new skills. For example, you are expected to:

- develop existing skills;
- be willing to learn new ways of studying;
- develop analytical skills;
- learn to think logically and see issues from both sides;
- be willing to challenge your existing perceptions and receive new ideas with an open mind;
- be prepared to consider information and ideas critically.

You will find more information about transferable skills in **Ch 6** and on critical thinking in **Ch 22**.

PLANNING YOUR STUDIES

University courses are challenging and the way subjects are taught will be different from one area of study to another. Sometimes you will have to attend lectures, other times tutorials, laboratory sessions or other kinds of practical sessions – and you are expected both to prepare for these and participate fully, even if no one explicitly states this. In some disciplines how you do both of these things is assessed.

? **How much am I expected to study?**

This is a frequently asked question, but the answer depends on many factors, including your abilities and the nature of your course work. Official bodies assume that, during term time, a full-time student is studying 40 hours per week. This figure includes contact time (lectures, tutorials, practicals, etc.) and non-contact time (reading, working on assessments, for example).

Here are some examples of things you will need to do:

Every day

- Prepare for lectures and other learning activities by doing some background reading. This may include printing out lecture notes or PowerPoint handouts for use in the lecture (**Ch 15, Ch 17**).
- Attend and take notes as appropriate (**Ch 17**) in all the scheduled lectures and other programmed activities.
- Obey safety instructions and follow rules and regulations, especially for lab and fieldwork and when using IT facilities.

Every week

- Follow up the lecture or other activities by doing supplementary reading, worked examples, or reviewing and condensing notes.

- Contribute actively in all forms of teaching and assessment, for example, by asking and answering questions.

- Engage fully with teaching materials and other facilities offered online. For example, you should look at your VLE modules several times a week to see announcements and participate in discussions.

At other times

- Attend class debates, year meetings and formal assessments.

- Attend all meetings with tutors – punctuality is expected.

- Submit work on time.

- Participate in field trip activities, as appropriate to your discipline (remember that this is something that you will have to work into your budget).

- Register for examinations at the times given.

- Provide feedback on your course when required to do so, for example, online or in class.

- Speak to your course director, adviser of studies/personal tutor or tutors in the academic advice service (sometimes called learning support centre) if you are having difficulty with your course or your learning. Information about these services is usually found on your university's web pages.

LOOKING AFTER YOURSELF

Universities are not as anonymous as they might seem on the surface and if you find yourself in difficulties there is usually someone to whom you can turn for help or advice that is freely available and confidential (see Information Box page 22). You'll find information about these services from noticeboards, your university's website and from information leaflets that will be displayed in prominent places in university buildings.

It's expected that, if you need help, you will take the initiative in asking for it. This should not be about crisis management, but about recognising potential queries, issues or difficulties before they become problems. Seeking advice at an early stage is not a sign of weakness, but a mature decision in problem-solving.

PRACTICAL TIPS FOR DEALING WITH THE UNIVERSITY SYSTEM

Recognise that going to university is like moving to a new community. A university has its own culture and conventions. Although it might seem confusing at first, the information you need is usually available somewhere. A good starting point is the institution's web pages. From the university's home page, you can usually find what you want, using the search facility or A–Z index.

Think for yourself. University is not like school and people generally will not tell you what to do or when (**Ch 5**). It is up to you to organise your time and to follow the necessary procedures explained in your course handbook in order to fulfil the course requirements.

If you have any queries, ask. If you don't know who to approach, or are in doubt about what needs to be done and when, ask the departmental secretary or administrator – who will usually be a mine of information.

Get together. If you feel that you don't understand course materials, probably there are others in the same boat. Ask around and discuss the difficulty with fellow students. Between you, it may be possible to work out the answer. If this doesn't work, ask a lecturer or tutor for help.

Seek support at an early stage. If you find that personal issues are beginning to interfere with your studying, then go to the support service that seems most appropriate for advice. It is better to seek advice while things are low-key than wait until the issues escalate into big problems.

5

WHAT MAKES UNIVERSITY EDUCATION DIFFERENT

How to get off to a good start

> It is useful to understand how university differs from other places of learning such as schools and further education colleges. By realising at an early stage that you will be responsible for your learning, you can adapt more easily to this new learning environment.

The differences between university and other educational environments stem largely from the fact that classes tend to be much larger than elsewhere. Lecture classes of 250–300 are quite normal, especially at early stages. It may seem like a contradiction to say that you are alone in a crowd, but it is true in the sense that this situation means that your learning is largely up to you. Although some syllabuses are quite prescriptive, no one will chase you up to see whether you did the preparation for a lecture, whether you attended a lecture, whether you are on track to hand in your work on time or monitor you very much in any other respect.

University attendance rules

i

While most departments do not monitor individual attendance at lectures, there are exceptions. For example, where a professional body has requirements that need to be met in order to achieve professional recognition of your qualification, it is generally a condition of passing a course that you attend all lectures. Attendances are recorded, sometimes electronically. Note that with effect from March 2009 UK legislation requires institutions to monitor the attendance of international students. If the 'expected contacts' within a course are missed, the university is required to report the student to the UK Border Agency.

TEACHING APPROACHES

Look now at Table 5.1, which compares secondary school, further education college, university and workplace in a number of key areas. It's fairly obvious that the 'university' column has much more detail than the other three and this is because there is so much that is different in higher education. Realising what makes university education distinctive from the beginning of your studies will help you adjust to the differences on a day-to-day basis.

Table 5.1 What makes university different? University is a special kind of place for learning. People come to it with different perceptions of what they might encounter and these perceptions may well be coloured by earlier learning experiences and environments. This table shows key aspects of four learning environments and how learning in each of them takes place. This will help you identify things that may be different from what you expected or have experienced elsewhere.

Aspect	Secondary school	Further education college	University ('higher education')	Workplace
Control	• Directed by teaching staff	• Directed by lecturers	• Directed by each college, faculty/school/department	• Directed by management at department level
Attendance	• Mandatory and monitored	• By choice and monitored	• By choice and selection, with varying degrees of monitoring dependent on discipline	• By choice and selection
Classes	• 40+ minutes per lesson	• 60+ minutes per lesson	• Multiples of one hour per lesson (typical lecture 50 minutes)	• Meetings: 15 minutes to 2–3 hours
Communication	• Daily bulletins and announcements • Noticeboards • Some electronic	• Handbooks • Classroom announcements • Noticeboards • Some electronic	Largely electronic: • Web pages • Virtual learning environments (VLE) • Electronic newsletters • Subject handbooks	Largely electronic: • Web pages • Circulars • Electronic newsletters • Staff handbook
Learner's position in the class	• One of a few • Small classes • Pupils generally known by name	• One of a few • Smallish classes • Students generally known by name	• One of many • Large classes, maybe in hundreds • Students generally not known by name	• Individual – people at different stages in organisation
Preparation required by student	• Regularly, homework for submission; finishing off class work	• Regularly, homework for submission; finishing off class work	• Preliminary reading, researching around topic • Largely self-directed	• Reading minutes, relevant papers • Sometimes, preliminary discussion to identify position

Aspect	Secondary school	Further education college	University ('higher education')	Workplace
Teaching input	• Teacher controlled • Feedback provided	• Lecturer controlled • Feedback provided	• Lecturer controlled in lectures • Less controlled in tutorials, practicals and labs • Little feedback	• Company controlled • In-house training programmes, not necessarily delivered by those trained to teach
Teaching strategies	• New learning presented, checked, revised and reinforced • Consolidated in subsequent lessons	• Interactive dialogue in lectures	• Traditionally, little dialogue in lectures • Little time to answer questions • In tutorials and labs, less formality and more interaction	• Open learning • On the job: peer-mentoring
Learning requirements	• Pace slow • Memorising information • One-word/short response answers • Teacher confirms correct response	• Medium pace • Dialogue in lecture • Mainly information transfer • Opportunities for questions	• Pace very rapid • Students need to think for themselves	• Pace varies • Continuing professional development requirements dictated by annual appraisal or personal ambition
Written work requirements	• Repeat what has been taught in class • Little need for original thinking	• Repeat what has been taught in class • Interpret questions and respond with syllabus content	• Evidence required of syllabus knowledge and understanding • Independent analytical thinking expected, especially at higher levels • Originality expected	• Graduate skills of critical thinking, ability to write appropriately to context and to explain things clearly and concisely
Presentational requirements	• Expressive • Often less emphasis on spelling, punctuation and grammar	• Presentation expected to be neat and correct in the main • Less monitoring of grammatical errors	• May be penalties for poor spelling, grammar and punctuation • Word-processed document may be mandatory	• Following house style and expected to be 100 per cent accurate in content and presentation • Sloppy work may be returned for revision

Table 5.1 (*cont'd*)

Aspect	Secondary school	Further education college	University ('higher education')	Workplace
Materials	• Colourful, visually explicit • Less text • Encouragement in earlier stages especially to use text word for word • Limited library facility	• Visually explicit, low on dense text • Class notes • Some use of more complex texts • Modest library facility	• Traditional textbook • Journal resources • Web-based resources • PowerPoint slides/class notes • Extensive on-site library with online journal access	• In-house library or records • Open-learning or distance-learning packages
Assessment procedures	• One-word/short responses • Teacher feedback expected and given	• Extensive feedback • Opportunities for multiple submissions before final assessment	• Little preliminary review at undergraduate level • One-time-only submission • Mark not negotiable	• Annual review or appraisal • May impact on promotion or salary increases
Examination strategy	• National level: repeat what has been taught in class in response to syllabus • Little need for original thinking • Externally moderated • Coursework forms part of assessment • No resit in same year	• Generally follow national exam format(s) • Local/national level: internally and externally moderated • Coursework forms part of assessment • Resit possibilities	• Internal examination: may contribute to final degree award • Moderated internally with oversight of external examiner • Continuous assessment may be included • Resit possibilities at early levels of study	• External exams may be a requirement of professional bodies

You will have made a definite choice to enter university, but it is important to recognise that the way lecturers teach is generally quite different from the teaching you had at school or college. Within any particular module, it may be that you are taught by more than one lecturer who may give two or three lectures and then be replaced by the next lecturer on the list. This, combined with large class sizes and a much tighter time frame, means that there is less opportunity in lectures for discussion or asking questions compared with school, college or workplace learning.

Most lecturers are willing to meet students at a mutually convenient time to discuss coursework. The crucial difference is that you are expected to make the first move – the assumption at university is that if you say nothing, you have understood everything. Other opportunities exist, however. For example, laboratory sessions and tutorials offer chances to ask questions and make sure you understand the material (**Ch 20**, **Ch 21**).

ASSESSMENT

In relation to assessment, there are really significant differences. At university, work is submitted by a deadline. Lecturing and other teaching staff do not routinely preview work that is to be submitted. This means that it is a one-time-only submission. For people who have come from traditions where it was the norm to submit a draft for review, sometimes more than once, this is a dramatic change. The tip, therefore, is to move from this culture of dependency to one where the support comes from within your peer group (**Ch 18**, **Ch 64**). Reading and commenting on each other's work is actually a contribution to learning for all parties. Alternatively, ask another family member to read over work for you. You can find out more about university assessment in **Ch 45**.

Challenging your marks

At university, marks are generally not negotiable. However, in some institutions, students are permitted to challenge marks. Where this is done under internal moderation, there is a potential risk of receiving a lower mark from the second marker and this will be the one that is recorded. If you feel that the mark you have received is not what your work deserves, it is probably more productive to seek an appointment with the marker to discuss the weaker elements in the work so that you can improve your next submission.

LEARNING TO LEARN

Nowadays, learning is considered a lifelong activity, so learning how to learn for yourself is fundamental. Critical to this is developing an ability to think things through for yourself, that is, not just accepting what textbooks or even world authorities on a topic tell you is the case.

There are many sides to most issues, and learning to make judgements of their merit is a key student skill. As you progress with your studies you will find that you refine this ability further until it becomes second nature. This means that, when you enter employment as a graduate, you will do so with a skill as an independent thinker that will distinguish you from others.

Another aspect to university learning is that you should be prepared to adapt the *way* you study and learn according to your preferred learning style (**Ch 13**), the subject material and the way in which you are taught (**Ch 16**). Your learning should also be active rather than passive (**Ch 61**).

> ✔ **Thinking for yourself**
>
> You are expected to reflect on what you hear and read at university. Lecturers will often argue for different cases or ideas to demonstrate the complexity of a problem. You have to decide what evidence has most validity in the light of the evidence they have presented.

🔧 PRACTICAL TIPS FOR ADJUSTING TO UNIVERSITY TEACHING APPROACHES

Start with an open mind and think for yourself. Everyone enters university with skills and talents, diverse knowledge and experience. However, university is about revisiting old ideas and values as well as exploring new areas and concepts. It is important to come to this new learning with an open mind where you explore ideas critically – and this may involve challenging your existing views and understanding.

Keep up with the work. The pace of university teaching can take many students by surprise. Things will not be repeated, and it will be routinely expected that you understand material covered at an earlier stage. No one will be monitoring how much studying you are doing and it is easy to let this slip, with consequent effects on later learning and exam results.

Manage your time carefully. This is vital, so you can balance your social life and term-time employment with your studying. There's more about this in **Ch 8**.

If in doubt, ask! It is regarded as *your* job to ensure you have understood all the course material and what you are expected to learn. If anything is unclear, ask your lecturer or tutor – you may need to make an appointment to do this. Many lecturers have consultation times posted on their office doors so you can go along at that time. Otherwise a quick email may be easier for you and for the lecturer.

Be your own person. Decide what you want to get out of your university studies and how hard you will need to work to achieve your goals. Don't be influenced by the laid-back attitude of some students: if they want to slack, that's their lookout. Also, don't be fooled by those who pretend to be doing little, but actually study quite hard behind the scenes. Stick to your personal work ethic, and study at times that suit you.

6

GRADUATE SKILLS AND ATTRIBUTES

How to learn what employers expect you to gain from being at university

What you learn at university is just as much about the skills you'll use in later life as it is about the subject you have chosen to study. This chapter provides an overview of the personal transferable skills that could apply in your circumstances.

Employers who recruit graduates expect more from a member of their workforce than someone who is simply a chemist, a historian or an engineer, for example. What they are looking for are graduates who possess a range of skills that can be applied in different situations. These are often referred to as 'personal transferable skills' or 'key skills'. There are essentially two types of such skills: those that are subject-specific and those that are generic. Subject-specific key skills are usually taught as part of the learning on degree programmes; generic key skills tend to apply across the disciplines.

KEY SKILL AREAS

Your degree will provide evidence to your future employer that you possess a range of specialist skills and knowledge for the work situation. However, providing evidence of what other transferable skills you possess can be more problematic – especially if you are unaware of what these skills are. Figure 6.1 shows five key areas in which transferable skills might be positioned. The five key skill areas highlighted are:

- personal development skills;
- interpersonal skills;
- communication skills;
- technical skills;
- intellectual skills.

You might like to use this figure as a reference checklist when working on your personal development planning (PDP) or compiling your curriculum vitae (CV) or a job application where you are required to outline skills you feel you have developed so far.

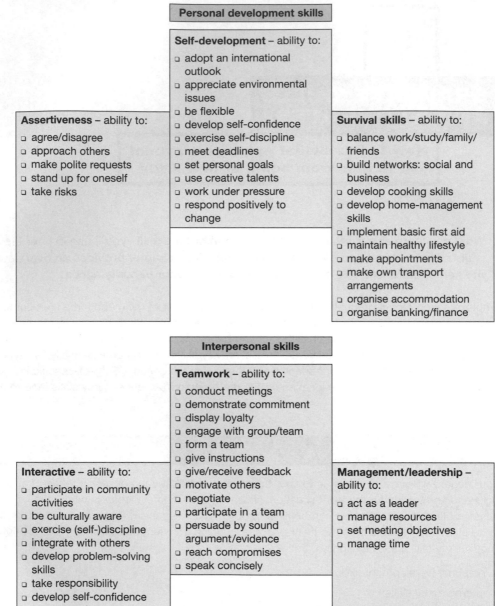

Personal development skills

Self-development – ability to:
- adopt an international outlook
- appreciate environmental issues
- be flexible
- develop self-confidence
- exercise self-discipline
- meet deadlines
- set personal goals
- use creative talents
- work under pressure
- respond positively to change

Assertiveness – ability to:
- agree/disagree
- approach others
- make polite requests
- stand up for oneself
- take risks

Survival skills – ability to:
- balance work/study/family/friends
- build networks: social and business
- develop cooking skills
- develop home-management skills
- implement basic first aid
- maintain healthy lifestyle
- make appointments
- make own transport arrangements
- organise accommodation
- organise banking/finance

Interpersonal skills

Teamwork – ability to:
- conduct meetings
- demonstrate commitment
- display loyalty
- engage with group/team
- form a team
- give instructions
- give/receive feedback
- motivate others
- negotiate
- participate in a team
- persuade by sound argument/evidence
- reach compromises
- speak concisely

Interactive – ability to:
- participate in community activities
- be culturally aware
- exercise (self-)discipline
- integrate with others
- develop problem-solving skills
- take responsibility
- develop self-confidence
- participate in a team

Management/leadership – ability to:
- act as a leader
- manage resources
- set meeting objectives
- manage time

Figure 6.1 Skills and attributes. Here is a fairly comprehensive list of what are commonly called personal transferable or key skills. Tick all the boxes where you think you already have some degree of skill, then underline all those with ticks that you think you could or should develop further while at university.

Communication skills

Written – ability to:
- write for academic purposes
- work accurately
- construct a CV
- conduct correspondence
- write formal articles/papers
- give a poster presentation
- write a product evaluation report
- write a project/technical report
- take minutes of meetings
- write for specific contexts

Visual and aural – ability to:
- use design techniques
- construct and present a PowerPoint presentation
- make a poster presentation
- listen to the views of others

Verbal – ability to:
- speak formally/informally to a range of people
- converse confidently
- present case/project
- debate formally and informally
- contribute to discussion in meetings
- conduct telephone interactions and negotiations

Technical skills

Computing skills – ability to:
- manage a database
- use desktop publishing
- use a keyboard
- organise file storage
- produce graphics
- handle statistical data
- word process
- use a spreadsheet
- produce graphics
- search the Web

Numerical – ability to:
- handle numerical information
- produce numerical reports
- understand numerical terms
- present numerical results

Technical/creative – ability to:
- appreciate the aesthetic
- be creative
- drive a vehicle
- use work-related technology

Intellectual skills

Problem-solving – ability to:
- analyse
- collect data
- think critically
- reflect on own learning
- develop learning strategies to suit personal learning style
- evaluate information
- generate new ideas
- organise and plan
- evolve problem-solving strategies
- reason objectively
- redesign and restructure
- research
- understand task organisation
- undertake career planning
- summarise information
- work on own initiative

Figure 6.1 (cont'd)

Once you have reviewed your skills in this way, you should then be able to compile three lists:

- skills that are reasonably well developed;
- skills that you would like to develop further;
- skills that are not developed at all and that you might consider developing as you progress.

In some cases, there will be an expectation that this is done as part of your PDP (see **Ch 7**).

As a university student your aim will be to do as well as you possibly can, for it is the combination of subject skills and key skills that you will develop on the road to becoming a graduate that will make you an attractive prospect to a future employer.

The concepts of 'graduateness' and 'employability' will be explored more fully in the section 'Planning for the future'.

PRACTICAL TIPS FOR ENHANCING YOUR SKILLS

Consult your course handbooks for references to key skills. These will probably highlight opportunities for you to gain and develop skills, and will indicate the terminology in favour at your institution and in your discipline.

Identify which extra-curricular activities and experiences could contribute to your skills. Make sure you add details of these to your CV.

Bear skills in mind when you consider optional elements of your course. For example, don't pick a supplementary module just because it is 'easy' – choose one that will enhance your skills.

Sign up for workshops and training courses. First-aid courses, IT workshops, short language courses and training for mentoring are all examples of readily available training options that you could use to develop your skills.

7

PERSONAL DEVELOPMENT PLANNING

How to reflect on your achievements and set yourself future goals

Personal development planning involves reflecting on your learning, performance and achievements. This process will help you organise your personal, educational and career development.

There's a lot to gain from thinking more deeply about what you are doing at university and where this might take you in terms of employment and career development. To help you with this, you may be asked to take part in personal development planning by your department, faculty, school or college. The exact process may go under a different name, but the outcome is usually similar: you will be asked to complete some form of personal development plan (PDP). Many professional bodies that validate degrees encourage PDP activities and there is a drive to introduce PDP schemes for most degrees.

PERSONAL DEVELOPMENT PLANNING

The aims of personal development planning include:

- recording your personal qualities, achievements and skills and monitoring their development;
- clarifying your personal and career goals;
- understanding more fully what and how you are learning;
- taking responsibility for your own development by setting yourself personal and academic targets and evaluating progress towards these;
- improving your employability;
- bringing together information for your CV and evidence to support job applications;
- starting the process of continuing professional development in your chosen career area.

i Benefits of personal development planning

Some research suggests that students who carry out PDP activities perform better in their academic courses than those who don't. These students also have better motivation, self-awareness and understanding of 'employability' and career options.

The process of personal development planning usually includes the following elements:

- **Thinking:** about where you stand now, where your interests lie, what your strengths and weaknesses are and the improvements you would like to achieve.
- **Planning:** where you want to go, what skills and knowledge you need to get there and how you might acquire them.
- **Action:** setting yourself goals and specific targets and monitoring your progress towards them.
- **Reflecting:** reviewing your achievements and deciding on further areas for personal, academic and career development.

This is seen as a continuous cycle of self-review, rather than a one-off event. Your university's PDP scheme will encourage you to go through the process and provide a mechanism for recording your thoughts and progress.

> **Definition: reflecting**
>
> In the PDP context, this is the process of looking back over past events; analysing *how* you have learned and developed as a person and your feelings about this; and re-evaluating your experience on the basis of your thoughts.

COMPONENTS OF PROGRESS FILES

Your PDP will generally be allied to a progress file. This will consist of all or some of the following components:

- **An academic transcript.** This is the ongoing record of your learning and achievement as recorded by the university. It would normally include details of the modules you are taking or have taken and the marks or grades you have obtained in them. It may also include a breakdown of assessed skills and other achievements (for example, attending a safety course or field excursion, or participating in an IT induction session). The style and content of the transcript will depend on your institution and the mechanism it uses for recording your achievements.

> **Checking your academic transcript**
>
> There will normally be a mechanism for doing this (you have the right to see it under the Freedom of Information Act 2000). If your transcript seems to be incorrect or incomplete, you should ask for it to be corrected as soon as possible, as it may be copied to employers at a later date.

- **A portfolio.** This is a collection of evidence to support your PDP and CV. This might be stored on paper or electronically. Depending on your discipline and modules, it might include outcomes of various tasks you have completed, such as: essays; literature surveys; posters; analysis of a problem or issue; research project reports; designs and artwork; practical reports; fieldwork project reports; or evidence of the use of IT and software, such as a completed spreadsheet. You can use this evidence as part of the process of reflection on your achievements and goals, and also to show to potential employers to demonstrate your skills and abilities.

- **A personal development plan.** This involves a reflective analysis of who you are, what you've done and what you plan to do. Some universities have created a structured process to assist in this – for example, a system that allows you to 'rate' your abilities and skills in different areas, and see how these have changed and should change in future. The outcome is often a series of short-term targets that you are set (by yourself, or in discussion with a tutor) to try to achieve by the time of your next personal review.

- **A career planning component.** The aim of this part, if included, is to encourage you to think about your career options at an early date, and to assist you to decide what qualities and qualifications you may need to achieve your goals.

- **A developing curriculum vitae.** The above features of the progress plan all feed into the CV that you will eventually submit to a potential employer. Focusing your thoughts on this end product is a good way of assessing the relevance of your studies and extra-curricular activities and how you can communicate information about your skills and personal qualities (in short, what *evidence* you will be able to present for this). The components of a CV and options for presenting them are covered in **Ch 70**.

✔ **Targeted CV**

It is important to realise that while you may work on a 'generalised' CV as part of personal development planning, a different, targeted CV should be submitted for each type of position for which you apply. The work you do on the generalised CV will allow you to pick and choose relevant components and make appropriate minor adjustments to the wording.

The way in which you will be invited to compile your progress file will depend on your institution and possibly your department or degree. Some PDP models focus on personal transferable skills (**Ch 6**), while others concentrate on career planning aspects. Many professional bodies define the content and presentation. Some PDP schemes are paper-based, involving worksheets, files, reports and plans; others are electronic, allowing you to access and work on your PDP online, by lodging materials in your own dedicated server space.

✔ **Filing your PDP materials**

If you are working with a paper-based scheme, it makes good sense to invest in a portable file system in which to keep all the materials.

THE HIGHER EDUCATION ACHIEVEMENT REPORT (HEAR)

This report was proposed by a committee led by Principal Burgess of Leicester University. The aim is to respond to employers' needs to identify more specifically the skills, attributes and achievements of their potential graduate employees. The HEAR is intended to be a document produced by universities that, over the period of a student's career, outlines their strengths and weaknesses in particular modules. The record may reflect performance in presentations, projects, group work, dissertations and timed examinations, but may also include additional information about extra-curricular activities, volunteering, work experience and professional recognition. These proposals are undergoing pilot development in some institutions and will take some time to implement.

REFLECTING ON YOUR PROGRESS AND PLANNING AHEAD

Try to answer the following questions. You may wish to record your answers and note opportunities and targets for each area. Table 7.1 illustrates one potential method for organising your thoughts.

What are your aspirations and goals? You might want to think in long, middle and short term:

- where you would like to be, career-wise, in 10 years' time?
- what sort of degree will you need to get on the first step on that career ladder?
- what steps can you take within the current year to help towards your degree goals?

What interests and motivations do you have? While some personal interests will always have 'hobby' status, others may be 'occupational interests', which might drive forward your selection of modules, degree subjects and even a career. Like interests, motivating factors will be intensely personal, some career-related, others only indirectly related to a career. You might have a desire to become rich, to help those less well off than yourself, to teach, to heal, to work with animals, to have a stable and predictable life, to raise a family. It isn't the easiest thing to identify what these factors are, but if you are able to, you can use this information to find a more satisfying educational and career path.

What key skills are you gaining – both during your academic studies and in your extra-curricular activities? The material in **Ch 6** should be useful here, but you will find other information about the skills you are covering in your course handbook and in subject benchmarking statements on the Quality Assurance Agency website (**www.qaa.ac.uk/students/ guides/understandcourses.asp**). Opportunities for gaining new skills should be incorporated into your plan – for example, attending a workshop to learn about a new software package.

What personality traits and personal qualities do you have, and how might these help you direct your future? Have a look at **Ch 69** and carry out the personality audit on pages 425–6 (or carry out a similar audit as part of your university's PDP scheme). How might the qualities you have identified in yourself relate to your potential career paths? Examine websites that provide ideas (for example, **www.prospects.ac.uk**).

What is your learning style? Reflecting on this might help you become a better learner. Have a look at **Ch 13** to help you decide whether you need to modify your current approach.

Table 7.1 Organising and summarising your personal development planning activities

Name: Date:

Topic	Current status	Action points	Target date	Notes
Long-term aspirations and goals				
Medium-term aspirations and goals				
Short-term aspirations and goals				
Key interests and motivations				
Key skills – strengths and areas for development				
Important personality traits and personal qualities				
Preferred learning style or preference				

PRACTICAL TIPS FOR PERSONAL DEVELOPMENT PLANNING

Revisit your PDP regularly. Try to look at it after each section of your course (could be a topic, semester or term, module, year) and review what you've written, update plans as appropriate.

Talk to others about your plans. Discuss your options and opportunities with as wide a range of people as possible – from personal tutors and academic staff to friends and family. Explaining how you feel will in itself help you to crystallise your thoughts, and any feedback or ideas given in return may also be helpful.

Make resolutions. At the start of each new teaching block, take time to make a set of fresh goals and plans based on thinking about what you achieved in the previous session and experience between, such as vacation work. Give yourself reasonably ambitious targets – but don't be afraid of failing. As long as you get part-way towards your goal, you will have achieved something. Not having a goal at all would be a problem.

8

TIME MANAGEMENT

How to balance study, family, work and leisure

Managing your time effectively is an important key to a fulfilling university career. This chapter provides ideas for organising your activities and tips to help you focus on important tasks.

Successful people tend to have the ability to focus on the right tasks at the right time, the capacity to work quickly to meet their targets, and the knack of seeing each job through to a conclusion. In short, they possess good time-management skills. Time management is a skill that can be developed like any other. Here are some simple routines and tips that can help you improve your organisation, prioritisation and time-keeping. Weigh up the following ideas and try to adopt those most suited to your needs and personality.

As a student, you will need to balance the time you devote to study, family, work and social activities. Although you probably have more freedom over these choices than many others, making the necessary decisions is still a challenging task. Table 8.1 demonstrates just how easy it is for students' study time to evaporate.

DIARIES, TIMETABLES AND PLANNERS

Organising your activities more methodically is an obvious way to gain useful time.

Diaries and student planners

Use a diary or planner to keep track of your day-to-day schedule (for example, lectures, sports activities) and to note submission deadlines for university work.

- Work your way back from key dates, creating milestones such as 'finish library work for essay' or 'prepare first draft of essay'.
- Refer to the diary or planner frequently to keep yourself on track and to plan out each day and week. Try to get into the habit of looking at the next day's activities the night before and the next week's work at the end of the week. If you use a diary with the 'week-to-view' type of layout, you will be able to see ahead each time you look at it.
- Number the weeks, so you can sense how time is progressing over longer periods, such as a term or semester.
- Consider also numbering the weeks in reverse 'count down' fashion to key events such as end of semester/term exams and assignment submission dates.

Table 8.1 Some of the ways in which students' study time evaporates. Do you recognise any of these traits in yourself?

Personality type	Typical working ways . . . and the problems that may result
The late-nighter	Luke likes to work into the small hours. He's got an essay to write with a deadline tomorrow morning, but just couldn't get down to doing it earlier on. It's 2.00 a.m. and now he's panicking. Because the library's shut, he can't find a reference to support one of his points; he's so tired he won't be able to review his writing and correct the punctuation and grammatical errors; and he feels so shattered that he'll probably sleep in and miss the 9.00 a.m. deadline. Oh well, the essay was only worth 25 per cent – he'll just have to make up the lost marks in the exam . . .
The extension-seeker	Eleanor always rationalises being late with her assignments. She always has good reasons for being late, and it's never her fault. This is beginning to wear rather thin with her tutors. This time her printer packed up just before submission, last time she had tonsillitis and the time before she had to visit her granny in hospital. She's asked for an extension, but will lose 10 per cent of the marks for every day her work is late. It's only a small amount, but as she's a borderline pass in this subject, it could make all the difference . . .
The stressed-out non-starter	Shahid has to give a presentation to his tutorial group. Only thing is, he's so intimidated by the thought of standing up in front of them, that he can't focus on writing the talk. If only he had his PowerPoint slides and notes ready, he'd feel a whole lot more confident about things, but he can't get going because of his nerves. Maybe if he just goes out for a walk, he'll feel better placed to start when he comes back . . . and then, maybe another cup of coffee . . .
The last-minuter	Lorna is a last-minute person and she can only get motivated when things get close to the wire. She produces her best work close to deadlines when the adrenaline is flowing. However, her final-year dissertation is supposed to be a massive 10,000 words, there's only a week to go and she hasn't felt nervous enough to get started until now . . .
The know-it-all	Ken has it all under control. The lecture notes are all on the Web, so there's really no need to go to the lectures. He'll catch up on sleep instead and study by himself later on. Then he'll just stroll to the exam looking cool, get stuck in and amaze everyone with his results. Trouble is, the professor gave out a sheet changing the learning outcomes at her first lecture, missed out one of the topics (which Ken has revised carefully) and told the other students that the exam format now involves two compulsory questions . . .
The perfectionist	Pat wants to do really well at uni. She signed up for a vocational degree and has plans to land a plum job on graduation to start her climb up the career tree. Mum and Dad want her to do really well in her assignments and it's vital that the essay that she's working on starts with a cracking first sentence. Just can't phrase it right though – she's tried 15 different ways and crossed them all out. Time is running out now, and she will have to put off going to the Globetrotter's Dance. Well, who needs a social life anyway . . .
The juggler	Jeff is a mature student and is working part-time to make ends meet. Although it started as 10 hours a week, it's now up to 25. He's juggling his shifts so he can attend lectures and tutorials, and might be able to do a bit of coursework in the breaks at work, providing the staffroom is empty. He can't get into the library to work on the short-loan material, so he'll have to miss that out. And he's so tired at the end of each day, he just can't summon the energy to read the core texts. Doesn't know how long he can keep this pace up . . .

Choosing a diary or planner

Some universities and many bookshops sell academic diaries that cover the year from September to August. Alternatively, some sell academic planners with diary features, such as *The Smarter Student Planner* (see references), which provide templates for planning that allow you to keep track of assignment dates, plan for exam revision as well as providing reviews of key points of grammar, spelling, punctuation and maths.

Timetables

Create a detailed timetable of study when you have a big task looming (e.g. before exams, or when there is a large report or literature survey to write up). The use of revision timetables is covered further in **Ch 60**, and the same principles apply to other tasks. You could:

- break the task down into smaller parts;
- space these out appropriately;
- schedule important activities for when you generally feel most intellectually active (e.g. mid-morning).

One advantage of a timetable is that you can see the progress you are making if you cross out or highlight each mini-task as it is completed.

Wall planners

These are another way of charting out your activities, with the advantage, like a timetable, that you can see everything in front of you.

Advantages of being organised

If you organise your time well, you will:

- keep on schedule and meet deadlines;
- reduce stress caused by a feeling of lack of control over your work schedule;
- complete work with less pressure and fulfil your potential;
- build your confidence about your ability to cope;
- avoid overlapping assignments and having to juggle more than one piece of work at a time.

Being organised is especially important for large or long-term tasks because it seems easier to put things off when deadlines seem a long way off.

LISTING AND PRIORITISING

At times you may run into problems because you have a number of different tasks that need to be done. It is much better to write these tasks down in a list each day, rather than risk forgetting them. You will then have a good picture of what needs to be done and will be better able to prioritise the tasks.

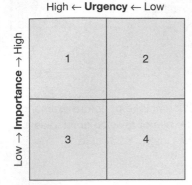

Figure 8.1 **The urgent–important approach to prioritising.** Place each activity somewhere on the axes in relation to its importance and urgency. Do all the activities in sector 1 first, then 2 or 3, and last 4.

Once you've created a list, rank the tasks by numbering them from 1, 2, 3 and so on, in order from 'important and urgent' to 'neither important nor urgent' (see Figure 8.1). Your 'important' criteria will depend on many factors: for example, your own goals, the weight of marks given to each assessment, or how far away the submission date is.

Each day, you should try to complete as many of the listed tasks as you can, starting with number 1. If you keep each day's list achievable, the process of striking out each task as it is completed provides a feeling of progress being made, which turns into one of satisfaction if the list has virtually disappeared by the evening. Also, you will become less stressed once high-priority tasks are tackled.

Carry over any uncompleted tasks to the next day, add new ones to your list and start again – but try to complete yesterday's unfinished jobs before starting new ones of similar priority, or they will end up being delayed for too long.

i Deciding on priorities

This involves distinguishing between important and urgent activities.

- **Importance** implies some assessment of the benefits of completing a task against the loss if the task is not finished.
- **Urgency** relates to the length of time before the task must be completed.

For example, in normal circumstances, doing your laundry will be neither terribly important nor particularly urgent, but if you start to run out of clean underwear, you may decide otherwise. Hence, priorities are not static and need to be reassessed frequently.

ROUTINES AND GOOD WORK HABITS

Many people find that carrying out specific tasks at special periods of the day or times of the week helps them get things done on time. You may already do this with routine tasks like doing your laundry every Tuesday morning or visiting a relative on Sunday afternoons. You may find it helps to add work-related activities to your list of routines – for example, by making Monday evening a time for library study, to work on your next assignment.

Good working habits can help with time management:

- **Do important work when you are at your most productive.** Most of us can state when we work best (Figure 8.2). When you have worked this out for yourself, timetable your activities to suit: academic work when you are 'most awake' and routine activities when you are less alert.

- **Make the most of small scraps of time.** Use otherwise unproductive time, such as when commuting or before going to sleep, to jot down ideas, edit work or make plans. Keep a notebook with you to write down your thoughts.

- **Keep your documents organised.** If your papers are well filed, you won't waste time looking for something required for the next step.

- **Make sure you always have a plan.** Often, the reason projects don't go well is because there is no scheme to work to. Laying out a plan for an essay, report or project helps you to clarify the likely structure behind your efforts. Writing out a fairly detailed plan – not just a few headings – will save you time in the long run.

- **Extend your working day.** If you can deal with early rising, you may find that setting your alarm earlier than normal provides a few extra minutes or hours to help you achieve a short-term goal.

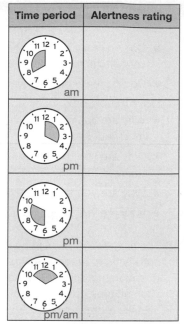

Time period	Alertness rating
am	
pm	
pm	
pm/am	

Figure 8.2 Are you a morning, afternoon, evening or night person? Rate yourself (marks out of 10) according to when you find yourself most alert and able to study productively.

HOW TO AVOID PUTTING THINGS OFF

One of the hardest parts of time management is getting started on tasks. Procrastination is all too easy, and can involve the following:

- convincing yourself that other low-priority work is more important or preferable;
- switching frequently among tasks, and not making much progress in any of them;
- talking about your work rather than doing it;
- planning for too long rather than working;
- having difficulty starting a piece of writing (having 'writer's block');
- spending too long on presentational elements (e.g. the cover page or a diagram), rather than the 'meat' of the project.

Definition: procrastination

This is simply putting off a task for another occasion. As the poet, Edward Young, wrote: 'Procrastination is the thief of time'.

A particular type of procrastination involves displacement activity – doing things that help you to avoid a difficult or distasteful task. For example:

- Do you really need to check and answer all your texts and emails or update your status on your social networking site before getting down to work?
- Do you really need to watch that TV programme or have another spell at that computer game?
- Why are you cooking tonight, rather than eating fast food and getting down to your studies much quicker?
- Why are you drawing such a neat diagram, when creating a less tidy one will let you get on to the next topic?
- Why are you so keen to chat to your friends rather than go to the library?
- Why are you shopping today, when you could easily leave it until later?

The first step in preventing the syndrome of procrastination, and especially displacement activity, is to recognise what your subconscious is doing. You need to make a conscious effort to counteract this side of your personality, by analysing your behaviour and possibly setting yourself time or other targets with 'rewards' to tempt you into meeting these. For example, 'I'll take a break when I've written the next section, 200 words . . .'

You might also make a list of things that need to be done and prioritise these into 'immediate', 'soon' and 'later' categories. Convince yourself that you will not start on the 'soon' and 'later' categories until you have fulfilled all those items on the 'immediate' list. And don't be tempted to think that if you get the smaller things out of the way that will free up your mind for the bigger issues – all that will happen is that more lower-category issues will creep into your attention.

Delaying completion of a task, in itself a form of procrastination, is another aspect of time management that many find difficult. It's a special problem for those afflicted by perfectionism. Good time managers recognise when to finish tasks, even if the task is not in a 'perfect' state. At university, doing this can mean that the sum of results from multiple assignments is better, because your attention is divided more appropriately, rather than focusing on a single task at the expense of others.

Tips for getting started on tasks and completing them on time are provided in Table 8.2.

Table 8.2 Ten tips for getting started on academic tasks and completing them on time

1 **Improve your study environment.** Your focus and concentration will depend on this.
   - Create a tidy workplace. Although tidying up can be a symptom of procrastination, in general it is easier to start studying at an empty desk and in an uncluttered room.
   - Reduce noise. Some like background music, while others don't – but it's generally other people's noise that really interrupts your train of thought. A solution might be to go to a quiet place like a library.
   - Escape. Why not take all you need to a different location where there will be a minimum of interruptions? Your focus will be enhanced if the task you need to do is the only thing you can do, so take with you only the notes and papers you require.

2 **Avoid distractions.** If you are easily tempted away from tasks by your friends, you'll have to learn to decline their invitations politely. Hang up a 'do not disturb' sign, and explain why to your friends; disappear off to a quieter location without telling anyone where you will be; or switch off your phone, TV or email program. One strategy might be to say to friends, 'I can't come just now, but how about having a short break in half an hour?'

3 **Work in short bursts while your concentration is at a maximum.** After this, give yourself a brief break, perhaps by going for a short walk, and then start back again.

4 **Find a way to start.** Breaking initial barriers is vital. When writing, this is a very common problem because of the perceived need to begin with a 'high impact' sentence that reads impressively. This is unnecessary, and starting with a simple definition or restatement of the question or problem is perfectly acceptable. If you lack the motivation to begin work, try thinking briefly about the bigger picture: your degree and career, and how the current task is a small but essential step to achieving your goals.

5 **Focus on the positive.** You may be so anxious about the end point of your task that this affects your ability to start it. For example, many students are so nervous about exams or speaking in public that they freeze in their preparation and put the whole thing off. One way to counter this would be to practise – perhaps through mock exams or rehearsing an oral presentation with a friend. Focus on positive aspects – things you do know, rather than those you don't; or the good results you want to tell people about, rather than those that failed to provide answers.

6 **In written tasks, don't feel you have to work in a linear fashion.** Word-processing software allows you to work out of sequence, which can help get you going. So, for a large report, it might help to start on a part that is 'mechanical', such as a reference list or results section. Sometimes it's a good idea to draft the summary, abstract or contents list first, because this will give you a plan to work to.

7 **Cut up large tasks.** If you feel overwhelmed by the size of a job and this prevents you from starting it, break the task down to manageable, achievable chunks. Then, try to complete something every day. Maintaining momentum in this way will allow you to whittle away the job in small pieces.

8 **Work alongside others.** If you arrange to work alongside others, you can spur each other on with sympathy, humour and the promise of a drink or break after each study period.

9 **Ask for help.** You may feel that you lack a particular skill to attempt some component of the task (e.g. maths, spelling, or the ability to use a software program) and that this is holding you back. Don't be afraid to ask for help. Rather than suffering in isolation, consult a fellow student, lecturer, or skills adviser; or visit one of the many websites that offer assistance.

10 **Don't be too much of a perfectionist.** We all want to do well, but doing your very best takes time – a commodity that should be carefully rationed so that all tasks are given their fair share. Perfectionism can prevent or delay you getting started if you feel your initial efforts need to be faultless (see 4 above). Also, achieving fault-free work requires progressively more effort, with less return as you get nearer to perfection. The time you need to spend to attain the highest standards will probably be better used on the next task.

Invest in items to support your time management. Helpful items could include a diary, wall planner, mobile phone with diary facility, and alarm clock – then use them!

Investigate how you really use your time. Time-management experts often ask clients to write down what they do for every minute of several days and thereby work out where the productive time disappears to. If you are unsure exactly what you waste time on, you might like to keep a detailed record for a short period, using a suitable coding for your activities. When you have identified the time-wasting aspects of your day, you can then act to cut these down (or out). Those of a more numerical bent might wish to construct a spreadsheet to do this and work out percentages spent on different activities. Once you have completed your time sheet, analyse it to see whether you spend excessive amounts of time on any one activity or may not have the balance right. As you think about this, remember that universities assume you will be carrying out academic-related activities for roughly 40 hours per week.

Create artificial deadlines. Set yourself a finishing date that is ahead of the formal submission deadline for your assignment. That way you will have the time to review your work, correct errors and improve the quality of presentation.

Build flexibility into your planning. We often end up rushing things because the unexpected has interrupted a timetable that is too tightly scheduled. To avoid this, deliberately introduce empty slots into your plans to allow for these contingencies.

Try to prioritise the items on your 'to do' list. If you produce a daily list of tasks, spend some time thinking about how you wish to prioritise and order them through the day. You might adopt a numerical system or one using stars, for example.

Ask yourself whether your lifestyle needs radical surgery. You may find that little in this chapter seems relevant because your time is dominated by a single activity. This might be socialising, caring for others, outside employment or travelling, for example. In these cases, you may need to make fundamental changes to your lifestyle to place greater emphasis on your studies. In some cases a student counsellor might be able to help you decide what needs to be done.

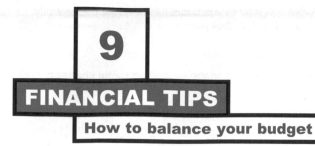

9

FINANCIAL TIPS

How to balance your budget

Many students report that keeping to a budget is one of the hardest parts of student life. This chapter provides information to help you predict likely costs, advice on keeping costs down and hints on what to do if your budget isn't working out.

Being at university will almost certainly result in a change in your financial status. Much depends on your personal circumstances, and in particular the degree of support your family is able to provide; however, being a student will probably restrict your earning potential and almost certainly increase your expenses. These days, many students expect to carry a debt following their studies – one that you will probably wish to minimise.

CREATING A BUDGET

A budget contains predictions about your income and your expenditure over a defined period. The main reasons you should set up a budget are:

● you will have a realistic view of the costs of being a student, especially in relation to less easily predicted expenses (**Ch 2**);

● you will be less likely to overdraw your bank account past any agreed limit and will therefore avoid incurring penalties;

● by forecasting expenditure on essentials, you can have a better idea of any surplus available for lower priority or luxury items;

● you can reserve sums of money for anticipated costs;

● if you predict ahead of time that you will need to take out a loan, you may be better placed to borrow an appropriate amount and negotiate a more advantageous interest rate;

● you can feel more confident that any debt you do incur will be controlled.

> ### Studying and living in a large city
>
> This can be much more expensive than at a campus-based or smaller-town university. Additional costs arise mainly from accommodation, transport (it is often difficult or very expensive to live near the campus) and food. For example, costs in London are estimated to be about 18 per cent higher than elsewhere.

The table in the Appendix on page 446 can be used as the basis for a budget over weekly, monthly or yearly periods. To predict your costs, you should:

- use past expenditure as a guide, adding a suitable amount for inflation;
- use other sources of information, such as Figure 2.1 (page 6), agreed rental contracts and student-focused financial websites;
- use a well-educated guess, perhaps based on discussions with other students or family members.

If you feel that budgeting over short periods is inappropriate for you because your expenditure is irregular, you could try working to an annual cycle, dividing infrequent but large outgoings by 12 to give average monthly costs. You can then create a budget for each month, but should take care to carry over any monthly surplus, rather than spending it. You can also use standing orders or direct debits to smooth out costs over the year.

> ✔ **A spreadsheet could help with budgeting**
>
> If you are familiar with this kind of program, consider using a spreadsheet to set up your budget as on page 446. You will be able to adjust the income and expenditure headings to suit your circumstances. You can also monitor your income and outgoings more easily by updating with real values.

BANKING AND LOAN OPTIONS

Setting up a bank account

Many people only start 'serious' banking when they become students. Even if you already have an account, it may pay to change your bank either for convenience or because of the incentives on offer. Some matters, such as overdraft facilities, are decided at branch level and you may find it may be useful to be able to talk face to face with staff when arranging such facilities.

Banks are keen to attract students as customers, because of their relatively stable careers and future earning potential. You should therefore shop around to find the best bank and the best type of account to suit your needs. You can speak to representatives of different banks who attend Freshers' Week fairs in the early stages of the new academic year. Alternatively, you can make online comparisons of bank account offers (but note that some offers may *not* apply to students). Some useful sites include:

- **www.nus.org.uk** – information provided by the National Union of Students;
- **www.studentloans.co.uk** – information on a selection of banks offering student banking; and
- **www.studentbanking.co.uk** – current information on offers for student banking provided by the main high street banks.

Here are some important aspects to consider:

- **Convenience and facilities.** Is there a branch or cash dispenser (ATM) on campus, or is a good telephone or internet banking facility available? Would you like associated debit or credit cards?
- **Costs and potential gains.** Will your account be free to run? Will you incur large charges if you accidentally overdraw? Might you gain interest when, however briefly, your account is in credit?
- **Overdraft facilities and interest rates.** How much will the bank lend you? What will it cost in interest (if anything)? When will you have to pay your debt back?
- **Incentives.** What will the bank give you to join them?

To set up an account, you will need to provide evidence of your identity and status. Typically, a bank will ask to see your birth certificate or passport, evidence of your address and some indication of your student status, such as an acceptance letter or matriculation card. They may also require an initial deposit, such as a loan cheque.

Loan options

There are various options to borrow money or receive grants to finance your studies, including tuition fee loans, maintenance loans, bursaries and scholarships. Your ability to access these will depend on where you study and your personal circumstances. In most cases, loans will only need to be repaid after you graduate, and in certain cases only when you are earning in excess of a salary threshold. Some grants, generally awarded to students from less well-off backgrounds, do not have to be repaid.

Ideally, of course, you will be trying to minimise the debt you carry into your later career – at that time you will have other priorities for your earnings, such as setting up a home. Two ways in which you can reduce your debt are by:

- taking on part-time work so you increase your income;
- budgeting carefully so that you reduce your outgoings.

How can I get the work–study balance right?

For most students, the clear priority should be degree-course work and not term-time employment. Conditions of your employment (timing and length of shifts, for example) may tend to interfere with your studies or even attendance at lectures and other parts of your course. You should avoid this conflict if at all possible.

TERM-TIME AND VACATION WORK

Naturally, universities and their staff expect you to study hard to earn your degree. In fact, they expect you to put in the equivalent of a full-time working week. Not all of this is taken up in 'contact' with staff in lectures, tutorials and practicals, but it is expected that you read, revise and work on essays and other assessments during the remainder of the time. If you take on term-time paid employment, this may affect your study effort and it may reduce time you would otherwise spend socialising or in sport, leisure or rest. Many sources recommend taking on no more than 15 hours' paid work per week.

The university vacations will provide you with opportunities for longer, more intensive periods of employment, which can replenish your bank account without affecting your studies. Many of these opportunities will involve seasonal occupations, but some of these fall into the category of 'internships', which, while often less financially rewarding, may provide vital career-related experience and are worth pursuing.

Term-time and vacation work and your later employability

Remember to include on your CV any employment you have had while at university, as this will indicate that you have a work ethic, experience and skills that could be valuable in a future career. Your term-time employers may also be willing to provide a reference for you (Ch 71).

University towns and universities themselves provide many opportunities for paid term-time and vacation work and there is usually a contact point where these are advertised, for example, at the students' union or support services ('job shop', or similar).

WHAT TO DO IF YOUR FINANCES SEEM OUT OF CONTROL

If your budget doesn't seem to be working out or if you are approaching or in danger of exceeding your authorised overdraft limit, it is vital to talk to someone about your finances. You might approach a family member, your university's student finance specialist (often working within student services), or people at your students' union. Your bank adviser may be able to point you in the direction of additional sources of money (loans) or extend your overdraft facility. Most of these people will be sympathetic to your needs, perhaps surprisingly so, as long as you are open and honest with them.

Always respond promptly to all correspondence regarding debt

Explain what you intend to do and take notes of the names of the staff to whom you spoke and what was said. Keep a note of times and dates of all communications.

Whoever you approach, you should try at all times to maintain a good relationship with your bank and its staff and, in particular, develop or preserve your credit status. This will be important in later life when you may wish to take on a substantial debt such as a car loan or mortgage. Your credit rating may be at risk if you exceed debt limits or fail to make expected payments.

PRACTICAL TIPS FOR COST-SAVING AND BUDGETING

Actively control your weekly or monthly expenditure. From your budget calculations (page 446), work out how much you should be taking out of the bank each week – and try to keep to this. Limit your 'pocket' money (the cash in your pocket or purse for day-to-day expenses). That way you will not be tempted to buy small treats, the cost of which add up. If you spend more than you planned in a given period, think of it as a loan from yourself and make do with less cash in the following week(s). Bear in mind that expenditure at the beginning of an academic session is always higher, and slows down as the year progresses.

Keep track of your account balance. By doing so you can avoid going into the red or exceeding your overdraft limit. In particular, don't forget to take a note of how much you take out of the 'hole in the wall' (ATM) to top up your wallet or purse. Try to pay predictable bills by standing order or direct debit, so that you can have a better idea of your outgoings and will not receive a surprise bill – but make sure that you always have enough in your account to service these payments and remember to cancel them when your obligation to make these payments terminates.

Keep money back for known costs and contingencies. When grant and loan money comes in, allocate some of this to known recurrent costs, predictable one-off expenses and 'emergencies'. Use only the remainder for day-to-day expenses.

Bank smartly. Put loan or other income that comes at the start of term/semester or year into an interest-bearing account, so you can benefit from this. When borrowing, try to do this from as few sources as possible and at as advantageous an interest rate as possible. However, if you need to borrow, do so in instalments, so you are not tempted to spend any lump sum you receive too quickly. Shop around if necessary and look for special deals. Move your debt if necessary. Credit cards differ greatly in interest rate and may have good introductory deals. Try not to use store cards as they generally have very high interest rates unless you pay off the entire balance each month.

Save on insurance costs. It's always worth shopping around to find the best deal and some companies have special polices for students. You should also find out whether your family's insurance policy for contents covers your possessions while you are away from home and under what circumstances and with what excesses. Likewise, check on your family's travel insurance policies. It may be cheaper overall if your family policy shifts to one that covers you too.

Shop smartly at the supermarket. If you have to buy food, play the supermarkets at their own game to save money:

- Find out which supermarket group is the cheapest for the goods normally on your shopping list.
- Find out the times that perishable goods are taken off the main shelves to be sold cheaply before their sell-by date – and time your shopping trips to suit.
- Check which cheap or own-brand items are acceptable, and buy these, but note that some of these may represent a false economy, either because there's less in the packet or tin, or because the quality is significantly reduced.
- Be aware of supermarket ploys to encourage impulse buying. When you visit, make a shopping list and stick to it.
- Take advantage of two-for-one offers to stock up – but only if you would normally buy the product.
- Use loyalty schemes and student discounts to your advantage.
- Don't shop when you are hungry. This sounds daft, but it works, as you won't be tempted as much to stock up.

Gain full benefits from vacation work. If you can get a job during the vacations, you may wish to try the following:

- Put a proportion of your earnings in an 'untouchable' account to cover your expenses for term-time.
- Take full advantage of 'perks' of the job such as free meals or cheap goods.
- Save any tips separately for a treat or special item.
- Ensure you aren't being taxed at an inappropriate 'emergency' rate: contact your local tax office if unsure, quoting your National Insurance (NI) number.
- When relatively flush with cash, do not be tempted to splash out on luxury items you don't really need.

10

CAMPUS ORIENTATION

How to identify the key facilities at your university

Knowing your way around campus is essential if you don't want to waste time or miss lectures or meetings, but it isn't always straightforward. Familiarising yourself with your new environment will be easier if you follow the tips within this chapter.

The physical area covered by university buildings is usually referred to as a campus. Some universities are in the middle of cities, while others are located at a distance from city life. Your university may have a traditional layout with quadrangles and lawns, or its buildings may be placed within busy city surroundings. Often, universities are spread over more than a single campus.

Whatever kind of campus you inhabit, initially you will need to find your way about. Lectures and tutorials often take place in buildings that are widely dispersed and you'll need to recognise these buildings, learn the shortest routes between locations, and find out where certain key resources are housed. Often buildings are named after important benefactors or famous alumni or researchers who have a connection with the institution. Campus maps usually have a key, with these names in alphabetical order.

CAMPUS TOURS

You may find that your university's website has a virtual tour of the campus, which will help you explore it online before you arrive.

Universities usually run campus tours in the early days of Freshers' Week. These tend to be led by senior students, so you get the chance to ask questions and benefit from their knowledge. Even if you are local, it is unlikely that you will have discovered the inner parts of the university campus, so it is worthwhile attending. It's also a good way to meet people and explore in company.

Maps

Most universities provide campus maps with their enrolment documentation; these will also be available at the central reception facility and are often also available electronically on university websites. Most campuses are well signposted but, if you are in doubt, stop someone and ask. An A–Z style of street map for the town may be a useful addition to help you find your way around the surrounding area.

After you've done the tour, it's worth going walkabout armed with your maps to ensure that you know how to get to the places you'll need to be at and take note of how long it actually takes to move from one place to another – make allowance for extra time needed when paths and roads may be busy as people move from class to class. You'll find out where your lectures and other learning activities are going to take place from the timetable given out when you matriculate or when you register for a specific course.

KEY BUILDINGS AND LOCATIONS

Among the important buildings to identify in your first few days are:

- where to matriculate and/or register for classes;
- where your lectures will be held;
- where tutorials, practicals and labs will take place;
- where IT facilities can be accessed;
- where to eat and socialise (for example, the students' union);
- where you can study.

The checklist in the Information Box below includes these and itemises additional buildings and locations that you should be able to find.

---

i

Some key buildings and locations – a checklist

❏ Bookshops

❏ Buildings where your lectures will be held

❏ Buildings where your tutorials or labs will take place

❏ Campus bank and/or cash dispenser (ATM)

❏ School/faculty building for your discipline

❏ School/faculty (admin.) office

❏ Finance/cash office

❏ Informal learning spaces

❏ IT suites

❏ Main or subject library

❏ Registry/academic administration office

❏ Residences office

❏ Students' union or association

❏ Student 'help desk'

❏ Support services

❏ Student union shop

❏ University health centre

Some buildings will be large and navigation skills will be required to find your way around inside. For example, the university library is one place where, initially, you may feel rather lost. The librarians will be happy to answer queries about facilities at any point in the year, but in the early weeks of the academic year they usually offer special library tours. These are valuable not only because they show you where books and other resources are kept, but also because they show you how to use the library catalogue to find out what book and online resources are available and how to access them (Ch 23).

TOWN INFORMATION

Depending on the size of the local town or city, universities often run bus tours to help students who are not local to become familiar with the local area. This is important if you do not want to become too campus-oriented with your activities. Speaking with students living at home will also help you find your way about, since they have local knowledge and will be able to help people new to the area to find their bearings.

Some useful locations – a checklist

Maintenance:
- ❑ Bank
- ❑ Post office
- ❑ Medical practice
- ❑ Supermarkets
- ❑ Chemist
- ❑ Launderette
- ❑ Recycling point

Public facilities:
- ❑ Police station
- ❑ Public library

Travel:
- ❑ Bus station
- ❑ Rail station
- ❑ Airport links
- ❑ Taxi ranks

Entertainment:
- ❑ Cinemas and theatres
- ❑ Football grounds
- ❑ Sports centres
- ❑ Swimming pools
- ❑ Restaurants
- ❑ Clubs and pubs

Another useful source of local information is the people who work in your institution. They will often live locally and will be able to provide you with information that might otherwise be difficult to find. For example, they might be able to tell you where would be the best place to buy a set of second-hand pots and pans, or where you can find a shop selling halal or kosher food.

TRANSPORT INFORMATION

You'll need to work out how best to travel from your accommodation to the campus. This may be a simple walk or cycle ride, but if you live some distance away from the campus it may be necessary to find out about public transport options. The local *Yellow Pages* will have contact details under 'Bus, coach and tramway services' and 'Train information'. Associated websites advertised alongside may offer online public transport timetables and route-planning information. Local tourist offices will also have this kind of information, including places to go and things to do within the area. Check out student travel offers and discounts.

Where students have to travel between campuses, or between a residence and the campus, universities may provide shuttle buses timed to fit in with lecture schedules. If you will have to undertake such trips regularly, make sure that you know the timetable as well as the pick-up and drop-off points. Find out about late-night bus services too, since off-peak services may be less frequent – important to know if you are working late in the library or are out socialising later in the evening.

Plan your days ahead. Before you get to know your routine and the tracks you'll need to make between teaching venues, use your street map and the campus map to work out the shortest routes in advance.

Always carry your matriculation (ID) card when you are on campus. This is usually required for access to buildings and facilities, such as the library and Students' Union.

Take care over personal safety. Exploring a new town or city is interesting, but it is better to do this in company, particularly at night. Students' Unions often run late-night bus services so that it should not be necessary to walk alone at night. If you feel a personal alarm would make you feel safer, these are normally sold in campus shops such as those run by Students' Unions.

11

SOCIAL LIFE AT UNIVERSITY

How to create new social networks and support existing ones

> For nearly all students, university involves great changes to their social relationships. There will be changes to contacts with family, old friends and groups. New friendships will be formed, but they won't happen overnight. This chapter shows how new networks and friendships evolve and suggests ways of maintaining existing relationships.

A university is like a city within a city. Its community is populated by people who live locally as well as those who have come from other parts of the UK and beyond. It is enriched by the variety of people who live, work and study on the campus. As a member of this cosmopolitan society, you will begin to build up social and learning networks and will make many new and long-lasting friendships. However, this will not happen immediately. It takes time to create these contacts and friendship groups and that process will depend especially on where you live.

LIVING IN HALLS OF RESIDENCE AND OTHER RENTED ACCOMMODATION

Many institutions try to offer first-time students the opportunity to live in a hall of residence. Here you will immediately have the potential, within a very short time, to meet a diverse range of new people, and will often live in close contact with students from different backgrounds. Although most accommodation offices try to 'match' people in the way they distribute students in residences, this is not always possible. It may take you some time to locate someone doing the same course as you, or with the same social interests, or a group of people with whom you feel comfortable in terms of personality.

One thing you may share with others is living away from the family home, so social events are usually organised to help new students to feel at home and to encourage people to mix. Taking part in these activities will help you to feel part of your new community. Queuing for meals, doing your washing in the in-house launderette or making a cup of tea also provide opportunities for meeting people and striking up conversations.

You may have chosen to live in shared private rented accommodation. This has the potential advantage of introducing you to the closer friendship group of your flatmates. On the other hand, it may limit the number of new people you meet, and to compensate you may need to make extra efforts to take part in social activities on the campus.

International students

Often students from other parts of the world come to the UK to study, hoping to experience British life and develop their skills in English. This can be quite difficult to do if they are routinely housed in the same residences, thus creating an international 'ghetto'. If you are an international student, introduce yourself to home students and ask them questions about language and customs. This gives you a chance to interact with native speakers and become less reliant on your own national or ethnic group. Join societies and clubs as a means of broadening your circle of friends and experience of university life.

LIVING AT HOME

In many universities, a considerable number of students live at home. This may be for financial reasons or, in the case of many mature students, because they have an established home within the immediate area. In these cases, it is important to see your university friendships as complementing your home-based social networks. Your university contacts are more likely to relate to the nine-to-five experience of campus life. This means that friendships are more likely to be formed with fellow students you meet in lectures, tutorials, practicals or labs.

For many home-based students, transport arrangements or family responsibilities may make it impractical to attend many of the social functions that may take place in the evenings or at weekends. However, in the early weeks, if you can manage to attend one or two of these events, you will be present at a critical point in the establishment of potential friendships.

Mature students

Increasingly, mature students are forming a larger part of university communities. If you are a mature student, it is important that you participate in the wider life of your institution so that your voice and interests are reflected in university activities and policies. Many mature students find it refreshing to count among their friends students who may be the same age as their own children – and this can work in reverse also.

MAKING THE FIRST MOVES

Even if you are shy, you will recognise that it is important to mix and to work at forming new relationships. We all have different ideas of what makes someone a possible kindred spirit and, if you are a 'people watcher', you may find it interesting to look out for the personality types in Table 11.1. You might even recognise yourself!

Table 11.1 Social stereotypes you may meet at university. Of course, there may be others, and it is unlikely that everyone you meet will be so well defined as these characters.

Social stereotype	Description	How you might relate to them socially
The butterflies	Want to be everybody's friend and flit from one group to another; seem to know and be known by everyone.	If you also are a butterfly, this is alright. If you're not, accept this type of person for the open, sharing, but short-term acquaintance they may prove to be.
The lions	Usually go around in an exclusive group or clique; very difficult to infiltrate unless you share their value systems or shared experience.	If you have an 'intro' to the group of lions through an existing member, it may be possible to break into it. These groups can start out as apparent opinion formers, but, as other (non-clique) networks are formed, the influence potential of the lions diminishes.
The elephants	Lovely but loud extroverts – you will hear them before you see them. They always seem to need to make a noise – processing along the corridors, talking at full volume and oblivious to the fact that others are trying to work/sleep/study.	If you are an elephant, you will probably find and go around with other elephants. If you're not an elephant, making friends with an elephant allows you entry to an alternative, but often larger-than-life, world.
The worker bees	Tend to feel insecure in their own abilities and try to make up for this by working extra hard. Others who like to work may just be workaholics.	Worker bees may come across as serious-minded, and tend to find their friendship groups among similar types.
The moles	Shy, modest types who frequently may give an impression of being academically weak. However, often they are highly competent, but they just don't project this loudly.	These are people to watch because they will have sussed out how the course works, what the strategic learning points are and how best to succeed. Generally, they don't say much, but they observe a lot. If you need to know something about the course, they will probably have read all the information – and know what it means.
The cuckoos	May have swallowed all the hype about the great uni social life but may have played too hard and too long. Generally, they do not make it through the first year of university.	These people may simply have come to university because they see it as a rite of passage on to the next phase in their lives. Their priorities may not be studying towards a degree. If you find yourself mixing with such a group, you probably need to take stock of your own goals and how you aim to achieve them.
The homing pigeons	May live on or off campus but feel the tug of home very strongly. Consequently, they may make too few opportunities to mix with other students, preferring the security of home.	These people may find university so different from home and their previous learning environment that they return home at every opportunity or preserve their home networks to the exclusion of potential university ones.
The grasshoppers	Share characteristics with elephants, lions and butterflies. Hop from party to party and generally live it up. Fatigue often takes over and they lose sight of the primary activity of studying.	These people tend to have developed a set of values and behaviours that may not equate with success or achievement of full potential. If you wish to succeed, you can certainly go along with the grasshoppers but on your own terms – that is, on condition that you keep up with your academic work and will not be available to party every night of the week.
The hares	These folk are often doing too many things: for example, by leaping from one part-time job to another part-time job in order to keep themselves financially solvent.	These types will have little time for making friends although they may need, of necessity, to cultivate a few friends from whom they can borrow notes and general information.

On the academic scene

Many friendships emerge by sharing experiences. The most obvious way is by meeting people who are in the same classes as you. You will find that you get to know people through tutorial or lab groups, as well as from striking up casual conversations as you wait outside a class or lecture room. In some lectures, you will be encouraged to work with people sitting around you and this is an effective way of widening your circle of acquaintances. One way of ensuring that you get to know people studying the same subject is to volunteer to be a class representative (**Ch 12**).

> ✔ **Taking the initiative**
>
> Make a point of introducing yourself to the people next to you in lectures. Vary the position in which you sit in lectures so that you maximise the number of people you encounter – but avoid the back row if you want to have a good view of the board and hear clearly. Sitting nearer the front ensures that you avoid some of the distraction of noise from others.

On the social scene

Membership of the students' union or students' association is automatic in most institutions. This gives you access to all the facilities and activities provided within the union. These services are managed by a student executive, although some of the commercial activities such as bars, cafés and restaurants are managed by professionals. Office-bearers of the union/association are elected by the student body and the process is conducted under the scrutiny of a returning officer nominated from the staff body. You may feel that you would like to participate in this aspect of student life by standing as a year representative (**Ch 12**).

Joining one of the university's many clubs or societies is a way of finding people who share the same interests as you. The range of possible activities is vast and you will need to decide how many societies you can realistically afford to join. Being a fully participating member will not be possible for more than a few, and membership fees soon add up. Some subjects have their own societies, which may organise their own subject-specific events.

Pubbing, clubbing and partying are all part of student life. You'll need to strike a balance between night-time fun and the need to be bright and attentive in daytime classes. Also, there is a limit to the amount of money you can afford to spend on these social activities. Conversely, staying in your room and being abstemious can be limiting also. It is perfectly possible to go out and *not* spend a lot of money – hard drinking is not a prerequisite for a good social life, but pub or students' union life may offer the setting that helps consolidate friendship groupings.

> **i** **Examples of university societies**
>
> - Army Cadet Corps
> - Poker Club
> - Chemistry Society
> - Debating Society
> - European Society
> - Lesbian, Gay and Bisexual Society
> - Mature Students' Society
> - Public-speaking Club

On the sports scene

People often quote the old saying 'a healthy mind in a healthy body' in relation to university study. In more modern language this might translate to 'work hard and play hard'. Joining your sports union or institute is a way of keeping fit and making friends with people who enjoy the same sporting activities as you. It will also help you to perform well in your academic studies. On campus, there are numerous possibilities of sporting activities and facilities available at moderate costs. Many institutions offer family memberships, so that for mature students, for example, this is a way of involving your family in your university life.

Typical sports activities

- Badminton
- 5-a-side football
- Golf
- Hockey
- Judo
- Karate
- Keep-fit
- Squash
- Swimming
- Tennis
- Volley ball
- Water polo

MAINTAINING CONNECTIONS

Through time, you will become involved in many extra-curricular activities and form a wide range of new friendships. The possible links between these networks and your existing ones are illustrated in Figure 11.1.

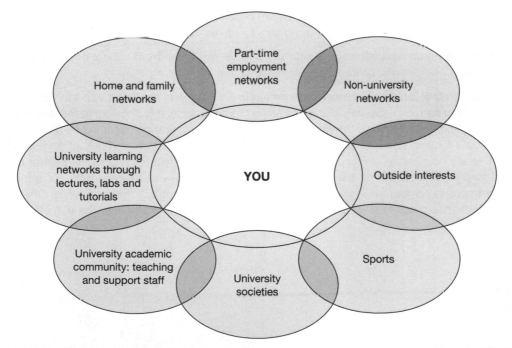

Figure 11.1 Your personal networks. Pre-existing networks are denoted in grey, while potential new university groupings are shown in colour. These groupings may overlap, but the common feature is you.

It's important not to take old relationships for granted. Your family and pre-existing friends will miss you and will want to find out how things are going. Especially if you are living away from home, try to keep in contact and arrange to meet up with your old friends from time to time. You might earmark an evening each week to phone home, or send an email update, or arrange a Skype call.

PRACTICAL TIPS FOR ESTABLISHING YOUR UNIVERSITY SOCIAL LIFE

If you are living away from home, try not to go back within the first month. This may seem harsh but you need to make the break. If you go back home too soon, you may miss out on a number of induction and social events and this may make you feel isolated on your return. It takes time to settle into any new setting and it is better to keep in touch by phone, texting or email so that you maintain your home support networks while building new university ones.

If you are living at home, try to arrange things so that you can attend evening social activities. Some people feel that living at home isolates them from the social life of the university. This need not be the case. If you can manage to attend some activities that are of particular interest to you – and there are many early evening events that mean you don't have to worry about when the last bus is – you will meet people who share something in common with you.

Take the initiative by introducing yourself to others and engaging them in conversation. It helps if you can expand on the conversational gambits of: 'What's your name?' 'Where are you from?' and 'What are you studying?' By the nth time these questions have been answered, both the responses and your interest in them become rather mechanical. Ask people secondary questions about their feelings and responses to events; this usually gets the conversation going.

Try not to go around exclusively with the people you know from school or college. Branch out. Meet new people. Learn about different cultures and communities.

Expect to feel lonely or homesick sometimes. Having made radical changes to your lifestyle, this is only natural, especially at the beginning of your course. It is possible to feel alone in a crowd, and university might seem to be just such a place. If you do begin to feel that this is the case for you, speak to someone about how you are feeling. With a little support from your university counselling service, someone from the chaplaincy team or a personal tutor or adviser of studies, or maybe even a student who is in the year above you, you can work out some strategies to combat these feelings so that you begin to feel part of the community. Often you can integrate more easily by getting involved in some extra-curricular activities (**Ch 12**).

12

CONTRIBUTING TO THE ACADEMIC AND OUTSIDE COMMUNITY

How you can benefit as well as give something back by participating in non-academic activities

Extra-curricular activities have the potential to contribute hugely to the richness of your university experience and to the academic and non-academic communities. There is a wide range of activities to choose from, but balancing these with your academic studies is vital to your success at university.

Your time as a university student is one where you are studying within a small 'campus community' within your university town. This campus community, like all communities, is made up of people with different interests and enthusiasms. You can become involved in what university has to offer in many different ways, and you can also seek outside activities to provide a release from campus life. Some may choose to pursue activities such as a sport or skill with others who share their interest; some may wish to carry out charitable work, while others might opt to become involved in student representation through their students' union or students' association. Participating in these kinds of extra-curricular activities can result in life-changing experiences – from developing relationships with soulmates to finding a vocation that influences your future career, as well as bringing a sense of balance to your life.

Extra-curricular activities

These are voluntary activities that are generally not examined as part of your university qualification, although some may be recognised by an outside body or certified as part of your university transcript. Certain universities give credit for activities whose extent and quality they can verify.

IDENTIFYING WAYS TO PARTICIPATE

The opportunities to take part in extra-curricular activities will vary from campus to campus, town to town. Whatever is on offer on your campus, you will find a variety of options that would rarely be found outside university. Many campus activities are generated for students by other students, while outside opportunities tend to be supported by the local community. In either case, your participation will help you to develop personal qualities and skills such as leadership, team-building and problem-solving – in short, many of the key skills sought by employers that are outlined in **Ch 6** and **Ch 69**.

As indicated in Table 12.1, there is an almost bewilderingly wide array of pursuits in which you can choose to take part. Your reasons for selecting from these might include:

- Having a past involvement with the same or similar groups, and hence confidence, skills and experience that might assist you and others;
- Having an interest or desire to participate in the main area of activity – for example, a wish to 'give something back' through charitable work, or a wish to participate in a specific sport;
- The social benefits of joining a club, society or sporting team (**Ch 11**);
- A relationship between the activity and your academic interests – for example, participating in a debating society if you are studying law; taking part in a student exchange if you wish to develop language skills; or joining a hill-walking club if you are aiming for an ecology degree;
- The potential value of the experience on your CV – for example, activities that might develop and/or demonstrate your leadership, honesty or other personal qualities (**Ch 69**);
- A chance to earn money to support your studies, where the activity is rewarded in this way;
- The prospect of gaining work-related experience and connections – for example, via a weekend job or a summer internship/placement;
- The opportunity to develop your religious faith through charitable acts;
- The benefits of keeping up connections if you are studying close to your home – for example, by continuing with a group you have previously been involved with;
- A chance to involve yourself in the local community and 'real world', rather than spend all your time on campus.

? Where can I find out more about voluntary activities?

There are several ways. As a first step, do a web search on charities or areas that interest you. Many organisations are national and have a generic website that links to local listings or contact information. Alternatively, approach local libraries, Citizens' Advice Bureaux or local authority offices: these will hold lists of local charities that might welcome your support and participation. You might also be able to obtain information from the university support services.

✔ Special requirements for volunteers

For some activities involving children and older people, it may be necessary for volunteers to undergo some criminal record check (sometimes termed 'disclosure'). This can take some time and there is a cost implication to the organisation wishing to recruit a volunteer. You should check this with your chosen organisation at the outset in case you have to wait for a lengthy period before being able to make a contribution.

Table 12.1 Examples of extra-curricular activities

Activity	Examples
Charities	Working in a charity shop; collecting on charity days; asking people to donate on a regular basis
Exchanges	Spending part of your degree abroad; working abroad in summer; helping with exchange students
Faith-based organistations	Taking part in church services; teaching at a Sunday school or equivalent; visiting parishioners
Internships and placements (see Ch 69)	Working for a local firm, a large conglomerate or government body
Representation	Putting yourself forward as a class representative; standing for election to the students' union or students' association; carrying out a special-interest survey
Skills-related	Learning a language; joining a student entrepreneurship organisation; gaining a first-aid qualification
Societies	Joining and taking part in a debating society, the poker club, or a musical group
Sports	Joining a local hockey team; playing for a university badminton team; playing squash with your friends
Volunteering and community engagement	Peer mentoring; working on a conservation project; writing for the student newspaper

PLAYING YOUR PART IN DECISION-MAKING

Representing your fellow students can be considered to be a special type of extra-curricular activity. You can contribute in three particular ways. The first is to stand as a candidate for the executive committee of your students' union or association, possibly in a sabbatical post in the students' union. Sabbatical officers are students who suspend their studies for a fixed period in order to undertake students' union duties. These paid positions are elected, but may have responsibilities related to reviews of the curriculum, running student facilities and interacting with university officials.

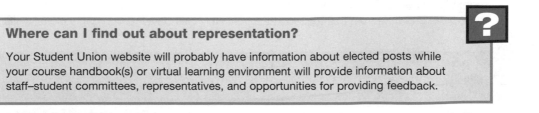

Where can I find out about representation?

Your Student Union website will probably have information about elected posts while your course handbook(s) or virtual learning environment will provide information about staff–student committees, representatives, and opportunities for providing feedback.

The second way in which you can become involved in representation is to become involved in school/department boards or committees at higher levels. To take part in these, you might need to become elected as a class, school or college representative. Some might regard committee activity as boring, and it often is, but it gives you a chance to see the bigger picture, to observe the conduct of meetings and to make a bigger difference for your fellow students. For example, this process might involve asking others for their views, or receiving these by email, then representing views at staff–student liaison committee or equivalent, which might meet once or twice a semester or term.

The third way in which you can affect decision-making is in providing evaluative feedback regarding your course. This is of particular relevance to the design and review of courses – an important, if not vital, part of the process of developing the course content and enhancing its delivery. In general, academics and external reference points are the main influences on the design of the curriculum, but student input helps to ensure that teaching is felt to be relevant and is provided in the most effective way.

Feedback forms are circulated at the end of most courses and sometimes after each topic. You should try to be fair and helpful in your ratings and comments – the course organisers will take them very seriously. Ideally, they will let you know what they have done as a result of your comments. If you feel that waiting until the end of the course will delay necessary action, just speak directly to your lecturer, the course leader or your class representative. In some cases you will be able to relay these comments via email or the virtual learning environment.

> **?** **Why give feedback?**
>
> You may be tempted to ask what you personally will gain from giving feedback. In fact, this is probably an inappropriate question to ask – it is really a matter of taking on an inherited obligation. This is because you will undoubtedly have gained from the comments provided by your predecessors. You therefore owe a debt to them, but instead of repaying it directly, you actually pass on the favour to the next generation who follow you.

STRIKING THE RIGHT BALANCE IN YOUR ACTIVITIES

The danger in taking part too enthusiastically in extra-curricular activities is that you will lose track of your academic responsibilities. This should not be a problem if you limit your involvement carefully and use appropriate time-management approaches (**Ch 8**). A positive aspect is that employers may note the extent of your involvement (it should be recorded in your CV, **Ch 70**) and take from this that you have relatively well-developed organisational skills.

PRACTICAL TIPS FOR EXPLORING OPPORTUNITIES FOR EXTRA-CURRICULAR AND REPRESENTATION ACTIVITIES

Look at your students' union notice boards or website to find out about clubs and their meeting times. Alternatively, go along to the Societies' Fayre often run by the students' union at the beginning of each academic year. Such events allow you to see the full range of societies active in your university. Where your special interest appears to be missing, approach a member of the Student Executive Committee to find out how to set up a new society to allow you to meet with others who might have a similar interest.

Think about the best activities to suit your interests and motivation. This may require a certain amount of introspection and reflection, so you could perhaps discuss it with a friend or a family member who knows you well.

Think forward to potential careers and which activities might have value when you apply for jobs or take up a position. The university careers service may be able to help you.

Find out more about representation in your university. Ask existing representatives about their experiences and find out exactly what the job involves and whether it is something you would like to do.

Take time to think about your course and what constructive criticism you can provide. How do different teaching approaches and models compare, in your view? How could they be developed further, given realistic resources?

Do something! The benefits of extra-curricular activities will only be available if you get involved. Taking the first step can be difficult, but thereafter, things will be a lot easier. Keeping busy will help you to adjust to your new life at university.

13

YOUR LEARNING PERSONALITY

How to identify and capitalise on your preferred learning style

In your role as a student, consider how you learn best and how this relates to your personality. This will help you to think more perceptively about how to tackle particular learning activities. This chapter explores approaches to determining your preferred learning style.

In real-world employment, a growth industry has developed in identifying employees' personality types and learning styles. The aim is to help managers identify the best way to approach the training of their employees and to build more effective work teams. In education, the potential for adjusting study techniques to produce a better fit with learning styles and preferences has long been recognised, and this is increasingly being promoted in university teaching.

i Definition: learning style

This is the way an individual takes in information, processes it, remembers it and expresses it. Some people refer to this as a learning preference. There are many different ways of categorising learning styles and it is probably true that no one category fits any person perfectly. We all have elements of one or more learning styles in our make-up and we may also change through time.

WHY KNOWING YOUR LEARNING STYLE IS IMPORTANT

Put simply, the potential exists to use information about your learning style to perform better at university. Recognising your learning style will help you to:

- identify your academic strengths and weaknesses;
- study more effectively;
- approach problem-solving more flexibly, especially when working with others.

Your natural learning style has already evolved significantly by the age of three and, as you go through your education, your style is influenced by the behaviours you learn. Trying to be true to your own learning style may have been difficult in the mass education system of school, where there is little scope to diverge from the predominant teaching methods. Your ability to favour your personal learning style may have been placed 'on hold' until you reach university, where you have more choice over what you learn and how you learn it.

However, as a student, for some activities you can probably adopt an approach that is suited to the subject and methods of teaching and assessment. If you know what your learning preferences are, you will be better placed to adopt an approach that is best suited to your 'natural' learning style. To help you do this, we have created a simple questionnaire to allow you to identify your preferences within a particular system, the Myers–Briggs Type Inventory (Tables 13.1, 13.2 and 13.3).

Words used to classify learning styles

Existentialist: describes someone who is sensitive to deep issues about human existence, especially belief in freedom and responsibility of the individual.

Extrovert: describes someone whose focus is on the external rather than themselves; generally outgoing and sociable.

Introvert: describes someone whose focus is on the internal self rather than the external; generally shy, withdrawn and reserved.

Kinesthetic: describes someone whose personality is often expressed through physical activity.

AN INTRODUCTION TO THE MYERS–BRIGGS TYPE INVENTORY

The Myers–Briggs Type Inventory (MBTI) has become a benchmark for identifying personality and learning-style attributes. It has been much used by managers, trainers and human resource specialists to explore team-building.

The MBTI is based on a list of 16 categories of personality (Briggs Myers and Myers, 1995). Look at Table 13.1 and do the short quiz that will help you to identify what your particular personality/learning type is. The 16 categories are derived from a list of four pairs of items. You are asked to opt for one or the other. If you have difficulty selecting, think about how you liked to do things as a child below the age of 10: that preference probably represents your underlying personality type. Once you have completed this quiz and found your category combination as a sequence of letters (for example, ENTJ), look at Table 13.2. This will 'decode' your style combination and its characteristics. After you have identified your attributes from the MBTI, go to Table 13.3, which identifies some of the implications for your learning.

Table 13.1 Personality/learning self-assessment quiz. This quiz is adapted from the Myers–Briggs Type Inventory (MBTI). There are four preference scales, with two choices in each – select what best describes you and tick the appropriate numbered box beneath each double selection. Note the letters you have selected in the self-assessment grid below and use this code in Tables 13.2 and 13.3.

Preference scale 1 – how you focus your attention and energy	
Extroversion (**E**)	**I**ntroversion (**I**)
• Like participation and socialisation; motivated by interaction with others • Act first and think second • Energised by outside world and people • Impatient of tedious jobs	• Prefer one-to-one communication and relationships; less comfortable in crowds • Think ideas through before speaking/acting • Want to understand the world • Need time to 'recharge batteries' regularly

1 My preference is   **E** ☐   **I** ☐

Preference scale 2 – how you take in information, become aware of others and events	
Sensing (**S**)	Intuitio**n** (**N**)
• Focus on the here and now • Observe what is going on all around; with good recall of past events • Instinctively use common sense and seek practical solutions to problems • Improvise solutions based on past experience • Like clear information; dislike unclear facts	• Focus on the future • Seek patterns and relationships between facts gathered • Trust instincts and imagination to evolve new possibilities • Improvise solutions based on theoretical understanding • Not fazed by unclear facts or information; guess meaning on information available

2 My preference is   **S** ☐   **N** ☐

Preference scale 3 – how you evaluate information, reach conclusions, make decisions	
Thinking (**T**)	**F**eeling (**F**)
• Analyse problem and logical impact of decisions objectively • Strong principles and need a purpose • Frankly honest rather than diplomatic • Accept conflict as a norm in dealing with people	• Reach decisions on basis of personal feelings and impact on others • Sensitive to needs of others and act accordingly • Seek consensus • Dislike conflict; intense dislike of tension

3 My preference is   **T** ☐   **F** ☐

Preference scale 4 – how you select your lifestyle, relate towards the outside world	
Judging (**J**)	**P**erceiving (**P**)
• Plan in detail in advance • Focus on task, finish and move on • Regulate life by routines, date-setting • Work best keeping ahead of deadlines	• Take things as they come, plan on the job • Multitask, good in emergencies, flexible and receptive to new information • Need flexibility; dislike being boxed in by arrangements • Not fazed by time pressure, work best close to deadlines

4 My preference is   **J** ☐   **P** ☐

Self-assessment:
Insert your four preferences **in order** and then look at Table 13.2 to find your definition

☐   ☐   ☐   ☐
1   **2**   **3**   **4**

Table 13.2 Personality/learning types (derived from MBTI). Check your personality characteristics from the letter combination that you derived in Table 13.1.

Extrovert types	
MBTI type	**Characteristics**
1 ENFJ	Friendly, outgoing, sociable and enthusiastic. Decide on basis of personal values. Empathetic but easily hurt; like to maintain stable relationships. Actively encourage personal growth in others. Attuned to others' emotions. *Keywords:* sensitive, innovative, optimistic, adaptable, resourceful
2 ENFP	Talkative, outgoing, curious and playful. Come up with new ideas, energise groups, proceed on the basis of patterns they see. May neglect details in planning. Enjoy experimentation and variety. *Keywords:* sensitive, innovative, creative, optimistic, adaptable, resourceful
3 ENTJ	Friendly, strong-willed, outspoken and logical. See the big picture. Demand much of selves and others. Natural leaders who organise people and processes towards completion. Develop systems to eliminate inefficiency. Less tolerant of people who do not come up to standard. *Keywords:* decisive, organised, efficient
4 ENTP	Friendly, outgoing, humorous, flexible and unpredictable. Make decisions on logical basis. Ingenious problem-solvers. Tend to ignore routine tasks. Like to initiate change. See obstacles as challenges to overcome. Sparkle in debate. Good at 'reading' people. *Keywords:* logical, analytical, creative, imaginative
5 ESFJ	Active, friendly, talkative and energetic. Good at hosting. Can't handle criticism or conflict. Encourage teamwork to overcome problems. Work hard at detail and meeting deadlines. Intensely loyal, need to belong. Decide on basis of personal values. *Keywords:* organised, responsible, conventional, realistic, literal
6 ESFP	Warm, gregarious, talkative, impulsive and curious. Live life in the fast lane, good company. Like harmony in relationships. Flexible, respond to life as it happens. Like troubleshooting, dealing with problems in fire-fighting mode. Can galvanise others into action. *Keywords:* impulsive, active, sensitive, caring, unpredictable
7 ESTJ	Energetic, outspoken, friendly and productive. Get things done. Deal with facts. Assume leadership roles. Bring order, process and completion. Decisions based on logic. Direct, tendency to be blunt to the point of seeming impersonal and uncaring. *Keywords:* practical, realistic, down-to-earth, traditional, accountable
8 ESTP	Active, adventurous, talkative, curious and impulsive. Live for today. Deal with facts objectively. Brevity in explanations: give recommendation and move on to next problem. Less interested in theories, more in practical action to solve problem. *Keywords:* observant, practical, logical, fun-loving

▶

continued overleaf

Table 13.2 (*cont'd*)

Introvert types		
MBTI type		**Characteristics**
9	INFJ	Independent, thoughtful, warm, reserved and polite. Preference for patterns and possibilities. Creative, bringing originality and flair to work. Personal sense of purpose. Like to have identified goals. Work hard at understanding others, helping them to develop their potential. *Keywords:* productive, original, kind, deliberate
10	INFP	Reserved, kind, quiet, sensitive and dedicated. Deeply committed to work. Generally flexible except when values are violated, then take up principled stance. Creative contributions but sometimes take on more than seems possible, yet get it done. Hidden warmth for people. *Keywords:* creative, original, imaginative, flexible
11	INTJ	Autonomous, intellectually curious, aloof, imaginative and innovative. Decisions after impersonal analysis. Strategist, enjoying putting theories into operation. Reserved but critical of self and others; set high standards of competence for all. *Keywords:* analytical, logical, organised, definitive
12	INTP	Private, quiet, sceptical and curious. Prefer dealing with patterns and possibilities. Decisions based on logic. Interested in new ideas, search for logical explanations. Meet complex problem-solving as intellectual challenge. Enjoy theorising, analysis and understanding for new learning. *Keywords:* non-conforming, adaptive, unpredictable
13	ISFJ	Cautious, gentle, friendly and thoughtful. Make decisions based on personal values. Accept considerable responsibility. Interest in people, working for their interests. Like stability and dislike conflict. Uncompromising in beliefs held. *Keywords:* diligent, conscientious, organised, decisive
14	ISFP	Kind, humble, empathetic, thoughtful and faithful. Adaptable, interested in people, loyal follower, supportive team member. Like harmony and working in small groups. Prefer own space and time parameters. *Keywords:* adaptable, responsive, curious, realistic
15	ISTJ	Conservative, quiet, realistic and practical. Very reliable group member, renowned for accuracy. Decisions after looking at options. Work towards achieving goals. Like structured routine in daily life. Like to be of service to others. *Keywords:* precise, honest, matter-of-fact
16	ISTP	Logical, pragmatic, quiet, autonomous and aloof. Like seeking new information and understanding. Detached appraisal, decisions based on logic. Analyse information in order to solve organisational problems. Like to be free to implement solutions. *Keywords:* realistic, flexible, resourceful, objective, curious

Table 13.3 Implications of the MBTI for you as a learner. From the letter code you identified in Table 13.1, mark your four types on the matrix below to see the traits that could impact on the way you learn. These are only a guide, but should help you to think about how to adapt to improve on the way you learn. Particularly relevant chapters are shown beside the recommended study approaches.

☐ **Extrovert (E)**

Learn best:
- by discussion
- by physical activities
- by working with others

Challenges:
- studying alone
- reading, writing, researching
- any solo activity

Recommendation: study buddying; study as if preparing to teach someone else – **Chs 14, 23, 25, 64**

☐ **Introvert (I)**

Learn best:
- by quiet reflection
- by reading
- by listening carefully to lectures

Challenges:
- shyness in group discussion
- taking time for thinking
- fast lecture delivery

Recommendation: contribute to discussions by writing down what you wish to say – **Chs 15, 16, 21, 22 and 49**

☐ **Sensing (S)**

Learn best:
- if material can be memorised
- by step-by-step approaches
- by following practical applications
- from real-life scenarios

Challenges:
- impatient with complex situations
- lecturers rapidly covering topics
- finding out exactly what is required of them

Recommendation: move from familiar facts to abstract concepts; use multimedia techniques for learning – **Chs 15, 16, 19, 20, 22**

☐ **Intuitive (N)**

Learn best:
- if given theory
- by focusing on general concepts
- by using insight not observation
- from general outlines

Challenges:
- reading instructions thoroughly
- lecturers who pace material too slowly (for them)
- find repetition/practice boring

Recommendation: look for opportunities to use self-instruction modes, e.g. using multimedia – **Chs 22, 24, 27, 28, 63**

☐ **Thinking (T)**

Learn best:
- by using objective material
- when course topics and objectives are clearly defined

Challenges:
- when lectures seem in illogical order
- outlining a logical order, e.g. in textbooks and handouts

Recommendation: seek guidance/explanation from lecturer if course appears to lack coherence – **Chs 14, 17, 22, 24, 26, 28, 30, 63**

☐ **Feeling (F)**

Learn best:
- by relating ideas to personal experience
- by working in small groups
- by helping others

Challenges:
- abstract topics, e.g. those that do not relate to people
- lecturers who seem distant and detached

Recommendation: try to establish rapport with lecturer by asking questions, seeking more explanation – **Chs 14, 15, 16, 18, 22, 24, 28, 61, 63**

☐ **Judgement (J)**

Learn best:
- working on one thing at a time
- knowing marking criteria

Challenges:
- last-minute changes in syllabus
- timetable changes

Recommendation: build flexibility into work plans to accommodate unexpected changes – **Chs 14, 22, 24, 45, 48, 58, 61, 63**

☐ **Perceiving (P)**

Learn best:
- on tasks that are problem-based
- when under pressure

Challenges:
- procrastination
- difficulty completing tasks
- impulsiveness

Recommendation: find novel ways to tackle assignments; break longer assignments into smaller sub-tasks – **Chs 8, 14, 22, 24, 33, 45, 67**

Deep and surface learning

It has been suggested people are either 'deep' or 'surface' learners – for example, good at theoretical learning for long-term retention or, alternatively, better at short-term memorising of facts. This idea has been dispelled by researchers, who demonstrated that people tend to use either of these approaches strategically, depending on the context in which they are trying to learn.

What do the results of these tests mean? First, it is important to recognise that all combinations have merit: there are no 'right–wrong' or 'best–worst' types in MBTI or any of the other systems you may try.

Second, it is important to recognise that the *process* of reaching a measured conclusion is important. Each of these systems helps you analyse how you learn successfully, what your strengths are and how this information can guide you when thinking about how you learn best. Thinking at this deeper level will almost certainly help you to improve your study methods.

How you do this will depend on your diagnosed learning style, your subjects and how they are taught. Some examples might include:

● a person who finds they are 'ESFP' in the MBTI might decide to set up a study-buddy partnership as part of their revision effort (Table 13.3; **Ch 64**);

● someone who has a pronounced bodily–kinesthetic intelligence or kinesthetic learning style (Table 13.4), might focus their studies on recalling real-life examples and case studies, or on remembering the details of specific lab or tutorial exercises;

● an individual who has a preference for sensing (Table 13.1), or has a visual learning style (Table 13.4), might translate their lecture notes into diagrams and flowcharts rather than lists (**Ch 17, Ch 26**). They may also find that their learning style impacts on their role(s) as team members (**Ch 19**).

Critique of MBTI

This inventory has had its critics whose concerns emanate, amongst other things, from the fact that Briggs Myers and Briggs had no institutional academic affiliation. Their work is derived from the teaching of Carl Jung and was based on observation and the evidence of numerous tests. Criticism not withstanding, it remains in use as a psychometric test instrument used in employee selection contexts. For the purposes of this book, it demonstrates a broad range of personality types, but does not explicitly deal with learning unless extended, as in Table 13.3, to consider how the traits identified are likely to affect learning.

Three further well-known profiling instruments are introduced in Table 13.4, which provides a snapshot of the approaches used. The Information Box on page 76 gives references so that you can follow up any that you find interesting.

Table 13.4 Three further approaches to categorising learning styles. These approaches are all based on validated academic work and some are commonly used in employment interviews. See references on page 76 for more information. Some terms are explained in the Information Box on page 69.

Kolb cycle learning styles (Honey and Mumford, 1982)	Multiple intelligences (Gardner 1983, 1993)	VARK learning styles (Fleming, 2001)
Types of learner based on a cyclic model of the learning process	A subdivision of intelligence into various categories that are said to be more or less pronounced in different people and which influence the way we process information	A subset of learning preferences derived from Gardner's Multiple Intelligences and the Myers–Briggs Type Inventory (see text)
• **Activator:** has an open-minded, unbiased approach to new experiences • **Reflector:** looks at issues from all angles, collects data and works towards a conclusion • **Theorist:** analyses and synthesises information that is then placed into systematic and logical theory • **Pragmatist:** likes to experiment with new ideas and theories to see if they work	• **Verbal–Linguistic:** shows good verbal skills; aware of sounds and rhythms • **Logical–Mathematical:** an abstract thinker seeking logical/ numerical patterns • **Visual–Spatial:** good at processing visual images, accurately and abstractly • **Musical:** good with rhythm, pitch and timbre • **Bodily–Kinesthetic:** has good body movements; skilled at handling objects • **Interpersonal:** responsive to others' moods and motivations • **Intrapersonal:** aware of own inner feelings, values, beliefs and thought processes • **Naturalist:** has an empathy with the environment, living organisms and other natural objects • **Existentialist:** sensitive to deep issues about human existence	• **V**isual: preference for learning from visual media; highlighting notes, using books with diagrams • **A**ural: preference for discussing subjects; attending tutorials and lectures rather than reading textbooks • **R**eading–Writing: preference for text in all formats and language-rich lectures; converting diagrams to text • **K**inesthetic: preference for experience using all senses; recalling by remembering real things that happened
Critique: said to narrowly pigeonhole people whereas in real-life situations individuals adjust their learning approach to the situations facing them	**Critique:** theoretical basis perceived as abstract, but people can build on strengths for effective learning. This summary shows 9 intelligences – others describe 7, 8 and up to 11 used in different treatments	**Critique:** styles strongly related to learning input, strategies and outputs; treatment accepts that some people may have multimodal learning preferences

Additional reading on learning styles

Biggs, J., 1999. *Teaching for Quality Learning at University*. Buckingham: Society for Research into Higher Education and Open University Press.

Briggs Myers, I. and Myers, P. B., 1995. *Gifts Differing: Understanding Personality Types*. Palo Alto, California: Davies-Black Publishers.

Fleming, N.D., 2001. *Teaching and Learning Styles: VARK Strategies*. Christchurch: Neil D. Fleming.

Gardner, H., 1983. *Frames of Mind*. New York: Basic Books.

Gardner, H., 1993. *Multiple Intelligences: The Theory in Practice*. New York: Basic Books.

Honey, P. and Mumford, A., 1982. *Manual of Learning Styles*. London: Peter Honey.

Honey, P. and Mumford, A., 1995. *Using Your Learning Styles*. London: Peter Honey.

PRACTICAL TIPS FOR CAPITALISING ON YOUR IDENTIFIED LEARNING STYLE

Think about what your learning style means for aspects of your studying. How might it affect the following important processes?

- How you take notes in lectures (**Ch 17**) and make notes from texts (**Ch 26**).
- How you revise (**Ch 61**).
- How you study with others (**Ch 64**).
- How you express yourself in assessments (**Ch 45–Ch 50**).
- How you answer in exams (**Ch 65**).

Look at the big picture. Be aware that your preferred learning style may not be entirely applicable in some situations. Think about how you can modify it to meet such circumstances, perhaps by exploiting a different aspect of your personality.

Watch your lecturers. If students have different learning styles, it follows that this is also the case for lecturers. Observe the people who teach you and try to identify their learning style. This could be helpful in understanding why they present information in particular ways and may allow you to be more accommodating in dealing with the content of their lectures and tutorials.

Talk about learning styles. Discuss learning styles with friends in order to find like-minded colleagues with whom you could work collaboratively in lectures, researching and learning – especially if you are an extrovert who finds it difficult to cope with studying alone.

14

STUDYING INDEPENDENTLY

How to organise yourself and develop good study habits

> One of the distinctive traditions of university is that students are expected to set their own learning agenda within the confines of their course of study. This chapter covers practical ways for organising yourself for study, and ways of organising the material you need to support your learning, assignments and exam revision.

At university, learning is very much up to you. This means that you have to organise yourself by planning ahead, prioritising different study activities, and making sure that you meet deadlines. You may also need to decide what to learn and how deeply you need to understand it (**Ch 22**). An audit of what you will need and what needs to be done will help you to organise yourself. Examining learning objectives/outcomes (**Ch 63**) and taking account of assessment feedback (**Ch 58**) are good ways of assessing whether you are hitting the right level with your work.

Too much information?

Especially at the beginning of a new academic year, students are often bombarded with information, leaflets and publicity items. Take some time to sift through this to separate the gimmicks from the substantive information that may be of use to you in helping you to study. Keep it all in a spare file and then when you do need that information, it will be there for you.

SOURCES OF INFORMATION FOR YOUR SUBJECTS

At university, most key information is given in printed format and students are expected to read this intensively in order to map out their own schedule of personal study. The most common places for finding this information include:

- **Course handbook:**
  - gives information about lecture topic, numbers of lectures, names of lecturers;
  - gives dates and venues of practicals, lab dates and tutorials;
  - gives reading lists for written work, for tutorial or practical work;
  - gives some guidance on subject-specific or preferred referencing styles;

- may give some guidance on essay-writing as required in that subject area;
- provides learning objectives/outcomes;
- refers to marking criteria (**Ch 63**).

- **College/faculty/school timetable:** gives venues and times of classes and exam dates.
- **Noticeboards:** give important information, including late changes to printed information. You should find out where the relevant departmental, school and faculty noticeboards are and consult them regularly.
- **Emails:** provide updates, reminders and other information. Group and individual emails are the preferred means of communication with students. Thus, it is essential to keep checking your university email account regularly.
- **Virtual learning environment:** gives access to much of the above information, online. Course information may be posted on the electronic noticeboard or announcement page. Frequent attention to such announcements is vital for keeping up to date with what is happening on your courses.

ORGANISING YOUR STUDY SPACE AND YOUR NOTES

Everyone needs a place to study, and, ideally, this should be a location that is exclusively 'yours'. However, if this is not possible, investigate facilities such as study rooms in your department or study zones in your library. Alternatively, some people find that going to a public library or another specialist library on the campus provides the anonymity that allows them to study uninterrupted. Working in a comfortable temperature with adequate light and ventilation is important. Your desk and chair should be complementary in height so that you are not sitting in a crouched position; conversely, if you are 'too comfortable' it is easy to drop off to sleep – easy chairs or on top of your bed are not recommended.

Keeping your work organised is something that some people do intuitively, while others need to work hard at it. Each subject you study on your course will generate a lot of paper. Whether you receive this in hard copy or it is offered to you via websites or your university's virtual learning environment, you will have to keep it where you can find it easily and relate the content to other elements of the course. You will generate other material yourself in the form of notes taken in lectures or notes you make yourself as a result of your research and further reading. It is important to record the sources of this information. Table 14.1 gives practical ideas for organising the extensive amount of information that you will gather.

> ✔ **Finding your 'own' space**
>
> This can vary according to your mood, the task or what's available at the time you are free. Some people are creatures of habit and like to lay claim to a particular niche in the library; others prefer home study. Whatever suits you, your learning style and temperament is the right approach. Don't worry if it differs from approaches adopted by others on your course.

Table 14.1 Tips for organising key information arising from your studies

Day-to-day 'housekeeping'
• Use time when you are at an 'energy low' to undertake routine clerical activities by writing up and filing your notes; use your 'high energy' time for intensive study.
• Be systematic – date everything as you receive or create it.
• Store your material in an organised way – invest in a series of large ring-binder folders, one per subject, with coloured dividers to section different elements of the course. This will help you to retrieve things quickly. You could arrange the subjects alphabetically or chronologically, for example. This is a matter of personal preference. The important thing for retrieval purposes is to be consistent.
• As soon as you start to use material from any kind of source, *always* note down all the reference information required to relocate the source should you need it at a later point. This information will also be needed should you wish to cite some of the information from this source in your text. This means that you should record all the information required for the reference system you may customarily use, for example, the Harvard style of referencing (**Ch 35**).

Formulae
• Create a formula sheet (**Ch 47**) for each of your subjects by listing *all* the formulae, along with a list of what the symbols mean. Keep this in your subject file in a position that can be easily located.
• Make sure that you have copied formulae down correctly. In particular, make sure that you have used capital (upper case) or small letters (lower case) and also subscript and superscript correctly. For example, V_{max} = peak of dc voltage, as opposed to v_{max} = peak of an ac voltage.
• By keeping your formulae sheets in a polythene pocket at the front of your file, you will prevent them from becoming dog-eared. If you have access to a laminator, then laminating your formulae sheet allows you to keep a hard-wearing reference readily accessible.

Electronically retrieved or created material
• Create separate folders for each topic within the course you are studying. This will make it easier for you to locate work.
• Save your material using a file name that will make sense to you even when you try to locate it several months later. It may be useful in some cases to add a date reference to the file name, for example: Dental caries 170406.doc
• Keep a back-up of all work done on a personal computer. This includes saving any electronic work that you have to submit so that you can produce additional copies if required to do so.
• Insert page numbers and the date on which you last worked on the document as a footnote (some packages will alter the date automatically every time you work on a document). This will avoid confusing different versions.
• Explore the software package you are using to find out how to print the file name and complete pathway in the footer section of your document.

DEVELOPING YOUR SKILLS

Initially, early on in your undergraduate career, it will help you tremendously if you review the learning and studying skills you need to develop. These include:

- learning how to use IT facilities (**Ch 27**);
- being competent in relatively advanced features of a word-processing package – Microsoft Word is possibly the most commonly used package on most university networks (**Ch 27**);

- learning how to use subject-specific software (**Ch 27**);
- using keyboard skilfully (**Ch 27**);
- knowing the location in your library of books, reference materials and other subject-specific resources (**Ch 23**);
- being able to use your library efficiently by accessing its electronic catalogue and other electronic resources (**Ch 23**);
- internet searching for reliable source material at the correct level (**Ch 23, Ch 27**);
- being able to organise, structure and write a competent piece of text appropriate to higher-level learning in your subject area (**Ch 32–Ch 44**).

Being able to do these things to some degree of competence will be of enormous value to you throughout your study years. If you feel that you need further assistance in any skill mentioned, go to the relevant service in your university and make enquiries about courses or inductions that will help you to develop your skills. You will find information about how to find support services on the university home page. Look for:

- **IT support service:** word-processing, software packages or keyboard skills.
- **Learning centre:** for help from study advisers.
- **Library:** for a familiarisation or induction programme. For specific queries there will be an information desk position where you can get help with your search or query.

GETTING DOWN TO THE TASK

Think about what you need to do, work out how much time you can allocate to finishing the task, decide how you are going to tackle the task and then get on with it. You may find that the first 10 minutes is hard going, but then the ideas begin to flow.

Types of studying to be done

Studying is a multifaceted activity and one that differs according to discipline and subject. The first thing you need to consider is what you need to do to learn within your specialism. This could include:

- reviewing new material from lectures by annotating or rewriting notes;
- finding and reading related hard-copy material;
- finding material on a virtual learning environment or other web-based source;
- preparing or writing up reports or essays;
- preparing for exams.

Once you work out for yourself the activities that are necessary for learning in your field, then you will be able to assign the time and priority you give to each activity.

Recognise the importance of *thinking* about the subject material as a vital part of studying (**Ch 22**) rather than passively reading it. Table 22.1 (on page 122) summarises the different types and 'levels' of thinking that tutors expect you to be doing.

Displacement activity

As noted in **Ch 8**, displacement activity is a form of procrastination where you find other ways of using your time to avoid getting down to work. Examples include:

- persuading yourself that you can study in the sun (or the pub!);
- washing your car/windows/dog;
- going window-shopping;
- tidying your DVD collection or room.

Planning and overplanning are other kinds of displacement activity. Although planning is essential, there is the risk of overplanning: try to achieve the right balance between planning and productivity.

If the total number of displacement tasks or the time that you allocate to them is preventing you from making real progress with your studies, maybe you need to make hard decisions about time management (**Ch 8**).

Asking questions

Although learning is up to you at university, if you do not understand something even after you have attended the relevant lectures, delved into the recommended texts and spoken to others on the course, go to your department and ask to see someone who can help you. Departmental secretaries are usually good people to speak to first in order to find out about availability of academic staff. Otherwise, email your lecturer to make an appointment or to pose the question directly. Staff welcome being asked questions and within a few minutes may iron out the difficulty for you. This may also highlight to the staff member that a topic may need to be revisited with the whole class.

HOW TO STUDY ACTIVELY

It's all too easy to go through the mechanics of studying by copying out notes or reading a chapter from beginning to end. While this could be *part* of process, it's important to think about what you're doing and why. Table 14.2 lists some typical activities along with the questions you should be asking yourself as you do them. Being aware of these different aspects of studying will prevent you from working 'on autopilot' and will help you to internalise your reading and writing.

Using your 'visual' brain

Generally, most people tend not to exploit their visual memory. If you use highlighters for headings and sticky place tabs on key sheets in your file, this will help you find things more readily and also help you remember content because of the layout of the page or the positioning of notes within your file.

Table 14.2 Typical study activities, with questions to ask yourself as you do them

Rewriting notes from lectures (see also Ch 17)

- What are the key ideas?
- Do I need to reorganise these to create a logical sequence that matches my understanding?
- Is this taking up too much of my time? If so, try to take your original notes more neatly. If you think that rewriting notes helps you to learn, could you synthesise the notes into bulleted lists/flow charts/diagrams rather than lengthy sentences?

Making notes from texts (see also Ch 26)

- How is the information organised?
- How can I identify the key ideas quickly to provide an overview? How can I restructure information into concise notes?
- How much detail do I need for:
  - learning about the topic?
  - eliciting information for an assignment?
  - revising for exams?
- What is the best method for framing my notes?

Thinking/reflecting (see also Ch 22)

- What do I think about this topic? It's important that you don't just take what someone else tells you as the only approach on the topic. Think critically by questioning your own ideas. Be prepared to redefine your view in the light of new approaches, information or evidence.
- What should I be looking for – information or concepts? If information, how reliable is your source and can you cross-check from another resource? If concepts, what evidence is there for each viewpoint? How good is the evidence? What other evidence might be available? Where will you find this?
- Are any patterns emerging? Look for relationships or themes, such as:
  - cause and effect (reason and result);
  - comparisons and similarities, contrasts and differences;
  - threads of arguments, supporting evidence and counter-arguments;
  - problem and solution information.

Working through problems and examples (see also Ch 29 and Ch 47)

- Is the answer sensible and are the units correct?
- Have I done what has been asked?
- Is there anything else asked for?
- Have I used the correct formula?
- Have I used all the information given in an appropriate way?

Thinking about the wider picture (see also Ch 63)

- How does this topic or aspect fit in with the earlier lectures and learning?
- How does this match up with the learning objectives on my course?
- What areas do I need to explore or develop in further reading or practice?
- What should I specifically highlight for revision purposes?

Know your best time to study. You are at your most effective as a student at particular times (Ch 8); exploit this by doing intensive learning activities at these times.

Check out the hours that facilities are open. Find out the library, study centre or computing facility opening times. Plan your study periods around those if you prefer studying in these settings.

Plan ahead. Keep an eye on things you have to do over the following week/month and plan your time to fulfil all the assignments, lab and tutorial work on time (Ch 8).

Develop a personal filing system. Learn to be methodical in the way that you store notes, handouts and any other printed material within your filing system (Ch 17).

Think about the underlying principles involved in your learning. Keep your focus on the bigger picture and avoid becoming bogged down in the minutiae.

Take breaks. When working on your own it is essential to take breaks. It is also important to maintain your social networks, and taking regular short breaks with colleagues helps you to maintain perspective on your work.

Work with a buddy. Although studying is something that you need to do primarily on your own, coming together with another person on your course to compare notes, confirm understanding of more difficult points and discuss a set assignment can help the learning of all involved. This contributes to the consolidation of your learning and helps identify gaps in your knowledge (Ch 18, Ch 64).

Develop your professional vocabulary. For subject-specific and general language, it will help you to remember words If you write them down along with a simple definition (Ch 42). A small, cheap telephone address book marked off with alphabetical sections makes an instant glossary reference notebook. You can record new words/specialist terms easily in alphabetical order, which makes retrieval easier than if you had recorded these indiscriminately in a long list.

Reinforce your learning. You will need to be able to use the language of your subject appropriately and make sure terms are spelled correctly; if studying a quantitative subject, you may need to master key formulae so that they become second nature to you. This is a reflection on your command of your subject. Make a habit of checking through your glossary or formulae lists frequently so that you can make a conscious effort to learn how to spell the more difficult words or lay out formulae accurately.

Tackle tutorial questions. Do *all* the examples in a set of tutorial questions, even when you don't have to submit them. Check your answers from the answer key, if provided. If you have difficulty in working out a particular solution, ask one of your lecturers or tutors to give you some guidance – staff will often go to considerable lengths to help with difficulties. Once you are satisfied that you have the correct answers, file the tutorial sheets alongside the related topic notes.

15

LECTURES

How to learn effectively from this teaching method

The lecture is the fundamental component of most campus-based university teaching. For many students, lectures represent a new way of learning. You'll need to decide how to deal with different lecture styles and how to adapt to a wide range of different approaches to the use of lecture time in modern higher education.

The word 'lecture' comes from the Latin word *lectura* – a reading; it is worth remembering that, even in modern times, a lecture begins its life as a piece of text and that some lecturers do, indeed, read their lectures from that text. However, many lecturers adopt a less formal delivery and use their notes simply as a reference rather than as a text they read aloud.

---

i Timing of lectures

The timetable of lectures is organised at faculty level. Tutorials, practicals, laboratory and fieldwork are all normally timetabled by schools/departments. Generally, lecturers have no say about when the lectures or other teaching take place. These are usually decided by a central timetabling unit on the basis of availability of the facilities required.

WHAT IS A LECTURE?

The normal pattern is that a lecture:

- usually lasts for 50–60 minutes;
- is given by a subject specialist;
- provides different perspectives on learning depending on the topic and discipline – factual information, ideas, analysis, argument, contrasting viewpoints, methods or examples;
- guides you in your study of a topic – this means that you may have to do a lot of supplementary reading on your own, or that you need to work through examples, or conduct experiments, to add to your understanding and knowledge;
- may provide introductory or complementary material that is later followed up in tutorials, laboratory practicals, fieldwork or site visits;
- may relate to some form of assessment, either in class or in an e-learning format after the lecture.

Been there, seen that, done that

In some subjects you may find that you have covered a topic at school or college or even in another subject. It's easy to think that you can skip those lectures or stop taking notes. The reality is that the topic will probably be taught in a different way and for a different purpose. The changes are often subtle, but important, so you mustn't switch off. The lecturer may also take you further than your previous studies, so it's wise to revisit the 'old' stuff and be ready to absorb the different approach and emphasis.

KEY FACTS ABOUT LECTURES

People have differing expectations of where lectures fit into the learning within a particular subject area. Here are some key facts that will help you to understand and adapt to this form of course delivery.

- What you hear in the lecture will not necessarily be found in textbooks.
- A lecture is not meant to be a comprehensive treatment of any topic. The aim is generally to give an overview of the key issues or topics and a framework to assist you with further study.
- Lecturers may present views that do not necessarily represent their own position; they may simply be exploring different approaches and attitudes within the field.
- Although some lecture notes are made available through virtual learning environments (VLEs), generally these notes will not reflect all that was said in the corresponding lecture.
- Approaches differ between one lecturer and another, even in the same subject area.
- Style differs from one subject to another and from one discipline to another (**Ch 16**).
- Some lectures are compulsory, for example, in vocational subjects, such as law, medicine or nursing. Even if they are not, it is important to attend as listening to your lecturer explain the topic (**Ch 16**) lays down the foundation for understanding and recall.

In some disciplines, the programme of lectures is divided into topic areas, with different lecturers taking responsibility for the delivery of their specialist topic.

WHAT YOU ARE MEANT TO DO IN LECTURES

Although students do not generally participate in the delivery of the lecture in terms of interaction with the lecturer, sometimes they are asked to perform some kind of task, perhaps in collaboration with someone sitting beside them. Otherwise, students are expected to take responsibility for exploiting the information covered in the lecture, and, in particular, to take a personal set of notes (**Ch 17**). Some important ways in which students can contribute before, during and after the lecture are given in Table 15.1.

Materials for lecture note-taking

You will need appropriate materials for your chosen subject: paper, pens, highlighters, calculator, dictionary.

Table 15.1 Ideas for getting the most from lectures

Before the lecture	In the lecture	After the lecture
This information is usually available in the course handbook or on the VLE.	Always write the name of the lecturer, the subject and the date on your lecture notes. This helps you to keep your files organised sequentially and will aid your revision.	Clarify any points you didn't understand. Ask a fellow student, consult a text or website and, if still in doubt, speak to the lecturer.
Find out when and where your lectures are – be there. Lectures provide the framework of the knowledge base of your course. If you miss lectures, your understanding rapidly becomes incomplete.	Ensure that you keep a written record of each lecture:	Soon after the lecture, go over your notes. Some people feel completely rewrite their lecture notes: they feel rewriting notes is a valuable means of consolidating the information and ideas. However, others regard this as a pointless and time-consuming exercise. Their view is that the time would be better spent doing supplementary reading on the lecture content.
Find out how changes in the timetable are notified to students, e.g. via noticeboards or as virtual learning environment announcements or emails.	– If the lecturer gives handouts, highlight, underline or make additional notes on the handout as the lecture progresses. This is called 'annotating'.	
Identify the lecture topic and prepare by doing some basic reading beforehand.	– If you are not given handouts, choose a note-taking style that is appropriate to the content and discipline of the lecture. Take the lecturer's style into account as well (**Ch 17**).	Follow up references and think about the ideas that were covered in the lecture. As your course progresses you should then begin to think about connections between topics and the theory that relates to them.
Review the learning objectives or outcomes for the lecture or topic. This will help you to focus your attention on key aspects.	Evolve your 'own' abbreviations for note-taking. This could include some contraction of words, text-message language or standard abbreviations drawn from mathematical or punctuation symbols (**Ch 17**).	There may be additional material and coursework to complete after the lecture – make sure you do this as it will almost certainly be related to later assessment (**Ch 63**).
Note how many lectures are allocated to each topic. This can often be important in balancing your effort when it comes to revising.	Look at the lecture template in **Ch 16** (Table 16.2) and listen for the statement at the beginning of the lecture that outlines the aims and the way that the lecturer intends to achieve these and the 'signpost' words that are used to provide a transition from one phase to the next within the lecture.	Try matching the lecture content with the learning objectives or outcomes. This helps you understand the fuller context of your course; what you are being taught and why; and, specifically, where any particular lecture fits in the greater scheme of things.
Be on time. Late arrivals are disruptive and interrupt the lecturer's flow of thought and this will affect the delivery. You should aim to be sitting in your seat 5 minutes before the start of the lecture.	Note any particular points of emphasis – these topics may crop up later in assessment.	
Switch off your mobile phone.	Learn to adapt your note-taking style to the different styles of delivery you encounter (**Ch 17**).	Get into the habit of noting down your own ideas and questions in your notes in a way that allows you to remember that these were not part of the lecture but your reaction to what you heard. Think about such issues further, as these points show your ability to think critically.
Recording lectures is not the norm and you must seek the permission of each lecturer *before* the lecture if you wish to do this. Some lecturers may refuse to give permission for reasons of copyright. Visually or aurally impaired students can make special arrangements directly with the lecturer and the disability support service on your campus.	Note any references (usually author surname and date) that crop up in the lecture.	

DIFFERENT LECTURE FORMATS

Be prepared to experience different lecture formats – not all will involve listening and note-taking. While some lecturers may consistently follow a particular format, others may alter their delivery depending on the topic, the size of the class, or the stage in the module that has been reached. Some typical formats are:

- **Traditional lecture:**
  - 50-minute non-stop monologue;
  - aims of the lectures are listed;
  - the method of approach is explained;
  - the content is covered in detail;
  - the key points are summarised.
- **'Split' lecture:**
  - 25-minute lecture; then
  - 5-minute break, allowing students to catch up with colleagues on any points that have been missed in the first phase of the lecture; then
  - 25-minute lecture, giving further coverage by the lecturer.
- **'Activity' lecture:**
  - 20 minutes (approximately) of content; then
  - 10 minutes of in-class activity (possibly working with partner(s)); then
  - 15 minutes' general discussion relating to the work with partners; then
  - 10 minutes' summary by the lecturer of key issues arising from the lecture, small group work and plenary: this could consist of clarification of points, identification of argument and counter-argument and balance of argument.

Introductions and summaries

Most lectures begin with an outline of what will be covered; if you miss this, you could fail to understand the logic of the lecture structure and content. Don't be late – you may miss the whole point of the lecture for the sake of a few minutes. Often key 'housekeeping' announcements occur at the start and you may miss these too. Lecturers usually summarise key issues, facts, theories or processes at the end of the lecture and sometimes introduce their next lecture in general terms to demonstrate the linkage between one phase of their teaching and the next. Apart from being discourteous, leaving early means that students miss this key guidance and interpretation of the lecture series.

VISUAL AIDS USED IN LECTURES

Some lecturers will appear to talk spontaneously without prepared notes, but lectures are not off-the-top-of-the-head streams of words. They are the product of planning and research, as well as careful thought about the best way to present the topic.

Many lecturers use visual aids to assist them in their explanations. These may include:

Overhead transparencies

Some lecturers may prefer to write up their overheads as they proceed through the lecture. This means that you have to pay particular attention to what is written on the slide and to decode often erratic handwriting. However, if overheads are prepared ahead of time by the lecturer, they can be particularly useful and some lecturers may be willing to provide copies in advance or after the lecture.

Slides

In some disciplines there is a strong reliance on visual images that cannot be reproduced readily except on photographic slides, for example, where the lecturer might wish to show you examples of micro-organisms or fine art. In such instances, it is helpful to note details of each slide and a record of the comments that are made by the lecturer, both as an aid to recall and in case you have a question afterwards. The examples and conclusions may be extremely important to the topic.

PowerPoint presentations

Many lecturers now structure their presentation around projected slides of this kind. PowerPoint-style slides are beneficial in that they allow you to listen, rather than write. However, it is vital not to switch off – the points on the slides will only be the skeletal framework and if you have a printout, you should be annotating this throughout the lecture, adding detail or personal interpretation.

> **✔ If you are dyslexic, or have any disability**
>
> There may be special arrangements in place to help you with lectures. For example, dyslexic students are entitled to ask for larger print handouts or may be permitted to record lectures. Ask for information from a lecturer or from the disability support service on your campus, or consult your university's website.

🔧 PRACTICAL TIPS FOR LEARNING EFFECTIVELY FROM LECTURES

Approach the lecture experience with a positive, open-minded attitude. For example, you can bring:

- motivation for learning (**Ch 13**);
- an interest in the subject (**Ch 2, Ch 4**);
- prior knowledge of the subject (**Ch 26**);
- understanding of the learning objectives, gained from the course handbook (**Ch 63**);
- critical thinking skills (**Ch 22**).

Prepare for the lecture. Particularly in topics you find hard, preparing by printing out and reading any published notes, reading the textbook or trying example questions will greatly improve what you take home from lectures.

Attend all lectures. You may be tempted to miss them for a number of reasons, but in most cases the lectures are the foundation of your course. If you miss even one lecture, it is very easy to continue this practice so that, in the end, you don't attend any. This is not advisable as it is very hard to catch up with the material later on. Don't be lulled into a false sense of security because the material (you think) will be accessible from the VLE. The printed notes are simply outlines – there is no substitute for hearing what was actually said. Moreover, don't assume that the lecture content is all that you have to learn for assessment in assignments or exams; lectures provide a framework for learning but you are expected to develop your understanding by further reading and critical thinking.

Listen intelligently. This means recognising the lecturing style of the lecturer, the structure of the lecture and the thought process that is being demonstrated (**Ch 16**). This will enable you to identify key points and tailor your note-taking strategy to the style, method of delivery and lecture format. Adopting positive body language sends the signal that you are engaged with the lecture topic.

Take account of the importance of visual information. If you are shown something on a photographic slide, a PowerPoint slide, an overhead transparency or on the chalk-/whiteboard, then you should write the important details down. Your lecturer would not present it to you visually if this information were not important.

Note down references. Take particular note of any references that are given by the lecturer. Often only the author will be mentioned and maybe the date of publication. You will usually find full details in the course handbook. Make a point of consulting the references as soon after the lecture as possible. Add any notes you gain from these sources to your lecture notes.

16

LISTENING SKILLS

How to understand what lecturers say and how they say it

Lectures are about passing on information, ideas and arguments. This chapter introduces you to some different lecturing styles; suggests strategies for adapting to each of these examples; and provides some illustrations of the language frequently used to frame and structure lectures.

In the course of your academic career you'll encounter many lecturers: some good, some less so, some you will like and some you will not. However, it is the lecture content that is important, and whatever you think about the lecturer or the topic, you will need to engage with the material that is being delivered.

LECTURING STYLES

You will find some common lecturing approaches given in Table 16.1. This table also provides strategies for dealing with these delivery styles. These examples are only a selection of lecture types – each lecturer has a unique approach. Your challenge is to adapt your listening strategies and note-taking style to meet the idiosyncrasies of each lecturer. Listening carefully and developing an ability to take meaningful notes comes with practice. As you develop this skill you will be better able to evaluate and extract what is relevant from each lecture.

✔ **Differing preferences for lecturing styles**

One person's ideal lecture is another person's nightmare. Some people like a measured, systematic delivery, while others dislike this intensely and find a more dynamic delivery more stimulating. You need to adapt to the different styles you encounter.

Table 16.1 Examples of lecturing styles and the strategies that can be used to cope with them

Type of lecturer	Potential strategies
The entertainer. This sort of lecturer tells good jokes and can 'ad lib' them throughout the lecture. Many people like these lectures, but what you need to do is separate the ideas from the banter. Good lecturers who adopt this style are not really comic 'turns', but are usually simply using humour as a vehicle to deliver their ideas by keeping the listeners' attention.	Listen for the 'signpost' words and phrases in their lecture, that is, when they state how they are going to deal with the topic, and then pick these out as the lecture unfolds (see Table 16.2). Keep a note of the lecture structure as an aid to revision and a record of your understanding. Remembering the jokes and comic business may help you remember the content afterwards, although it may also create a smokescreen that you need to see through.
The drone. This type of lecturer specialises in a monotonous delivery, that is, without any modulation of voice or expression. Material to be covered may be difficult to absorb, even if it is fundamentally interesting.	You have to listen carefully for the specific words used that express meaning rather than rely on the intonation to highlight changes in the stages of a lecture, for example, when the lecturer is moving on to another theme.
The rambler. Some lecturers ramble. They appear to stray from the point, get carried away by their own eloquence or simply lose the thread. However, in some instances what seems like a series of disjointed thoughts may be pulled together as underpinning for a tight and logical argument.	Don't 'switch off' – take notes! Listen for the individual points and note these down as the lecture progresses. Gradually, the rationale may become clearer and you will have the bare bones of the points made at the earlier stage to support the conclusions. Later, imposing your own order on the content of the lecture, perhaps by referring to the texts, may help you to make the material more easily remembered.
The mumbler. Not everyone is a gifted public speaker and lecturers are no exception. Some very gifted and talented people just do not perform well in front of large groups of people. Consequently, they may not project their voices well and the bigger the lecture theatre, the more this becomes a problem.	In this case coping strategies are less easy to evolve. Sitting near the front of the room will at least place you nearer the speaker and this may assist a little. A more subtle approach is to make eye contact with the lecturer, smile and look interested. This confidence-building strategy may encourage the lecturer to speak more clearly. Another strategy might be to raise the issue with your class representative who can draw it to the attention of the department concerned. Otherwise, simply make an appointment to speak with the lecturer to explain the difficulty – they may be unaware that they cannot be heard beyond the third row. Asking that lecturers uses a lapel microphone or one attached to the lecturer may solve the problem of audibility.
The fidget. Some people think best when they move around. It may be that, as they deliver the lecture, they move back and forth across the dais or wave their arms like windmills or absent-mindedly fiddle with equipment.	The lecturer's mannerisms can be distracting, but try to rise above these irritations and follow the flow of information coming your way. Try to identify whether this idiosyncrasy is a form of 'code'. For example, does the lecturer use hand, arm or body movements as a means of reinforcing important points? Watching the lecturer as you take notes can be important to obtaining the most from the lecture.

continued overleaf

Table 16.1 (*cont'd*)

Type of lecturer	Potential strategies
The techno-wizard. Some lecturers thrive on the use of gadgetry and you may find that your lecturers prefer the medium of slides, video, or PowerPoint presentation instead of the traditional oral presentation. Good teachers use the medium that is best suited to their message and sometimes PowerPoint presentations provide greater clarity and precision than the traditional acetate slides. One advantage is that it is possible to obtain handouts of the PowerPoint presentation (sometimes available on the module VLE facility), but do not assume that this will always be the case.	Getting down the detail of the slides may be difficult and it might be helpful to request that the slides are made available on the course VLE, if this is used, so that you can look at the presentation again later and print it out if you feel that it would be useful. PowerPoint presentations might present a good opportunity for some team work. If the slide is packed with information, agree with a fellow student that one of you will make a note of what is said about the slide while the other will copy down what is on the slide. In this way, you can share the notes later, confident that you have the complete information that was delivered – both oral and visual.
The egotist. Many of the people who lecture to students are so absorbed in their own ideas that they sometimes ignore the bigger picture. They may have been asked to deliver the lecture series because of their expertise and research background. However, this can result in a rather narrow perspective on a topic and you need to be aware that there may be other viewpoints or approaches to be considered in order to achieve a balanced perspective.	Listen carefully for references to the work of others. After the lecture, go to the library and check out other 'big names' in the field by looking at the catalogue for recent publications on the same topic area. Look at journals for articles by your lecturer and identify from the reference list other experts in the field.

THE STRUCTURE AND LANGUAGE OF LECTURES

Although lecture styles differ among disciplines and from one lecturer to another, it is possible to identify some common features that apply to most. Table 16.2 links these typical structural elements with the characteristic language that is associated with them.

The lecture 'experience' is a partnership between listener and lecturer where both engage with the content. Lecturers will aim to give their undivided attention to their material which will have involved many hours of research and preparation taking into account level and relevance. Student listeners are expected to give their undivided attention to the lecturer. Without that, key points could be missed or the thread of an argument misunderstood.

The implication is that you should not only be listening to what is being said, but also considering what is being said. This can help greatly when deciding what type of notes to take (**Ch 17**).

Table 16.3 provides examples of appropriate and inappropriate approaches to lectures.

> ✔ **Disability issues**
>
> If you have problems with hearing or sight, special facilities or equipment will be available to help you in lectures: contact your university's disability service to establish what provision can be made to meet your needs.

Table 16.2 Structural elements of lectures and their characteristic 'signpost' language. These speech samples are typical examples your lecturers might use. This is not a comprehensive list of elements of a lecture; nor will all of the elements appear in every lecture. Once you have developed the capability to listen for such phrases, you can use this information to create better notes (Ch 17). For example, you can hear when a list is being initiated; when a definition requires to be taken down exactly as spoken; or when emphasis is being given to an important point.

Lecture element	Characteristic language
At the beginning of the lecture	
Introduction – outlining the topic to be covered	'In today's lecture I'll be considering . . .'
Aims – defining what the aim of the lecture is	'I'm going to look at a number of aspects of . . .'
Lecture format	'I'll begin by . . . and then I'll go on to . . . and I'll end by . . .'
In the body of the lecture	
Providing a definition	'I'm going to start by defining . . .'
Giving examples	'Let's look at some examples of . . .'
Describing: • processes • events • position	'The first stage is . . .' 'To begin with . . . then . . .' 'At the centre is . . .'
Presenting a theory or argument: • stating the key points in support • explaining the perspective of each point • justifying the evidence supporting these points • presenting a counter-argument • justifying the evidence supporting these points	'This viewpoint is supported by . . .' 'This means that . . .' 'It can be seen from this evidence that . . .'; 'This evidence suggests that . . .' 'The opposing viewpoint is that . . .'; 'This contradicts the view that . . .' 'It can be noted that there is some variance with . . .'
Going through a worked example of a calculation	'I'm going to show you how to approach this type of problem . . .' 'Here's a typical set of data that we might use with xxx's formula . . .'
Drawing logical connections	'Thus, it can be seen that . . .'
Identifying main issues	'The critical factors are . . .'
Stressing importance	'It is essential that . . .'
Repeating a point for clarification or emphasis	'Let me put that in another way . . .'
Moving on to a new theme	'Passing on to the next theme in my discussion . . .'
At the end of the lecture	
Pointing out themes	'This links to what I was saying in Tuesday's lecture . . .' 'Tomorrow, I'm going to take this topic forward and . . .'
Concluding – drawing together the lecture's key messages	'To summarise the key aspects I've covered, let's remind ourselves of . . .'; 'The "take-home messages" are . . .'

Table 16.3 Examples of students' approaches to lectures

Type of listener	Implications of approach
The dreamer	Listens with a faraway look, gazing on the horizon through the window, missing out on references and examples – needs to stay focused and make a conscious effort to stay with the subject by consistent note-taking throughout.
The listener	Listens for content paying attention to the 'cue' words and phrases that lecturers use to map their lectures (Table 17.2) and takes 'intelligent notes' – uses style suited to content to record key points with supporting information, examples or references (see **Ch 18**).
The networker	Uses the opportunity of the lecture to charge up laptop/mobile, monitor emails, update *Facebook* status, or play games in the belief that multitasking is their forte and that they can assimilate lecture content while dealing with networking demands. Experienced lecturers can identify those students doing this and may well ask the networker to leave the lecture room – needs to ditch the gadgets and give 100% attention to the lecture, making meaningful notes.
The sound technician	Records the lecture. This is an infringement of the lecturer's copyright (**Ch 36**) and they may be asked to leave the lecture – needs to enhance personal independent learning by taking notes. *Note that students with certain disabilities may be given individual permission to record lectures exclusively for their own use.*
The squirrel	Listens intently and tries to take down almost every word but actually misses out on understanding because not taking notes selectively – needs to develop selective note-taking, rather than a verbatim record.
The techno-artiste	Uses different technologies to take notes. While a laptop-based record of lecture content has merit, but can be lost if the technology malfunctions – needs to develop manual note-taking as a way of developing fast hand-writing skills for exam writing.
The whisperer	Whispers throughout to companions to left and right causing distraction to the lecturer and inconvenience to others – needs to be less selfish by concentrating on substance of lecture rather than providing running commentary and so allow others to concentrate on the lecture.

PRACTICAL TIPS FOR BETTER LISTENING

Think about your position in the lecture room. Sitting near the front may allow you to hear better, but it may not be the best spot to see visual aids. Try not to sit next to others who may distract you. The 'back row' ethos may be good for a laugh, but it doesn't really help you learn.

Understand the jargon. Your comprehension will be better if you are familiar with the technical terms and jargon being used – so a little preparation beforehand may help, for example, by reading the appropriate chapter of the textbook.

Be well organised. Make sure you have all the necessary equipment e.g. pens, paper, highlighters.

Don't try to take down all the lecturer's words as if they were dictation. There may be spells when this is appropriate, and the lecturer should make this obvious. Otherwise, listen to the main points of what is being said and recast this in words that you understand (**Ch 17**).

17

NOTE-TAKING IN LECTURES

How to refine what you hear into note form

> The aim of lectures, regardless of discipline, is to present a topic for study in ways that introduce key points and develop understanding through explanation, examples or citation of references for further reading. This chapter outlines approaches to attending lectures, and taking notes from what you hear and see.

University lectures should be seen as a guide to a topic rather than the final word on a subject (**Ch 15**). Lectures provide essential information delivered in a particular sequence for a particular course. In many subjects, the lecture is an introduction to the topic rather than a comprehensive analysis. For some subjects, lectures are compulsory. This may be dictated by professional associations that validate many professional qualifications and is not simply a university regulation.

YOUR ROLE IN LECTURES

Since lectures do not provide you with a full understanding of the subject, and certainly not the total requirement for exam revision, some input on your part is assumed (**Ch 16**). For example, this may involve writing up the notes in a style that is more comprehensive and comprehensible. Alternatively, you may use the original lecture notes as the basis for note-making from texts cited from the reading list. In many subjects, this process is assumed as part of the learning process.

Routine lecture note housekeeping

In each lecture, note the date, the lecturer's name, the lecture topic or title, and number your pages in sequence (1, 2, 3 . . .). Also note the aims of the lecture as outlined at the beginning.

You will attend many lectures in a week, maybe several in a day. It makes sense to keep some record of what you have seen and heard. It is important to consider what your purpose is when you take notes, since this will affect your strategy. For example, this may be:

- to keep a record of what was said for future reference and exam revision;
- to note key points to allow you to do follow-up reading on the topics in your own time;
- to provide a record of a constructed argument, a sequence of ideas or a process;
- to derive a proof or formulae.

APPROACHES TO NOTE-TAKING

How you lay out notes in lectures will depend on:

- your ability to listen for specific information and the thread of an argument, discussion or sequence of a process (**Ch 16**);
- the neatness of your handwriting;
- your particular learning personality or style (**Ch 13**);
- the styles of delivery you encounter in lectures (**Ch 16**);
- the subject you are studying and its conventions;
- specific lecturer content.

Notes made as a result of reading provide you with the chance to design a layout that reflects your learning style and understanding (**Ch 26**). This is less possible in a lecture because you are following someone else's train of thought without having the chance to reflect on this too much. As a result, the design of your lecture notes has to be spontaneous and is less under your control. However, as you become a more experienced note-maker and note-taker, you will become more attuned to ways in which the format of the lecture can be adapted to particular types of note-taking design.

> ### ✔ Tips for good note-taking
>
> - Listen for and note the key ideas – avoid trying to write down every word (verbatim notes). It's impossible – you'll miss out on understanding ideas, explanations and examples.
> - Develop a note-taking style that will provide you with notes that will be meaningful in six days, weeks or months.
> - Cultivate your own 'code', for example:
>   - underlining or highlighting points emphasised by the lecturer;
>   - asterisks (*) for points or new words to look up later;
>   - BLOCK CAPITALS for sub-headings or keywords;
>   - special abbreviations for your subject that are in general use or that you create for yourself;
>   - a symbol (e.g. #) that indicates your thought or response to a point made by the lecturer.

Table 17.1 outlines four different lecture delivery modes that are commonly used and makes suggestions as to how you might extract key information for your notes.

Figure 17.1 illustrates four possible formats for notes and suggests ways in which these different strategies can be used to suit different note-taking needs within lectures. Adding to these strategies, note-making approaches are covered in **Ch 26**.

Table 17.1 Note-taking scenarios. Each lecture is unique and the strategies adopted by the lecturers will vary from individual to individual, topic to topic and according to discipline conventions. You will need to adapt your note-taking style to the mode of presentation, the style of the individual lecturer and the content. Four possible scenarios that you might encounter are shown in this table.

Scenario 1	Scenario 2	Scenario 3	Scenario 4
'Straight' lecture: delivered without handouts or special visual aids	**Lecture supported with printed handouts**	**Lecture delivered using overhead transparencies**	**Lecture delivered using PowerPoint software**
Listen for: • Aims of lecture or outline of structure of lecture. • References to authors, dates of publication. This is the usual way of citing sources in a lecture. You need to then consult the reading list for details of title, chapter or page references. • Key personalities, dates or events relating to specific aspects of the topic. • Discourse markers – the signpost words (**Ch 16**, **Ch 33**) that indicate stages and shifts of emphasis within the lecture. • Structuring of an argument and the supporting evidence; stages of a process; sequence of events. • Repetition of points or oral emphasis using exaggerated stress or intonation. • Summarising of points at mid- and end-points in the lecture.	If handouts are available before or at the lecture: • Use highlighters to mark key points. • Use a contrasting colour, e.g. red or green, to annotate notes with additional information, examples or explanations given in the lecture. This will make it easier to distinguish from the printed text. • Make additions as described in scenario 1. If handouts are available after the lecture, use your own notes taken in the lecture to expand the lecture notes.	Follow scenario 1 but in addition: • Copy points shown on overheads as the skeleton for your own expanded notes. • For this kind of presentation it is sometimes helpful to work with a friend where one person copies the slide and the other notes what is said when the lecturer 'talks to the slide'. After the lecture, merge the notes to create a more comprehensive record of what was actually covered in the lecture. To do this, you will need to work together in order to agree the synthesis of your notes and this will offer opportunities to discuss and clarify points. This will reinforce your learning.	Use of this software provides a slick and professional presentation that permits good images of the detail of graphs or diagrams, and the lecturer can build these up stage by stage. However, this can often create an amount of detail that is very difficult to note down completely in the lecture. If this is the case for you, try to follow the steps for scenario 1 and ask for the PowerPoint slides to be made available for downloading before or after the lecture. This has cost implications but note that there are options to print out slides as handouts of two, three, four, six or nine slides to a page using grayscale or black and white rather than colour (**Ch 28**).

Warning: Notes from lectures, whether borrowed from a colleague or made available by the lecturer, are not a substitute for attending the lecture. Lecturers expand on certain points or add examples to clarify understanding. They may also deviate from the notes and expand points outside the notes.

Keyword notes

Topic Lecturer Date

Aims

- Good for lecture where there are clear divisions to its structure.
- Easy read-back using keywords in shaded boxes on left of the sheet.
- The printed margins could be used to separate keywords from corresponding text.

Concept maps/mind maps

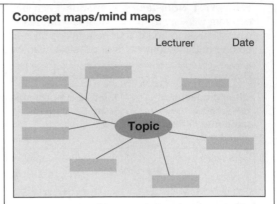

- Works best using page in landscape position.
- Good for the meandering lecture where there is back-tracking, re-emphasis and repetition.
- Suits some learning styles better than others.
- Easily annotated but can become cramped.
- Needs tidy writing.

Linear notes

Topic Lecturer Date

1. Heading
    1.1 Sub-point
    1.2 Sub-point

2. Heading
    2.1 Sub-point
    2.2 Sub-point

3. Heading
    3.1 Sub-point
    3.2 Sub-point
    3.3 Sub-point

- Good for scientific subjects and other subjects that follow processes or procedures where a hierarchy of events or stages is often relevant.
- Again, easy read-back using decimal notation to identify sub-points. A mix of numerical and lettered referencing (e.g. 1, 1a, 1b . . .) could also be used.
- Effective use of white space makes this memorable.

Matrix notes

Topic Lecturer Date

Aspect	View 1	View 2	View 3	View 4
A				
B				
C				
D				
E				

- Good for laying out different/contrasting viewpoints across a number of aspects of an argument. Works well if this is a declared aim of the lecture.

Figure 17.1 Note-taking strategies. Four models of note-taking with the benefits of each style.

Before the lecture. Try to read some fundamental background information on the topic. This could be the introduction to that topic in a basic recommended textbook or from a good encyclopaedia. Beware of internet sources, because these can be unreliable in terms of accuracy and truth.

Obtaining supporting material. Some lecturers make use of virtual learning environments available in many universities to provide lecture notes, handouts, overhead transparency or PowerPoint slides before or after the lecture. Downloading this kind of material when it is made available may assist you to make more comprehensive notes. Note that the provision of this material remains at the discretion of the lecturer. If you have a hearing impairment, are dyslexic or have another visible or invisible disability, you may be able to request that lecture notes or handouts are made available to you before lectures. You should consult the disability support service in your institution with regard to any special needs you may have.

In the lecture. Choose a seat that allows you to see the whiteboard, projection screen or television monitor easily. Avoid sitting near the door, the back of the room (most commonly inhabited by the chatterers and latecomers) or underneath noisy air-conditioning vents. If you have a disability, you can ask for special arrangements to be made to enable you to access a lecture theatre or room without difficulty and also, if necessary, to ensure that a particular seat is reserved for you. In some instances, you may be permitted to record the lecture electronically.

Paper size. A4 is the standard paper size for handouts and printers and so it makes sense to be consistent by using A4 paper and file size for your own notes. It is probably more economical to use narrow-lined paper with a margin, as this allows you to optimise the use of paper. Some subjects might require blank rather than lined paper to allow for diagrams and mathematical calculations. Otherwise, your own handwriting style and ability to write neatly at speed will dictate your choice. If you are neat by nature, lined or unlined paper is probably immaterial (you can get more text on unlined paper!); if you are generally untidy in your writing, the lines will discipline your note-taking. Small reporter-style notebooks are not recommended, because the volume of notes that you will generate will fill one of those pads in a very short time.

Storing your notes. Decide on a strategy for filing your notes that is systematic and foolproof. Foolscap or A4 files with two holes are the most readily available and therefore cheaper. You may prefer to keep separate thinner files for each subject, or to use a single lever arch-file for a subject and use colour-coded section dividers to separate topics within the subject area. Get into the habit of filing notes immediately after the lecture so that they don't sink to the bottom of a rucksack or sports bag.

Adapting your style. There is no single way to take notes that will suit all styles, content or circumstances. You will need to adapt your style to suit individual delivery styles as well as content.

'Writing up' lecture notes after the lecture. Views differ on this. You need to ask yourself a difficult question – what do you gain from this exercise? Some people feel that this is an essential aspect of the learning process, is an aid to understanding and aids their recall. Others start off doing this but quickly find that there is simply not enough time to revisit lecture notes in order to remodel them to make them neater, more legible or more meaningful. If writing up lecture notes is just to make your notes look neat, colourful or simply pretty, you need to consider whether the time might not be better spent doing some follow-up reading using your 'raw' lecture notes as a guide and possible skeleton for notes you make from sources (see **Ch 26**).

18

CO-OPERATIVE LEARNING

How to study successfully with others

> University education involves learning for yourself, but this doesn't mean that you have to do it alone. Support networks can help. Your fellow students are a learning resource for you, and you for them. By studying together in groups formally and informally you can develop mutually supportive 'buddy networks' with others on your course.

Learning in a group has advantages – people learn in a different way by listening and interacting, compared with listening passively in a lecture. Groups work because of the different personalities and learning styles represented in them. If everyone in the group were the same, it is likely that the group would be rather dull; each person brings something unique and this adds to its effectiveness. It is the interaction of diverse personalities and learning types that creates a 'group dynamic', with members feeding off each other's ideas, working more intensively and, at times, competing with each other.

FORMAL (STAFF-SELECTED) GROUPS

Studying formally as a group normally means that you are participating in a learning activity that has been initiated by an academic staff member. This could be a formal tutorial, lab activity or practical facilitated by a tutor, or it may take the form of a group project that is conducted independently of the staff member. In all these situations, it is likely that you will have had little choice in the composition of the group. For effective learning to take place, however, you will have to adopt the basic practices described in this chapter.

✔ Groupwork pointers

Here are some ground rules for working effectively as a group, whether in a formal or informal setting:

- Learn to listen as well as speak.
- Respect the views of others and understand that criticism of your views is not a personal slight.
- Ensure that everyone is allowed space to give their views.
- Prevent anyone from dominating the discussion or activity.

Staff-led groups

- Ensure that you are prepared adequately for the group activity.

- Participate in the discussion and do not leave one or two people to do all the talking.

- Have the confidence to express your views, even if these seem to be at variance with those of others.

- Be prepared to defend your views or suggestions with reasoned argument supported by well-considered evidence.

- Use the group-learning experience as an opportunity to explore issues or ideas in greater depth with an expert to guide you.

- Recognise that a tutor may act as 'devil's advocate' to push you into exploring alternative scenarios, options or strategies.

- Take notes in these meetings, as these will complement your lecture notes and additional reading. They may also cause you to reflect on your own understanding or opinions.

Unsupervised student groups

- Work out and agree some ground rules, such as setting goals, responsibilities and deadlines.

- Ensure that the work allocation is evenly distributed across the group.

- Create a positive learning environment by addressing the task in hand and ensuring that people do not feel constrained in presenting their ideas.

- Engage in analytical thinking to tackle the task in hand.

- Encourage everyone to contribute ideas.

- Encourage exploration of ideas, their implications and also counter-arguments.

- If you don't understand something, ask others in the group if they can explain it to you.

- If more than one meeting is required, ensure that the assigned contributions are completed for presentation at the next meeting.

- If you have real difficulties within your group, approach the staff member who set up the activity to discuss these with the whole group.

Advantages of unsupervised group learning

This learning context:

- Allows people to learn from each other.
- Encourages a positive-thinking approach to the task.
- Broadens the horizons of thinking.
- Breaks down barriers.
- Supports weaker students and develops the mentoring abilities of stronger students.
- Allows all members to be less inhibited in expressing ideas or opinions or offering solutions.
- Enhances your skills for future employment.

INFORMAL (STUDENT-SELECTED) GROUPS

Studying informally as a group is more likely to have come about because a self-selected group of students has decided to tackle a particular issue or topic independently of staff input. Groups that students set up spontaneously are less likely to need to agree ground rules and a method of working, because the very creation of the group is evidence of a less formal social arrangement. Some tips for working in this way include:

- Allocate a specific time and location to tackle the task you've decided to address.
- Ensure that the location is appropriate – for example, in the open discourse area of the library rather than in the union bar where distractions could interfere with the purpose of the group. Increasingly institutions are providing seating facilities in 'open-space' locations that are relatively quiet to enable students to work together informally.
- Agree targets and work towards fulfilling these within a certain time span.
- Recognise that not all the things you wish to tackle can be solved in this way and that it is sometimes appropriate to seek help from a staff member.
- Accept that people work at different speeds and so try to accommodate this in how the group breaks down the tasks it wishes to fulfil.
- If the group works well, try to maintain the co-operative spirit by sharing resources, debating lecture issues, and exploring new techniques or approaches that you encounter in your learning.

The interplay in informal groups can be complex and rewarding, as the example in Table 18.1 illustrates: those helping others at one level can often benefit themselves from the process.

? How can you set up your own study group?

Here are some possibilities to consider. In each case, explain what you are trying to set up and ask if anyone would be interested in participating:

- Speak to your lab partners or fellow members of formal groups.
- Speak to people before or after lectures, or as you walk between lecture theatres.
- Place a message on a discussion board on your virtual learning environment.
- Email fellow class members.
- Ask your class rep or the lecturer to make an announcement ('anyone interested meet after the lecture . . .').

Table 18.1 is a case study that shows how this approach can work.

Table 18.1 Case study: Gary's informal study group

The problem and a solution
Gary is a former Further Education (FE) student who came to university from a local college.
He is finding it really difficult to grasp some aspects of the new topic being covered in lectures. He has done this subject before at college, but it was taught in a completely different way. Gary is a direct-entry student, which means that he has gone straight into second year at university. He thinks he's possibly missed out on something that everyone else has covered in first year. After a bit of soul-searching, he plucks up the courage to ask a couple of other students, whom he knows only by sight, if they are also finding the topic difficult. Their response indicates that they too are finding it difficult, but less so than Gary, so he suggests that they meet up after the lecture to try a couple of tutorial questions together.
By pooling their knowledge, these three are able to work through the new topic and method of tackling it. The others are able to explain the missing bit of Gary's knowledge and he is able to explain from his college learning some aspects the others don't quite understand. As a result, the learning they gained from working with others on the problem areas was probably much deeper than if they had each studied alone. The three decide to meet up again when it is time to revise for the end-of-module exam.

Underlying message
Students giving the explanation of a concept to a colleague reinforce their own understanding, while students receiving the explanation are often able to understand the explanation given by a friend better than when it was covered in a lecture or tutorial by a member of staff.

PRACTICAL TIPS FOR STUDYING IN GROUPS – IN BOTH FORMAL AND INFORMAL SETTINGS

Effort in; benefit out. What you gain from working in a group will reflect the effort that you and your colleagues put into the activity.

Believe in yourself and your ideas. Your ideas are as valid as anyone else's; do not be put off by the person who sounds extremely eloquent and well-read – sometimes there is little substance behind what they say.

Treat group working as a positive learning experience. Use the group experience as an opportunity to explore your own ideas, and learn from those of others.

Know when to ask for help. Sometimes groups simply do not work as a functioning entity – there may be no explicable reason and the 'fault' may not be attributable to any individual or group of individuals within the group. The group dynamic simply fails. If this seems to be happening, talk to a member of staff who may have some strategies to resolve the situation.

Learn more about how groups and teams work. This topic is covered in **Ch 19** and **Ch 64**.

19

PARTICIPATING IN A TEAM

How to make a contribution when working with others

Working within a team is a rewarding way to learn and it can reflect workplace practice. This chapter introduces the theory of team roles and discusses some essential teamwork skills.

There are many situations at university where you will be expected to act as a member of a team – sometimes in the academic context and sometimes in a sporting or social situation. The academic focus is usually on assessed group exercises, but the principles are applicable in other areas, such as club membership or employment. Generally, your team will be expected to work together to produce some outcome such as a poster or report. Your actions within the team may be assessed by your tutors and in some cases by your fellow group members (peers).

You may already have built up teamwork skills without realising it. Perhaps you have played team games, been a member of a fund-raising group, organised a social event or been employed as part of a team. This experience will help greatly as you learn more about your character as a team worker and develop the necessary skills even further.

TEAM ROLES

Research suggests that there are many distinct team personalities and that each of us has a 'natural' team role. During group work at university you can discover which role suits you best. Thinking about your group activities will help you develop as a team member. What you find out about yourself may even influence your eventual choice of career and job.

A part of the tension in being a team member is that you, or a fellow member, may be asked to play a different role from the one that is natural. This can lead to problems as you try to adapt to the requirements of the role, or when someone else tries to assume a different role from the one they have been assigned. Also, when you work in a small team, you may be asked to play multiple roles or to switch between roles at different times as the project progresses.

Examples of teamwork at university

- Preparing a group poster (**Ch 56**).
- Writing a joint report (**Ch 54**).
- Some types of problem-based learning (**Ch 45**).
- Practical and project work (**Ch 20, Ch 51**).
- Running a society or sports club.

Table 19.1, which is based on the work of Meredith Belbin, gives a breakdown of main team roles and the personality features associated with them (Belbin, 2006). His analysis recognises that there are both 'good' character traits and 'allowable weaknesses' for each role. This notion is valuable, because it eliminates the feeling that any one role is superior. For example, you may have the impression that 'team leader' is the star role in any group, and perhaps one to which you might want to aspire. However, leader types are generally poor at coming up with ideas and can be weak at putting them into practice (Table 19.1); these are functions vital to the success of the group and they may well be your strength.

Simplified team roles

You may feel that the analysis of roles in Table 19.1 is too complex and detailed for your needs. A simplified grouping of roles, using the role numbering of that table, could be:

- Leader: A + B
- Creative person: C + E
- Organiser: F + G
- Worker: H + I
- Critic: D

To help decide which role might suit you, think whether you would describe yourself as action-oriented, people-oriented, or as a thinker. Belbin classified the nine roles in this way and, by narrowing the options, this may help you to decide which fits you best:

- Those who prefer action should be a shaper, implementer or a completer–finisher (types B, F or G in Table 19.1).
- Those who are people-oriented should be a co-ordinator, a resource investigator or a team worker (types A, E or H in Table 19.1).
- Those who are thinkers should be an innovator, a monitor–evaluator or a specialist (types C, D or I in Table 19.1).

Delegation

If you like to be 'in control' of your work, giving over tasks to others can be stressful. In teamwork, you should accept that others may take a different approach from you and allow them to learn from their mistakes.

Table 19.1 The nine team roles identified by Belbin. Use this table to identify the role(s) that best fit your personality. Refer also to Ch 13 regarding learning styles and their relevance for team-work roles.

Team role	Key attributes and beneficial functions in a team	Allowable weaknesses
A The co-ordinator	A 'caring' leader type who is calm and authoritative. Takes a balanced view and displays sound judgement. Makes the team work towards its shared goal. Good at spotting others' talents and at delegation.	May be less creative or intelligent than others and have no special expertise.
B The shaper	A 'manipulative' leader type who is a dynamic go-getter but impatient for results. Good at generating action, troubleshooting and imposing a pattern. Provides drive and realism to team activities.	Can be headstrong, emotional and impatient with others.
C The innovator	An intelligent, creative, ideas person, who generates solutions to problems and often uses unusual approaches. A source of originality for the group's activities.	May work in isolation and ideas may be impractical. May not communicate well.
D The monitor–evaluator	The 'critic' who analyses what the team is doing in a detached and unemotional way. Good at evaluating the group's ideas and making sure they are appropriate.	May lack drive and have a low work rate. Critical comments may act to demotivate others.
E The resource investigator	An extrovert, communicative sort, who enthusiastically investigates new information and ideas. Good at exploiting resources and developing external relations.	Can be over-optimistic and may have a short attention span.
F The implementer	A hard worker who uses energy, discipline and common sense to solve problems. Turns ideas into actions. Good at making sure things get done.	May lack flexibility and resist new ideas.
G The completer–finisher	A conscientious individual who is anxious that tasks are completed to a high standard. Painstaking, orderly and well-organised. Good focus on fulfilling objectives.	Obsessive about details and may wish to do too much of the work to control quality and outcome.
H The team worker	A social type whose aim is to support others and provide cohesion to the team. Perceptive of others' feelings – helpful and diplomatic in approach. Promotes team spirit.	Doesn't like to lead or make decisions.
I The specialist	The kind of person who provides essential expertise and skills to the group. Adds a professional dimension but can be single-minded and may not suffer fools gladly.	Narrow outlook. Can be obsessed by technical detail and not see the big picture.

Communication

The success of any team depends on its ability to communicate. The larger the group, the more important this becomes, as shown in Figure 19.1. Group members need to understand what is expected of them by the team and by the teaching staff who have set the task. Time-frames have to be defined, as do team roles, arrangements for meetings and the interchange of information or files. Face-to-face meetings are usually important at some early stage; thereafter, email, mobile phones and discussion boards are useful ways of keeping in touch. Agreeing and setting up these communication channels should be one of the first things your group does, for example, by exchanging email addresses.

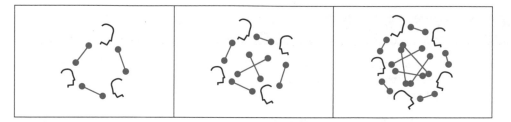

Figure 19.1 Team interactions. As the number of people in a group increases, so does the complexity of potential contacts between them. With three people, the number of one-to-one relationships possible is three; with four people it is six and with five it is ten. The larger your group, the more important communication becomes.

Time management

There will always be a deadline for your team's work and this implies that planning will be required to meet your goal (Ch 8). You may find it difficult to arrange mutually suitable meeting times if the group members have diverse timetables and responsibilities, so intermediate targets (milestones) and diary dates should be set as early as possible. This is an important responsibility of the co-ordinator or shaper.

Compromise

Give and take is essential to team function at many levels. One concession you may need to make is in the team role(s) you adopt, as discussed above: this may require self-awareness and flexibility on your part. In addition, you may not have chosen your team and you may not even like some of its members – but to succeed as a group you will have to get along together. This may require diplomacy and tact. Team membership requires everyone to be able to give and receive criticism constructively and not as personal disapproval. If you are a perfectionist, you may need to accept that some aspects of the group's activities may be below your normal standards – but this may be essential to ensure that the team as a whole fulfils its remit.

Focus and commitment

Teamwork exercises are often demanding in time and effort; everyone needs to show commitment and a high work rate if the highest standards are to be achieved. Your group must keep its collective eye on its goals and targets, to ensure that it meets these, otherwise the overall mark may suffer. Facilitating this is one of the leader's duties.

> **✔ Finding the right person for the job**
>
> At different times your team will need someone to co-ordinate the task; someone to come up with bright, inventive ideas; someone to keep everyone else on target; someone who can find useful facts; someone who is good at design; someone who can organise materials; and someone to act as a spokesperson. If the right person does each of these tasks, the overall output from the team will be improved.

MAKING SURE THAT YOUR TEAM WORKS WELL TOGETHER

Issues can often be anticipated and defused before they become problems. Difficulties are best treated by discussing them as soon as they become apparent, either within the team or with the staff supervising the task.

- Try to ensure that team members have sufficient time collectively to complete the task. If this is not possible, you may need to consider how you modify the task or the method you have agreed upon. This may result in an outcome less ambitious, but still of a high standard.
- If some members do not feel sufficiently motivated, the group as a whole may lack drive. One of the leader's roles is to stimulate the group. If this is your responsibility, from time to time remind the team of the relevance of the task and the rewards for doing it well.
- Where possible, try to ensure that people are assigned roles that fit best with their personality. Otherwise, they may feel uncomfortable.
- Sometimes, personalities clash when it is felt that someone is not pulling their weight, or when someone acts as an outsider (or is treated as one). Early discussion is essential and a 'team worker' may need to act as mediator.

🔧 PRACTICAL TIPS FOR BEING A SUCCESSFUL TEAM MEMBER

Behaviour:

- Be considerate by respecting the different abilities and contributions of others.
- Be positive, praise others' work whenever you can and discourage ridicule of other team members' ideas.
- If you feel you need to be critical, try to do this without arousing hostility.
- Don't form cliques within teams.
- Remember that if someone has flaws in some areas, they may be compensated for in other areas (and perhaps at a later time).
- From time to time, reflect on your contribution and your role-playing.

Communication:

- Make sure you talk to other team members and try to encourage them to talk to you.
- Distribute contact numbers and email addresses; reply promptly to messages.
- Talk through all problems as soon as possible.
- Understand that other team members may be shy or nervous.
- Contribute if your team has to 'defend' your work.
- Learn to listen to others and recognise that views that differ from your own may have value. Don't monopolise discussions or impose your views.

Effort:

- Try to 'do your bit'. Don't be a lazy team member. The more effort everyone makes, the sooner the work will be completed.
- Produce work of the highest quality you can.
- If you feel your contribution is overloading you or is disproportionate to the contribution of others, call the group together, explain the problem and explore some solutions with the whole team participating.
- Tailor your collective effort to the reward on offer, remembering that good marks in assessed coursework can make it easier to gain a pass or good grade overall.
- Keep the final objective of your exercise in mind at all times.

Assessment and evaluation:

- Make sure you know how you will be assessed, and use this information to the team's advantage.
- Be scrupulously fair in your assessment of colleagues, if this is required.
- Don't award peer-assessment marks from loyalty if they are not deserved.
- After the event, think about what you learned from it – not only about the subject, but about your own behaviour and teamwork in general.

20

LABORATORY SESSIONS AND FIELD VISITS

How to gain hands-on experience and skills

Many courses, especially in the sciences, include laboratory sessions and field visits. These practicals provide valuable opportunities to observe specimens, carry out standard procedures and refine a range of valuable skills. You can gain a lot from these parts of the curriculum if you approach them correctly.

In many scientific subjects, more than a third of the course time may be allocated to laboratory sessions and/or field visits. This proportion will also be reflected in the marks given for related in-course assessments and formal practical exams, so you should treat these practical elements just as seriously as lectures and tutorials.

Practical work is given emphasis because it:

- allows you to see and interact with real examples of organisms, specimens, artefacts, processes and reactions;
- helps you to develop new skills in areas such as observation, measurement, manipulation and data analysis;
- lets you gain an appreciation of 'scientific method', perhaps by imitating original experiments carried out in your field;
- demonstrates equipment and gives you 'hands-on' experience of using it;
- allows you to explore field locations relevant to your studies;
- gives you practice in writing up your work in formats that you may later use to report project work and theses at a higher level.

In many cases, practical sessions are carried out in pairs or as part of a small group, so there is a chance to learn from your fellow students and to work as a team (**Ch 18, Ch 19**).

---

i

Examples of skills covered in practicals and field visits

- Observation
- Handling samples and organisms
- Using equipment
- Designing experiments
- Working safely

- Measuring and recording
- Creating tables and graphs
- Data analysis
- Reporting in written and spoken forms
- Teamwork

PREPARING FOR PRACTICAL SESSIONS

If you want to gain the most from your practicals, good preparation is essential. Often lab sessions and field visits are tightly scheduled and you may be expected to be 'up and running' almost from the start. Practicals may also involve new concepts and terms and if you don't understand these, you may not gain much from your efforts.

- Read through the schedule beforehand, making sure you understand the terminology – try to gain an overall impression of what you will be expected to do, and why.
- Consult textbooks or websites if you don't understand any of the underlying theory.
- Make sure you have the appropriate equipment ready to take to the practical.
- Ensure you arrive at the lab or assembly point in good time.

APPROPRIATE CONDUCT IN THE LAB AND FIELD

Any rules associated with lab or fieldwork will have your safety as their primary concern, so you must pay attention to them. You may be asked to work with toxic chemicals, dangerous instruments or in hazardous environments, so care is essential. At an initial meeting of your class, you will be introduced to basic safety measures and legislation, told about the fire drill and shown relevant hazard symbols (Figure 20.1).

 Explosive

 Oxidising agent

 Extremely or highly flammable

 Toxic or very toxic

 Corrosive

 Harmful or Irritant

 Dangerous for the environment

Figure 20.1 **Some of the main EU hazard symbols**

In the lab, you will be asked to wear a lab coat – which should always be buttoned up – and, if you have long hair, asked to tie it back. Eye protection goggles may be necessary for some procedures, and those who normally wear contact lenses may be subject to special rules because vapours of corrosive laboratory chemicals may be trapped between the lens and the cornea of the eye. You should never eat or smoke in a lab. You should also keep your bench space tidy and quickly dispose of specimens or sharps as instructed.

Definition: COSHH

This stands for 'Control of Substances Hazardous to Health' – a UK regulation that came into force in 1999. It lays out the legal framework for risk assessment whenever hazardous chemicals, agents or procedures are used. Normally the person in charge of your lab or field visit (an academic or senior lab technician) will carry out a COSHH assessment, which should be displayed prominently and/or communicated to you. In certain situations you may be asked to complete the paperwork yourself, but will be given guidance on how to do this.

Where hazardous materials or procedures are involved, you will be told about any risk assessment that needs to be carried out, including, where appropriate a COSHH risk assessment (see Information Box on page 111) and you have a duty to read this carefully.

When working with chemicals or live organisms like bacteria, take appropriate precautions:

- be aware of possible modes of ingestion, including inhalation by nose or mouth, ingestion by mouth, absorbtion through exposed skin, inoculation through skin;
- take special care with procedures such as pipetting or transferring samples between vessels;
- note where eye washes and emergency showers are located in your lab and understand the appropriate procedures when you come into contact with chemicals;
- know what to do if you spill any chemicals;
- make sure you know what type of fire extinguisher or fire blanket to use for the reagents being used, and where these are located;
- always wash your hands thoroughly after each lab session.

For field visits, you will be advised about appropriate clothing. You should take special care to use appropriate footwear and be prepared for a change of weather conditions. If in a group, you should stay close to the main body of people; otherwise, try always to work with a partner, rather than alone. Any fieldwork group should:

- take a first-aid kit;
- leave full details of where they are going and when they expect to return;
- consult a weather forecast before they leave, and if working on the seashore find out about the state of the tides.

CARRYING OUT INSTRUCTIONS AND NOTING RESULTS

Lab and field visit schedules usually contain the following components:

- **Theory, background and aims.** This contains information essential to your understanding of the practical, interpretation of instructions and approach to any assessed components, so do not be tempted to skip this and move directly to the instructions.
- **Instructions.** The language used here is generally very precise and should be followed to the letter or number. Success will often depend on, for example, the precision with which you measure out reagents, or the exact timing or temperature you use. When reading the schedule beforehand, you may wish to highlight key points in the instructions so you can follow them better during the session, or lay out tables ready to record your data. Before you start, the person in charge of the lab may tell you about any late changes that have had to be made – it is therefore important to arrive in good time and to listen carefully while this is done, making appropriate notes.
- **Results section.** This part provides space for you to record observations, data and comments. Increasingly, a 'workbook' style of lab schedule is provided, with spaces and prompts for drawings, results and conclusions, but this is not always the case, and, especially in later years, you will be expected to organise your own notes.

The language of practical reports

There are specific conventions about language use that should be adopted. In the 'Introduction' and 'Materials and methods', the past tense, passive voice and third person (see **Ch 54** for definitions) are generally used (for example, 'Sturrock and Dodds (1984) were the first to show . . .' and 'the data were recorded at 5-minute intervals'). However, present tense might be used when describing figures and tables (for example, 'Table 3 shows the relationship between . . .'). Read research reports in your subject area to gain a feel for the style usually adopted.

Being able to record accurately what you see and measure is a vital skill in the sciences, and will be practised and tested throughout your university career. The following are key tips for recording your observations:

- Don't rely on your memory – write down everything.
- Never write on scraps of paper (you'll lose them) – use a proper lab book.
- Always date each page and provide full details of the specimen or experiment.
- If recording data, develop the skill of writing this information clearly – for example, ones and sevens are easily confused and you may wish to adopt the practice of crossing the latter (i.e. 7̵).
- If you are recording numbers, use an appropriate number of significant figures (**Ch 29**) to take account of the precision (or, perhaps more strictly, the lack of precision) of your method.
- If drawing diagrams, make sure these have a descriptive title and are well labelled.
- In the field, be prepared for bad weather – buy a special wet-weather notebook or take a clear plastic bag to enclose your notebook, and use a pencil as this will write on damp paper.
- Write down any final answers or results *in the form specified* – you may lose marks otherwise.
- Draw any graphs or tables according to the normal scientific conventions (**Ch 33**).

Defined report formats

If you are asked to use a specific format or template for writing up lab or field sessions, make sure you do this, or you may lose marks (and the sympathy of your marker!).

You may be asked to submit a selection of completed workbook schedules for marking. In some cases, you will be required to hand in lab reports. Table 20.1 details the key components of a typical lab report and outlines what's expected for each part. Further advice on practical assessments and oral exams is provided in **Ch 50**.

Table 20.1 Typical components of a lab or field report. This is the standard format used for scientific reports (see also **Ch 54**): for write-ups of single experiments or a laboratory practical, normally only the parts marked * would be included. *Always adopt the precise format specified in your course handbook.*

Section or part	Expected content
Title page*	A descriptive title that indicates what was done and sometimes describes the 'headline' finding. Also the full names of the author or authors, the module title or code and the date.
Abstract	A brief summary of the aims of the experiment or series of observations; the main outcomes (in words) and conclusions. This should allow someone to understand your main findings and what you think they mean.
Abbreviations	A list of any abbreviations for technical terms used within the text (for example, 'DNA: deoxyribonucleic acid'). These are also given within the text at the first point of use, for example '. . . deoxyribonucleic acid (DNA)'.
Introduction*	An outline of the background to the experiment, the aims of the experiment and brief discussion of the techniques to be used. Your goal is to oriente the reader and explain what you have done and why.
Materials and methods*	A description of what was done. You should provide sufficient detail to allow a competent person to repeat the work.
Results*	A description of the experiments carried out and the results obtained, usually presented in either tabular or graphic form (never both for the same data). You should point out meaningful aspects of the data, which need not be presented in the same order in which the work was done.
Discussion (or conclusions)*	A commentary on the results and an outline of the main conclusions. This could include any or all of the following: • comments on the methods used; • mention of sources of errors; • conclusions from any statistical analysis; • comparison with other findings or the 'ideal' result; • what the result means; • how you might improve the experiment; • where you would go from here, given more time and resources. Sometimes you might combine the results and discussions sections to allow a narrative to develop – to explain, for example, why one result led to the next experiment or approach. Bear in mind that a large proportion of marks may be given for your original thoughts in this section.
Acknowledgements	A list of people who helped you.
References	An alphabetical list of sources cited in the text, following one of the standard formats (**Ch 35**).

How should I title my report?

This is something that many students get wrong. The title should be a simple descriptive summary of what you are reporting, for example:

- Effect of chemical x on response y of specimen z;
- The relationship between factor A and factor B under condition C;
- Yield of reaction p in the presence of different catalysts q, r and s;
- Characteristics of specimens of c found in location d.

If no other hints or tips are provided, you should consult the literature in your subject area for typical examples of style.

PRACTICAL TIPS FOR GETTING THE MOST FROM LABORATORY SESSIONS AND FIELD VISITS

Focus on the aims and 'learning outcomes' of the session. When reading schedules beforehand, or listening to your lecturer introducing a procedure, make sure you understand what the purpose and likely 'take-home message' of the session is going to be. This will help you work much more effectively during the practical.

Use lab assistants and demonstrators fully. These people are there to help you, so make the most of them. Often, they may be recent graduates, and sympathetic to any problems you may be facing. If in doubt, ask – it could save you lots of time and help you gain marks. Be prepared to ask questions yourself rather than wait to be asked – but don't expect the demonstrator to give you the answers directly. They will be under instruction to make *you* do most of the thinking, but will be happy to help you along the way.

Learn how to draw up informal tables and figures quickly. Rough tables will help you to record your results neatly and quickly, while 'instant' graphs will give you an early visual indication of how the experiment is proceeding. Your tables should include a column describing what is being measured or the number or timing of the measurements, and include sufficient 'cells' in the rows for each replicate or repeated measurement you will make. When constructing graphs, you will need to assess the largest and smallest figures you are likely to obtain, so you can determine what the limits of the graph axes should be. For all tables and figures, no matter how quickly drawn up, remember to state the measured quantity and the units of measurement.

Take plentiful notes and provide detailed labels. Note down anything that might be useful at a later date – and be prepared to use most of your senses, with caution: note colours, sounds and feel, but only taste and smell when specifically instructed. Label any diagrams fully and add a time and date. As well as stating what a component is, add relevant detail such as colour and texture. All diagrams should include a scale.

Use 'empty' time effectively. During lab experiments, there may be delays between parts of your work as reactions develop, or gaps if you are ahead of the rest of the class. Use this time to look ahead in the schedule to see what you will be doing next, to create tables or graphs ready for recording your results, or jot down ideas for your conclusions.

Write up your practical work when it is fresh in your mind. You may be tired after a lengthy lab session, but if you delay for too long you may forget useful details.

21

TUTORIALS

How to prepare and participate

| Tutorials differ from discipline to discipline and from institution to institution. This chapter outlines approaches to the conduct of tutorials that you may encounter in your field of studies.

Tutorials have a long history in university education. Their function is to involve students actively in the learning process by meeting in small groups to tackle a set topic or problem.

Most tutorials will involve 5–12 students, although there are some universities where tutorials are conducted on a one-to-one basis. The tutor's role is to facilitate discussion or, for problem-solving tutorials, to assist students encountering difficulties. In addition, they may be required to make an assessment of your participation and performance.

? Who are my tutors?

It is unlikely that the people who deliver your lectures will conduct your tutorials. Some may be freelance tutors who are brought in for the sole purpose of taking tutorials; others may be postgraduate students who are studying in your department (this may be an element of their postgraduate training).

Think a little more strategically about what you can learn from tutorials beyond the subject-based agenda on which your group will work. For example, a tutorial is a kind of meeting and through your participation you will be expected to develop interpersonal skills that will transfer to meetings in other professional contexts once you graduate.

TUTORIAL TYPES

There are essentially two types of university tutorial. One is common in subjects related to arts, social sciences, law and social work, for example, the kind of tutorial where a preset topic is considered in a discussion format. The second type of tutorial is more common in scientific and engineering disciplines, and is conducted alongside the lecture and practical programme. Here, students discuss answers to a series of problems or calculations under the guidance of a tutor. This approach is also found in numerical subjects such as accountancy.

Whatever your discipline, your role in tutorials requires preparation and participation.

Your tutorials will be held at regular intervals over a term or semester. You will normally be allocated to a tutorial group by the course director or administrator, and details of dates, times and venues for these meetings will be provided in your course handbook, on the departmental noticeboard or posted on your university's virtual learning environment. Tutorial topics and problems will be given to you under the arrangements that prevail in your department. For example, sometimes this information is provided in handout form, sometimes it is included in the course handbook.

Preparing for tutorials

Particularly for tutorials that involve working through examples or problems, it may be helpful to prepare for the tutorial with others. If you work together on problems that have been tricky, you might find a solution together. If not, then asking as a group for help from the tutor will ensure that your problems are addressed and may guide the meeting to cover key issues for your learning.

Before each tutorial, depending on the subject you are studying, you will be expected to have done some preparation.

- **For tutorials in practical or numerical subjects, you should have:**
  - tackled the full set of problems or done the prescribed reading;
  - where required, submitted answers on time;
  - thought about difficulties that you may have found with the tutorial problems or about possible issues that might arise in the discussion;
  - reflected on how this topic or set of problems fits into the wider course structure and learning process;
  - prepared any questions about the work that you might like to ask the tutor or group.
- **For discussion-style tutorials in non-scientific subjects, you should have:**
  - done the required reading;
  - identified and analysed the topic or theme;
  - reflected on the key issues that arise;
  - considered the topic from different angles, for example, arguments for and against a particular set of ideas or proposals;
  - prepared any questions about the work that you might like to ask the tutor or group.

Sometimes your tutorial will be held in an unfamiliar location such as a staff office – take the time to find out where this is beforehand and allow sufficient time to get to the location promptly.

Ch 49 outlines how your tutorial performance may be assessed.

Informal meetings

There are occasions when you might have a meeting with a lecturer on an informal basis to go over a particular piece of work or to ask for an explanation of a point covered in lectures that you have had difficulty understanding. This type of meeting is conducted more as a conversation than as a tutorial in the more usual sense outlined in this chapter.

PARTICIPATING IN TUTORIALS

There can be a time lapse between one tutorial and the next, and it may be that you don't meet your fellow tutees except in that tutorial situation. Some people may not feel as comfortable about participating in problem-solving or debating issues with relative strangers as they would among friends. This may be because they feel unsure of the situation as well as feeling unsure of the mode of learning that they are experiencing. No two students are the same and it is the richness represented within a student group that can make a tutorial a stimulating experience. How you participate in tutorials will very much depend on what kind of a student you are and what type of tutorial you are attending.

STRATEGIES FOR DIALOGUE IN TUTORIALS

Most communication is a two-way process, where one person speaks and the other listens. In tutorials, the situation is much the same except that there are more listeners, all with views of their own and all with something to say, if given the opportunity. You will need to develop some skills in interpersonal communication to ensure that you have the chance to be both a speaker and a listener. Table 21.1 introduces some tutorial 'characters' and suggests ways in which you can interact with them by using appropriate conversational gambits that are part of the turn-taking in group dialogue. These strategies are not only useful in tutorials – they can apply in meetings and group work situations.

Can I ask my tutor to explain things I wasn't sure about in the lecture?

This is not really the function of a tutorial in most subjects. In fact, your tutor may have no first-hand knowledge of your lecture course and will not be in a position to undertake discussion of any queries you might have. If you do have questions about the lectures, it is advisable to seek an appointment with the lecturer either via email or through the departmental secretary.

Table 21.1 Tutorial characters. Tutorial groups comprise many different types of student with different personalities, views and experience. Learning to interact with these individuals can be as challenging as the content of the tutorial. The column on the far right presents some approaches that might be useful to stimulate an even balance of participation in tutorials.

Tutorial character	Characteristic behaviour in tutorials	Typical oral strategies	Oral gambits in response
The quiet student	Shy and retiring. Never, or rarely, offers an opinion on topic. Takes lots of notes. Avoids eye contact with others. Speaks only when spoken to.	• I don't know. • Says nothing.	• What do you think about this? • What do you think about X's theory?
The know-it-all student	Has an opinion on almost everything. May have done reading but no reflection on deeper meaning; or has done problems but omits key steps.	• In my opinion . . . . • I think . . . . • It's my view that . . . . • If you ask me	• I think you're taking rather a narrow view on this. What about . . . ?
The centre-stage student	Likes to be the centre of attention. Attempts to monopolise the attention of the tutor and prevents others from asking questions or from contributing.	• I see this breaking down into 10 areas. The first one is . . .; the second one is . . . the tenth one is	• Could I come in here? • Actually, I have a related point . . . • I'd like to make a point here.
The conversation-monopolising student	Has read up about the subject and thought about it a lot, therefore has much to say and goes on and on. Is so preoccupied with his/her own thoughts that he/she tends to forget that others might wish to make their own points.	• My understanding of X's work is that . . . furthermore . . . on the other hand . . . I'd also like to say that . . .	• Could we hear other views? • Let's summarise what you've said so that I can make sure I understand your point.
The interrupting student	Not a good listener. Keeps talking over others or interrupting when others are speaking.	• If I could come in here . . . . • I can't let that point go unchallenged . . .	• Could I just finish my point? • That's really a digression.
The uncertain student	Not very confident of own understanding or abilities – usually unfairly. Doesn't ask questions to confirm understanding. Rarely offers opinion except when asked directly.	• I'm not sure. • I don't think I know.	• How would you tackle this? • That's a really good point. I quite agree with you.
The uninterested student	Only took the subject to make up the module numbers at matriculation. Gazes out of the window, plays with mobile phone.	• Don't know. I'm only here until the union opens. • This is really boring, isn't it?	• Ignore.
The active student	Contributes and listens. Has done the preparation; sorted out some of the ideas; not too sure about some points. Asks for clarification.	• Could you explain . . . ? • There are three points to make. • What do other people think?	• I think that is a well-considered point. • Could you expand on it further? • That's an interesting question. What do others think about this?

General pointers for problem-solving tutorials

Think about the underlying principles involved in the exercises. Consider how the examples fit into the wider scheme of things, especially your lectures.

Make sure that you have done the full set of examples beforehand. Identify those that have caused difficulty or raised questions in your mind so that you can discuss these points with the tutor.

Don't feel that your question is stupid. The chances are that there will be others in the group who will be having the same difficulty.

Get your question in early on in the session. Make sure you ask your question before people who may not have done the preparatory work divert the tutor's attention with trivial or irrelevant questions.

Useful general pointers for tutorials based on discussion.

Make sure that you do contribute. It is better to say something that you have an opinion about rather than be asked a direct question by the tutor about something where you have very little knowledge to support an opinion.

Make your points clearly and objectively. While you may hold strong views on a topic, you will be expected to explain these on the basis of supporting evidence and argument, not on emotion.

Be aware that your ideas are as valid as anyone else's. This means that you can contribute effectively to the discussion.

Don't take criticism of your ideas personally. This is an objective academic exercise and the tutorial would be dull and possibly pointless if everyone agreed.

Learn to listen as well as to speak. The convention in tutorials is that everyone has space to speak and be heard. Although you may not agree with the views of others, at least listen to what they have to say and consider their argument for its merits as well as its flaws.

Don't assume that your tutor is expressing a personal view when they present a point. Tutors may be taking the role of 'devil's advocate' simply to stimulate discussion by making the group consider alternative viewpoints.

22

THINKING CRITICALLY

How to develop a logical approach to analysis and problem-solving

> The ability to think critically is probably the most transferable of the skills you will develop at university – and your future employers will expect you to be able to use it to tackle professional challenges. This chapter introduces concepts, methods and fallacies to watch out for when trying to improve your analytical capabilities.

How can you apply theory and technique to help you think better? Many specialists believe that critical thinking is a skill that you can develop through practice – and this assumption lies behind much university teaching. Your experience of the educational system probably tells you that your marks depend increasingly on the analysis of facts and the ability to arrive at an opinion and support it with relevant information, rather than the simple recall of fact. If you understand the underlying processes a little better, this should help you meet your tutors' expectations. Also, adopting a methodical approach can be useful when you are unsure how to tackle a new task.

THINKING ABOUT THINKING

Benjamin Bloom, a noted educational psychologist, and colleagues, identified six different steps involved in learning and thinking within education:

- knowledge
- comprehension
- application
- analysis
- synthesis
- evaluation.

Bloom *et al.* (1956) showed that students naturally progressed through this scale of thought-processing during their studies (Table 22.1). Looking at this table, you may recognise that your school work mainly focused on knowledge, comprehension and application, while your university

> ## ℹ Definition: critical
>
> People often interpret the words 'critical' and 'criticism' to mean being negative about an issue. For university work, the alternative meaning of 'making a careful judgement after balanced consideration of all aspects of a topic' is the one you should adopt.

Table 22.1 Classification of thinking processes by Bloom *et al.* (1956) (Bloom's Taxonomy)

Thinking processes (in ascending order of difficulty)	Typical question instructions
Knowledge. If you know a fact, you have it at your disposal and can *recall* or *recognise* it. This does not mean you necessarily understand it at a higher level.	• Define • Describe • Identify
Comprehension. To comprehend a fact means that you *understand* what it means.	• Contrast • Discuss • Interpret
Application. To apply a fact means that you can *put it to use*.	• Demonstrate • Calculate • Illustrate
Analysis. To analyse information means that you are able to *break it down into parts* and show how these components *fit together*.	• Analyse • Explain • Compare
Synthesis. To synthesise, you need to be able to *extract relevant facts* from a body of knowledge and use these to *address an issue in a novel way* or *create something new*.	• Compose • Create • Integrate
Evaluation. If you evaluate information, you *arrive at a judgement* based on its importance relative to the topic being addressed.	• Recommend • Support • Draw a conclusion

tutors tend to expect more in terms of analysis, synthesis and evaluation. These expectations are sometimes closely linked to the instruction words used in assessments, and Table 22.1 provides a few examples. However, take care when interpreting these, as processes and tasks may mean different things in different subjects. For example, while 'description' might imply a lower-level activity in the sciences, it might involve high-level skills in subjects like architecture.

Some disciplines value creativity as a thinking process, for example, art and design, architecture, drama or English composition. In such cases, this word might take the place of 'synthesis' in Table 22.1. Some also propose that in certain cases creativity should be placed higher than 'evaluation' in the table.

When you analyse the instructions used in writing assignments (**Ch 32**, especially Table 32.2) and other forms of assessment (**Ch 46–Ch 57**), you should take into account what type of thinking process the examiner has asked you to carry out, and try your best to reach the required level. To help you understand what might be required, Table 22.2 gives examples of thought processes you might experience in a range of areas of study.

> **i   Contexts for thinking critically**
>
> Examples of university work involving high-level thinking skills include:
>
> - essay-writing in the arts and social sciences
> - problem-based learning in medicine and nursing
> - engineering problems based on real-life machines and buildings
> - scenarios in law
> - project-based practical work in the sciences.

Table 22.2 Examples of Bloom's classification of thinking processes within representative university subjects

Thinking processes (in ascending order of difficulty)	Law	Examples	
		Arts subjects, e.g. History or Politics	Numerical subjects
Knowledge	You might know the name and date of a case, statute or treaty without understanding its relevance	You might know that a river was an important geographical and political boundary in international relations, without being able to identify why	You might be able to write down a particular mathematical equation, without understanding what the symbols mean or where it might be applied
Comprehension	You would understand the principle of law contained in the legislation or case law, and its wider context	You would understand that the river forms a natural barrier, which can be easily identified and defended	You would understand what the symbols in an equation mean and how and when to apply it
Application	You would be able to identify situations to which the principle of law would apply	You might use this knowledge to explain the terms of a peace treaty	You would be able to use the equation to obtain a result, given background information
Analysis	You could relate the facts of a particular scenario to the principle to uncover the extent of its application, using appropriate authority	You could explain the importance of the river as a boundary as being of importance to the territorial gains/losses for signatories to the peace treaty	You could explain the theoretical process involved in deriving the equation
Synthesis	By a process of reasoning and analogy, you could predict how the law might be applied under given circumstances	You could identify this notion and relate it to the recurrence of this issue in later treaties or factors governing further hostilities and subsequent implications	You could be able to take one equation, link it with another and arrive at a new mathematical relationship or conclusion
Evaluation	You might be able to advise a client based on your own judgement, after weighing up and evaluating all available options	You would be able to discuss whether the use of this boundary was an obstacle to resolving the terms of the treaty to the satisfaction of all parties	You would be able to discuss the limitations of an equation based on its derivation and the underlying assumptions behind this

USING METHOD TO PROMPT AND ORGANISE YOUR THOUGHTS

Suppose you recognise that critical thinking is required to solve a particular problem. This could be an essay question set by one of your tutors, an issue arising from problem-based learning, or even a domestic matter such as what type of car to buy or where best to rent a flat. The pointers below help you to arrive at a logical answer. You should regard this as a menu rather than a recipe – think about the different stages and how they might be useful for the specific issue under consideration and your own style of work. Adopt or reject them as you see fit, or, according to your needs, chop and change their order.

- **Decide exactly what the problem is.** An important preliminary task is to make sure you have identified this properly. Write down a description of the problem or issue – if this is not already provided for you – taking care to be very precise with your wording. If a specific question has been given as part of the exercise, analyse its phrasing carefully, to make sure you understand all possible meanings (**Ch 32**). If you are working in a group, ideally all members should agree on the group's interpretation.

- **Organise your approach to the problem.** You might start with a 'brainstorm' to identify potential solutions or viewpoints. This can be a solo or group activity and typically might consist of three phases:

  - **Open thinking.** Consider the issue or question from all possible angles or positions and write down everything you come up with. Don't worry at this stage about the relevance or importance of your ideas. You may wish to use a 'spider diagram' or 'mind map' to lay out your thoughts (**Ch 17** and **Ch 26**).

  - **Organisation.** Next, you should try to arrange your ideas into categories or sub-headings, or group them as supporting or opposing a viewpoint. A new diagram, table or grid may be useful to make things clear (see Figures 26.1–26.7 for examples of layout).

  - **Analysis.** Now you need to decide about the relevance of the grouped points to the original problem. Reject trivial or irrelevant ideas and rank or prioritise those that seem relevant.

? **Can a methodical approach inspire you creatively?**

You may doubt this, and we all recognise that a solution to a problem often comes to us when we aren't even trying to think about it. However, technique can sometimes help you clarify the issues, organise the evidence and arrive at a balanced answer. This should help inspiration to follow.

 Sharpening your research skills

Consult the following chapters for further information and practical tips:

- library and web-search skills: **Ch 23**, **Ch 27**
- collecting information that will allow you to cite the source: **Ch 35**
- avoiding plagiarism: **Ch 36**.

- **Get background information and check your comprehension of the facts.** It's quite likely that you will need to gather relevant information and ideas – to support your viewpoint or position, provide examples or suggest a range of interpretations or approaches. You also need to ensure you fully understand the information you have gathered. This could be as simple as using dictionaries and technical works to find out the precise meaning of key words; it might involve discussing your ideas with your peers or a tutor; or you could read a range of texts to see how others interpret your topic.

- **Check relevance.** Now consider the information you have gathered, your thoughts and how these might apply to your question. You may need to re-analyse the question. You will then need to marshal the evidence you have collected – for example: for or against a proposition; supporting or opposing an argument or theory. You may find it useful to prepare a table or grid to organise the information (see Figure 26.6 for an example) – this will also help you balance your thoughts. Be ruthless in rejecting irrelevant or inconsequential material.

- **Think through your argument, and how you can support it.** Having considered relevant information and positions, you should arrive at a personal viewpoint, and then construct your discussion or conclusion around this. When writing about your conclusion, you must take care to avoid value judgements or other kinds of expression of opinion that are not supported by evidence or sources. This is one reason why frequent citation and referencing is demanded in academic work.

- **Get cracking on your answer.** Once you have decided on what you want to say, writing it up should be much easier.

Value judgements

These are statements that reflect the views and values of the speaker or writer rather than the objective reality of what is being assessed or considered (**Ch 37**). For example, if the person is sympathetic to a cause they may refer to those who support it as members of a 'pressure group'; if they disagree with the cause, its members become 'activists'; similarly, 'conservationists' versus 'tree-huggers'; 'freedom fighters' versus 'insurgents'. Value judgements often imply some sense of being pejorative (negative). For example: 'Teenagers are unreliable, unpredictable and unable to accept responsibility for their actions'.

RECOGNISING FALLACIES AND BIASED PRESENTATIONS

As you consider arguments and discussions on academic subjects, you will notice that various linguistic devices are used to promote particular points of view. Identifying these is a valuable aspect of critical thinking, allowing you to rise above the argument itself and think about the way in which it is being conducted.

There are many different types of logical fallacies, and Table 22.3 lists only a few common examples. Once tuned in to this way of thinking, you should observe that faulty logic and debating tricks are frequently used in areas such as advertising and politics. Analysing the methods being used can be a useful way of practising your critical skills.

Table 22.3 Common examples of logical fallacies, bias and propaganda techniques found in arguments. There are many different types of fallacious arguments (at least 70!) and this is an important area of study in philosophical logic.

Type of fallacy or propaganda	Description	Example	How to counteract this approach
Ad hominem (Latin for 'to the man')	An attack is made on the character of the person putting forward an argument, rather than on the argument itself; this is particularly common in the media and politics	The President's moral behaviour is suspect, so his financial policies must also be dubious	Suggest that the person's character or circumstances are irrelevant
Ad populum (Latin for 'to the people')	The argument is supported on the basis that it is a popular viewpoint; of course, this does not make it correct in itself	The majority of people support corporal punishment for vandals, so we should introduce boot camps	Watch out for bandwagons and peer-pressure effects and ignore them when considering rights and wrongs
Anecdotal evidence	Use of unrepresentative exceptions to contradict an argument based on statistical evidence	My gran was a heavy smoker and she lived to be 95, so smoking won't harm me	Consider the overall weight of evidence rather than isolated examples
Appeal to authority	An argument is supported on the basis that an expert or authority agrees with the conclusion; used in advertisements, where celebrity endorsement and testimonials are frequent	My professor, whom I admire greatly, believes in Smith's theory, so it must be right	Point out that the experts disagree and explain how and why; focus on the key qualities of the item or argument
Appeal to ignorance	Because there's no evidence for (or against) a case, it means the case must be false (or true)	You haven't an alibi, therefore you must be guilty	Point out that a conclusion either way may not be possible in the absence of evidence
Biased evidence	Selection of examples or evidence for or against a case. A writer who quotes those who support their view, but not those against	My advisers tell me that Global Warming isn't going to happen	Read around the subject, including those with a different view, and try to arrive at a balanced opinion
Euphemisms and jargon	Use of phrasing to hide the true position or exaggerate an opponent's – stating things in mild or emotive language for effect; use of technical words to sound authoritative	My job as vertical transportation operative means I am used to being in a responsible position	Watch for (unnecessary) adjectives and adverbs that may affect the way you consider the evidence
Repetition	Saying the same thing over and over again until people believe it. Common in politics, war propaganda and advertising	'Beans means Heinz'	Look out for repeated catchphrases and lack of substantive argument
Straw man/false dichotomy	A position is misrepresented in order to create a diversionary debating point that is easily accepted or rejected, when in fact the core issue has not been addressed	Asylum seekers all want to milk the benefits system, so we should turn them all away	Point out the fallacy and focus on the core issue

One way of avoiding bias in your own work is consciously to try to balance your discussion. Avoid 'absolutes' – be careful with words that imply that there are no exceptions, for example, *always*, *never*, *all* and *every*. These words can only be used if you are absolutely sure of facts that imply 100 per cent certainty.

> ## Definitions
>
> - **Fallacy:** a fault in logic or thinking that means that an argument is incorrect.
> - **Bias:** information that emphasises just one viewpoint or position.
> - **Propaganda:** false or incomplete information that supports a (usually) extreme political or moral view.

PRACTICAL TIPS FOR THINKING CRITICALLY

Focus on the task in hand. It is very easy to become distracted when reading around a subject, or when discussing problems with others. Take care not to waste too much time on preliminaries and start relevant action as quickly as possible.

Write down your thoughts. The act of writing your thoughts is important as this forces you to clarify them. Also, since ideas are often fleeting, it makes sense to ensure you have a permanent record. Reviewing what you have written makes you more critical and can lead you on to new ideas.

Try to be analytical, not descriptive. By looking at Table 22.1, you will appreciate why analysis is regarded as a higher-level skill than description. Many students lose marks because they simply quote facts or statements, without explaining their importance and context, that is, without showing their understanding of what the quote means or implies.

When quoting evidence, use appropriate citations. This is important as it shows you have read relevant source material and helps you avoid plagiarism (**Ch 36**). The conventions for citation vary among subjects (**Ch 35**), so consult course handbooks or other information and make sure you follow the instructions carefully, or you may lose marks.

Draw on the ideas and opinions of your peers and tutors. Discussions with others can be very fruitful, revealing a range of interpretations that you might not have thought about yourself. You may find it useful to bounce ideas off others. Tutors can provide useful guidance once you have done some reading, and are usually pleased to be asked for help.

Keep an open mind. Although you may start with preconceived ideas about a topic, you should try to be receptive to the ideas of others. You may find that your initial thoughts become altered by what you are reading and discussing. If there is not enough evidence to support *any* conclusion, be prepared to suspend judgement.

Balance your arguments. If asked to arrive at a position on a subject, you should try to do this in an even-handed way, by considering all possible viewpoints and by presenting your conclusion with supporting evidence.

Avoid common pitfalls of shallow thinking. Try not to:

- rush to conclusions
- generalise
- oversimplify
- personalise
- use fallacious arguments
- think in terms of stereotypes
- make value judgements.

Keep asking yourself questions. A good way to think more deeply is to ask questions, even after you feel a matter is resolved or you understand it well. All critical thinking is the result of asking questions.

Look beneath the surface. Decide whether sources are dealing with facts or opinions; examine any assumptions made, including your own; think about the motivation of writers. Rather than restating and describing your sources, focus on what they *mean* by what they write.

23

THE LIBRARY AS A RESOURCE

How to make the best use of the facilities

At university you will find that you will be expected not only to seek out the books on your reading list, but also to source additional material for yourself. Learning more about information literacy and how to access resources is a priority. The pace of progression in relation to libraries and information dissemination is rapid and detailed institution-specific information soon becomes outdated. Hence, this chapter focuses on key aspects of information retrieval and related skills.

The library is a key resource for any student. A modern university library is much more than a collection of books and journals – it co-ordinates an electronic gateway to a massive amount of online information. Accessing these resources requires library skills that are essential for your studies.

FIRST STEPS FOR NEW STUDENTS

- Find the university library and activate your membership. This usually cannot be done until you have matriculated.
- Find out when library tours that are offered to new students take place. Register for one of these, since this will enable you to familiarise yourself with the layout and facilities available.
- Obtain leaflets or library maps to which you can refer later when you explore the library on your own.

Your library record

When you join your university library, a record is established in your name. Most libraries use an electronic system that allows you to check your record of books out on loan at any time.

Deciding whether to buy textbooks

Sometimes reading lists are lengthy and the recommended textbooks are expensive. Check what the library holds, although you may encounter access problems if everyone else in the class is looking for the same thing at the same time. In this case, use the catalogue to find alternatives – there are usually other options. Consider purchasing your own copy of books that you need to refer to frequently and that relate strongly to the lecture content and coursework.

Most university libraries offer the following facilities:

- quiet study areas
- groupwork areas where discussion is allowed
- photocopiers and printers
- computing terminals, and possibly a wireless network
- online catalogue access
- support from expert staff, both in person and via the library website.

Apart from books, most UK university libraries will hold some of the following, in hard copy:

- selected daily and weekly newspapers
- periodicals and academic journals
- reference materials
- slides (e.g. for art or life sciences)
- video and DVD resources.

Table 23.1 indicates the type of content you can expect from these resources. The precise holdings will depend on factors such as the degrees taught, any teaching specialisms, the research interests of staff and past bequests of collections. Each library is unique and, in this respect, will hold particular archive material that is not available elsewhere.

Digital and web-based resources

Many current items are now available online in each of the categories listed in Table 23.1. For example, libraries take out subscriptions to e-book repositories, e-journals, e-newspapers and online dictionaries and encyclopaedias. Your institution will have its own method of giving access to these digitised and web-based resources, probably via the library electronic desktop. A password may be required (see below).

The main advantage of this method of accessing information is that it is available 24 hours per day from any computer connected to the internet. In some cases, more than one person can access the e-book at any one time. Some e-book facilities, such as ebrary, offer additional facilities, such as searching, note-making facilities and linked online dictionaries for checking the meanings of words.

Electronic databases make it easier to access information from public bodies, and much of that kind of information is also now more readily available online. For example, statistical population details are available through the National Statistics website (**www.statistics.gov.uk**); papers and publications produced by the Houses of Parliament can also be accessed electronically at **www.parliament.uk**; European Commission information can be found at **ec.europa.eu**. Specialist organisation provide extensive information. As an example, the Forestry Commission (**www.forestry.gov.uk**) and Woodland Trust (**www.woodlandtrust.org.uk**) provide detailed data about UK forests and woods.

Table 23.1 Some of the types of content that can be obtained from library resources. These may be available as hard copy or online.

Type of resource	Examples	Indication of content
Books	Prescribed texts	Provide linkage with the course content
	General textbooks	Give an overview of the subject
	Supplementary texts	Discuss subject in greater depth
Reference books	Standard dictionaries	Provide spelling, pronunciation and meaning
	Bilingual dictionaries	Provide translation of words and expressions in two languages
	Subject-specific dictionaries	Define key specialist terms
	Thesauri (plural); Thesaurus (singular)	A–Z versions are easier to use than the original Roget's Thesaurus. The A–Z versions give synonyms (words similar in meaning) and, in some, antonyms (words opposite in meaning).
	General encyclopaedias	Provide a quick overview of a new topic
	Discipline-specific encyclopaedias	Focus on in-depth coverage of specific topics
	Biographical material	Sources of information on key figures both contemporary and in the past
	Yearbooks	Provide up-to-date information on organisations
	Atlases	Provide geographical or historical information
	Directories	Provide up-to-date access to information on organisations
Newspapers	Daily or weekly newspapers	Provide coverage of contemporary issues
Periodicals and academic journals	Discipline- or subject-specific publications produced three or four times per year	Provide recent ideas, reports and comment on current research issues
Popular periodicals	*Nature*; *New Scientist*; *The Economist*	Provide coverage of emerging themes within broad fields, such as their titles suggest
Search engines and databases	Electronic repositories of academic journals and other material	Access will depend on the journal subscriptions held by your library

Shared library resources

Many university libraries share resources with those of neighbouring institutions and all are linked to the British Library, the national library of the UK. This receives a copy of every publication produced in the UK and Ireland, and its massive collection of over 150 million items increases by 3 million items every year. Some university libraries are designated as European Documentation Centres (http://ec.europa.eu/europedirect). These centres hold key documents of the European Union.

WHAT YOU NEED TO KNOW AS A BORROWER

You should find out the answers to the following questions regarding book borrowing.

- **How many books can you borrow at any one time?** This depends on your status as a borrower: staff and postgraduate students can usually borrow more books than undergraduate members.

- **What is the maximum loan period?** This will depend on the type of resource you wish to borrow. For example, some books that are heavily in demand because they are prescribed texts may be put on a short-loan system within the library. The basic idea is that readers are limited to a shorter borrowing time for these books. This period may be as short as a few hours, or perhaps a few days. Standard loans are usually for several weeks.

- **What are the fines if you keep a book after the due date?** Fines usually apply to all borrowers, whether they are staff or students. The fine will be dictated by the status of the book that is overdue. Short-loan books have higher fines; standard loans are lower. While a few pence may not seem much on a standard loan, if you have 10 books all overdue for two weeks, you can be looking at a double-figure in pounds.

- **How can you renew the loan?** Most libraries accept telephone renewals, but, increasingly, online facilities enable you to renew books from wherever you access the university home page.

Electronic book tagging

To protect their valuable assets, most universities operate a system of electronic 'book tagging' to ensure that resources cannot be withdrawn without being logged out to a particular user. This means that all books need to be 'de-activated' before you can take them out of the library.

REGULATIONS AND CODES OF CONDUCT

All libraries have these; they generally serve to protect the resources and respect the needs of other library users. You will be alerted to these rules by notices, leaflets and websites. In particular, you have important legal responsibilities under copyright law, which sets out limits on the amount you can photocopy (**Ch 36**).

Always personalise your photocopy cards

If your library operates a card system for photocopying, write your name and a contact number on your card, in case you absent-mindedly leave it on a machine. This will allow the library staff to arrange for the card to be returned to you.

KEY INFORMATION LITERACY SKILLS

Information literacy has been defined as: *'knowing when and why you need information, where to find it, and how to evaluate, use and communicate it in an ethical manner.'* (CILIP, 2012). Seven key information skills are associated with information literacy (SCONUL, 2011):

1 the ability to identify a personal need for information ('identify' information)
2 the ability to assess current knowledge and identify gaps ('scope' information)
3 the ability to construct strategies for locating information and data ('plan' information)
4 the ability to locate and access the information and data needed ('gather' information)
5 the ability to review the research process and compare and evaluate information and data ('evaluate')
6 the ability to organise information professionally and ethically ('manage' information)
7 the ability to apply the knowledge gained: presenting the results of their research, synthesising new and old information and data to create new knowledge and disseminating it in a variety of ways ('present' information).

You should assess how well you can carry out each of these skills. Consult library staff for assistance if necessary.

In terms of the ability to locate and access information, these are the basic skills you will need to master:

- **How to use the electronic catalogue.** Most systems offer a function where you can search by author, by title, or by subject, although there may be more alternatives on the system you will use.

- **How to find a book or periodical.** When you identify the book that you want from the catalogue, then you need to be able to find where it is shelved in the library. This means that you need to take a note of two things: the location (the book might be shelved in another site library, for example) and the class number (not the ISBN number, which is irrelevant). The catalogue number may comprise a sequence of letters and/or numbers depending on the system used in your library. This number corresponds to the number on the spine of the book – universities generally use one of two systems (see Information Box on page 134). Books are shelved sequentially according to these numbers, in stacks labelled to assist you to find what you want. If you have difficulty in locating a particular book, library staff can help.

> ### Catalogue searches
>
> It is useful to remember that there are often several ways to spell surnames, for example, Brown/Browne or Nichol/Nicol/Nicoll. To find a book by an author's name that you may only have heard mentioned in a lecture, you may have to try various options in order to find the one you want. Check with the book list in your course handbook, as this may give details, including catalogue information.

- **How to borrow a book or journal from another library.** Sometimes books are not available in your own library and you may wish to request a loan from another UK library. There will be a particular librarian responsible for inter-library loans who will arrange this. However, there are cost implications in this process. Usually, the cost is borne by the borrower.

- **How to access your university library's e-resources.** This is normally done via the library's website. Some resources are open-access, but others will require a password that allows publishers to verify that your library has subscribed to an e-resource and that you have access rights. Systems may vary but information and training on how to access material using e-resources will usually be available to students in a special training session during a lecture or your library may provide independent training sessions that you can attend. The important thing is not to be puzzled by the range of resources available to you. Ask a librarian to help you find your way around this 'e-world'.

---

i Library cataloguing systems

The system your library uses will be explained in leaflets or during the library tour. The two main possibilities are:

- **The Dewey decimal system:** each book is given a numerical code. For example, editions of *Hamlet* by William Shakespeare are filed under 822.33.
- **The Library of Congress system:** each book is given an alphanumeric code. For example, editions of *Hamlet* by William Shakespeare are filed under PR2807.

Additional numbers and letters may be used to define editions and variants on a subject area. Each system may be interpreted slightly differently in different libraries.

Of course, finding information within the library and associated online facilities is only the first step in using it for your studies. The next stage is to evaluate it (**Ch 22** and **Ch 24**) and use it appropriately in your academic writing (**Ch 32**, **Ch 33**), note-making and revision (**Ch 26**, **Ch 61**). In these contexts, citing sources of information correctly (**Ch 35**) is important, to avoid plagiarism (**Ch 36**).

🔧 PRACTICAL TIPS FOR MAKING THE MOST OF LIBRARY RESOURCES

Go on a library tour. Be prepared to ask questions if you are shown things that you don't understand or that seem strange to you. University libraries are unlike public libraries in many ways and have much more to offer. This is a chance to learn about these opportunities. If tours are not available, see if a virtual tour can be made from your university library's website.

Take advantage of reciprocal arrangements. Some university libraries have agreements with other similar libraries in the area, including national libraries. This enables you to use and sometimes, depending on the agreement, borrow books from partner libraries.

Find and join the local public library. This may hold some texts that would be relevant to your course and will not be so heavily in demand as those in the university library.

Explore all the library locations available to you. You may find different areas that are more convenient or that suit your moods, learning preference or personality. You may find spots that are out of the way and quieter or zones with a buzz that gets you going.

24

ANALYSING AND EVALUATING INFORMATION

How to filter and select reliable material and discuss it appropriately

> Since so much information is available nowadays, through many different media, the evaluation of evidence, data and opinions has become a core skill. This chapter will help you understand the origin of information and ideas, the reliability of sources, and differences between fact, opinion and truth.

Whatever subject you are studying at university, the ability to evaluate information and ideas is essential. This is a multifaceted skill that will differ according to the task in hand. Your analysis may centre on the accuracy or truth of the information itself, the reliability or potential bias of the source of the information, or the value of information in relation to some argument or case. You may also come across contradictory sources of evidence or conflicting arguments based on the same information. You will need to assess their relative merits. To do any or all of these tasks, you will need to understand more about the origin and nature of information.

THE ORIGIN OF INFORMATION AND IDEAS

Essentially, facts and ideas originate from someone's research or scholarship. These can be descriptions, concepts, interpretations or numerical data. At some point, information or ideas must be communicated or published, otherwise no one else would know about them. Information and ideas usually appear first in the primary literature and may be modified later in the secondary literature (Table 24.1). Understanding this process is important when analysing and evaluating information and when deciding how to cite evidence or references in the text of your own assignments (**Ch 35**).

The nature of evaluation

In 'scientific' subjects you will need to interpret and check the reliability of data. This is essential for setting up and testing meaningful hypotheses, and therefore at the core of the scientific approach.

In 'non-scientific' subjects, ideas and concepts are important, and you may need to carry out an objective analysis of information and arguments so that you can construct your own position, backed up with evidence.

Table 24.1 Characteristics and examples of primary and secondary sources of information

Primary sources: those in which ideas and data are first communicated.	• The primary literature in your subject may be published in the form of papers (articles) in journals. • The primary literature is usually refereed, that is, judged, by experts in the authors' academic peer group, who check the accuracy and originality of the work and report their opinions back to the journal editors. This system helps to maintain reliability, but it is not perfect. • Books (and, more rarely, articles in magazines and newspapers) can also be primary sources, but this depends on the nature of the information published rather than the medium. These sources are not formally refereed, although they may be read by editors and lawyers to check for errors and unsubstantiated or libellous allegations.
Secondary sources: those that quote, adapt, interpret, translate, develop or otherwise use information drawn from primary sources.	• It is the act of recycling that makes the source secondary, rather than the medium. Reviews are examples of secondary sources in the academic world, and textbooks and magazine articles are often of this type. • As people adopt, modify, translate and develop information and ideas, alterations are likely to occur, whether intentional or unintentional. Most authors of secondary sources do not deliberately set out to change the meaning of the primary source, but they may unwittingly do so. Others may consciously or unconsciously exert bias in their reporting by quoting evidence only on one side of a debate. • Modifications while creating a secondary source could involve adding valuable new ideas and content, or correcting errors.

ASSESSING SOURCES OF 'FACTS'

Not all 'facts' are true. What you read could be misquoted, misrepresented, erroneous or based on a faulty premise (foundation principle). This is particularly true of web-based information because it is less likely to be refereed or edited. Logically, the closer you can get to the primary source, the more consistent the information is likely to be with the original. Clearly, a lot depends on who wrote the source and under what patronage (who paid them?). Hence, another important way of assessing sources is to investigate the ownership and 'provenance' of the work (from whom and where it originated, and why).

- **Authorship.** Can you identify who wrote the piece? If it is signed or there is a 'by-line' showing who wrote it, you might be able to judge the quality of what you are reading. This may be a simple decision, if you know or can assume the author is an authority in the area; otherwise a little research (for example, by putting the name into a search engine) might help.

  Of course, just because Professor X thinks something, this does not make it true. However, if you know that their opinion is backed by years of research and experience, you might take it a little more seriously than the thoughts of an unknown web author. If no author is cited, this may mean that no one is willing to take responsibility for the content. Could there be a reason for this?

- **Provenance.** Is the author's place of work mentioned? This might tell you whether there is likely to have been an academic study behind the facts or opinions given. If the author works for a public body, there may be publication rules to follow and they may even have to submit their work to a publications committee before it is disseminated. They are certainly more likely to get into trouble if they include scurrilous or incorrect material. Another issue to consider is whether a company or political faction may have a vested interest behind the content.

Determining authorship and provenance

This information is easy to find in most published academic sources, and may even be presented just below the title for convenience. In the case of the Web, it may not be so easy to find what you want. However, often relevant clues can be obtained from the header, body and footer information.

FACTS, OPINIONS AND TRUTH

When dealing with a large reading list and a wide diversity of viewpoints, you can easily become confused and lose sight of the differences between fact, opinion and truth. Becoming aware of this issue is fundamental to study in many subjects, particularly in the arts, social sciences and law.

In many fields, for example, in arts and social sciences, there is often no 'right' or 'wrong' answer, simply a range of stances or viewpoints. It is therefore possible that your answer may differ significantly from the viewpoints of your fellow students and possibly also that of your tutor. You will probably be given credit for constructing your own argument with evidence to substantiate your position, rather than simply following a 'line' expounded in lectures or a standard text. Even if your tutors disagree personally with your conclusions, they will mark your work according to the way you have presented it.

Table 24.2 provides a checklist for assessing the reliability of information you may read.

Table 24.2 A checklist for assessing the reliability of information. These questions are based on commonly adopted criteria; the more 'yes' answers you can give, the more trustworthy you can assume your source to be.

Assessing authorship and the nature of the source	Evaluating the information and its analysis
❏ Can you identify the author's name?	❏ Is the source cited by others?
❏ Can you determine what relevant qualifications the authors hold?	❏ Is the date of the source likely to be important regarding the accuracy of the information? For example, is it contemporary to events, or is it written with the benefit of hindsight?
❏ Can you say who employs the author?	❏ Have you focused on the substance of the information presented rather than its packaging?
❏ Do you know who paid for the work to be done?	❏ Does the language used indicate anything about the status of the information?
❏ Is this a primary source rather than a secondary one?	❏ Is the information fact or opinion?
❏ Has the source been refereed or edited?	❏ Have you checked for any logical fallacies in the arguments?
❏ Is the content original or derived?	❏ Have possible errors associated with any numbers been taken into account?
❏ Does the source cite relevant literature?	❏ Have the data been analysed using appropriate statistics?
❏ Have you checked a range of sources?	❏ If there are graphs, are they constructed fairly?

However, in some subjects, such as History, Politics and Economics, it is very easy to stray into opinionated and biased conclusions. Sometimes these might be referred to as 'value judgements' (**Ch 37**). If your work includes these unsubstantiated viewpoints, you may be marked down.

Truth is a concept that can be problematic, because it involves a host of philosophical concepts, which may be confusing. In debate, something is only true when all sides of the argument accept it. If a particular line of argument can be shown to lack credibility or to be in some way unacceptable, this will add weight to the counter-argument.

Concepts of truth and fact involve the notions of objectivity and subjectivity:

- **objective** means based on a balanced consideration of the facts;
- **subjective** means based on one person's opinion.

Most academics aim for a detached, objective piece of writing. Nevertheless, it is important to state your own opinion at some point in the work, particularly if some of the evidence might point to a contrary view. The key is to produce valid reasons for holding your opinion.

> ### The provisional nature of information
>
> There are countless examples where what was once seen as an unassailable 'fact' is now seen as ridiculous (consider the once-accepted orbit of the Sun around the Earth); and where what was once considered ridiculous is now generally accepted (for example, continental drift in the field of plate tectonics). In other cases, the mainstream view of society may change through time, such that it radically alters the whole frame of discussion (for example, on slavery or emancipation of women). For this reason, one of the central tenets of academia is that it is seen as acceptable and often desirable to challenge accepted fact and opinion. Keeping an open and enquiring mind is therefore valued, so long as a viewpoint is supported by up-to-date and reasoned reference points.

BACKING UP YOUR OWN OPINION OR CONCLUSION

Your grade will probably depend on how convincing your argument is and how well you use supporting evidence to support your position. Evidence comes in many forms: from statistical/numeric sources, from quotations, or from observation. You should assess all potential evidence for relevance and value, and you must make sure you cite the source of the information in your own writing, otherwise the evidence may be invalidated by the marker and you may be accused of plagiarism (**Ch 35, Ch 36**).

Above all, you should try to produce a *balanced* conclusion. This is one where you are open about counter-arguments and counter-evidence that does not, at least on the face of it, support your case. You must explain what others think or might think, then explain why you have arrived at the conclusion you have made.

Example: fact and opinion

The world record for the 100-metre sprint in athletics was 9.79 seconds at 30 September 1999. This is a *fact*. The record may change over time, but this statement will still be true. Some claim that many world records are created by athletes who have taken drugs to enhance their performance. This is an *opinion*. There is evidence to back up this position, but recent controversies have highlighted the problem of proof in these cases. Claims about drug misuse are open to conjecture, claim and counter-claim, not all of which can be *true*. Your task might be to identify the difference between fact and opinion and write with that knowledge. Do not avoid the controversy, but be clear about the facts, the truth and your opinion of the evidence as well as the reliability of the source(s) of that evidence.

PRACTICAL TIPS FOR EVALUATING INFORMATION

Be selective in your choice of sources you cite. Always try to read and cite the primary source if you can. Do not rely on a secondary source to do this for you, as you may find the author uses information selectively to support their case, or interprets it in a different way from you.

'Triangulate' uncertain information by making cross-referencing checks. This means looking at more than one source and comparing what is said in each. The sources should be as independent as possible (for example, do not compare an original source with one that is directly based on it). If you find the sources agree, you may become more certain of your position. If two sources differ, you may need to decide which viewpoint is better.

Consider the age of the source. 'Old' does not necessarily mean 'wrong', but ideas and facts may have altered between then and now. Can you trace changes through time in the sources available to you? What key events, works or changes in methods have forced any changes in the conclusions?

Look at the extent and quality of citations provided by the author. This applies particularly to articles in academic journals, where positions are usually supported by citations of others' work. These citations may indicate that a certain amount of research has been carried out beforehand, and that the ideas or results are based on genuine scholarship. If you doubt the quality of the work, these references might be worth looking at. How up to date are they? Do they cite independent work, or is the author exclusively quoting him/herself or the work of one particular researcher?

Analyse the language used. Words and their use can be very revealing. Have subjective or objective sentence structures been employed? The former might indicate a personal opinion rather than an objective conclusion. Are there any telltale signs of propaganda? Bias might be indicated by absolute terms, such as 'everyone knows . . .'; 'I can guarantee that . . .'; or a seemingly unbalanced consideration of the evidence. How carefully has the author considered the topic? A less studious approach might be indicated by exaggeration, ambiguity, or the use of journalese and slang. Always remember, however, that content should be judged above presentation.

Assess substance over presentation. Just because information is presented well, for instance in a glossy magazine or particularly well-constructed website, this does not necessarily tell you much about the quality of its content. Try to look beyond the surface.

Try to maintain a healthy, detached scepticism. However reliable a source of a piece of information seems to be, it is probably a good idea to retain a degree of scepticism about the facts or ideas involved and to question the logic of arguments. Even information from primary sources may not be perfect – different approaches can give different outcomes, for reasons not necessarily understood at the time of writing. Also, try not to identify too strongly with a viewpoint, so you can be detached when assessing its merits and failings.

Try to distinguish fact from opinion. To what extent has the author supported a given viewpoint? Have relevant facts been quoted, via literature citations or the author's own researches? Are numerical data used to substantiate the points used? Are these reliable and can you verify the information, for example, by looking at a source that was cited? Might the author have a hidden reason for putting forward biased evidence to support a personal opinion?

Spot fallacious arguments and logical flaws. Concentrate on analysing the method being used to put the points over, rather than the facts themselves. Perhaps you can see one of the common fallacies in arguments that indicate a flaw in logic (**Ch 22**).

Look closely at any data and graphs that are presented and the way they have been analysed. If the information you are looking at is numerical in form, have the errors of any data been taken into consideration, and, where appropriate, quantified? If so, does this help you arrive at a conclusion about how genuine the differences are between important values? Have the appropriate statistical methods been used to analyse the data? Are the underlying hypotheses the right ones? Have the results of any tests been interpreted correctly in arriving at the conclusion? Look closely at any graphs. These may have been constructed in such a way as to emphasise a particular viewpoint, for example, by biased selection of axis starting points (**Ch 30**).

Don't be blinded by statistics. Leaving aside the issue that statistical methods don't actually deal with proof, only probability, it is generally possible to analyse and present data in such a way that they support one chosen argument or hypothesis rather than another ('you can prove anything with statistics'). To deal with these matters, you will need at least a basic understanding of the 'statistical approach' and of the techniques in common use (**Ch 30**).

Look at who else has cited the author's work, and how. In many scientific subjects you can use the Science Citation Index to find out how often an article or author has been cited and by whom (available via Thompson Reuters Web of Science). You may then be able to consult these sources to see how others have viewed the original findings. Works that review the same area of study, published after your source, may also provide useful comments.

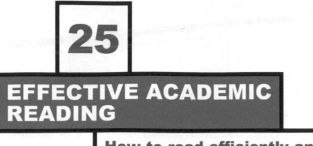

25

EFFECTIVE ACADEMIC READING

How to read efficiently and with understanding

Whatever your discipline, you will find that you are required to do a lot of reading as a university student. This chapter explains how to develop the speed-reading skills that will help you to deal more effectively with academic text.

Much of the material you will read as part of your studies will be books and chapters written following traditional academic style, and may appear, at first glance, to be heavy going. However, by taking advantage of the way printed academic resources are organised and understanding how text within them is structured, you should find it easier to read the pages of print in a way that will help you gain an understanding of the content while saving you time.

Reading and note-making

This chapter is concerned mainly with reading and comprehension as a prelude to note-making (**Ch 26**). While it is possible to read and make notes at the same time, this is not always the most effective form of studying, as your notes may end up simply as a rewrite of the source text. Notes framed after you have scanned the prescribed section of text will be better if you have a clearer idea of their context and content.

SURVEYING THE OVERALL ORGANISATION OF A TEXT

A text may be suggested by tutors; alternatively, when expanding your lecture notes or revising, you may come across a resource in the library that looks as if it might be relevant. In either case, carry out a preliminary survey to familiarise yourself with what it contains. You can use elements of the structure to answer key questions about the content, as follows:

- **Title and author(s).** Does this text look as though it is going to be useful to your current task? Are the authors well-known authorities in the subject area?
- **Publisher's 'blurb'.** Does this indicate that the coverage suits your needs?
- **Publication details.** What is the date of publication? Will this book provide you with up-to-date coverage?

- **Contents listing.** Does this indicate that the book covers the key topic areas you need? Do the chapter titles suggest the coverage is detailed enough?

- **Index.** Is this comprehensive and will it help you find what you want, quickly? From a quick look, can you see references to material you want?

- **General impression.** Does the text look easy to read? Is the text easy to navigate via sub-headings? Is any visual material clear and explained well?

The answers to these questions will help you to decide whether to investigate further: whether you need to look at the whole book, or just selected parts; or whether the book is of limited value at the present time.

? What is your reading goal?

It is always a good idea to think about your purpose before you start reading any piece of text (see 'question stage' in Table 25.3).

- If you are looking for a specific point of information, this can often be done quickly, using the index or chapter titles as a guide.

- If you wish to expand your lecture notes using a textbook, you might read in a different way, which might result in note-making (**Ch 26**).

- If your aim is to appreciate the author's style or the aesthetics of a piece of writing, perhaps in a work of fiction, you may read more slowly and reread key parts.

Sometimes, different methods may be required, for example, in English literature, 'close reading' techniques. These specialised methods will probably be taught as part of your studies.

HOW TO EXAMINE THE STRUCTURE OF THE WRITING ITSELF

Well-structured academic texts usually follow a standard pattern with an introduction, main body and conclusion in each element. Sometimes the introduction may comprise several paragraphs; sometimes it may be only one paragraph. Similarly, the conclusion may be several paragraphs or only one. Figure 25.1 represents a layout for a piece of text with five paragraphs, comprising an introduction and conclusion with three intervening paragraphs of varying length.

Within the structure of the text, each paragraph will be introduced by a topic sentence stating the content of the paragraph. Each paragraph performs a function. For example, some paragraphs may describe, others may provide examples, while others may examine points

---

i Reader as author

The points in the main text about the organisation of printed material and the structure of text are important for you as a reader or decoder of text, and they also come into play when you become an academic author and have to put your own ideas clearly – they help your reader (often 'the marker') to decode your written text.

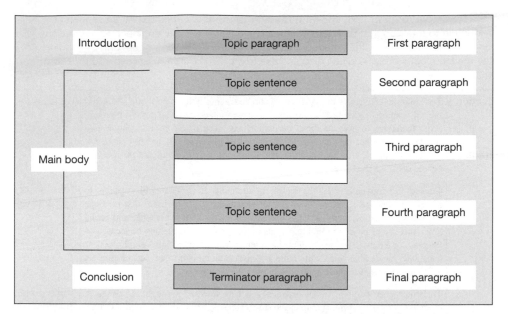

Figure 25.1 Sample textual layout. Most academic texts will be similarly organised.

in favour of a particular viewpoint and others points against that viewpoint. For more about paragraph types, see Table 38.3 on page 249.

The function of these paragraphs, and the sentences within them, is usually signalled by use of 'signpost words', which guide the reader through the logical structure of the text (Table 38.2). For example, the word 'however' indicates that some contrast is about to be made with a point immediately before; 'thus' signals that a result or effect is about to be explained. A breakdown of text structure is given in Table 25.1.

Use this knowledge of text structure to establish general meaning by:

- reading topic and terminator paragraphs, or even just their topic sentences, to gain a quick overview of the text;
- scaning through the text for key words related to your interest. This may indicate particular paragraphs worthy of detailed reading. Sometimes headings and sub-headings may be used, and these will facilitate a search of this kind; and
- looking for signpost words identify the underlying 'argument'.

Origin of speed-reading

The basic techniques were developed in the 1950s by Evelyn Wood, an American educator. She set up institutes to teach students to develop an ability to read hundreds of words per minute. Those who have studied her method include businessmen and politicians, who have to learn to read lengthy papers quickly but with understanding. US Presidents Jimmy Carter and John F. Kennedy were both regarded as famous speed-reading practitioners.

Table 25.1 Sample reading text, showing reading 'signposts'. This text might represent the introduction to a textbook on modern communications in electrical engineering, journalism, marketing or psychology. The light shaded areas indicate the topic sentences; darker shading indicates the signpost words. You can also use this text of 744 words to assess your speed of reading (see Table 25.2).

Introduction Topic paragraph	Technological advances and skilful marketing have meant that the mobile phone has moved from being simply an accessory to a status as an essential piece of equipment. From teenagers to grandmothers, the nation has taken to the mobile phone as a constant link for business and social purposes. As a phenomenon, the ascendancy of the mobile phone, in a multitude of ways, has had a critical impact on the way people organise their lives.	Topic sentence
	Clearly, the convenience of the mobile is attractive. It is constantly available to receive or send calls. While these are not cheap, the less expensive text-message alternative provides a similar 'constant contact' facility. At a personal and social level, this brings peace of mind to parents as teenagers can locate and be located on the press of a button. However, in business terms, while it means that employees are constantly accessible and, with more sophisticated models, can access internet communications also, there is no escape from the workplace.	Topic sentence Signpost word Signpost word
	The emergence of abbreviated text-message language has wrought a change in everyday print. For example, pupils and students have been known to submit written work using text message symbols and language. Some have declared this to mark the demise of standard English. Furthermore, the accessibility of the mobile phone has become a problem in colleges and universities where it has been known for students in examinations to use the texting facility to obtain information required.	Topic sentence Signpost word Signpost word
	The ubiquity of the mobile phone has generated changes in the way that services are offered. For instance, this means that trains, buses, and restaurants have declared 'silent zones' where the mobile is not permitted, to give others a rest from the 'I'm on the train' style mobile phone conversation.	Topic sentence Signpost words
Transition paragraph	While the marked increase in mobile phone sales indicates that many in the population have embraced this technology, by contrast, 'mobile' culture has not been without its critics. Real concerns have been expressed about the potential dangers that can be encountered through mobile phone use.	Topic sentence Signpost words
	One such danger is that associated with driving while speaking on a mobile. A body of case law has been accumulated to support the introduction of new legislation outlawing the use of hand-held mobile phones by drivers while driving. The enforcement of this legislation is virtually impossible to police and, thus, much is down to the common sense and responsibility of drivers. Again, technology has risen to meet the contingency with the development of 'hands-free' phones that can be used while driving and without infringing the law.	Topic sentence Signpost word
	A further danger is an unseen one, namely the impact of the radiation from mobile phones on the human brain. Research is not well advanced in this area and data related to specific absorption rates (SARs) from the use of mobile phones and its effect on brain tissue is not yet available for evaluation. Nevertheless, although this lack of evidence is acknowledged by mobile phone companies, they advise that hands-free devices reduce the SARs levels by 98 per cent.	Topic sentence Signpost word

Table 25.1 (*cont'd*)

	Mobile phone controversy is not confined only to the potential dangers related to the units alone; some people have serious concerns about the impact mobile phone masts have on the area surrounding them. The fear is that radiation from masts could induce serious illness among those living near such masts. While evidence refuting or supporting this view remains inconclusive, there appears to be much more justification for concern about emissions from television transmitters and national grid pylons, which emit far higher levels of electromagnetic radiation. Yet, little correlation appears to have been made between this fundamental of electrical engineering and the technology of telecommunications.	Topic sentence Signpost word Signpost word
Conclusion Terminator paragraph	In summary, although it appears that there are enormous benefits to mobile phone users, it is clear that there are many unanswered questions about the impact of their use on individuals. At one level, these represent an intrusion on personal privacy, whether as a user or as a bystander obliged to listen to multiple one-sided conversations in public places. More significantly, there is the potential for unseen damage to the health of individual users as they clamp their mobiles to their ears. Whereas the individual has a choice to use or not to use a mobile phone, people have fewer choices in relation to exposure to dangerous emissions from masts. While the output from phone masts is worthy of further investigation, it is in the more general context of emissions from electromagnetic masts of all types that serious research needs to be developed.	Topic sentence Signpost words Signpost words Signpost word Signpost word

SPEED-READING TECHNIQUES

Before describing techniques for improving reading speed, it is useful to understand how fast readers 'operate'. Instead of reading each word as a separate unit, these readers use what is called peripheral vision (what you see, while staring ahead, at the furthest extreme to the right and the left). This means that they absorb clusters of words in one 'flash' or 'fixation' on the text, as shown in Figure 25.2(a). In this example, four fixations are required to read that single line of text.

A reader who does this is reading more efficiently than the reader who reads word by word (Figure 25.2(b)). This reader makes 12 fixations along the line, which means that their reading efficiency is low. Research has also indicated that people who read slowly in this way are less likely to absorb information quickly enough for the brain to comprehend. Therefore, reading slowly can actually hinder comprehension rather than assist it.

As a practised reader, you will probably have developed these fast-reading skills to some degree. They can be improved using techniques like the 'eye gymnastics' exercise in Figure 25.3.

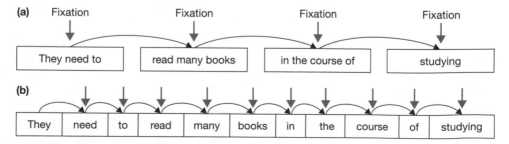

Figure 25.2 Eye movements when reading. (a) Reader who makes eye fixations on clusters of words. (b) Reader who reads every word one by one.

Learning to read quickly	is a skill	that needs to be developed.
If you have to read	a new piece of text,	you will find it useful
first of all	to read	the first paragraph
and the last paragraph	of the section, chapter or article.	From this
you should be able	to gauge	the context
and general outline	of the topic under discussion.	While it is true
that all academic texts	should have been well edited	before publication,
it does not follow	that every text	will follow these conventions.
However,	a well-written piece	of academic writing
should follow this pattern	and, as a reader	you should exploit
this convention	in order to help you	to understand
the overall content	before you embark	on intensive reading
of the text.		

When you are about to	take notes from texts	you should not begin
by sitting	with notepad ready	and the pen poised.
Certainly	make a note of	publication details needed
for your bibliography,	but resist the temptation	to start taking notes
at the same time as	beginning	your first reading of the text.
It is better	to read first,	reflect, recall
and then write notes	based on	what you remember.
This gives you	a framework	around which
you ought to be able	to organise your notes	after you have read
the text intensively.	People who start	by writing notes
as soon as	they open the book	will end up
copying	more and more from the text	as their tiredness increases.
In this case	very little	reflection or learning
is achieved.		

Figure 25.3 'Eye gymnastics' exercise. Try to read the following text quite quickly. Read from left to right in the normal way. The aim of the activity is to train your eyes to make more use of your peripheral vision when you are reading. In this way, you will learn to make fewer fixations on the text by forcing your eyes to focus on the centre of a group of words, which are printed in naturally occurring clusters – usually on the basis of grammatical or logical framing. It may be that you experience some discomfort behind your eyes, which indicates that they are adjusting to this less familiar pattern. If this is the case, you should keep practising using this text as a means of developing the speed of your eye movements.

Other things you can do include 'finger tracing', where you run your finger below the line of text being read to follow your eyes' path across a page, starting and stopping a word or two from either side. This is said to increase your eye speed, keep your mind focused on the words being read and prevent you from skipping back to previous sentences or jumping forward to text that follows. Some people find it helpful to use a bookmark placed horizontally along the line they are reading, because it makes a useful guide that prevents the eye jumping ahead of the text they are reading.

Increasing your reading speed using finger tracing

- Select a reading passage of about two pages in length (you could use the sample text in Table 25.1). Note your starting and finishing time and calculate your reading speed using Method B in Table 25.2.

- Take a break of 40–60 minutes. Return to the text and run a finger along the line of text much faster than you could possibly read it.

- Repeat, but more slowly, so that you can just read it ('finger tracing'). Again, note your starting and finishing times, and work out your reading speed. You should find that your reading speed has increased from the first reading.

- Carry out this exercise at the same time of day over a week, using texts of similar length and complexity.

The average reading speed is said to be 265 words per minute (wpm). Reading speeds for university purposes may be slightly lower, as aspects like difficulty of the text, unfamiliarity with the terminology used and the complexity of the concepts being discussed in the text have the potential to slow down reading. However, as you become more familiar with the subject and the issues being covered in your course and, thus, with your supplementary reading, then your reading speed will increase.

Things that can reduce your reading speed

As well as trying methods to read faster, you should be aware of circumstances that might slow you down. These include:

- distractions such as background noise of television, music or chatter (see Table 8.2 on page 45);

- sub-vocalisation (sounding out each word as it is read aloud);

- reading word by word;

- over-tiredness;

- poor eyesight – if you think your eyes are not 20:20, it might be worth going for an eye test; your eyes are too important to neglect and a pair of reading glasses may make a huge difference to your studying comfort;

- poor lighting – if you can, read using a lamp that can shine directly on to the text; reading in poor light causes eye strain and this, in turn, limits concentration and the length of reading episodes.

Table 25.2 How to calculate your reading speed. Two examples.

Method A (specified reading time)	
a Select a chapter from a textbook (this is better than a newspaper or journal because these are often printed in columns)	
b Calculate the average number of words per line,	
e.g. 50 words counted over 5 lines	= 10 words per line
c Count the number of lines per page	= 41 total lines
d Multiply (b × c) = 10 × 41	= 410 words per page
e Read for a specific time (to the nearest minute or half-minute)	
without stopping	= 4 minutes' reading
f Number of pages read in 4 minutes	= 2.5 pages read
g Multiply (d × f) = 410 × 2.5	= 1025 total words read
h Divide (g ÷ e) = 1025 ÷ 4	**= 256 words per minute**

Method B (specified text length)	
a Find a piece of text of known word length (see method A)	= 744 words
b Note the time taken to read this in seconds	= 170 seconds
c Convert the seconds to a decimal fraction of minutes = 170 ÷ 60 = 2.8 minutes	
d Divide (a ÷ c) = 744 ÷ 2.8	**= 266 words per minute**

You can assess your normal reading speed using either method described in Table 25.2. The text of Table 25.1 is a suitable piece of writing whose word length is already known, should you wish to try method B. If your reading speed seems slow, you can work on improving it by using a similar level and length of text at the same time each day. Go through the reading speed process and, gradually, you should see your average creeping up.

Other strategies you can develop to read and absorb content quickly include:

● **Skimming.** Pick out a specific piece of information by quickly letting your eye run down a list or over a page looking for a key word or phrase, as when seeking a particular name or address in a phone book.

● **Scanning.** Let your eye run quickly over a chapter, for example before you commit yourself to study-read the whole text. This will help you to gain an overview of the chapter before you start.

● **Picking out the topic sentences.** As seen above and in Figure 25.1 and Table 25.1, by reading the topic sentences you will be able to flesh out your overview of the text content. This will aid your understanding before you study-read the whole text.

● **Identifying the signpost words.** As noted above, these help guide you as the reader through the logical process that the author has mapped out for you.

● **Recognising clusters of grammatically allied words.** Subliminally, you will group words in clusters according to their natural sense. This will help you to read by making fewer fixations and this will improve your reading speed. You can improve your speed by using the eye-gymnastics exercise (see page 146).

● **Taking cues from punctuation.** As you read, you will gain some understanding by interpreting the text using the cues of full stops and commas, for example, to help you gain understanding of what you are reading. The importance of punctuation to comprehension is vital (**Ch 40**).

To be effective, reading quickly must be matched by a good level of comprehension; reading too slowly can hamper comprehension. Clearly, you need to incorporate tests of your understanding to check that you have understood the main points of the text. One method of reading that incorporates this is called the SQ3R method – survey, question, read, recall and review (Table 25.3). This is also a helpful strategy for exam revision as it incorporates the development of memory and learning skills simultaneously.

Table 25.3 Reading for remembering: the SQ3R method. The reader has to engage in processing the material in the text and is not simply reading on 'autopilot', with very little being retained. SQ3R and note-making are covered in **Ch 26**.

Survey stage
<ul><li>Read the first paragraph (topic paragraph) and last paragraph (terminator paragraph) of a chapter or page of notes</li><li>Read the intervening paragraph topic sentences</li><li>Focus on the headings and sub-headings, if present</li><li>Study the graphs and diagrams for key features</li></ul>
Question stage
<ul><li>What do you know already about this topic?</li><li>What is the author likely to tell you?</li><li>What specifically do you need to find out?</li></ul>
Read stage
<ul><li>Read the entire section *quickly* to get the gist of the piece of writing; finger-tracing techniques may be helpful at this point</li><li>Go back to the question stage and revisit your initial answers</li><li>Look especially for keywords, key statements, signpost words</li><li>Do *not* stop to look up unknown words – go for completion</li></ul>
Recall stage
<ul><li>Turn the book or your notes over and try to recall as much as possible</li><li>Make key pattern headings/notes/diagrams/flow charts (**Ch 26**)</li><li>Turn over the book again and check over for accuracy of recall; suggested recall periods – every 20 minutes</li></ul>
Review stage
<ul><li>After a break, try to recall the main points</li></ul>

READING ONLINE RESOURCES

Of course, you can always print out material sourced from the Web, in which case, similar principles apply to those described elsewhere in this chapter. However, due to cost or environmental considerations, or simply the fact that that you need to assess the material before committing yourself to a printout, you may prefer to read directly from the screen. The following points are worth considering when doing this:

- Web page designers often divide text into screen-sized chunks, with links between 'pages'. This can make it difficult to gain an overall picture of the topic being covered. Make sure you read through the whole of the material before forming a judgement about it.

- One benefit of web-based material is that it is often written in a 'punchy' style, with bulleted lists and easily assimilated take-home messages, often highlighted with graphics. Bear in mind, however, that this may lack the detail required for academic work, for example, in the number and depth of any examples given.

- The ease of access of web-based materials might cause a bias in your reading – perhaps towards more modern sources, but also, potentially, away from the overtly academic – always check to see whether 'standard' printed texts are advised on reading lists or are available in your library.

- The skimming method described on page 148 can be accelerated if you use the 'find' function (control + F in MS Word and Internet Explorer) to skip to key words.

- If you are likely to spend lengthy spells at a screen, make sure you are positioned well, with your eyes roughly level with the mid point of the screen.

- Take frequent breaks – stand up, walk around for a while and then return to the task.

- If you wear spectacles, you may find that an additional pair for use when reading on-screen material is helpful. You can find out more about this from your institution's health and safety office or from an optician.

If you do decide to print out a resource, check on the screen for an icon that might give you a 'print-friendly' version.

🔧 PRACTICAL TIPS FOR READING EFFECTIVELY AND WITH UNDERSTANDING

Be selective and understand your purpose. Think about why you are reading. Look at the material you have already collected relating to the subject or topic you aim to study. For example, this should include lecture notes, which ought to remind you of the way a topic was presented, the thrust of an argument or a procedure. Are you reading to obtain a general overview or is it to identify additional specific information? Use a technique and material that suits your needs.

Adjust your reading speed according to the type of text you have to read. A marginally interesting article in a newspaper will probably require less intensive reading than a key chapter in an academic book.

Grasp the general message before dealing with difficult parts. Not all texts are 'reader friendly'. If you find a section of text difficult to understand, skip over that bit; toiling over it will not increase your understanding. Continue with your reading and when you come to a natural break in the text, for example, the end of a chapter or section, then go back to the 'sticky' bit and reread it. Usually, second time round, it will make more sense because you have an overview of the context. Similarly, don't stop every time you come across a new word. Read on and try to get the gist of the meaning from the rest of the text. When you have finished, look the word up in a dictionary and add to your personal glossary (**Ch 42**).

Take regular breaks. Reading continuously over a long period of time is counter-productive. Concentration is at a peak after 20 minutes, but wanes after 40 minutes. Rest frequently, making sure that your breaks do not become longer than your study stints.

Follow up references within your text. When you are reading, you need to be conscious of the citations to other authors that might be given in the text; not all will be relevant to your reading purpose, but it is worth quickly noting the ones that look most interesting as you come across them. You'll usually find the full publication details in the references at the end of the chapter/article or at the end of the book. This will give you sufficient information to supplement your reading once you have finished reading the 'parent' text.

26

NOTE-MAKING FROM TEXTS

How to create effective notes for later reference

Keeping a record of the content of your reading is essential when you are a student. There is simply too much information to remember and retain. This chapter outlines practical ways in which you can keep a record of what you read and think in appropriate note form so that it is meaningful to you at a later date. You should also note connections, critical thoughts and ideas that arise while you read.

Most courses provide a reading list of recommended resources. Depending on your subject, these include textbooks, journal articles and web-based materials. Sometimes you will be given specific references; at other times you will have to find the relevant material in the text for yourself. The techniques described in **Ch 25** will help you identify the most relevant parts of the text quickly and provide basic information for your note-making.

You will develop note-making skills as you progress in your studies. It takes time and experimentation to achieve a method that suits you. This will need to fit with your learning style (**Ch 13**), the time that you can allocate to the task and be appropriate for the material and the subject area you are tackling. This chapter suggests a range of methods you can choose from in order to abstract and write down the key points from your sources.

The time you spend making notes is an investment. Your notes could be an essential resource for your future studies, so never throw them away. In particular, notes taken for specific coursework assignments may prove useful at exam time. They can help with the revision process by refreshing your memory on difficult concepts; and they can provide examples, detail or 'colour' for your answers.

Note-making formats

Sometimes notes may be better suited to being laid out on paper in the landscape rather than the portrait position. This clearly suits methods such as mind maps (Figure 26.5). Similarly, you can take advantage of the landscape format when making matrix (grid) notes (Figure 26.6) by creating columns across the page.

WHY ARE YOU TAKING NOTES?

Students usually make notes for assignment writing and/or revision. Therefore, some texts will simply be 'dip in and out', while some will require intensive reading. You need to decide what your purpose is in making the notes. For example, it may be to:

- frame an overview of the subject;
- record a sequence or process;
- enable you to analyse a problem;
- extract the logic of an argument;
- compare different viewpoints;
- borrow quotes (with suitable citation – see **Ch 35**);
- add your own commentary on the text, perhaps by linking key points with what has been discussed in a lecture or tutorial.

This will influence the style, detail and depth of your notes.

✔ Essentials of note-making

You will save time if you develop good practice in making your notes.

- On all notes record the full details of source, that is:
    - author surname and initials
    - title in full with chapter and pages
    - date of publication
    - publisher and place of publication.

    You will need this information to enable you to cite the source of information if you decide to use any of this information in your own writing (**Ch 35**).

- It's a good idea to add the date(s) you made the notes.
- Your notes have to be as meaningful in six days, weeks or months. Personalise them by using:
    - underlining
    - highlighting
    - colour coding
    - numbered lists
    - bullet points
    - distinctive layout
    - boxes for important points
    - mnemonics (Using a sequence of letters or words to help remember a key point, e.g. '**R**ichard **o**f **Y**ork **g**oes **b**attling **i**n **v**ain to remember colour spectrum: **R**ed, **O**range, **Y**ellow, **G**reen, **B**lue, **I**ndigo, **V**iolet).

WHAT DO YOU NEED TO RECORD?

One of the pitfalls of making notes is that people often start off with a blank sheet, pen in hand, and then begin to note 'important' points as they read. Within a short time, they are rewriting the book. To avoid this, the trick is to:

- identify your purpose;
- decide on the most appropriate note-making style and layout for the task;
- scan the section to be read;
- establish the writer's purpose, for example:
  - a narrative of events or process
  - a statement of facts
  - an explanation of reasoning or presentation of a logical argument
  - an analysis of an issue, problem or situation
  - a critique of an argument;
- work out their 'take' on the subject, and how this relates to your purpose;
- jot down ideas that arise during your reading;
- make links between this text and others, if any;
- ensure you paraphrase in your own words rather than transcribe, and if you do transcribe, use quote marks and note reference details (**Ch 35**, **Ch 36**).

HOW ARE YOU GOING TO LAY OUT YOUR NOTES?

There are several strategies that you might consider using. Figures 26.1–26.7 illustrate some examples (see also **Ch 17**). Not all will be relevant to your subject, but some will. Some techniques may not seem directly suitable, but, with a little adaptation, they may work for you. Table 26.1 compares the advantages and disadvantages of each method.

It may be that one of these note-taking strategies has attractions for you because it seems to fit with your learning preferences (**Ch 13**). For example, a 'visual learner' might prefer the concept map shown in Figure 26.5.

Other methods might suit a specific task: an assignment that requires you to analyse a complex set of viewpoints or positions might best be approached using the matrix approach shown in Figure 26.6, while one that asked you to review two sides of an argument could be tackled using the herringbone map idea shown in Figure 26.7, or a variant of it.

Table 26.1 A comparison of the different methods of note-making from texts (illustrated in Figures 26.1–26.7)

Note type	Figure	Advantage	Disadvantage
Keyword notes	26.1	Good as a layout for easy access to information	Dependent on systematic structure in text
Linear notes	26.2	Numbered sequence – good for classifying ideas	Restrictive format, difficult to backtrack to insert new information
Time lines	26.3	Act as memory aid for a sequence of events; stages in a process	Limited information possible
Flow-chart notes	26.4	Allow clear path through complex options	Take up space; may be unwieldy
Concept maps/ mind maps	26.5	Good for recording information on a single page	Can become messy; can be difficult to follow; not suited to all learning styles
Matrix notes/ grid notes	26.6	Good layout for recording different viewpoints, approaches, applications	Space limitations on content or amount of information
Herringbone maps	26.7	Good for laying out opposing sides of an argument	Space limitations on content or amount of information

---

Topic: DEPOPULATION OF THE COUNTRYSIDE   Source: Ormiston, J., 2002. Rural Idylls.
                                                          Glasgow: Country Press.

Problem: Population falling in rural areas
                 Traditional communities disintegrate
                 Incomer settlement – dormitory villages

Reasons: Mechanisation of farming
                 Creation of farming combines
                 Bigger farms, fewer employed
                 Decline of traditional farming & related activities

Effects: Families dispersed – fewer children
                 Closure of shops, post offices, schools, surgeries
                 Transport links less viable

Solutions: Housing subsidies to encourage families to remain
                 Diversify economic activity, e.g. tourism/action holidays
                 Stimulate rural economy – farm shops, farmers' markets
                 Diversify from traditional crops – seek new markets

Figure 26.1 Example of keyword notes

(a)

Topic: OBESITY IN CHILDREN

Source: Skinner, J., 2001. Diet and Obesity. Edinburgh: Castle Publishing.

1. Lifestyle
   1.1 Television, computer-games generation
   1.2 Unsupervised leisure time – sedentary
2. Diet
   2.1 Constant 'grazing' – junk food
   2.2 Additives/processed foods
   2.3 Lack of adequate fresh food, including fruit & vegetables
3. Exercise
   3.1 Sport by spectating rather than participating
   3.2 Decline in team sports in schools
   3.3 Children over-protected from 'free play' outdoors
4. Family
   4.1 Parents overeat; children likewise
   4.2 Instant food
   4.3 Food as an incentive & reward
5. Schools
   5.1 School meals spurned in favour of snack bar/chip shop
   5.2 Health-eating programmes as part of curriculum
6. Health service
   6.1 Less emphasis on prevention
   6.2 Limited health education of parents and children

(b)

Topic: GENERAL FEATURES OF ORGANIC MATERIALS

Source: Barker, J., 2001. Chemistry for University. Manchester: Midland Publishing.

1. Solid state – molec. crystal – powder, poly. Thin films
2. Unique physical properties – exploit for high-tech applications
3. Advantages
   3.1 Versatile properties – reg. by organic chemistry
   3.2 Readily accessible – via organic synthesis
   3.3 Low cost – cheap raw materials
   3.4 Tractable – fusable, soluble: easy to fab.
4. Disadvantage
   4.1 Relatively fragile
5. Important types
   5.1 Conducting CT salts
   5.2 Conducting poly

(c)

Topic: OPERATIONAL AMPLIFIERS

Source: Scott, D.I., 1977. Operational Amplifiers. Coventry: Circuit Publishers.

1. Usually an integrated circuit; can be discrete
2. Uses all technologies: bipolar; FET; MOS; BI-FET
3. Effectively a highly stable differential amplifier
4. Advantages
   4.1 High voltage gain – typ. 100,000
   4.2 High input impedance – typ. 1 MΩ – can be much higher, FET, MOS
   4.3 Low output impedance – typ. 600 Ω
   4.4 Low drift, BI-FET best
   4.5 Wide voltage supply range
5. Disadvantages
   5.1 Relatively narrow bandwidth – GBP typ. 1 MHz (but operates to DC)
   5.2 Very unstable in discrete versions – requires matched transistors
6. Common types
   6.1 741 – most common
   6.2 LM 380 – common AF AMP
   6.3 TDA 2030 – common power amp. – 20 W into 4 Ω

Figure 26.2 Examples of linear notes. These are drawn from three diverse disciplines where topics lend themselves to hierarchical approaches.

Figure 26.3 Example of time-line notes. This design is good for showing a sequence of events, in this case, the development of European organisations.

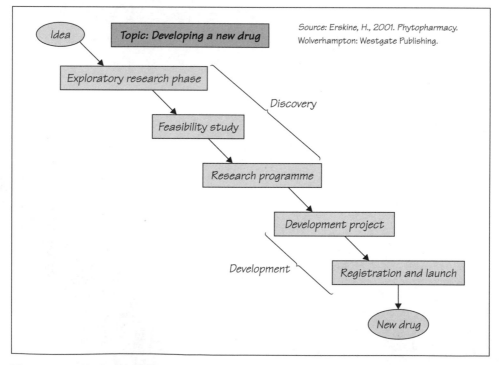

Figure 26.4 Example of flow-chart notes. These are particularly useful for describing complex processes in visual form.

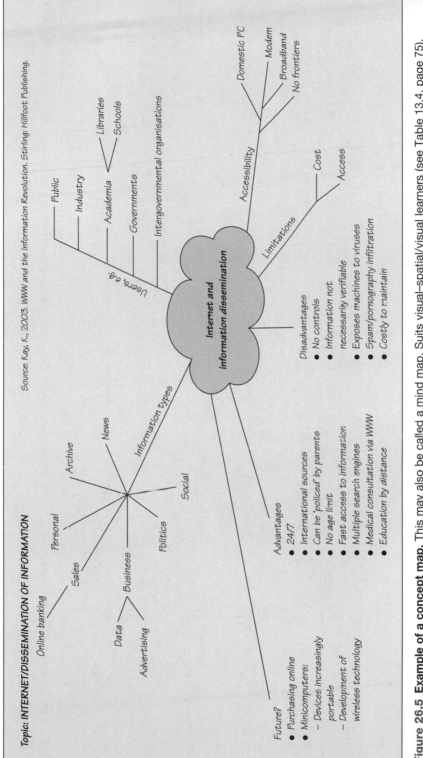

Topic: INTERNET/DISSEMINATION OF INFORMATION

Source: Kay, K., 2003. WWW and the Information Revolution. Stirling: Hillfoot Publishing.

Internet and information dissemination

Users, e.g.
- Public
- Industry
- Academia
  - Libraries
  - Schools
- Governments
- Intergovernmental organisations

Accessibility
- Domestic PC
- Modem
- Broadband
- No frontiers

Limitations
- Cost
- Access

Disadvantages
- No controls
- Information not necessarily verifiable
- Exposes machines to viruses
- Spam/pornography infiltration
- Costly to maintain

Information types
- News
- Archive
- Personal
- Sales
- Data
- Business
  - Advertising
- Politics
- Social
- Online banking

Advantages
- 24/7
- International sources
- Can be 'policed' by parents
- No age limit
- Fast access to information
- Multiple search engines
- Medical consultation via WWW
- Education by distance

Future?
- Purchasing online
- Minicomputers:
  – Devices increasingly portable
  – Development of wireless technology

Figure 26.5 Example of a concept map. This may also be called a mind map. Suits visual-spatial/visual learners (see Table 13.4, page 75).

Topic: TRAFFIC CONGESTION

Source: Walker, I.M.A., 2005. Urban Myths and Motorists. London: Green Press.

Solutions	Council view	Police view	Local business view	Local community view
Pedestrianisation	+ Low Maintenance – Initial outlay	+ Easier to police + Less car crime + CCTV surveillance easier	+ Safer shopping and business activity – Discourages motorist customers	+ Safer shopping + Less polluted town/city environment
Park and ride schemes	+ Implements transport policy – Capital investment to initiate – Car park maintenance	+ Reduce inner-city/town traffic jams + Reduce motor accidents – Potential car park crime	– Loss of custom – Lack of convenience – Sends customers elsewhere	+ Less polluted town/city environment – Costly
Increase parking charges	+ Revenue from fines – Costly to set up	– Hostility to enforcers	– Loss of custom – Delivery unloading problematic	– Residents penalised by paying for on-street parking
Restrict car journeys, e.g. odd/even registrations on alternate days	+ Easy to administer	+ Easy to police	– Seek exemption for business vehicles	+ Encourage car-sharing for daily journeys – Inconvenience
Levy congestion charge for urban journeys	+ Revenue raised – Cost of implementing tracking system	– Traffic jams on alternative routes	– Cost of loss of custom	– Inhibit work/leisure activities – Cost

Figure 26.6 Example of matrix notes. This particular analysis lays out positive (+) and negative (–) viewpoints on an issue from a range of different perspectives.

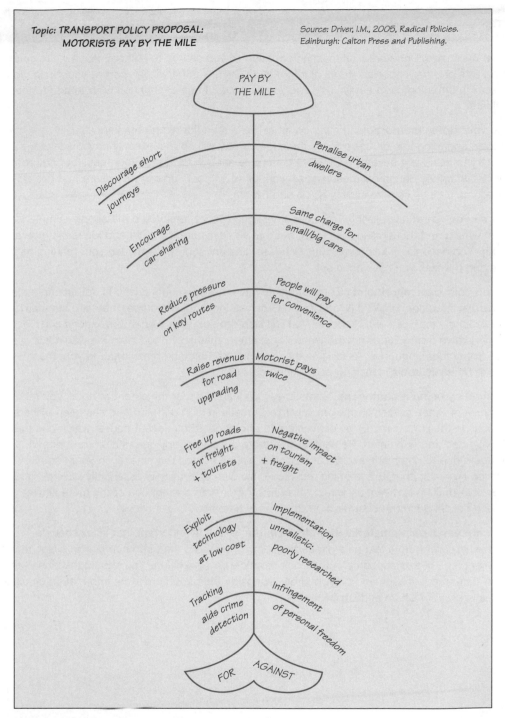

Topic: TRANSPORT POLICY PROPOSAL:
MOTORISTS PAY BY THE MILE

Source: Driver, I.M., 2005, Radical Policies.
Edinburgh: Calton Press and Publishing.

PAY BY
THE MILE

Discourage short
journeys

Penalise urban
dwellers

Encourage
car-sharing

Same charge for
small/big cars

Reduce pressure
on key routes

People will pay
for convenience

Raise revenue
for road
upgrading

Motorist pays
twice

Free up roads
for freight
+ tourists

Negative impact
on tourism
+ freight

Exploit
technology
at low cost

Implementation
unrealistic:
poorly researched

Tracking
aids crime
detection

Infringement
of personal freedom

FOR   AGAINST

Figure 26.7 Example of a herringbone map. This design is good for showing, as in this case, two sides to an argument. May be particularly appealing to visual learners (see Table 13.4 on page 75).

Use white space. Don't cram as much information as you can on to a sheet; leave white space around lists or other important items of information. By using the 'visual' part of your brain, you will recall information more easily. This additional space can be used if you wish to add further detail later.

Make your notes memorable. It's important to make sure that your notes are visually striking. However, spending lots of time making them look pretty will not necessarily pay dividends. Again, try to achieve a balance – visually memorable enough to trigger your recall but not so elaborate that they become a meaningless work of art without substance. Ensure that this does not become a displacement activity (**Ch 8** and **Ch 14**).

Think as you write. It is essential for deeper learning (**Ch 22**) that you don't simply summarise others' writing and thoughts in note form, but that you evaluate the facts and ideas that you are reading. You need to make connections between different sources, between your reading as a whole and the task you have been set.

Develop your own 'shorthand'. Some subjects have their own abbreviations, for example MI (myocardial infarction) or WTO (World Trade Organisation) and, of course, there are standard abbreviations – e.g., i.e., etc. However, you will also develop your own abbreviations and symbols drawn from your own experience, for example maths symbols, text messaging or words from other languages. As long as these are memorable and meaningful to you, then they can be useful tools in making and taking notes (**Ch 17**).

Save time by using a photocopy. Sometimes you may find that the extent of notes you require is minimal, or that a particular book or other resource is in high demand and has been placed on short loan in the library. It may be convenient to photocopy the relevant pages, which can then be highlighted and annotated. Remember that there are photocopying restrictions imposed on readers due to copyright law (**Ch 36**) – details will be posted prominently in your library. However, note also that as a learning technique this type of activity is essentially passive, and, if your note-making is meant as an aid to revision or for memorising, one of the more active methods described in this chapter or in **Ch 61** may be better.

Take care when using material straight from the text. It is important that, if you decide to use an excerpt from a text as a direct quotation, you record the page number on which that particular piece of text appeared in the book or article you are citing. You should then insert the author, date of publication and page number alongside the quotation. More information on citing sources is given in **Ch 35** and **Ch 36**.

27

COMPUTING LITERACY

How to make the best use of computers and software in your learning

Information and communications technology (ICT) is a vital element of modern university education. Software tools are invaluable aids for many aspects of your work, and some specialist programs may be essential. This chapter focuses on effective use of ICT in a university context and makes suggestions for developing your computing skills.

Most employers will expect graduate job applicants to possess advanced skills in information and communications technology (ICT). This is often reflected in the tasks set by academic staff in university, where ICT will routinely be used as a means to an end – for example, in word-processing an essay or report; or in using a spreadsheet to produce a graph for a lab report.

Many students will feel that their ICT skills are satisfactory, but most people who work with computers agree that no matter how much you know, there is always something new to learn. This chapter offers general tips for using the applications commonly available at university level. You will find other useful advice on electronic information retrieval in **Ch 23** and on e-learning in **Ch 28**. Online assessment (computer-aided assessment) is covered briefly in **Ch 46**.

USING NETWORKED FACILITIES

As a signed-up university student you will gain access to many computing facilities free of charge. You will be issued with a username and asked to select a private password (see overleaf). When you log on, your screen will probably show a student 'desktop' with icons for a range of 'office'-type software and other facilities, such as email and a browser. This is sometimes called the SOE or standard operating environment. You will also be allocated space on a networked drive on which to store your files. It's worth spending some time becoming familiar with what's on offer and if the software differs from what you are used to, getting to know the special features of these new programs.

Most universities have a set of conveniently located computing suites and you are likely to find widespread wireless facilities, for example, in the library study areas and some social venues. If you can set it up, broadband access to the internet at your accommodation will be valuable, as so much course information is now available online and you will probably wish to work late at night to finish coursework. There may be a charge for connecting, however, and you may need technical help.

Password security

You should follow these guidelines:

- Never share your password or write it down in an obvious way.
- Use different passwords on different systems.
- Change your password regularly.
- Mix letters and numbers to create nonsense words.
- Try to make each password memorable.
- Be aware that others could be watching your keystrokes.
- Never leave a computer logged on in an open environment.

There will probably be an ICT induction session, where you are introduced to the specific facilities available to you, the university's code of conduct and where you can find help. Regulations regarding the use of network facilities have been created to protect you, your fellow students and the university, and should be respected. Academically, the most important will be those concerning plagiarism and copyright (**Ch 36**).

Typical network and IT-suite facilities

It is likely that you will have access to:

- banks of computers and/or wireless connection zones
- 'office'-type programs, centrally licensed
- certain specific programs, such as those for image manipulation and statistical analysis
- the internet
- email
- networked printing
- CD/DVD burning hardware
- an ICT helpdesk

There will probably be a charge for printing and you will need to supply your own consumables, such as blank CDs.

USEFUL SKILLS WITH 'OFFICE'-TYPE SOFTWARE

The three core 'office'-type programs deal with word-processing, spreadsheets and delivering presentations. Table 27.1 summarises useful applications of word-processing and spreadsheets in university coursework. Use of presentation software is covered in **Ch 57**. Databases are included in many software suites, but are more specialised and generally harder to learn to use (but see the spreadsheet section of Table 27.1 if you only need basic database functions).

Table 27.1 Key word-processing and spreadsheet skills for university coursework. How many of these do you feel competent about?

Word-processing skills	Spreadsheet skills
You will be expected to use word processors to write and edit written coursework. Key elements include:	If your coursework involves numbers or graphs in any form, a spreadsheet can be a valuable time-saving resource. Key elements include:
❑ **Word count and page numbering.** Many submissions will be limited to defined length and these functions will help you keep track of your progress.	❑ **Arithmetical and mathematical calculations.** Error-free addition and multiplication, and the capability to use complex formulae to calculate results. Of course, formulae need to be set up correctly to get the right answers, so always test them with a dummy set of data for which you know the expected answer.
❑ **Spellchecker.** Helpful for a quick check of glaring errors, but is *not* a substitute for a careful read through at draft stage, as words you can easily mistype like 'form' and 'from' will not be highlighted (**Ch 43**). Also, the default spellcheckers may suggest Americanised spellings (like Americanized, for example), which may not be suitable.	❑ **Repeated calculations.** Excellent when you need to repeat a calculation from different starting values. Just set up a formula and enter fresh values to obtain instant results.
❑ **Thesaurus.** Great for adding variety to your vocabulary and finding a word that is at the tip of your tongue (**Ch 42**).	❑ **Formatted calculations.** For example, financial statements, financial analysis and projections in accountancy.
❑ **Grammar checker.** Helps spot basic errors, like sentences without verbs, but do not rely on its advice as it can be faulty; moreover, you will frequently wish to reject some of its valid suggestions as these may not be tuned to academic or technical styles of writing.	❑ **Graphs.** Probably the most valuable spreadsheet application. Takes tabular input and uses it to create a range of graph types to suit your needs. Useful for trying out different graph styles without having to redraw. It's worth learning how to manipulate aspects like axis presentation and background, as automatic settings tend to be set up for 'business' use. Integrated 'office' suites allow export of graphs to a word-processed document.
❑ **Print preview.** Valuable for seeing how your work will look on the printed page and can help you to save on print costs.	
❑ **Copy and paste.** Useful for moving blocks of text around your document at review stages (**Ch 43**) – but use with extreme caution for copying and pasting text or images from electronic sources because of plagiarism and copyright issues (**Ch 35, Ch 36**).	❑ **Elementary database functions.** Spreadsheets can be used to carry out simple database functions (for example, you can sort number and text columns). You can also use alphanumeric and logical functions to 'interrogate' bodies of text/number information.
❑ **Tables.** Apart from the obvious, useful for laying out your work in columns and grids. You may wish to alter borders if set automatically.	❑ **Statistics.** Many statistical needs are catered for, including calculation of descriptive and hypothesis-testing statistics. These functions save a lot of calculation time, but you need to know some statistical theory to use them most effectively.
❑ **Drawing facilities.** Useful for creating simple diagrams.	
❑ **Footnotes.** Handy for some styles of citation and referencing (**Ch 35**).	

---

i

Learning to use new software

Specialist training will generally be given by departments if you are required to use advanced features of spreadsheets, database or statistical software as an integral part of your coursework.

FILE MANAGEMENT

You only need to lose or accidentally delete an important file or forget where you have stored a vital piece of writing once to realise that file management is an important skill. A power cut or accidental key stroke can lead to a program shutting down or part of a file being corrupted or lost. The solution is obvious: back up your files frequently. This should involve saving frequently, either manually or using an auto-save function, and keeping copies of your files in more than one location. Take special care when using memory sticks or CDs to carry files between computers, as these could be lost. In case this happens, make sure you can identify your own storage medium, and ensure that others can find return details. You may wish to password-protect some of your files.

Storing files on network drives

This is generally a good idea, as the files will probably be automatically backed up on a daily basis. If you happen to lose or corrupt a file, contact the ICT helpdesk staff.

As you progress, you will collect a large number of files and will need to be able to track these down when required. The start of each term or semester is a good time to organise or reorganise your file folders and sub-folders. For example, you may wish to set a folder up for each subject you are taking and for other activities that might generate files. Naming your files appropriately is important, too. File names should indicate contents, date and draft version (where appropriate). This is highly useful when trying to track down information later.

Basic computer security and safety

- Take extreme caution when opening files attached to emails from unknown sources – they may contain viruses.
- Never give away any information about bank accounts, even if the request appears to come from your bank – this will be a scam, as your bank will never request information in this way.
- Do not circulate 'round-robin' or chain-letter emails – they can clog up the system.
- Take care with food and drink next to computers – spilled drinks can short-circuit electrical components and food can make keyboards dirty, for example.
- At home, make sure you have installed appropriate firewall and virus detection software (university networks are protected centrally).

USING BROWSERS AND SEARCH ENGINES

A browser is your window into the internet and World Wide Web (WWW). By entering the URL, or address, of any website, you can access billions of web pages throughout the world. Browsers use HTTP, a protocol for transfer of web page data, and interpret code in HTML, the universal web-page-constructing language.

Internet Explorer, Netscape and Mozilla Forefox are examples of browsers. Their most important features are the address bar, where you enter the URL, and the favourites menu, where you can index sites you visit frequently. Most browsers will automatically be set to your university's home page, and from this you will be able to access many key facilities, such as the virtual learning environment (VLE) (**Ch 28**).

Examples of search engines

Search engines:
Google: **www.google.com**
Yahoo: **www.yahoo.com**
Ask.com: **www.ask.com**
Google Scholar: **www.google.co.uk/scholar**

Meta-search engines:
Dogpile: **www.dogpile.com**
Clusty: **http://clusty.com**

A search engine is a tool for accessing information on the internet. These are the equivalent of website indexes. Several types are available (see tip box above), each using a subtly different search mechanism – so you will get different results depending on which one you choose. Meta-search engines employ several search engines to come up with a result. Tips for using search engines effectively are presented in Table 27.2.

Most universities take a relatively relaxed view on the use of university computing facilities to do such things as booking travel tickets or purchasing items online. They will, however, expect you to give up your terminal if another student needs to use it to carry out academic work. Activities involving gaming and gambling, unauthorised business transactions, unauthorised downloading of copyright files (such as music files), transmitting viruses and accessing porn, racist and other dubious material are completely forbidden. Note that the ICT department will be able to track such activities and you may be held accountable for them, with, in some cases, severe penalties, including expulsion from your course and even legal action.

Of course, finding information is not the same as deciding whether it is relevant or using it to answer questions, construct viewpoints, summarise situations and carry out other academic activities. Arguably, the ability to *evaluate* information is the most important skill you will develop while at university – see **Ch 24**.

Definitions: key web concepts

Home page: the entry page for any large website, often with links to key areas.

HTML: hypertext markup language – the coding language used to create pages on the World Wide Web.

HTTP: hypertext transfer protocol (why most web addresses begin with **http://**).

Hypertext: text that when clicked on moves the browser to a new web page.

Surfing: using a search engine to look for web sources (implies you may not have a particular website in mind).

URL: the uniform resource locator, or address, of a website or other type of resource on the internet, for example: **http://www.prospects.ac.uk**

Web page: strictly, any content at a specific URL.

Table 27.2 Tips for effective web searching. There is so much information on the Web that finding exactly what you want can be difficult. The hints here will help you narrow down a search when this is required. They use formats acceptable for the Google search engine.

Tip	Comment
Plan your search before starting	Spend a little time thinking through what you really want to achieve: this may influence your choice of search terms (key words)
Select *specific* key words	Take care with spelling and try to choose combinations of words that will narrow down the search
Search for key phrases using inverted commas ('xxxx')	This will result in the exact phrase (that is, words in the order specified and with same letter case)
If a search is unsuccessful, double-check your spelling	Some common misspellings may be identified automatically by the search engine, which will prompt you to confirm your spelling or select an alternative. Some terms are spelled differently in the USA and Europe
Use capital letters with proper names	Some search engines will prioritise results by case match
Use * to indicate a wildcard part of a word or phrase	All possible options for * will be searched for – this may expand rather than narrow a search, but can help if you are unsure of an exact term, or do not wish to exclude certain results
Try using numbers rather than words, or adding numbers as part of a search	For example, if you know a phone number or product reference number, it may help narrow things down
Restrict your search using search-engine options	For example, you can choose only sites from the UK or to search solely for images
Use logical (sometimes called Boolean) operators	This is advanced searching. If you add 'and' ('&' will work too), between two phrases this will only produce results with both phrases present. If you use OR it will select sites with either phrase, while 'not' will exclude the phrase
Use + or – between words	These have the same effect as 'and' and 'not' as described above
Search for proximity of terms in the website	If you enter 'near' between two words or phrases, this will prioritise results according to how close the words are
Use the search engine's 'Advanced search' feature	This will present you with several options to help you narrow the search
Find the word(s) you searched for in a web page	To find where a word you searched for is located on a large web page, use Control + F, enter the word or phrase, and click on search
Try a different search engine	You may find that another search engine, or a meta-search engine (page 165) produces different and possibly more useful results

EMAIL AND DISCUSSION-BOARD ETIQUETTE

Two commonly used routes of online communication are email and discussion boards. These allow you to communicate with tutors and classmates, giving each person the choice of when and where they contribute. Web-based email software allows you to check messages from any networked computer, while discussion boards are most likely to be operated within a VLE (**Ch 28**).

'Synchronous' discussions are sometimes arranged, where participants must log in at the same time to take part in a live discussion.

- Check your university email account and discussion boards frequently (preferably daily). You may receive important messages from tutors in this way (for instance, changes to lecture locations).

- Bear in mind that without the normal conversational body language and voice tone, e-messages can seem abrupt and may be misconstrued. Always read through a message after you have written it with this in mind, before sending. If in doubt, leave it for 30 minutes or so, perhaps using the 'send later' function, and then reconsider.

- Avoid 'spectating' during e-discussions. Contribute positively if you can. Even if someone has already said something you would have liked to have said, agreeing with them may help to continue the e-conversation.

PRACTICAL TIPS FOR IMPROVING YOUR ICT LITERACY

Enrol on a course or workshop. If you do feel you need to update your skills or expand the range of software you feel competent to use, you may be able to enrol on an ICT module to improve your skills or attend special workshops. Enquire at the ICT helpdesk or reception to find out what is available.

If you're new to computing, don't be frightened to experiment. Computers can't break because of things you do at the keyboard. If you get in a tangle, you can always switch off/shut down and start again afresh. The main danger is losing information, so always save files before carrying out any operation about which you are not confident.

Learn the fundamentals, then improve. You don't have to learn all parts of a program at once. Pick up the basics, then develop your skills further, perhaps using the tips here.

Use the 'Help' facility to expand your knowledge about a program. If you don't know how to do something, a query here may provide the answer.

Invest in a simple manual. The standard manuals for software can be rather technical – a wide range of manuals is published that use simpler terms and that make few assumptions about your knowledge (for example, *Word for Dummies*).

Watch how your friends use programs and swap tips. This can result in exchanges of really useful suggestions. For example, some people like keyboard shortcuts (such as 'Control + C', 'Control + V' for copy and paste functions), while others prefer menu options.

Explore menu options. If you have the time, it can be worth going over every menu option in a program to see what it does.

Don't suffer in silence if you have a computing query. Contact helpdesk staff. They will probably have come across your problem before and can offer an advanced set of skills, for example to unscramble corrupted files.

28

E-LEARNING

How to make the most of online teaching

E-learning systems offer you many useful facilities and the capacity to access course materials at a time and place of your choosing. This chapter discusses how to adapt your study methods to learn more effectively from online course components.

E-learning is a term used to cover a range of online methods of delivering materials and resources for learning. Most universities use a web-based virtual learning environment (VLE), such as Blackboard or WebCT. Others favoured in the UK are Moodle, First Class and Desire2Learn. These platforms provide an integrated route to learning resources from a single login. Systems for computer-aided assessment (also known as online assessment) may be provided in addition. You may be given online access to all these facilities via a portal, which you might be able to customise.

Online teaching is often mixed with traditional on-campus teaching – so-called 'blended learning'. Alternatively, and especially if you are a distance learner, you may find that nearly all of your course material is delivered online. Whatever the mix, you will need to adapt to the specific challenges of the web-based component.

---

i Definitions: e-learning terminology

Blended learning: a mix of e-learning and traditional teaching methods.

Computer-aided assessment (CAA): tests and exams delivered (and marked) using software. If delivered via the Web, also known as **online assessment (OA)**.

Computer-based learning (CBL) or **computer-aided learning (CAL):** software-driven interactive learning activity.

Portal: a web-based gateway to various useful web services.

VLE (virtual learning environment): online software system that delivers educational materials and facilities for students. May include lecture notes, email and discussion boards, groupwork areas, communication tools, assessments and grade books.

EFFECTIVE E-LEARNING

There are three basic requirements if you are to make the most of your e-learning opportunities:

- You must have access to the Web through a reasonably speedy link.
- You will require basic IT skills to navigate websites and manipulate files.
- You will need to make frequent visits to your portal or VLE.

Access

Your university will provide a range of on-campus computing facilities and will specify minimum requirements for online access from home or other accommodation, probably at broadband data transfer rates (2 megabits per second or greater). Local authorities also provide free or low-cost facilities in libraries and study centres.

Skills

E-learning systems generally require only basic competence in computer use. If you are a computer novice, it is essential that you learn how to use these facilities, as so much of your future work will require this – and most universities offer some form of IT induction and training. Even if you feel fully conversant with computing from experience at school and home, these sessions will inform you about the special features of your local network and systems.

Visiting and participating in your VLE modules

You should visit each VLE module or portal on a daily basis if you can. If you fail to do this, you may miss out on announcements, messages, new work deadlines, ongoing discussions and fresh materials. Where opportunities are given, you should participate actively in online discussions, self-assessments and the like: these will have been designed by your tutors to add to your knowledge, experience and skills.

THE RANGE OF E-LEARNING FACILITIES AND HOW TO USE THEM

It's worth setting aside some study time early in the term or semester to investigate all the different VLE features that have been activated by staff – you will then know how to use these to your advantage later on. Components offered within a typical VLE module include:

- **Course information.** This may include the syllabus, timetable, learning outcomes and details about the teaching and administrative staff – it may take the place of the traditional course handbook. Aspects of using these elements are covered in **Ch 63**.

- **Announcements.** Information from the course administrator(s) may appear on the opening page of the VLE or portal, which is a good reason for checking this frequently. They may alert you to late timetable or location changes, forthcoming coursework deadlines, and events such as departmental seminars.

- **Lecture notes.** Such notes may include files from PowerPoint presentations. If lecturers use the VLE to let you access summary notes or slides from their lectures in advance, printing these out with space for your own extra notes will allow you extra time to follow the emphasis and take-home messages during the lecture, rather than simply transcribing what is covered (**Ch 16, Ch 17**).

- **Links to websites and e-books.** These provide you with supplementary information. Lecturers may help you by moderating or commenting on these website resources. You can use their critical remarks to improve your own skills for evaluating information (**Ch 24**).

- **Tailored resources.** These will support your learning and will include multimedia presentations, quizzes and interactive software. These can be extremely valuable as a substitute for a practical or other hands-on experience. Most will have self-contained instructions for their use, or this information will be given in the course handbook.

- **Learning tools.** Tools such as an online dictionary/thesaurus, online study guide or links to the library catalogue can be valuable when you are working on assignments, so it is worth the investment of time to learn what they contain and how to use them.

- **Discussion boards, blogs and chatrooms (both synchronous and asynchronous).** These are used to allow you to exchange comments and queries, and can be a useful way to sense how far ahead or behind you are with your learning. They are also used to facilitate groupwork, providing a forum for the team to exchange ideas and files. Don't be hesitant to start a new thread or to respond to someone else's query or comment. The system only works well if everyone takes part. However, when participating in online discussions, make sure you respect others' views and are polite about your peers and lecturers.

- **Links to support services.** These may range from the students' association to the careers service. This may be a faster and more convenient method of accessing information and contacts than the university website.

- **Email facilities.** You may have your own account or links to the university's specialist email software. This can be a very convenient part of the VLE because many tasks you will carry out online may be facilitated by using email – e.g. asking questions of lecturers, making contact with your peers in the class.

Taking notes from PowerPoint presentations

If you use the three-slides-per-page handout format (accessible from the 'File > Print > Print What > Handouts > Slides per page > 3 > OK' options) you can obtain a printout that looks like the following, with space for your notes beside each slide.

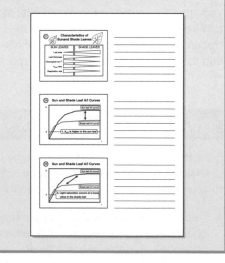

- **A digital 'dropbox'.** This is a convenient way of submitting files containing coursework online. Follow the instructions carefully to ensure your work is delivered safely. Keep a backup copy.

- **Gradebooks.** These allow you to see the marks that have been recorded for your coursework and final assessments. For obvious reasons, you will have read-only access.

- **Mechanisms for providing feedback on teaching.** If feedback questionnaires are presented on the VLE, this gives you a chance to provide considered comments in your own time, and in privacy. The VLE may also provide information about class representatives and a means of contacting them (for example, by email or discussion board).

ONLINE ASSESSMENT

Online assessment is increasingly used at university, especially for large classes in early years. The different sorts of questions commonly on offer are outlined in **Ch 46** and **Ch 47**. If you have the chance to test the program being used beforehand, do so, as this will make it easier to sit real high-stakes assessments, which are generally carried out under exam conditions within IT suites using identical software. In any case, you will probably find that formative online tests are a good way to learn, especially if they are 'open book' and you are allowed to look at notes and texts as you answer.

Take time at the start of each module to explore the online resources. Although some features may not be activated immediately, it will be valuable to know the scope of the resource at your disposal and to consider this in relation to your assessment tasks.

Get into a daily routine for visiting your VLE and carrying out the work. There may be a convenient time at the start of the day or between lectures for you to look at emails and announcements. If you get into the habit of doing this on a daily basis, you won't miss important new information.

Allocate some specific times to study online. Your course outcomes may require a significant and ongoing input.

Organise your online learning resources. You could do this by grouping them within folders using the bookmark facility on your browser. This will keep the browser interface uncluttered and help you access the resources quickly, without having to remember or enter URLs.

Check on the status of your home computer facility. Your access to online facilities from home will be greatly dependent on such factors as the speed of your internet connection, computer memory and what plug-ins you have installed. Each institution will publish a set of 'minimum standards' that they assume you will have, and instructions for downloading and enabling software.

Bear in mind that your tutors may be monitoring your activities. Although they may not contribute, lecturers may be able to see what you have written on discussion boards, for example. They may also be able to use the number of times you have visited the VLE as an indicator of your participation in the course (although generally speaking if they are going to do this, they should tell you beforehand).

Save on ink costs. When printing out lecture notes based on PowerPoint presentations or similar, you may wish to select 'Pure Black and White' from the 'Color/Grayscale' options on the 'Print' menu, or you are liable to use up a lot of coloured ink printing the slide backgrounds.

When working online, keep aware of the risks of plagiarism and copyright infringement. Although it is technically easy to cut and paste material into your own documents and essays, this is regarded as cheating and may be illegal (**Ch 36**). You should not contemplate plagiarism for moral reasons, but if tempted, you should also realise that lecturers nowadays have a range of sophisticated packages for detecting it, and the penalties for being caught are severe.

Remember to keep using 'traditional' sources of information. When a large proportion or all your teaching is provided online, it is important not to overlook conventional sources such as books and research journals. Increasingly, even these are available online, and many can be evaluated and reserved online, before visiting your library.

29

NUMBER CRUNCHING

How to solve problems in arithmetic and algebra

This chapter reviews common concepts and methods that will help you answer straightforward numerical questions from your coursework. The mathematical techniques covered are relatively uncomplicated, but you may not have used them since your schooldays.

Many university subjects include elements that require skills of numeracy, especially in the later stages of study. Examples include biology, economics, geography and psychology. If you've forgotten school maths or lack the required knowledge and technique, you may find these parts of your courses challenging. Dip into this chapter if you need to refresh your knowledge and skills.

Getting to grips with maths

The one certain way of making sure you understand and can carry out the mathematical parts of your courses is to practise. This will increase your confidence and reveal any misunderstandings, which you can then raise with a tutor. Once you get over the initial barriers, you may find that your overall marks improve greatly.

NUMBERS AND SYMBOLS

Numbers and symbols are the essence of maths. Having a good understanding of the following terms will help you work through problems confidently:

- **Constants.** These are unchanging values such as gravitational acceleration (g) or pi (π). These are often given in tables, but in some cases you will need to memorise them. In the 'straight line' equation $y = mx + c$, m and c, the quantities describing the slope and y-intercept are examples of constants. Their values stay constant in any one instance, but change for different lines.

- **Variables.** These are mathematical quantities that can take different values. For example, if x and y change according to a mathematical relationship between them, such as $y = mx + c$, then x and y would be described as variables.

- **Units and prefixes.** Constants and variables can be dimensionless, but most have units, such as metres (m), m s^{-2} ('metres per second squared'), or kg. The *Système International d'Unités*, or SI, provides agreed standard units and is widely adopted in the sciences (Table 29.1). Prefixes are often used to denote very large and small numbers (Table 29.2); alternatively scientific or engineering notation may be used (see pp. 177–8 and Table 29.3).

---

i **Definitions: sets of numbers**

Whole numbers: 0, 1, 2, 3 . . .

Natural numbers: 1, 2, 3, 4 . . .

Integers: –2, –1, 0, 1, 2, 3 . . .

Real numbers: integers and anything in between, e.g. 1.54, π, e^4.

Prime numbers: natural numbers divisible only by themselves and 1.

Rational numbers: p/q, where p is integer and q is natural and they have no common factor.

Irrational numbers: real numbers with no exact value, such as π. If the final digit is repeated, it is often shown thus: $4/3 = 1.\dot{3}$ or 1.3r.

Table 29.1 Some examples of SI units. For the prefixes normally used in association with these units, see Table 29.2.

Quantity	SI unit (and symbol)
Base units	
Length	metre (m)
Mass	kilogramme (kg)
Time	second (s)
Temperature	kelvin (K)
Amount of substance	mole (mol)
Electric current	ampere (A)
Luminous intensity	candela (cd)
Supplementary units	
Plane angle	radian (rad)
Solid angle	steradian (sr)
Some examples of compound units	
Energy	joule (J) = m^2 kg s^{-1} = N m
Force	newton (N) = m kg s^{-2} = J m^{-1}
Pressure	pascal (Pa) = kg m^{-1} s^{-2} = N m^{-2}
Power	watt (W) = m^2 kg s^{-3} = J s^{-1}
Electric charge	coulomb (C) = A s
Illumination	lux (lx) = cd sr m^{-2}

Table 29.2 SI prefixes. Note that after the first row, small number prefixes have the ending 'o', while large number prefixes have the ending 'a'.

Small numbers			Large numbers		
Value	Prefix	Symbol	Value	Prefix	Symbol
10^{-3}	milli	m	10^{3}	kilo	k
10^{-6}	micro	μ	10^{6}	mega	M
10^{-9}	nano	n	10^{9}	giga	G
10^{-12}	pico	p	10^{12}	tera	T
10^{-15}	femto	f	10^{15}	peta	P
10^{-18}	atto	a	10^{18}	exa	E
10^{-21}	zepto	z	10^{21}	zeta	Z
10^{-24}	yocto	y	10^{24}	yotta	Y

Zeros and unity

Some basic points to remember:

- subtracting a number from itself gives zero
- multiplying a number by zero gives zero
- multiplying a number by 1 gives the number itself
- dividing a number or expression by itself gives 1
- dividing a number or expression by zero gives infinity and is mathematically meaningless.

- **Operators.** These are the mathematical codes for carrying out operations with variables and constants. From day-to-day usage, you will be familiar with the basic ones, such as add (+), subtract (–), multiply (× or .) or divide (÷ or /), as well as equals (=), approximately equals (≈) and does not equal (≠). Note that a sign for 'multiply' is frequently omitted, so a term like mx means 'm multiplied by x'. You should also know the following: greater than (>), less than (<), greater than or equal to (≥) and less than or equal to (≤). However, you may wish to refamiliarise yourself with other functions such as logs and powers if these are relevant to your studies (see below). In complex expressions, and particularly when there are mixed operations, the order in which you carry out operations is important (see Table 29.3).

Basics of maths relevant to manipulation of equations

The order in which you carry out operations is important. The mnemonic BODMAS (**b**rackets, powers **o**f, **d**ivision, **m**ultiplication, **a**ddition, **s**ubtraction) describes the order you should use, working left to right.

Table 29.3 Exponents and scientific notation: tips and examples

Tips	Examples
If you multiply a number by itself, this gives a positive power	$y \times y =$ 'y squared' $= y^2$ or 'y to the power 2'
Dividing a number by itself gives that number to the power 0 and is equal to 1. Continuing to divide by the number gives a negative power	$8/8 = 8^0 = 1$ $1/y = y^{-1}$, $1/z^8 = z^{-8}$ $x^{-5} = 1 \div x \div x \div x \div x \div x$
When adding numbers expressed as powers of 10, if the exponents are the same, you can add the numerical parts, but keep the exponent the same. You may wish to change the exponent thereafter if the addition of the numerical part results in a large or small number	$(2.0 \times 10^{-3}) + (3.0 \times 10^{-3})$ $= 5.0 \times 10^{-3}$ $759 \times 10^5 + 605 \times 10^5$ $= 1364 \times 10^5$ $= 136.4 \times 10^6$
If adding numbers with different exponents, first express them to the same power before adding the numerical parts	$(7.3 \times 10^4) + (6.0 \times 10^3)$ $= (7.3 \times 10^4) + (0.6 \times 10^4)$ $= 7.9 \times 10^4$
Add the exponents when multiplying, but multiply the numerical parts	$(8 \times 10^5) \times (3 \times 10^4) = 24 \times 10^9$ note that: $x^m \times x^n = x^{m+n}$ and $x^m/x^n = x^{m-n}$
When using scientific notation to express large numbers, count digits up or down from the decimal point to work out what the exponent should be	$134.5 = 1.345 \times 10^2$ (count is two digits) $0.0029 = 2.9 \times 10^{-3}$ (count is three digits)
To work out engineering notation more easily, group digits in threes from the decimal point, using commas	$15039829 = 15,039,829$ $= 15.04 \times 10^6$ to four significant figures $0.000392 = 0.000,392$ $= 392 \times 10^{-6}$
When you are expressing numbers in either scientific or engineering notation, try to express the numeric part as a number between 0 and 1000	Rather than writing 0.1256×10^6, write 1.256×10^5 (scientific notation) or 125.6×10^3 (engineering notation)

MANIPULATING EQUATIONS

Numbers and symbols, usually letters, may be linked together in equations (formulae) or functions, such that one expression is said to equal another (or zero). The formula $y = mx + c$ is an example of an equation. These generalised expressions of the relationship between different quantities, or terms, are useful in modelling, estimation and prediction, and this branch of mathematics is called algebra.

You will frequently need to rearrange equations. For example, if you wish to find a particular variable or constant in a formula, you may wish to express it in terms of other variables and constants, whose values you already know. This key mathematical skill usually involves carrying out an operation on both sides of the equation so that a particular term 'disappears' from one side and reappears on the other. You may need to simplify some of the terms before doing this or express them in a different mathematical way (see Table 29.4).

Table 29.4 Manipulating numbers and equations: tips and examples

Tips	Examples
When working out results, carry out a bracketed calculation first, or you may obtain an incorrect result	$(ab) + c \neq a(b + c)$ $(3 \times 5) + 6 \neq 3 \times (5 + 6)$ because $15 + 6 \neq 3 \times 11$
Remove an 'isolated' constant or variable by adding it to or subtracting it from both sides. If you change the side, you change the sign	If $x = y - z$, then $x + z = y - z + z$, so $x + z = y$, and by rearranging, $y = x + z$
Remove a multiplying constant or variable by dividing both sides by it	If $x = yz$, then $y = x/z$ (divide both sides by z and rearrange)
Remove a dividing constant or variable by multiplying both sides by it	If $x = y/z$, then $y = xz$ (multiply both sides by z and rearrange)
Remove a power from one side by multiplying both sides by the reciprocal power or by taking logs	If $a = b^c$, then $b = a^{1/c}$ If $a = b^c$, then $\log a = c \log b$, and $c = \log a/\log b = \log(a - b)$
Combine powers and powers of powers	$a^b + a^c = a^{(b+c)}$ and $a^b - a^c = a^{(b-c)}$ $(a^b)^c = a^{(bc)}$
It can be useful to combine expressions or express them in different ways before doing any of the above. Use parentheses (. . .) to 'isolate' parts of formulae and calculations	$ab + ac = a(b + c)$ so if you wish to find the value of a in $y = ax + az$ $y = a(x + z)$ $a = y/(x + z)$ If $xy^2 - xz = 5 - p$, find x. First, take x out as a common factor, so $x(y^2 - z) = 5 - p$. Now divide both sides by $(y^2 - z)$, so $x = (5 - p)/(y^2 - z)$

DEALING WITH LARGE AND SMALL NUMBERS

Many calculations involve large and/or small numbers, which can be unwieldy to write down. Exponents and logarithms are useful ways of expressing these in brief.

Exponents

In a term like x^n, n is known as an exponent and denotes that a number has been multiplied by itself n times, or is *raised to the power n*. In this type of expression, n may also be called the index.

Using powers of 10 to express very large or small numbers

This is best explained with examples:

$2000 = 2 \times 10^3 \ (= 2 \times 10 \times 10 \times 10)$

$0.0003 = 3 \times 10^{-4} \ (= 3 \div 10 \div 10 \div 10 \div 10)$.

Numbers are often expressed as powers of 10, such as 2.172×10^5 (= 217,200). This is called scientific notation and it makes arithmetic with large or small numbers much easier. Engineering notation is similar but uses powers of 10 in groups of three, such as 10^3 or 10^{-9}, corresponding to the SI prefixes (see Tables 29.2 and 29.4).

> ### i Using SI prefixes
>
> These symbols (see Table 29.2) effectively make engineering notation neater. Use them in combination with a unit to indicate very large or small numbers. For example:
>
> 5 kHz = 5000 Hz
> 15 μm = 0.000015 m.
>
> Pay special attention to case, because, for example, 1.5 pg ≠ 1.5 Pg.

Logarithms ('logs')

A log to the base 10 is the power of 10 that would give that number. Thus, log (100) = 2, because $10^2 = 10 \times 10 = 100$. Natural logs (symbol ln) are powers of e (≈ 2.178), which is used because it is mathematically convenient in some situations.

The following relationships simplify some calculations with logs:

$log\ (a) \times log\ (b) = log\ (a + b)$

$log\ (a) \div log\ (b) = log\ (a - b)$

$log\ (a^n) = n\ log\ (a)$

An antilog is 10^x, where x is the log value. You can convert a log value into a simple numerical value by working out its antilog. The equivalent for natural logs is e^x. These values are best obtained using a calculator.

> ### i Use of logs
>
> Logs were exceptionally valuable tools when even complex calculations were done 'by hand'; old-fashioned mechanical calculators such as slide rules were based on them. Nowadays, digital calculators make most calculations straightforward. However, logs are still found in some formulae (for example, the degree of acidity, or pH, is calculated as pH = −log [H^+], where [H^+] is the molar hydrogen ion concentration), and it is therefore important to understand their mathematical origin.

PRESENTING NUMBERS: SIGNIFICANT FIGURES AND ROUNDING

Sometimes when you carry out a calculation, and especially when using a calculator, the answer may appear with a large number of digits, for example, 12.326024221867.

Deciding on how many digits or significant figures (s.f.) to quote in your answer is important. If you do not include these in intermediate steps, your final result may be incorrect to a surprising degree; on the other hand, if you include too many in your final result, this may imply a false degree of accuracy. For example, it is incorrect to refer to a temperature of 15.34°C if your thermometer can only be read to the nearest half degree at best.

In calculations you will often be asked to express your answer to a certain number of significant figures (s.f. for short). The number of significant figures can be worked out by counting the number of digits from the left. The first non-zero digit in a number is the first significant figure. 12.326024221867 has 14 significant figures and would be expressed as 12.326 to five s.f. and 12.33 to four s.f. (see also Table 29.5).

The process of deciding what the last digit is when you do this is called rounding. In essence, you take into account the digits to the right of the last significant digit, and if they are greater than 0.5, you round up to the next number, and if they are less then 0.5, you round down. What you do if the remainder is exactly 0.5 depends: to avoid bias, the usual rule is to round down if the preceding digit is even and up if it is odd. Thus, to three significant figures, 15.65 would be expressed as 15.6, while 15.75 would be rounded to 15.8. See the tip box below regarding the situation where zeros are present.

Table 29.5 Significant figures and rounding: tips and examples

Tips	Examples
For numbers with no leading zeros, the number of significant figures is equal to the number of digits	94.8263 has six s.f.
With leading zeros, the significant figures start after the last leading zero	0.0000465 has three s.f.
'Internal' zeros count as significant figures	0.00044304 has five s.f.
Trailing zeros are not regarded as significant figures in whole numbers	2300 has two s.f.
Trailing zeros can be significant if they come after the decimal point, as they imply a certain accuracy of measurement	10.10 cm has four s.f.
The number of decimal places is the number of digits after the decimal points. Round up or down as appropriate	56.78478 to two decimal places is 56.78 56.78478 to three decimal places is 56.785
When calculating with several values, the one with the least number of significant figures should be used to define the number of s.f. used in the answer (an exception is when using mathematical constants, which are assumed to have an infinite number of significant figures)	$12.232 - 9.2 = 3.0$ (*not* 3.032) $176 \times 1.573 = 276$ (*not* 276.848) converting 1456 m to km, this is 1.456 km, *not* 1 or 1.5 km
Always round after you have done a calculation, not before	The area in cm^2 of a rectangular piece of carpet where the sides have been measured to the nearest mm as 1286×1237 would be 15,908 cm^2, *not* 129×124 cm = 15,996 cm^2
If asked to work out an answer, but without guidance on the number of significant figures to use, consider the accuracy of your original measurements. Round up or down to the nearest whole number of your finest measurement division	The length of the piece of string measured by a ruler was 134 mm Converting millimetres to inches using the factor 0.03937, the length of the piece of string is given as 5.28 inches to three s.f. (not 5.27558 as found with a calculator)

Easier to carry out is the instruction to 'express your answer to *n* decimal places', although this may also involve rounding. Hence, if a calculator gives an answer as 60.466023 and you are asked to supply an answer to two decimal places, you should write 60.47 (see Table 29.5).

? What about zeros in rounded numbers?

Significant figures (s.f.) become a little complicated if there are zeros present.

- Counting from the left, the first non-zero digit in a number is the first significant figure. Hence, 0.00012 has two s.f.

- The final zero even in a whole number is not regarded as a significant figure, because it only shows the order of magnitude of the number. Thus, 141.35 is written as 140 to two s.f.

- Zeros included after the decimal point do imply accuracy of measurement and should be regarded as significant figures. Thus 12.30 has four s.f.

See Table 29.5 for further examples.

FRACTIONS, PERCENTAGES AND RATIOS

A fraction is simply one number divided by another. It does *not* have to be between zero and one. A common fraction involves two integer numbers (for example, $^3/_4$), while in a decimal fraction the denominator is always a factor of 10, such as $^3/_{10}$. Decimal fractions are often expressed using the decimal point (for example $0.34 = {}^{34}/_{100}$).

---

i Terminology of fractions

The upper number (or the first number) is called the **numerator** and the lower number (or the second number) is called the **denominator**. When the numerator is smaller than the denominator, the fraction represents a number between 0 and 1. When the numerator is bigger than the denominator, the fraction represents a number greater than 1.

Where numerators and denominators can both be divided by a common factor, it is normal practice to express the fraction with the lowest values possible. Thus, $^9/_{24} = {}^3/_8$.

A percentage value is a fraction expressed as a number of hundredths. This is used because it is easy to comprehend. To calculate a common fraction as a percentage using a calculator, divide the numerator by the denominator and multiply the answer by 100. Thus, $^3/_4 = 0.75 = 75$ per cent = 75%. To convert a percentage into a decimal fraction, move the decimal point two places to the left.

---

i Common decimal fractions

You should memorise the following common fractions in terms of decimals (where *r* indicates a repeating digit):

$^1/_2 = 0.50$	$^1/_3 = 0.33r$	$^1/_8 = 0.125$
$^1/_4 = 0.25$	$^1/_5 = 0.20$	$^1/_{10} = 0.10$

Table 29.6 Fractions, proportions and ratios: tips and examples

Tips	Examples
When adding fractions, you need to ensure that the denominators are the same. To do this, multiply *both sides* of one of the fractions by a number that will allow this, then add the numerator values. In complex examples, you may need to multiply both sides of the fractions by different numbers. This number will generally be the number you need to multiply the denominator by to obtain a common value (the 'lowest common denominator')	$3/4 + 1/2 = (3/4 + 2/4) = 5/4 = 1\,1/4 = 1.25$ (multiply both sides of the second fraction by 2 to obtain them both expressed as fourths) $3/8 + 2/3 + 7/9$ $= 27/72 + 48/72 + 56/72$ $= 131/72$
When multiplying fractions, multiply both the numerators and denominators	$3/4 \times 5/2 = 15/8$
Likewise, when dividing, divide both the numerators and denominators. Another way to do this sort of calculation is to turn the 'divided by' fraction round and multiply	$3/4 \div 1/2 = 3/2$ Alternatively, $3/4 \div 1/2$ $= 3/4 \times 2/1$ $= 6/4$ $= 3/2$
To work out one number as a percentage of another, simply divide the two and multiply by 100	Express 12 out of 76 as a percentage: $12/76 \times 100 = 16\%$ (15.78947 rounded up)
To find a percentage of a number, express the percentage as a decimal fraction and multiply the number by this	75% of 320 = $0.75 \times 320 = 240$
Don't get confused by percentages less than one	0.05% is 5 in 10000 or $5/10000$
It may be convenient to express ratios as decimal numbers in relation to unity	If there are 34 girls in a class of 56, the ratio of girls to boys is $34/(56-34):1 = 1.5:1$ (rounded to one decimal place)

A percentage does not need to be a whole number (for example 65.34 per cent is valid), nor does it always need to be less than 100 (as in 'Jane earns 143 per cent of what John earns'), except where you are expressing a fraction of a limited total (you cannot assert that '126 per cent of dogs prefer Bonzo dog food').

A ratio expresses two or more numbers or proportions in relation to each other. The norm is to divide the larger by the smaller (or divide the others by the smallest). If you had 6 red, 12 blue and 36 orange discs, the ratio of red:blue:orange would be 1:2:6 (note the colon (:) as notation; you would say this as 'red to blue to orange'). Ratios can involve real numbers, such as 1.43:1.

Tips for manipulating fractions mathematically are provided in Table 29.6.

CALCULATOR SKILLS

In many subjects, you are permitted to make use of a calculator freely, even during exams. It is important to know how to carry out the basic functions of your model when under time pressure. Incorrect use of calculator functions is a major source of errors in answers to numerical questions.

Consult the instructions for your calculator, or if you have lost these or are not allowed to take these into an exam, always test out any assumptions you make about the way it works by entering values for which you know the answer.

Practise, practise and practise. If you feel that mathematics is a weak spot for you, this is really the way to conquer it. Maths skills are easily forgotten and need to be used frequently to be maintained.

Get to know your calculator. Aspects you should consider include:

- What kind of notation your calculator uses (standard or reverse-Polish notation; most use standard) and what this means, in particular about how you do nested calculations;
- how the memory works;
- how to enter a constant and use it in several calculations;
- how to enter exponents;
- how to express one number as a percentage of another.

Check the units and scale of your answers. First, make sure that you convert any answer into the units requested in the question, and with the appropriate number of significant figures, either as specified or as seems sensible to you. Second, make sure that your answer is not absurdly high or low. Areas and volumes are particularly difficult to visualise. Try to relate these to 'real life' if you can – for example, imagine what the value you obtain might look like in relation to something you are familiar with, like a stamp, piece of paper, glass of beer, and so on.

If you are unsure about the algebra using symbols, insert real numbers. The first example in Table 29.4 provides an illustration of how this might work in practice.

Show intermediate calculations and express your answers neatly. If you work through the problem step by step in your answer, you can be given part marks even if you get a simple numerical calculation wrong. Show your answer by repeating what you have been asked to show and its value (including the number of significant figures, where relevant) and underlining it using a ruler, thus:

The total mass of the patient's brain is 1.34 kg (to three significant figures).

When working with formulae, express all values in terms of base units. Nearly all scientific and engineering formulae are expressed in terms of SI base units (i.e. metres, seconds, grams), so if you are given a length as 10 mm, do not enter 10 into a formula, enter 10×10^{-3}, expressing the length in metres.

In exams, take a moment to think through the problem. Don't jump to conclusions: read through the whole question, noting which formulae might apply and why. Make sure you know what you are aiming for in terms of an answer, and note aspects such as the number of significant figures required. **Ch 47** provides further tips for approaching numerical questions in exams.

30

INTERPRETING AND PRESENTING DATA

How to understand and produce graphs, tables and basic statistics

You'll come across data in many forms during your studies. You may be required to understand and explain graphs, tables and statistics, or be expected to generate them from raw information. The emphasis in this chapter is on data interpretation, but the principles of constructing graphs and presenting tables are also covered.

There are many ways of presenting data sets and the methods chosen can affect your analysis or favour certain interpretations. A healthily critical approach is therefore essential when you are examining graphs, tables and statistics. Equally, when creating these items to condense and display your own information, your primary aim should always be to do this in a manner that is simple to understand and unbiased.

Graph types

Some common forms are illustrated throughout this chapter, but a quick way of finding out about different options is to explore the forms available in a spreadsheet program like Microsoft Excel. Look at the 'Insert > Chart' menu, which illustrates sub-types and provides brief descriptions. This is also a good way of exploring ways of presenting your own data.

HOW TO 'READ' A GRAPH

The following elements are present in most graphs and charts (collectively known as 'figures'). Use them to work out what a specific graph means, referring to the example shown in Figure 30.1.

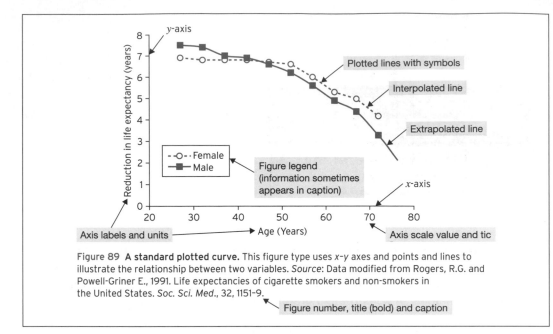

Figure 89 A standard plotted curve. This figure type uses *x–y* axes and points and lines to illustrate the relationship between two variables. *Source*: Data modified from Rogers, R.G. and Powell-Griner E., 1991. Life expectancies of cigarette smokers and non-smokers in the United States. *Soc. Sci. Med.*, 32, 1151–9.

Figure 30.1 The basic components of a graph

> ## ✔ Checklist for interpreting a graph
>
> ❑ Consider the context by reading the title, legend and main text.
> ❑ Recognise the type of graph.
> ❑ Examine what the axes show.
> ❑ Inspect the scale of the axes.
> ❑ Study the symbols and curves to work out what is being plotted and where.
> ❑ Evaluate what any error bars or statistics mean.
> ❑ From the trends in the lines, their maxima/minima or convergence/divergence, etc., work out what the results appear to show.

● **The figure title and its caption.** These should appear below the graph. Read them first to determine the overall context and gain information about what the graph shows. If the caption is detailed, you may need to revisit it later to aid your interpretation.

● **The type of figure.** With experience, you will come to recognise the basic chart types (Figure 30.2) and others common in your discipline. This will help you to orient yourself. For example, a pie chart is usually used to show proportions of a total.

● **The axes.** Many forms of chart represent the relationship between two variables, called *x* and *y* for convenience. These are often presented between a pair of axes at right angles, with the horizontal *x*-axis often relating to the 'controlled' variable (for example, concentration or time) and the vertical *y*-axis often relating to the 'measured' variable (for example, income, weight (mass), or response). More than one measured variable may be plotted on the same graph,

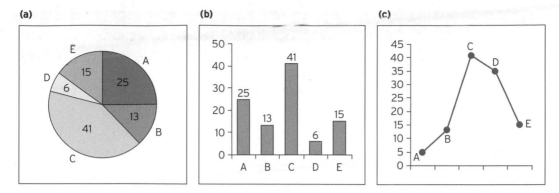

Figure 30.2 Common forms of graph. These are in addition to the standard plotted curve shown in Figure 30.1. (a) **Pie chart**, showing proportions of a total – here expressed as percentages. (b) **Histogram**, showing amounts in different categories. (c) **Frequency polygon**, showing distribution of counted data across a continuous range.

either using the same x-axis, or a second one (see Figure 30.2(b)). Some types of graph don't follow this pattern and if you are unfamiliar with the form being used, you may need to investigate further.

- **The axis scale and units.** An axis label should state what the axis means and the units being used. Each axis should show clearly the range of values it covers through a series of cross-marks ('tics') with associated numbers to indicate the scale. To interpret these, you'll also need to know the units. Some axes do not start from zero, or incorporate a break in the scale; others may be non-linear (for example, a logarithmic axis is sometimes used to cover particularly wide ranges of numbers). Pay attention in these cases, because this could mean that the graph exaggerates or emphasises differences between values, as demonstrated in Figures 30.3(a) and (b).

- **The symbols and plotted curves.** These help you identify the different data sets being shown and the relationship between the points in each set. A legend or key may be included to make this clearer. Your interpretation may focus on differences in the relationships and, inevitably, on the plotted curves (also known as 'trend lines'). However, it is important to realise that the curves are usually hypothetical interpolations between measured values or, worse, extrapolations beyond them; and, because they may involve assumptions about trends in the data, they should be examined with care. Symbols may also include information about variability in the data collected (for example, error bars), which provide useful clues about the reliability of data and assumed trends.

Plural terms

The following plurals are often misused or misunderstood:

Axis = singular

Axes = plural

Datum = singular

Data = plural (hence, the 'data *are* presented in Figure 14').

HOW GRAPHS CAN MISLEAD

You can learn a lot about data presentation by reviewing misleading graphs and learning why they might lead to incorrect interpretations. A selection of examples is shown in Figure 30.3. You should try to avoid confusing your audience by using these forms of misrepresentation when constructing your own figures.

> **i** **Definitions: trend lines on graphs**
>
> **Interpolation:** an assumed trend or relationship *between* available data points.
>
> **Extrapolation:** an assumed trend or relationship *before* or *after* (below or above) available data points. Extrapolation is risky because the assumption may be made that a trend will continue when there may be little evidence that this will happen.

CREATING GRAPHS

What follows is naturally a generalisation, but this sequence will suit many circumstances.

1 **Think carefully about what you want to plot and why, then choose an appropriate type of graph.** Recognising the type of data you want to present is essential for this, and reviewing the common options shown in Figures 30.1 and 30.2 may help. If you are choosing a plotted curve, you must decide which variable will appear on the x-axis and which on the y-axis. If you have selected an unfamiliar form of graph, you may wish to sketch out how this will appear for your data set. A spreadsheet (**Ch 27**) can be a valuable tool when working through this phase.

2 **Consider the range and units for the axes, where appropriate.** What are the upper and lower limits of your data? Should you start each axis at zero, and if not, will this act to distort the presentation (see Figure 30.3(a))? Will your axes be linear? Will they be in the same units as your measurements, or might you wish to work out ratios, percentages or other transformations (see **Ch 29** and below) before graphing the data? Once you have settled on these aspects, you can write the descriptive label for the axis, which should first state what is presented and then, usually in parentheses ( ) or after a solidus (/), the units used. Other forms of graph, such as a pie chart, may require a descriptive label for each segment, or you may prefer to use a legend or key.

3 **Choose elements of presentation.** For example, if you are using a pie chart, select colours or shading for the segments. If your graph has axes, decide how frequently you wish the tics to appear: too many and the axis will seem crowded, too few and it becomes less easy to work out the approximate values of data points. Decide which symbols will be used for which data sets, and if presenting several graphs in sequence, try to be consistent on this. If measures of location (Table 30.1) are plotted, consider whether you wish to add error bars to show the variability in the data.

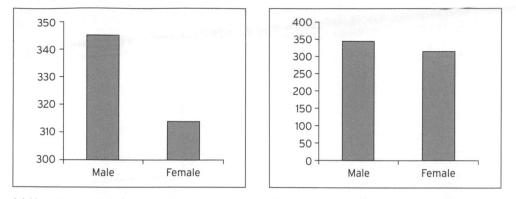

(a) Use of non-zero axis. In the chart on the left, it looks as if the differences between males and females are large; however, when the y-axis is zeroed, as on the right, the differences are much less noticeable.

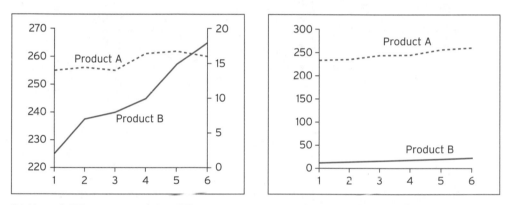

(b) Use of different y-axes for different curves. In the chart on the left it looks as if sales of product B (right-hand axis) are catching up with those of product A (left-hand axis); however, when the same axis is used for both curves, then it can be seen that product A vastly outsells product B.

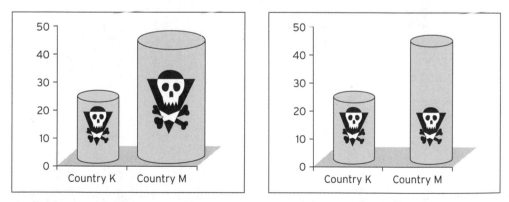

(c) Use of a two- or three-dimensional object to represent a linear scale. In the chart on the left, the barrel retains its shape in relation to the y-axis scale, so it makes it look as if country M produces much more toxic waste than country K. On the right, a truly linear representation is shown.

Figure 30.3 Three common examples of misleading graphs

Table 30.1 Descriptive statistics and their uses

Measure	Statistic	How to calculate*	Uses, advantages and disadvantages
Location	Mean	The sum of all the data values divided by the number of values, n	The most commonly used measure. It takes account of all the values in the data set, but can be influenced by the presence of outliers and is not representative of the whole body of data if this is asymmetric. Units are the same as the data
	Median	The mid-point of the data values when they are ranked in numerical order. For odd-sized data sets, it is the value of the middle datum, while for even-sized data sets, it is the mean of the two central values	May represent the location of the majority of the data better than the mean if the data set is asymmetric or there are outliers. Units are the same as the data
	Mode	The most common value in the data set	Easily found and unaffected by outliers; however, especially when the data set is small, it may be susceptible to 'random' variation in the distribution of values. Units are the same as the data
Dispersion	Range	The difference between the largest and the smallest values in the data set	Easy to determine, but its value is greatly affected by outliers and the size of the data set. Units are the the same as the data
	Semi-interquartile range	The difference between the first and third quartiles, which are the median values for the data ranked below and above the median value of the whole data set	Less easy to calculate than the range, but less affected by outliers and the size of the data set. Suitable to match with the median as a measure of location. Units are the same as the data
	Variance	The sum of the squares of the difference between each data value and the mean, divided by $n - 1$	Measures the average difference from the mean for all the data values. Good for data sets that are symmetrical about the mean. Units are the square of those of the data
	Standard deviation	The positive square root of the variance	A measure of the average difference from the mean for all the data values. Good for data sets symmetrical about the mean. Units are the same as the data, so preferable to the variance
	Coefficient of variation	The standard deviation multiplied by 100 and divided by the mean	A dimensionless (%) measure of variability relative to location. Allows the relative dispersion of data sets to be compared

* Note that these statistics are often expressed as mathematical formulae and are usually best calculated using a calculator or spreadsheet.

4 **Write the figure caption.** Your aim should be to ensure that the figure is 'self-contained' and that its essence can be understood without reference to detail normally given elsewhere, such as the material and methods section of a scientific report (**Ch 54**). Items to include here are:

- the figure number;
- the figure title;
- what the symbols and error bars mean (a legend or key within the figure may or may not be acceptable – check);
- if appropriate, how the plotted curve was chosen;
- any brief details about the data (for example, differences in the treatments) that will help your reader understand the figure better without having to refer to another section.

CREATING TABLES

A good table presents data in a compact, readily assimilated format. In general, you should not include the same data in a chart *and* a table. You might decide to use a table rather than a chart if:

- graphic presentation is not suitable for some or all of the data (for instance, when some are qualitative);
- there are too many data sets or variables to include in a chart;
- your audience might be interested in the precise values of some of your data;
- you wish to place large amounts of your data on record, for instance within an appendix to a report.

Think about and draw a rough design for your table before constructing a final version. Key elements include:

- **The title and caption.** Your table must have these as a guide to the content, just like a figure. Note that the numbering scheme for tables is independent from that of graphs. Titles and captions should always appear above the table.

- **Appropriate arrangement and headings.** Each vertical column should display a particular type of data, and the descriptive headings should reflect these contents, giving the units where data are quantitative. Each row might show different instances of these types of data. Rows and columns should be arranged in a way that helps the reader to compare them if this is desirable.

- **Rulings.** The default in word-processing programs such as Microsoft Word is to add boxed lines to tables; however, the modern style is to minimise these, often restricting their use to horizontal lines only.

- **Data values.** These should be presented to an appropriate number of significant figures. An indication of errors, if included, should be given in parentheses, and the heading should make it clear what statistic is being quoted.

- **Footnotes.** These can be used to explain abbreviations or give details of specific cases.

Figure 30.4 illustrates some important components of a well-designed table.

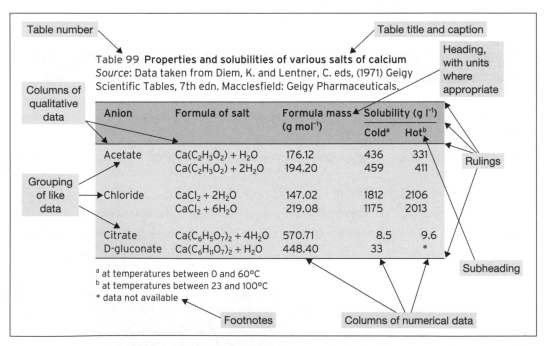

Figure 30.4 The basic components of a table. Note that shading is included here to emphasise the heading and data sections and would not usually be present.

IMPORTANT DESCRIPTIVE STATISTICS

Descriptive statistics are used to simplify a complex data set, to summarise the distribution of data within the data set and to provide estimates of values of the population frequency distribution. Two aspects that are often quoted are:

- a measure of location – this is an estimate of the 'centre' of the frequency distribution;
- a measure of dispersion – this is an estimate of the spread of data within the frequency distribution.

> ### Definition: frequency distribution
>
> This is a description of the frequency of occurrence of values of a variable. You may be interested in the actual distribution in the sample you have taken, and you might use a frequency polygon (Figure 30.2(c)) to represent this. You might also be interested in the underlying population frequency distribution. This is often theoretical in nature and a smooth curve representing a model function might be used to represent it.

Different measures of location and dispersion are outlined in Table 30.1 and many of these values can be obtained simply, using a spreadsheet or statistical program. More complex descriptive statistics such as standard error (describing the precision of a mean), or quantifying the shape of frequency distributions, are outside the scope of this book and a specialist text should be consulted.

CONCEPTS OF HYPOTHESIS-TESTING STATISTICS

Hypothesis testing in a statistical context is used to compare the properties of a data set with other samples or to compare the data set with some theory about it.

Error and variability exist in all data sets (see Tip Box, below), which means that it is impossible to be 100 per cent certain about differences between sets. Are the differences 'genuine' and due to a true dissimilarity between the samples, perhaps because of a treatment you have administered to one of them, or are the differences you observe just the result of random errors? Hypothesis testing works by trying to put a probability on these alternatives.

> ### Sources of random error and variability
>
> The following are reasons why the values and hence the descriptive statistics of samples of data may vary.
>
> - **Sampling error**, due to the selection of a small number of individuals from a larger, variable population.
> - **Measurement error**, due to the method of measurement of the variable.
> - **Rounding error**, due to an attempt to use an appropriate number of significant figures, but often compounded in calculations.
> - **Human error**, due to inaccurate writing or copying of data, mixing up of samples, and so on.
> - **Error from unknown sources**, or unappreciated effects of sampling.

The norm is to set up a 'null hypothesis' (NH) that says that the samples are the same or that they conform to some theoretical description. By making certain assumptions about the data, calculating a hypothesis-testing statistic, and looking up tables of probability (or calculating), you can find the probability P of the NH being true. The lower the P, the less likely you are to accept it in favour of the hypothesis that the differences were 'real' and due to your treatment or a genuine difference between the samples. Conventionally, if $P < 0.05$, then the NH is rejected.

Hypothesis-testing statistics differ in their assumptions about the data and what they set out to test. Some common ones and their uses are:

● **t-test:** for comparing two means;
● **χ^2 (Chi squared) test:** for comparing observed against expected values;
● **analysis of variance (ANOVA):** for comparing several means.

Precise details can be found in specialist texts.

PRACTICAL TIPS FOR PRODUCING GRAPHS, TABLES AND BASIC STATISTICS

Learn how to manipulate spreadsheet chart output. If you are using a spreadsheet to compose your graph, it is important not to accept the default values without making a conscious decision to do so. Altering these attributes of charts is usually possible, although it may require some advanced knowledge of the program. Things you might wish to change to meet discipline norms include scale (often automatically selected), background, gridlines, symbols and lines.

Learn the table functions in your word processor. You should know how to create a table, add and delete columns and rows, manipulate the width of columns and rows, add and remove borders to the table 'cells', merge and split cells and sort data within tables. This will help you produce more presentable and user-friendly tables.

Research further on statistics. Statistics can be a little daunting, but like maths it is a subject in which you can greatly improve if you apply yourself. If you lack confidence in your statistical abilities, you may wish to enrol on a supplementary module or buy additional texts to help you improve. This is another aspect of maths where practice makes perfect.

31

SHAPING UP IN MATHS

How to use basic geometry and trigonometry to solve spatial problems

Many numerical problems involve geometry and trigonometry. The principles involved in working out areas, volumes, angles and gradients are often relatively simple, but easy to forget. This chapter reviews the essential mathematical techniques you can apply to such problems and explains some of the terminology involved.

Being able to calculate angles, volumes and other features of shapes is a valuable skill in many subjects, from engineering to biology. This is not a maths textbook, however, and space does not allow a detailed treatment with examples and problems. Instead, we aim to introduce basic terminology and some relatively simple methods. If your subject requires more complicated maths, including differentiation and integration, you will need to seek help from specialist texts, or attend supplementary tutorials or modules.

CALCULATING AREAS AND VOLUMES OF COMMON SHAPES

Modelling exercises and problems frequently require you to quantify features of two- and three-dimensional shapes, such as their areas, perimeters and volumes. For standard shapes, these can generally be worked out using simple formulae, and it may be assumed by your tutors that you have memorised some of these from school work. If this isn't the case, Table 31.1 provides some reminders of commonly encountered examples.

WORKING OUT ANGLES

An angle occurs between two straight lines meeting at a vertex (Figure 31.1). If one of these lines is free to move, it can sweep round in a circle. Each full circle, working anticlockwise, by convention, is defined as 360 degrees – written as 360°. Another definition of angle is the radian (rad), such that there are 2π rad in each full circle.

About π

Pi is the ratio of the circumference of a circle to its diameter. It is an irrational number (**Ch 29**) with the symbol π and following value to 20 significant figures: 3.1415926535897932384.

Table 31.1 Formulae for calculating the perimeter, areas and volumes of objects

Shape and diagram	Perimeter (2D objects)	Area (2D objects) or surface area (3D objects)	Volume (3D objects)
Square	$4x$	x^2	
Cube		$6x^2$	x^3
Rectangle	$2(x + y)$	xy	
Cuboid		$2xy + 2xz + 2yx$	xyz
Circle	$2\pi r$	πr^2	
Sphere		$4\pi r^2$	$4\pi r^3/3$
Cylinder		$2\pi rh + 2\pi r^2$	$\pi r^2 h$
Ellipse	$\pi[(1.5a + b) - \sqrt{ab}]$ (approximation)	πab	
Ellipsoid		No simple formula	$\pi(abc)/3$
Triangle	$x + y + z$	$zh/2$	
Cone		$ph/2 + b$, where $p = 2\pi r$ and $b = \pi r^2$	$bh/3$
Pyramid		$ph/2 + b$, where $p = 4x$ and $b = x^2$	$bh/3$

Key: x, y, z = sides; a, b, c = axes; r = radius, h = height, or perpendicular height; p = perimeter of base; b = area of base.

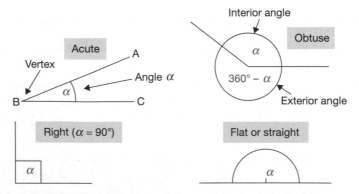

Figure 31.1 The terminology of angles. Angles are often denoted by Greek letters (for example α, β, γ, θ, ϕ, φ). They can be greater than 360°, continuing to sweep round the vertex in an anticlockwise direction; and negative, sweeping in a clockwise direction.

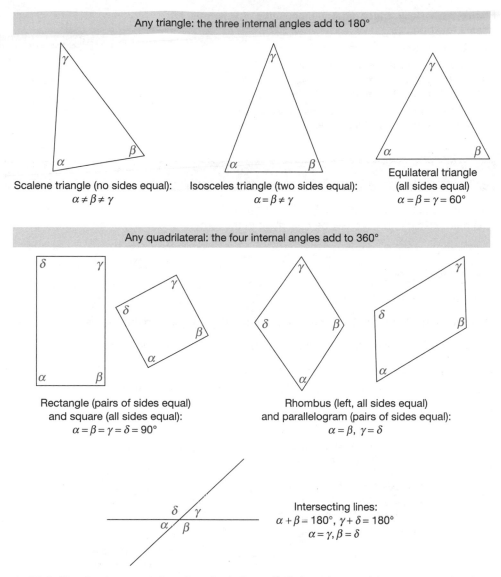

Figure 31.2 Simple shapes and angle calculations. At their easiest, problems may require the knowledge that the inside angles of a triangle always add up to 180°. Hence, if two of the angles are known, the third can be calculated by subtracting their sum from 180. Similarly, the angles in a four-sided shape (quadrilateral) add up to 360°, so if three are known, the fourth can be calculated. Symmetrical shapes simplify these problems, because they have equal angles at opposite sides.

A frequent challenge in geometry is to work out an unknown angle or side length in a triangular or four-sided shape. Some problems only require basic geometry to solve (Figure 31.2), while others require trigonometry and involve the use of sines, cosines and tangents (Figure 31.3). These mathematical functions have many applications, including in telecommunications, navigation, surveying and description of wave forms, where advanced trigonometric techniques are required.

Figure 31.3 Basic trigonometry: calculating side lengths and angles for triangles.

Pythagoras' theorem: $c^2 = a^2 + b^2$

Sin $\theta = a/c$ (opposite over hypotenuse)
Cos $\theta = b/c$ (adjacent over hypotenuse)
Tan $\theta = a/b$ (opposite over adjacent)

If required, rearrange these equations to find an unknown value if two out of the three variables are known.

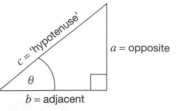

FUNCTIONS: SLOPES, INTERCEPTS, LIMITS AND ASYMPTOTES

A function describes a relationship where values of one variable determine the values of another. This relationship can generally be described in the form of a formula, or equation, such as:

$e = mc^2$,

$y = cos(x + z)$, or

$a = 5xy^2/(x^2 + y^4)$.

Many such functions can be represented graphically in x, y coordinate systems.

Generalised features of functions are illustrated in Figure 31.4. These include:

- the slope of the curve at any point (the tangent);
- the points where the function crosses the x- and y-axes, if it does;
- the intercept between two functions, if there is one;

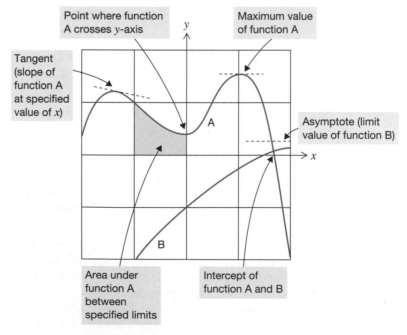

Figure 31.4 Some features of functions

- where a function has maximum or minimum values, if relevant;
- the limit value for a function (asymptote), if it has one;
- the area under a function curve, usually between specified limits.

Given a function, numerical values for these features can be worked out using advanced algebra and calculus. There are widespread applications for this sort of analysis: examples include the study of motion, optics and electromagnetism.

The straight-line equation $y = mx + c$ is one function that is frequently encountered. This has widespread uses, for example, in calibration curves, and when describing many relationships in biology, economics and physics. This equation has the following key features.

- The value of m describes the slope of the line. Higher positive m values result in a steeper line, and lower values give a shallower one, while negative values give a decreasing, or negative, slope (Figure 31.5).
- The value of c defines the y-axis intercept (this is where $x = 0$, so $y = c$). A zero value means the line passes through the intercept of the x- and y-axes and positive and negative values shift the whole line up or down respectively (Figure 31.5).
- The x-axis intercept is given by $-c/m$.

If the data points are scattered along a linear trend line, you can obtain 'best estimates' of m and c using linear regression analysis. This will also provide you with a value r, the correlation coefficient, which quantifies the relative scatter, or how well the line fits the points. The closer this parameter is to 1 (or −1 for negative slopes), the less the scatter. The statistic r can be used to test whether the slope of the line differs from zero; this will indicate whether the relationship between x and y is statistically significant.

Sometimes transformations are used to create a straight-line relationship between variables. A mathematical operation is carried out on the x values (and sometimes also the y values), so that a curved relationship becomes linear. This is done in some types of enzyme analysis, for example, where the reciprocals of x and y may be plotted against each other. However, if you employ linear regression on the transformed values, this is unlikely to be valid because concomitant changes in the error structure invalidate the assumptions of linear regression analysis.

Figure 31.5 Examples of straight-line relationships. Line A represents the equation $y = x$ (that is, in $y = mx + c$, $m = 1$ and $c = 0$). Line B, $y = x + 1$, shows how a change in y-intercept can be brought about through a change in c (here, $m = 1$ and $c = 1$). Line C, $y = 0.5x$, shows how a change in slope can be brought about by a change in m (here, $m = 0.5$ and $c = 0$). Line D, $y = -2x - 0.5$, shows a negative slope and intercept (here $m = -2$ and $c = -0.5$).

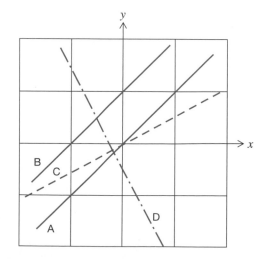

Find out what you need to know. Discover as soon as you can what maths and stats techniques might be required in your course (the module handbook may help, or your tutors may be able to assist). If you are rusty on these aspects, *take steps as soon as possible* to get up to speed. Some universities provide 'brush up your maths' type workshops or drop-in centres run as part of Maths departments or the academic support unit and these might help.

Translate your problem from 'ordinary' language into mathematical language. Allocate symbols for each dimension and note relationships between dimensions given in the problem.

Try to work out which formula applies. If you do not instantly recognise which equation applies to the problem you have been given, think through the values and dimensions you have been given and work out which of these appear in the 'candidate' formulae you are considering.

State your assumptions. If modelling using a 'perfect' shape or object, you should state the assumptions you are making (for example, 'the organelle was assumed to be spherical . . .'). While discussing your result, you may also wish to state why these assumptions might not be accurate in practice.

Use figures and graphs to 'visualise' a problem. This may make it easier to understand, although it isn't a suitable approach in all cases.

32

TACKLING WRITING ASSIGNMENTS

How to get started

Assignments at university challenge you to write in different forms. This chapter looks at the fundamental stages in preparing to respond to any assignment. It takes you through a step-by-step process to help you plan the structure of your submission.

Written university assignments take different forms. Examples include essays, reports, project dossiers, short-answer mini-essays, case studies or dissertations. The purpose is to give you an opportunity to demonstrate several things:

- your knowledge and understanding of a topic;
- your ability to research a specific aspect of the topic set in the assignment;
- your ability to organise supporting information and evidence in a structured piece of academic writing.

Especially for a longer piece of writing, or one that will count towards a module or degree mark, it is worth planning your work carefully and ensuring that you approach the task in a focused manner.

REALISTIC TIME PLANNING

Consult the course handbook for the assignment submission date. Work out how long you have between the starting point and due date, and then estimate how much of that time you can devote to completion of the work. Remember to take into account things you may need to do for other subjects, your need to attend lectures, tutorials or practicals, and any social or part-time work commitments (see also **Ch 8**).

Next, divide the available time into convenient working periods and decide how much time you wish to allocate to each aspect of the task (Table 32.1). Map these time allowances on to your available time.

Value of planning

Time spent deconstructing the task and planning your response will enable you to save time in the long run and, as with most jobs, the quality of the preparation will be reflected in the quality of the end product. Taking the time to ensure that you break down the question (or task) into its different elements will pay dividends by helping to make your response as focused on the task as possible.

Table 32.1 Subdivisions of a large writing task and their estimated timing. A possible method of organising your time when planning a lengthy written assignment.

Aspect of task	Time required	When I plan to do this
Analysing the task		
Doing preliminary reading		
Planning the response to the task		
Doing supplementary reading		
Writing the first draft		
Reviewing the first draft		
Editing/proof-reading the final copy		
Printing/writing out the final copy		
Time margin for the unexpected		

Good planning ensures that you can realistically complete the work before the submission date. It also allows you to balance the time spent on different components, devote sufficient time to aspects such as editing and proof-reading (**Ch 43**) and avoid penalties that might be imposed because of late submission.

RECOGNISING THE ELEMENTS OF THE TASK

Once you have thought about the amount of time you can allocate to the work, the next phase of analysing an assignment requires you to break the task down into its component parts by asking yourself the following questions:

- **What's the *instruction*?** Many assignments are not in the form of questions but framed as instructions introduced by an instruction word. It is important to interpret these instruction words properly (see Table 32.2).
- **What's the *topic*?** This will clarify the context of the discussion you will need to construct.
- **What's the *aspect* of the topic?** This will help you define a more specific focus within the wider context.
- **What *restriction* is imposed on the topic?** This will limit the scope of your discussion.

The example in the Information Box on page 201 shows you how this analysis might look for a sample question. You may already do this sort of thing subconsciously, but there is value in marking these elements out on paper. First, it helps you to recognise the scope and limitations of the work you have been asked to complete. Second, it means that you can avoid producing a piece of work that waffles or strays from the point. Once you have gone through this fairly quick process, you will be better able to work on planning your writing (**Ch 34**) and on adopting a suitable framework for your assignment (**Ch 33**).

Generally, instruction words fall into four categories, although this grouping may vary according to the context of the question. The list below defines these types. In broad terms, this suggests a hierarchy of approaches to tackling assignments that will dictate how you need to organise the information in your assignment (**Ch 33**).

> **Instruction word categories**
>
> One way of categorising instruction words is by looking at what they ask you to do:
>
> **Do:** create something, draw up a plan, calculate.
>
> **Describe:** explain or show how something appears, happens or works.
>
> **Analyse:** look at all sides of an issue.
>
> **Argue:** look at all sides of an issue and provide supporting evidence for your position.

Table 32.2 shows a range of typical instruction words, with definitions for each one. You should make sure you know what's expected of you when any of these instructions are used, not only in terms of these definitions, but also in relation to the thinking processes expected (see **Ch 22** and especially Table 22.1). However, always remember to take the whole question into account when deciding this.

EXPLORING THE TOPIC

Go back to the task and analyse the topic, its aspect(s) and restriction(s) more thoroughly. This is important because students often misread the task and, although they may submit a good piece of work, their response could miss the true focus of the assignment.

Next, create a brainstorm 'map' of the topic by writing down as many related aspects as you can in a free-flowing diagram (see Figure 26.5). Revisit the instruction word and consider how this applies to your initial response to the task. This may seem to be a strange approach, but these immediate thoughts are principally your own 'take' on the topic, perhaps influenced by lectures, but before your ideas have been influenced by any reading material. The most important aspect is that you are beginning to exercise your critical thinking skills (**Ch 22**), by analysing for yourself what you think is important about this subject.

Table 32.2 Instruction words for assignments and exams. These words are the product of research into the frequency of use of the most common instruction words in university examinations. The definitions below are suggestions. You must take the whole question into account when answering. See also Table 22.1.

Instruction word	Definition – what you are expected to do
Account [give an]	Describe
Account for	Give reasons for
Analyse	Give an organised answer looking at all aspects
Apply	Put a theory into operation
Assess	Decide on value/importance
Brief account [give a]	Describe in a concise way
Comment on	Give your opinion
Compare [with]	Discuss similarities; draw conclusions on common areas
Compile	Make up (a list/plan/outline)
Consider	Describe/give your views on the subject
Contrast	Discuss differences/draw own view
Criticise	Point out weak/strong points, i.e. balanced answer
Define	Give the meaning of a term, concisely
Demonstrate	Show by example/evidence
Describe	Narrative on process/appearance/operation/sequence . . .
Devise	Make up
Discuss	Give own thoughts and support your opinion or conclusion
Evaluate	Decide on merit of situation/argument
Exemplify	Show by giving examples
Expand	Give more information
Explain	Give reason for – say why
Explain how	Describe how something works
Identify	Pinpoint/list
Illustrate	Give examples
Indicate	Point out, but not in great detail
Justify	Support the argument for . . .
List	Make an organised list, e.g. events
Outline	Describe basic factors – limited information
Plan	Think how to organise something
Report	Give an account of the process or event
Review	Write a report – give facts and views on facts
Show	Demonstrate with supporting evidence
Specify	Give details of something
State	Give a clear account of . . .
Summarise	Briefly give an account
Trace	Provide a brief chronology of events/process
Work out	Find a solution, e.g. as in a maths problem

Brainstorming techniques

To create an effective brainstorm 'map', use a single sheet of A4 in the landscape position allowing more space for lateral thinking and creativity as well as for additions at later stages (see Figure 26.5 as an example). Alternatively, you might find it useful to construct your brainstorm as a grid or a herringbone (see Figures 26.6 and 26.7 as examples). These can form the basis of your writing plan.

FINDING THE MATERIAL AND SELECTING WHAT'S RELEVANT

As a preliminary to tackling the prescribed reading list, obtain some general background information about the topic. Typical additional sources are shown in the Information Box below.

Reading the literature that supports a subject is a routine part of student activity. Generally, reading lists are extensive to give some choice; they often list basic texts and then sources that go into greater depth. It is not usually expected that you read everything on these lists. In some subjects, you may only be expected to look at one or two recommended texts. In some other subjects, book lists are lengthy and the volume of reading may seem daunting, but the task will be more manageable if you approach it systematically.

Sources of information

Handouts/PowerPoint slides: should outline key issues and ideas, pose problems and provide solutions related to your topic.

Lecture notes: easy to locate if you've noted lecturer, topic and date.

General or subject encyclopaedias: provide a thumb-nail sketch of useful background information; give key points to direct your reading in more detailed texts. Electronic versions may be available through your university library (**Ch 23**).

ebrary: readily accessible, and reliable in its validity.

E-journals: often contemporary material that is reliable in its provenance.

Library resources: the electronic catalogue will enable you to locate many resources in addition to those listed above. However, you may also find things serendipitously by browsing in the relevant zone of shelving in the library, where it is possible to find books and journals that may not necessarily come up from the search headings you have selected when consulting the catalogue.

Unless specific chapters or pages are cited, students sometimes think that they need to read the whole book. This is usually not the case. Use the contents page and the index in partnership to identify which sections are relevant to your topic (**Ch 25**). Some authors often put key pages in bold type in the index and this will help you to focus your reading rather than cover every reference. At this stage also, preliminary encyclopaedia reading will help you to identify sections in a book resource that are more relevant to the present task.

Begin by doing the necessary reading and note-making (**Ch 23–Ch 26**). This has to be focused and you need to be reading with discrimination. As you move from basic texts to more specialist books or journal articles that give more detailed analysis, your understanding of the topic will deepen. This may mean, for example that you begin to build up a more informed picture of events, implications of a procedure or the possible solutions to a problem. What are you looking for? This could be, for instance, facts, examples, information to support a particular viewpoint, or counter-arguments to provide balance to your analysis of the topic. As you become more familiar with the issues, the easier it will be to think critically (**Ch 22**) about what you are reading and consequently building your response to the task you have been set. Continue to add to your initial brainstorm.

> ### ✔ The reporter's questions
>
> Sometimes it is difficult to identify the important from the unimportant, the relevant from the irrelevant. A well-tried strategy, for many subjects, is to ask yourself the questions that trainee journalists are advised to use:
>
> - **Who?** Who is involved in relation to this topic, for example, people/organisations?
> - **What?** What are the problems/issues involved?
> - **When?** What is the time-frame to be considered?
> - **Where?** Where did it occur?
> - **Why?** What reasons are relevant to this issue/topic?
> - **How?** How has this situation been reached?

ADOPTING AN ANALYTICAL APPROACH

Knowing what information to put aside and what to retain requires a more disciplined appraisal than the more wide-ranging approach you will have followed in your initial reading. Certain questions may help you to focus on what is important to your topic. For example:

- Who are the key actors in a sequence of events?
- What are the necessary events or conditions that explain particular situations?
- What explanations support a particular view?
- What patterns can be identified, for example, short-, medium- and long-term factors?

From your reading and note-making you will begin to find that different authors make similar or contradictory points. As you begin to identify the different schools of thought or approaches to an issue, you should begin to cross-reference your notes so that you can begin to group authors who subscribe to the same or similar viewpoints.

> ### ✔ Direct quotation
>
> It is important not to rely too heavily on quoting from the text. First, if this is overdone, it is plagiarism (**Ch 36, Ch 37**); second, it fails to give evidence that you understand the significance of the point being made.

University work needs more than simple reproduction of facts. You need to be able to construct an argument (Ch 33, Ch 34) and to support this with evidence. This means that you need to draw on the literature that you have read in order to support your position. In some instances, dependent on the topic and discipline, it may be appropriate to present differing viewpoints and evaluate arguments one over the others, and, if appropriate, address counter-arguments to these. What is important is to present a tight, well-argued case for the view you finally present as the one you favour.

Once you have evolved your own response to the task you have been set, you then need to place this within a framework that presents your response in a way that is well structured. Writing that follows a sequence of sound logic and argument will improve your potential for gaining better marks. This next stage in structuring your text is covered in **Ch 33**.

PRACTICAL TIPS FOR GETTING STARTED ON A WRITING ASSIGNMENT

Select from a wide range of sources. In the early years of university study many students follow the same practices as they used at school, often with too much reliance on handouts and notes from a single core textbook. At university you will be expected to read more widely by identifying source material beyond titles given as a basic starting point. It is worthwhile exploring your library on foot to browse in the areas related to your studies, where you may find a whole range of material that potentially expands your reading and understanding.

Keep a record of what you read. It is exasperating to know that you have read something somewhere but cannot find it again. It is good to develop the habit of noting page number, chapter, title, author, publisher and place of publication on notes you make. This makes citation and referencing much easier and less time-consuming.

Conserve what you read. In the process of marshalling information for a writing task you will probably obtain some material that proves to be irrelevant to the current writing task. It is well worth keeping this in your filing system because this topic may come up again at a later date in a subtle way. In exam revision, this personal cache of information could be useful in revitalising your knowledge and understanding of this topic.

Stick to your planned allocation of time for reading. This is a vital part of the writing process, but recognise the dangers of prolonging the reading phase beyond your scheduled deadline. This is an avoidance strategy that is quite common. Students may delay getting down to planning the structure and moving on to the writing phase because they are uncomfortable with writing. Facing up to these next phases and getting on with them is usually much less formidable once you get started, so it's best to stick to your time plan for this assignment and move on to the next phase in the planned sequence.

ACADEMIC WRITING FORMAT

How to organise your writing within a standard framework

Regardless of the type of writing assignment you have to complete, or your discipline, the structure follows a basic format. This chapter describes this design and explores some of the features that need to be included as you map your outline plan onto this structure.

This chapter describes the essential format of any piece of academic writing, namely, introduction–main body–conclusion. It is on this basic framework that different types of academic assignment are constructed, and these are examined in detail in **Ch 34**.

STANDARD FORMAT

The basic structure follows the convention of moving from the general (the introduction) through to the specific (the main body) and back to the general (the conclusion).

Introduction

Generally, this should consist of three components:

- a brief explanation of the context of the topic;
- an outline of the topic as you understand it;
- an explanation of how you plan to address the topic in this particular text – in effect, a statement of intent.

This introductory section can be quite long as it may take several sentences to lay out these three dimensions. It's important to do this with some thought because this indicates to your reader where you expect to take them in the main body of text. The introduction also lays down the parameters that you have set yourself for this piece of text. For example, your topic may be multifaceted and the word limit imposed on the total piece of text will not allow you to give a comprehensive coverage of all aspects. It is better to acknowledge the extensive nature of the topic and note that you are going to limit your discussion to only some of these aspects – usually those you consider to be most important. You need to explain the reasons for this decision at this stage.

The importance of the introduction

This is the first contact that your reader makes with you as the author of the text. This means that it has to be well organised and clear. However, to achieve this it is important to see this introductory section as 'work in progress' because, until you complete the entire text, you cannot really introduce the whole work accurately. Indeed, some people prefer to start writing the main body, move on to the conclusion, and then write the introduction.

Main body

This section lays out your work based on the approach you decide to adopt in organising the content (**Ch 34**). You will have explained the approach in the introduction and this will mean that you should have mapped out your route for explaining your points. In this section, you may need to generalise, describe, define or exemplify as part of your analysis. Here it's important to keep this part of the writing as brief, yet as clear, as possible. The construction of your paragraphs will be dictated by what you are trying to do at any particular point. Different types of paragraph structures are outlined in Table 38.3.

May I use sub-headings?

In some disciplines, and especially in report writing, sub-headings are acceptable. In others they are not. However, using sub-headings in drafts can help you maintain the focus of your writing. It helps to prevent you digressing into unrelated areas or presenting an apparently rambling paper. If you then 'translate' your sub-heading into a topic sentence (**Ch 38**), this will provide a link with the previous paragraph or an introduction to the next theme.

Conclusion

This summarises the whole piece of work. You should review the entire text in three elements:

- a restatement of the question and what you feel are the important features of the topic;
- a summary of the specific evidence that you have presented in support of your views;
- a statement of your overall viewpoint on the topic.

What mainly distinguishes the conclusion from the introduction is language. In the introduction, your explanation should be given clearly, avoiding jargon or technical words as far as possible. In the conclusion, you will be writing about the detail of the content and, therefore, the terminology you use is more likely to contain technical or more sophisticated language because you will have introduced this in the main body. You should avoid introducing new ideas in the conclusion that have not already been discussed in the earlier part of the writing.

Mini-conclusions

As you become immersed in the writing process you will become very familiar with the material and conclusions you have drawn along the way. By the time you come to write the conclusion to the whole work, this in-depth awareness may become diluted. To avoid this, it is a good idea, at the end of each section you write, to note down what main ideas you had considered and what your view is about these. If you note these down on a separate piece of paper, this will provide the substance for your final conclusion.

TAKING WORD LIMITS INTO ACCOUNT

Word limits are imposed, not to relieve tutors of marking, but to train you to be concise in your writing and to analyse the topic carefully to decide what to keep in and what to leave out.

As you plan and write your first draft, keep only a casual eye on word count at this stage. When you come to editing that draft you can prune and reshape your writing so that it becomes a tighter piece of prose that falls within the maximum–minimum word limits imposed by the regulations.

Counting words

Most word processors include a word-count feature. Microsoft Word has, in addition, a useful 'floating' toolbar that allows you to check running totals as you write or edit. You can access both features in this program from 'Tools > Word Count (> Show Toolbar)'.

It is important to note that falling short of the word limit is just as bad as overrunning the maximum. Some students keep a running total of words they have used and as soon as they reach the minimum word limit, they stop abruptly. This is not a good approach because it is more likely to leave a ragged and poorly considered piece of text that comes to an unexpected halt rather than one that is well-planned, relevant and concisely written.

Condense your text like a professional writer

Many eminent and prolific fiction and non-fiction writers admit to 'pruning' their work – not so much to meet word limits (although that is a consideration in professional publications), but to make the meaning clearer and sharper by cutting words out since repetitive expressions are often used in the first drafts of writing. For example, in draft material for this book we had written 'a definitive and final statement' but the word 'definitive' in this context, meant 'final', hence one of these words could be deleted, as could the word 'and' which was no longer necessary.

Keep the right proportions in your response. Make sure that the three elements within your writing framework are well balanced in extent. The main body should be the most substantial piece of the writing, whereas the introduction and conclusion should occupy much less space. A common problem for many students is that they devote too much time to outlining the context in the introduction and leave themselves with too little time and space to deal with the core of the essay and the conclusion.

Pay adequate attention to the conclusion. By the time that you come to write the conclusion, this is often done at some speed because there may be other demands on your time, or the initial interest in the subject has palled, or you may simply be tired. Thus, conclusions often don't get the attention they deserve. Do reserve some time to give your conclusion a critical appraisal, and even consider writing this section before finishing the perhaps more 'mechanical' earlier parts. Alternatively, as suggested above, you could 'write it as you go' by keeping detailed notes of key points separately, which you can use to frame your conclusion once you have written the main body.

Review the introduction. Once you have completed your draft, go back to the introduction and make sure that you have actually done what you set out to do when defining the parameters of your work and in your statement of intent. The act of writing your text may have stimulated new thoughts and your initial intentions may have altered in the process of writing.

Think about appendices. Sometimes the length of your text may be seriously beyond the word limit. This means that some drastic 'surgery' is required. One strategy might be to remove some parts of the text and, while remaining within the word limit, reduce the information contained to bullet-point lists. The detail can then be placed in an appendix or appendices (plural of appendix), making appropriate cross-references in the main text. In some disciplines, the use of appendices is discouraged and you may be penalised for using them. If in doubt, consult your course handbook or ask a member of staff.

Think about citations. In many disciplines you will be expected to include reference to recognised authorities within the field you are studying. In law, this could be cases; in the arts and humanities, it could be work by a distinguished academic. This does not mean that you need to quote substantial pieces of text; you can summarise the idea in your own words and then follow the rules about citation that are given in **Ch 35**. All this needs to be taken into consideration in planning and drafting your writing.

34

PLANNING WRITING ASSIGNMENTS

How to respond to the task

Once you have assembled the information for your assignment, you will be able to think about how you are going to respond to the set writing task within the standard framework. This chapter outlines some of the different options that you may need to consider when structuring your response into an outline plan.

The basic framework of an essay was described in **Ch 33**. The next step is to think about the particular assignment that you have to tackle and how you might organise your response to the task.

People and their thought processes are different and so individual approaches to planning an outline response to an assignment will vary. For some people, this can be a highly detailed process, for others, it may be a minimal exercise. Too much detail in a plan can be restricting, while too little can fail to provide enough direction. Therefore, a reasonably detailed plan should give some guidance while leaving you the flexibility to alter the finer elements as you write.

IDENTIFYING THE KEY THEMES IN YOUR TEXT

Planning your writing means that you need to return to your 'first thoughts' brainstorm (**Ch 32**), which should have been developed further as you have added key points from your reading and thinking. Consider whether any themes or recurrent issues are evident. It might be useful to 'colour code' all the items that are related, using a different colour highlighter for each category or theme. Then, you need to reconsider the instruction of the set task to help you construct your plan, that is, on the basis of description, analysis or argument (**Ch 32**).

? Lower- or higher-order thinking?

While, for some subjects, description would be a lower-order writing activity, for others this would be considered to be a higher-order skill (see **Ch 22** and especially Table 22.1). Often written assignments require some initial description of context or process to outline the background to the topic. This is then followed by in-depth consideration of the topic, using more analytical or critical approaches.

ADOPTING A STRUCTURAL MODEL

Brainstorming and then analysing the instruction should give you some indication of how you can construct the content of your paper as a logical discussion by considering how it would fit into one of several classic structural models or approaches (Table 34.1).

Table 34.1 Seven common structural models for written assignments

1 Chronological	Description of a process or sequence
2 Classification	Ordering objects or ideas
3 Common denominator	Identifying a common characteristic or theme
4 Phased	Identifying short-/medium-/long-term aspects
5 Analytical	Examining an issue in depth (situation – problem – solution – evaluation – recommendation)
6 Thematic	Commenting on a theme in each aspect
7 Comparative/contrastive	Comparing and contrasting (often within a theme or themes)

By adopting one of these models, it should be possible to map out the content of your answer in a way that provides a logical and coherent response to the task you have been set. Note that sometimes it may be necessary to incorporate one of these models within another. For example, within the common denominator approach it may be necessary to include some chronological dimension to the discussion.

Examples of each of these seven approaches are given below.

Chronological

An example of the chronological approach would be describing a developmental process, such as outlining the historical development of the European Union. This kind of writing is most likely to be entirely descriptive.

Classification

An example of this approach could be to discuss transport by subdividing your text into land, sea and air modes of travel. Each of these could be further divided into commercial, military and personal modes of transport. These categories could be further subdivided on the basis of how they are powered. Such classifications are, to some extent, subjective, but the approach provides a means of describing each category at each level in a way that allows some contrast. This approach is particularly useful in scientific disciplines. The rationale also is sympathetic to the approach of starting from broad generalisation to the more specific.

Common denominator

An example of this approach might be used in answer to the following assignment: 'Account for the levels of high infant mortality in developing countries'. This suggests a common denominator of deficiency or lack. This topic could therefore be approached under the headings:

● Lack of primary health care
● Lack of health education
● Lack of literacy.

Phased

An example of adopting a sequential approach to a topic might be in response to a task that instructs: 'Discuss the impact of water shortage on flora and fauna along river banks'.

- **Short-term factors:** e.g. drying out of the river bed occurs and annual plants fail to thrive.
- **Medium-term factors:** e.g. damage to oxygenating plant life and reduction in wildlife numbers.
- **Long-term factors:** e.g. the effect on the water table and falling numbers of certain amphibious species.

Note that topics amenable to this treatment do not always prompt this sort of response directly by asking for 'results' or consequences of an event; you could decide to use it in answer to a question such as 'Explain why water shortage has deleterious effects on riparian life.'

Analytical

This conventional approach might be used to approach complex issues. An example of an assignment that you could tackle in this way might be: 'Evaluate potential solutions to the problem of identity theft'. You could perhaps adopt the following plan:

- Define identity theft, and perhaps give an example.
- Explain why identity theft is difficult to control.
- Outline legal and practical solutions to identity theft.
- Weigh up the advantages and disadvantages of each.
- State which solution(s) you would favour and why.

> ### ✔ Taking the analytical approach – the SPSER model
>
> This tactic is particularly helpful in the construction of essays, reports, projects and case studies. It is also useful whenever you feel that you cannot identify themes or trends. The method helps you to 'deconstruct' or 'unpack' the topic and involves five elements, as follows:
>
> - **Situation:** describe the context and brief history.
> - **Problem:** describe or define the problem.
> - **Solution:** describe and explain the possible solution(s).
> - **Evaluation:** identify the positive and negative features for each solution by giving evidence/reasons to support your viewpoint.
> - **Recommendation:** identify the best option in your opinion, giving the basis of your reasoning for this. This element is optional, as it may not always be a requirement of your task.

Thematic

This approach is similar to the phased approach, but in this case themes are the identifying characteristics. Precise details would depend on the question, but examples could be:

- social, economic or political factors;
- age, income and health considerations;
- gas, electricity, oil, water and wind power.

Comparative/contrastive

This is a derivative of the themed approach. For example, consider a town planning task that instructs: 'Discuss the arguments for and against the introduction of car-free city centres'. You might approach this by creating a 'grid' as in Table 34.2, which notes positive and negative aspects for the major stakeholders.

Table 34.2 Model grid for planning comparison-type answers

Stakeholders		Column A	Column B
		Positive aspects	Negative aspects
1	Pedestrians	Greater safety, clean	Lengthy walk, poor parking
2	Drivers	Less stress; park and ride facilities	High parking fees; expensive public transport
3	Commercial enterprises	Quicker access for deliveries	Loss of trade to more accessible out-of–town shopping centres
4	Local authority	Reduces emissions	Cost of park and ride
5	Police	Easier to police	Reliance on foot patrols

There are two potential methods of constructing text in this comparative/contrastive approach:

- **Method 1.** Introduce the topic, then follow Column A in a vertical fashion, then similarly follow Column B and conclude by making a concluding statement about the merits and demerits of one over the other. In relation to the grid, this would result in the structure:

    introductory statement, then A1 + A2 + A3 + A4 + A5, then B1 + B2 + B3 + B4 + B5,

    followed by concluding statement.

- **Method 2.** Introduce the topic and then discuss the perspective of pedestrians from first the positive and then the negative aspects; now do the same for the viewpoints of the other stakeholders in sequence. This would result in the structure:

    introductory statement, then A1 + B1; A2 + B2; A3 + B3; A4 + B4; A5 + B5,

    followed by concluding statement.

A herringbone map, as illustrated in Figure 26.7 for pros and cons of a transport policy proposal, is an alternative method of laying out the different aspects of an issue.

Comparative/contrastive structures

Each method of structuring the points has advantages and disadvantages, according to the content and the context of the assignment. For example, in an exam it might be risky to embark on Method 1 in case you run out of time and never reach the discussion of column B. In this instance, Method 2 would enable a balanced answer.

Responding to question words

Not all tasks are based on instructions; some do ask questions. For instance, they may include words such as 'How . . . ?', 'Why . . . ?' and expressions such as 'To what extent . . . ?' In these cases, you will need to think about what these mean within the do–describe–analyse–argue instruction hierarchy. One way to do this is to reword the question.

For example, consider the question: 'To what extent has the disposal of sewage effluence in rivers contributed to depletion of fish stocks over the last decade?'

This might be reworded as: 'Evaluate the relationship between the disposal of sewage effluence in rivers and the depletion of fish stocks over the last decade'.

This would suggest using a phased approach to organising the content of the answer to the question.

EXPANDING YOUR OUTLINE

Once you have decided what kind of approach is required to cover your written assignment, then you can map this on to the main body of your essay plan and frame an introduction and conclusion that will 'top and tail' the essay. In this way, you can create the outline plan based on the introduction–main body–conclusion model that provides the framework for academic writing (**Ch 33**) in the English-speaking world.

PRACTICAL TIPS FOR PLANNING THE OUTLINE OF YOUR WRITTEN TEXT

Return to the outline plan. When you have completed your first draft it is a good idea to go back to your outline plan and check that you have not forgotten any points. You can also make sure that the links between sections that you noted in the plan have been achieved in the text.

Achieve balance in your response. Especially in the early years of university study, there is a tendency to adhere to the methods that had succeeded at school or college. This means that written work is often descriptive rather than analytical (see **Ch 22** for explanation). Ensure that the description you give is sufficient for the task, but if the instruction requires you to analyse or argue, then make sure this is the main focus of your response.

Explain your approach. Although the models outlined in this chapter are fairly standard approaches to tackling academic issues, it is still necessary to identify for your reader which approach you intend to adopt in the piece of text. Your reader should learn at an early point in your writing of the route you intend to follow. In most cases this would be in your introduction. This is dealt with more fully in **Ch 38**.

Seek 'your' answer rather than the 'right' answer. In subjects with a mathematical content, for example, there are clearly correct/incorrect answers, but in many other disciplines this is not the case. In these latter instances, you need to present *your* answer with supporting evidence. It is the merit of your appraisal that will most strongly influence your mark. It is essential to recognise that it is the structure of your argument, supported by relevant evidence, that is of importance and not, as some students think, a matter of reproducing the perceived viewpoint of those who lecture to you.

35

CITING AND LISTING REFERENCES

How to refer appropriately to the work of others

> In academic writing at all levels you must support your discussion of a topic by referring to the relevant literature. Several styles are in use and which one you will be required to adopt will depend on the conventions within your discipline. This chapter outlines four of the more common styles, showing you how to cite your source in text and list these in your reference list or bibliography.

When you write any kind of academic paper you must expect to give the sources of information and ideas you have drawn from your in-depth reading on the subject. You have to give your reader sufficient information to be able to locate your source. This is done in the body of the text at the point where you refer to (cite) the source, and then give full details of it either in a footnote, endnote or separate reference list at the end of the paper. Styles vary (see Table 35.1), but the preferred style for your discipline will be stipulated in your course handbook, or may be recommended by your lecturer or supervisor. However, you must be able to recognise the alternative styles in order to interpret the information given.

Definitions

Citation: the use of the idea presented by an author and expressed *in your own words* to support a point in your own work. Rules about citations in your text are given in **Ch 35**.

Quotation: the use of words drawn from the source you need. The words should remain faithful to the original. For layout of quotes see **Ch 25**.

Bibliography: a list at the end of your work of all source materials consulted as preparation for your paper. You do not need to have referred to all these sources directly in your text. In some styles the word 'bibliography' is used instead of the term 'reference list'.

Reference list: all the books, journals, web and online materials you have referred to in your paper. This list is usually at the end of the work.

WHY YOU NEED TO CITE YOUR SOURCES

Academic convention requires you to give this information in order to:

● acknowledge the use of other people's work – you must demonstrate clearly where you have borrowed text or ideas from others; even if you cite an author's work in order to disagree with it, you have made use of their intellectual property and you must show that you recognise this (there is more discussion on intellectual property and plagiarism in **Ch 36**);

- help your readers understand how your argument/discussion was assembled and what influenced your thinking – this will help them form opinions about your work;

- help your reader/marker evaluate the extent of your reading. This may help them to assess your work and to advise you on further or more relevant reading;

- provide your readers with sufficient information to enable them to consult the source materials for themselves, if they wish.

In many cases, if you do not provide a reference list you will lose marks. This must be in your department's preferred style (Table 35.1).

USING INFORMATION WITHIN YOUR TEXT

Essentially there are two means by which you can introduce the work of others into your text – by *quoting* exact words from a source, or by *citation*, which involves summarising or paraphrasing (**Ch 36**) the idea in your own words. In both instances you need to indicate the source material by means of the chosen style of citation (Table 35.1).

Quotation in the text

There are two possibilities (see also **Ch 44**). If the quotation is a short quotation, the exact words are placed within single inverted commas within the sentence (e.g. xxxx 'zzzz zz zzzz zz zzzz' xxx). If you are using a longer quotation, usually 30 words or more, then no inverted commas are used. The status of the text as a quotation is indicated by the use of indentation where several lines quoted from another source are indented within your own text and in single-line spacing. If you deliberately miss out some words from the original, the 'gap' is represented by three dots. This is called ellipsis. For example:

xxxxxxxx xxxxx xxxxx xxxx xxx xx xxxxxxxxx xxxx xx xxxxxx xx xx xxxx xxxxxx:

. . . zzzz z zzzzzz zzzzzzz zzz zzzzzzz zzzz zz z zz zzzz z zzzz zz z zzzzzz zzzzzzzzz.

(source)

xxxxxxx xxxx xxx xxxx xx xx xx xxxxxxxxxx xxxxx xxxxxxx xxxxx xxxxxxxxxxxxxxx.

> **i** **Quoting within a quote**
>
> British English uses single inverted commas to cover the whole quotation and double inverted commas (quotation marks) for the quotation within the quotation. For example, 'xxxxxx "zzzz" xxx'. The convention in American English is the opposite.

Footnotes and endnotes

In some disciplines, footnotes and endnotes, generally using superscript numbers, lead readers to the source information. However, in other disciplines, footnotes and endnotes are used simply to provide additional information, commentary or point of discussion about the content of the text. Footnotes generally appear at the bottom of the page where the link appears; endnotes are recorded in number order at the end of the body of the work.

Table 35.1 Choosing a referencing style. Departments normally specify the referencing style. Where no guidance is given, the choice is up to you. This table shows the most significant features, advantages and disadvantages of four common styles used in all forms of academic writing, including undergraduate and postgraduate assignments. It applies to all forms of writing – from essays to theses.

Method	Features	Advantages	Disadvantages
Harvard (Table 35.2)	• **Name/date** system used in the text (page number included only if making a reference to a specific quote or data) • Name of author can be included as part of the sentence (date in round brackets immediately after the name) *or* • Name and date both placed in round brackets at the end of the sentence	• Minimal typing: once-only entry in alphabetical order by author name in the reference list • Easy to identify contributors in a field from the citations shown in the text • Easy to make adjustments in the text and the reference list	• Name/date references can be intrusive in text • Not well-suited to citing archive material, e.g. historical documents, which may not have full details sufficient to comply with the system
Modern Languages Association (MLA) (Table 35.3)	• **Name/page** system in text; date at end of reference • Name of author can be included as part of the sentence (page number comes in brackets at the end of the sentence or clause) *or* • Name and page number(s) (no punctuation) both placed in brackets at the end of the sentence	• Minimal typing as details are printed only once in alphabetical order by author name in the reference list, which makes it easy to locate the source information • Easy to identify contributors in a field from the citations shown in the text	• Date of publication of source not in the text and not immediately evident in the reference list because of the position at the end of the reference • Indentation in 'follow-on' lines in the reference list can give a 'ragged' appearance to the layout of the reference list
Vancouver (Table 35.4)	• **Numerical** system with full-size numerals in brackets after the reported point • If another reference is made to a source in the text, the second and subsequent references use the number given to the reference when it was used for the first time	• Numbers are less intrusive in the text • Numbers are listed in numerical order at the end of the text, thus it is easy to locate the reference	• No bibliographical information in the text, thus difficult to gauge significance of the sources • Cumbersome to apply • Use of one number each time the source is used • Involves a considerable amount of checking and slows down the writing process
Chicago (Table 35.5)	• **Superscript numbers** used in the text • Relates superscript numbers to footnotes on the same page • Provides reference information in footnotes and reference list (note that the format differs between footnotes and reference list)	• Numbering system is unobtrusive and does not interrupt the flow of the text • Use of *op. cit.* and *ibid.* in the referencing saves retyping of bibliographical information	• First mention of a source gives full details, subsequent references give only name/page • More difficult to track the main contributors • Layout of footnote references differs from the bibliographical reference (if used) • Intensive checking to ensure that all superscript references are consistent after any changes

HOW TO CITE THE WORK IN THE TEXT

There are essentially two ways in which to do this: the information-prominent and author-prominent methods. These depend on the style of referencing you have elected to follow. Four commonly used styles are laid out in Tables 35.2–35.5. The broad principles, following the Harvard method, are outlined below.

- **Information-prominent method.** Here the statement is regarded as being generally accepted within the field of study. For example:

  Children express an interest in books and pictures from an early age (Murphy, 1995).

- **Author-prominent method.** Here the author and date of publication form part of the construction of the sentence. This formulation can be used with appropriate reporting words (see tip box) to reflect a viewpoint. For example:

  Murphy (1995) claimed that children as young as six months are able to follow a simple story sequence.

DIFFERENT REFERENCE STYLES

Styles of citing and listing references have evolved as technology and preferences have altered. Thus, some have followed conventions using name/date, name/page, and numerical notation to cite sources within text. These different approaches reflect different conventions in the layout of the corresponding reference or bibliography lists. Styles have been dictated by disciplines and their associated journals and this has led to modifications that create many variants of the original formats. Other styles, such as the American Psychological Association (APA) and the Modern Humanities Research Association (MRHA) used for literature and language, are extremely prescriptive. Their respective style guides extend the requirements to include a wide variety of features including such aspects as font, page layout, spelling, the use of active in preference to passive voice and much more. More information on these styles can be found at: www.apastyle.org and www.mhra.org.

The following tables illustrate four of the more commonly used styles:

- Harvard (Table 35.2, pages 220–221);
- Modern Languages Association (Table 35.3, pages 222–223);
- Vancouver (Table 35.4, pages 224–225);
- Chicago (Table 35.5, pages 226–228).

Software referencing packages

These can be used to fit your reference list to any of several conventions. However, it is worth reflecting on whether it is good use of your time to learn how to use a relatively complex package and key in the data to 'feed' the package, when you could achieve a similar end result with common-sense use of a list typed straight into a word-processed table, which can then be sorted alphabetically (usually sufficient for most needs).

PRACTICAL TIPS FOR CITING AND LISTING REFERENCES

Record all bibliographical details as a matter of routine. However you copy your notes – electronically, by photocopy or by writing – ensure that you record all the necessary bibliographical information, or you will waste time later on backtracking to find it.

Compile your reference list as you go along. Keep a list of the works you have read. Simply create a table or list within your software package and type in the relevant details immediately you cite the source in the text. Doing this from time to time as you write saves you having to embark on a marathon of typing at the completion of the task (a table makes the formatting easier and allows easy insertion of additional records). You will need to make a decision about your choice of reference style (page 312) at an early stage.

Don't mix referencing systems. Whichever style you use, make sure you follow its conventions to the letter, including all punctuation details. When no guidance is given, consult Table 35.1 to evaluate the possibilities.

Source quotations. If you note down a quotation speculatively for later use, make sure that you write down full reference details alongside it. Never rely on your memory for remembering reference details. Check everything and write it all down.

Check the detail. Allow plenty of time for final checking, especially consistency of layout.

Table 35.2(a) Outline of the Harvard style for citing references. This referencing system has the advantage of being simpler, quicker and possibly more readily adjustable than other systems. It is used internationally in a wide range of fields and provides author and date information in the text. Note that there are various interpretations of the style. This one generally follows BS5605:1990.

How to cite the reference in the text	How to lay out the reference list or bibliography
The cause of European integration has been further hampered by the conflict between competing interests in a range of economic activities (Roche, 2009). However, Hobart and Lyon (2012) have argued that this is a symptom of a wider disharmony which has its roots in socio-economic divisions arising from differing cultural attitudes towards the concept of the market economy. Morrison *et al.* (2011) have identified 'black market' economic activity in post-reunification Germany as one which exemplified this most markedly. Scott (2012) suggests that the black economy which existed prior to reunification operated on strong market economy principles. However, Main (2008 cited in Kay, 2010) has supported the view that black market economies are not culture dependent. Statistics presented by Johannes (2010) suggest that, in the UK, as many as 23 per cent of the population are engaged at any one time in the black economy. European-wide statistics indicate that figures for participation in the black economy may be as high as 30 per cent (Brandt, 2011).	Brandt, K-H., 2011. *Working the system* [online book]. Cardiff: Thornhill Press. Available at: http://www.hvn.ac.uk/econ/trickco.htm [Accessed 1 April 2011]. *Ferry Times*, 2012. Where the money moves. *Ferry Times*, 12 April, p. 24. Hobart, K. and Lyon, A., 2012. *Socio-economic divisions: the cultural impact*. London: Thames Press. Johannes, B., 2010. Functional economics. In M. Edouard ed., *The naked economy*. Cologne: Rhein Verlag, 2010, pp. 120–30. Kay, W., 2010. *The power of Europe*. Dover: Kentish Press. Morrison, F., Drake, C., Brunswick, M. and Mackenzie, V., 2011. *Europe of the nations*. Edinburgh: Lothian Press. Roche, P., 2009. *European economic integration*. London: Amazon Press. Saunders, C., ed., 2006. *The economics of reality*. Dublin: Shamrock Press. Scott, R., 2012. Informal integration: the case of the non-monitored economy. *Journal of European Integration Studies*, 3 (2), pp. 81–9.

Quotations in the text

The movement of money within the so-called black economy is regarded by Finance Ministers in Europe as 'a success story they could emulate' (*Ferry Times*, 12.4.11).

According to Saunders (2006, p. 82), 'black economies build businesses'.

Notes:

- In this version of the Harvard style only the first word of a title is capitalised. With the exception of proper nouns, other words are in lower case. Each entry is separated by a double line space.
- If you need to cite two (or more) pieces of work published within the same year by the same author, then the convention is to refer to these texts as 2005a, 2005b and so on.
- In some interpretations of this style the first line of every entry is indented five character spaces from the left margin. However, this can create an untidy page where it is difficult to identify the author quickly.
- Titles of books and journals are italicised.
- The first date in the internet citation is the date of publication, *if available*. Thus, the 'Accessed' date as shown in the second internet reference example will always be the same or later than the published date, never earlier.

Table 35.2(b) How to list different types of source following the Harvard style

Hard copy resources	Basic format: author surname | author initial | date | title | place of publication | publisher
Book by one author	Roche, P., 2009. *European economic integration*. London: Amazon Press.
Book by two authors	Hobart, K. and Lyon, A., 2012. *Socio-economic divisions: the cultural impact*. London: Thames Press.
Book with more than three authors	Morrison, F., Drake, C., Brunswick, M. and Mackenzie, V., 2011. *Europe of the nations*. Edinburgh: Lothian Press.
Book under editorship	Saunders, C., ed., 2006. *The economics of reality*. Dublin: Shamrock Press.
Chapter in a book	Johannes, B., 2010. *Functional economics*. In M. Edouard, ed., 2000 *The naked economy*. Cologne: Rhein Verlag, 120–30.
Secondary referencing – where the original text is not available and the reference relates to a citation in a text that you have read, then refer to the latter	Kay, W., 2010. *The power of Europe*. Dover: Kentish Press.
Journal article	Scott, R., 2012. Informal integration: the case of the non-monitored economy. *Journal of European Integration Studies*, 3 (2), 81–9.
Newspaper article	*Ferry Times*, 2012. Where the money moves. *Ferry Times*, 12 April, p. 24.
Online resources	
Internet references including e-books	Brandt, K-H. 2011. *Working the system* [online book]. Cardiff: Thornhill Press. Available from: http://www.hvn.ac.uk/econ/trickco.htm [Accessed 1 April 2011].
Internet references: e-journals online only	Ross, F., 2009. Coping with European fallout. *Journal of European Amity* [online], 5(14). Available at: http://jea,org/archive00000555/ [Accessed 11 Jan. 2010].
Journal article in print and online	Hunter, M., 2008. 'Europe: a group of friends or rivals?', *Journal of European Collaboration*, Available at: http://www.jec.org/3/35/hunter [Accessed 11 Aprill 2011].
Film, video or radio programme	Euro Yeti, 2010. Television programme. Kanal Alpha, Munich, 1st May.
Website	Transnational Co-operation Association. 2010. Available at: www.tca.org [Accessed 1st April 2012].

Notes: Further detailed discussion and layouts can be found in McMillan, K. and Weyers, J., 2012. *How to cite, reference and avoid plagiarism at university*. Harlow: Pearson Education.

For subsequent editions of a book, write the reference in the normal way, but insert the number of the edition after the title e.g. 4th ed.

Table 35.3(a) Outline of the Modern Languages Association (MLA) style for citing references.
This style provides author and page information in the text, but no date is included, only the page number(s). List alphabetically by author's surname in the works cited listing.

How to cite the reference in the text	How to lay out the works cited
The cause of European integration has been further hampered by the conflict between competing interests in a range of economic activities (Roche 180). However, Hobart and Lyon have argued that this is a symptom of a wider disharmony which has its roots in socio-economic divisions arising from differing cultural attitudes towards the concept of the market economy (101). Morrison *et al.* have identified 'black market' economic activity in post-reunification Germany as one which exemplified this most markedly (99–101). Scott suggests that the black economy which existed prior to reunification operated on strong market economy principles (83). However, Main has supported the view that black market economies are not culture dependent (qtd. in Kay 74). Statistics presented by Johannes suggest that, in the UK, as many as 23 per cent of the population are engaged at any one time as part of the black economy (121). European-wide statistics indicate that figures for participation in the black economy may be as high as 30 per cent (Brandt 12).	Brandt, K-H. 'Working the System.' Haven University 31 December 2010. Web. 1 April 2012. Hobart, K. and A. Lyon, *Socio-economic Divisions: the cultural impact*. London: Thames Press, 2012. Print. Johannes, B. 'Functional Economics.' *The Naked Economy*. Ed. M. Edouard. Cologne: Rhein Verlag, 2011: 120–30. Print. Kay, W. *The Power of Europe*. Dover: Kentish Press, 2010. Print. Morrison, F., *et al. Europe of the Nations*. Edinburgh: Lothian Press, 2011. Print. Roche, P. *European Economic Integration*. London: Amazon Press, 2009. Print. Saunders, C. ed. *The Economics of Reality*. Dublin: Shamrock Press, 2006. Print. Scott, R. 'Informal Integration: the case of the non-monitored economy.' *Journal of European Integration Studies* 2 (2012): 81–9. Print. 'Where the money moves.' *Ferry Times* 12 April 2011: 24.

Quotations in the text

The movement of money within the so-called black economy is regarded by Finance Ministers in Europe as "a success story they could emulate" (*Ferry Times* 24).

Some commentators appear to give approval to non-conventional economic activity: "black economies build businesses" (Saunders 82).

Long quotatations (normally more than four typed lines should be presented as indented text without quotation marks, that is, 2.5 cms from left margin and printed using double line spacing.

Notes:
- Successive lines for the same entry are indented by five character spaces.
- If two (or more) pieces of work published within the same year by the same author are cited, refer to these texts as 2012a, 2012b and so on.
- Titles are *italicised* (not underlined).
- MLA Style uses 'Works cited' rather than 'References'. The list should be printed on a separate sheet with the title 'Works cited' centred.
- MLA Style has discontinued use of URL's in citations for electronic resources.

Table 35.3(b) How to list different types of source following the Modern Languages Association (MLA) style

Hard copy resources	Basic Format: Author surname | author initial | title | place of publication | publisher | date | mode of publication |
Book by one author	Roche, P. *European Economic Integration*. London: Amazon Press, 2009. Print.
Book by two authors	Hobart, K. and A. Lyon. *Socio-economic Divisions: the cultural impact*. London: Thames Press, 2012. Print.
Book with more than four authors	Morrison, F. *et al. Europe of the Nations*. Edinburgh: Edinburgh City Press, 2011. Print.
Book under editorship	Saunders, C. ed. *The Economics of Reality*. Dublin: Shamrock Press, 2006. Print.
Chapter in a book	Johannes, B. "Functional Economics." *The Naked Economy*. Ed. Maurice Edouard, Cologne: Rhein Verlag, 2011. 120–130.
Anthology or collection	Henderson, J., ed. *The Euromarketplace*. Bochum: Wurtzig GMbH. 2010. Print.
Essay in a collection	Spark, L. "Talking shop" *Accessing European Networks*. Ed. A.L.R. Dyce. Glasgow: Glen Publications, 2009. 55–65. Print.
Secondary referencing*	Kay, W. *The Power of Europe*. Dover: Kentish Press, 2010. Print.
Journal article	Scott, R. "Informal Integration: the case of the non-monitored economy." *Journal of European Integration Studies* 2 (2012): 81–89. Print.
Newspaper article	"Where the money moves." *Ferry Times* 12 April 2011: 24. Print.
Online resources	
Internet reference including ebooks	Brandt, K-H. *Working the System*. Haven University 31 December 2010. Web. 1 April 2011
Internet references: e-journals online only	Ross, F. "Coping with European Fallout" *Journal of European Amity* [online only journal] 5.14 (2009) n.p. Web. 11 Jan 2010.
Journal article in print and online	Hunter, M. "Europe: a group of friends or rivals?", *Journal of European Collaboration*, 35.3 (2008): 120–129. Web. 11th April 2011
Film	*Euro Yeti*, Dir. David Royale, Perf. Ian Brown, Johan Black, Thomas Green, Antony Gray and Donna White. Kanal Alpha, 2010. DVD
Television/radio programme	"Europe and the Stars." *Euroknowledge Series*. Munich. 1 May 2011. Television.
Website	Co-operation Across Frontiers Online Transnational Co-operation Association, 2010. Web. 1 April 2012.

* Secondary referencing – where the reference relates to a citation in a text that was quoted in someone else's work, but which you have been unable to access in the original, then list only the source you read yourself.
* n.p. = no publisher   n.d. = no date
For subsequent editions of a book, write the reference in the normal way, but insert the number of the edition after the title e.g. 4th ed.

Note: Further detailed discussion and layouts can be found in McMillan, K. and Weyers, J., 2012. *How to cite, reference and avoid plagiarism at university*. Harlow: Pearson Education.

Table 35.4(a) Outline of the Vancouver style (numeric) for citing references. This system is widely used in Medicine and the Life Sciences, for example. In the text, numbers are positioned in brackets, that is, like this (1). These numbers relate to corresponding numbered references in the reference list. This style has the advantage of not interrupting the text with citation information. However, this means that the reader cannot readily identify the source without referring to the reference list. The Vancouver style resembles in some ways the style adopted by the Institute of Electrical and Electronic Engineers (IEEE).

How to cite the reference in the text	How to lay out the reference list or bibliography
The cause of European integration has been further hampered by the conflict between competing interests in a range of economic activities (1). However, Hobart and Lyon (2) have argued that this is a symptom of a wider disharmony which has its roots in socioeconomic divisions arising from differing cultural attitudes towards the concept of the market economy. Morrison *et al*. (3) have identified 'black market' economic activity in post-reunification Germany as one which exemplified this most markedly. Scott (4) suggests that the black economy which existed prior to reunification operated on strong market economy principles. However, Kay (5) has supported the view of Main that black market economies are not culture dependent. Statistics presented by Johannes (6) suggest that, in the UK, as many as 23 per cent of the population are engaged at any one time as part of the black economy. European-wide statistics indicate that figures for participation in the black economy may be as high as 30 per cent (7).	1 Roche P. European economic integration. London: Amazon Press; 2009. 2 Hobart K. and Lyon A. Socio-economic divisions: the cultural impact. London: Thames Press; 2012. 3 Morrison F., Drake C., Brunswick M. and Mackenzie V. Europe of the nations. Edinburgh: Lothian Press; 2011. 4 Scott R. Informal integration: the case of the non-monitored economy. Journal of European Integration Studies. 2012; 2, 81–9. 5 Kay W. The power of Europe. Dover: Kentish Press; 2010. 6 Johannes B. Functional economics. In Edouard M. The Naked Economy. Cologne: Rhein Verlag; 2000 p. 120–30. 7 Brandt K-H. Working the System. 2010 [cited 1 April 2011]. Available from: http://www.hvn.ac.uk/econ/trickco.htm. 8 Where the money moves. Ferry Times. 2011 April 12; 24. 9 Saunders C, editor. The economics of reality. Dublin, Shamrock Press; 2006.

Quotations in the text
The movement of money within the so-called black economy is regarded by Finance Ministers in Europe as 'a success story they could emulate' (8). According to Saunders, 'black economies build businesses' (9).

Notes:

- If two (or more) pieces of work published within the same year by the same author are cited, refer to these texts as 1999a, 1999b and so on.
- In some interpretations of this style, superscript numbers [8] are used instead of the full-size number in brackets (8) shown in the example in Table 35.4(a).
- In this system, titles are *not* italicised and only initial letter of first word is capitalised, unless a proper noun is used in the title.
- If a source is repeated, the number reference is reused for each occurrence of the repetition, regardless of its previous position in the text.

Table 35.4(b) How to list different types of source following the Vancouver style

Hard copy resources [# to demonstrate number of citation in the text]	The Reference List or Bibliography following the Vancouver style
	Basic Format: Author surname | author initial | title | place of publication | publisher | date |
Book by one author	# Roche P. <u>European economic integration</u>. London: Amazon Press, 2009.
Book by two authors	# Hobart K. Lyon A. <u>Socio-economic divisions: the cultural impact</u>. London, Thames Press, 2012.
Book with more than three authors	# Morrison F, Drake C, Brunswick M, and Mackenzie V. <u>Europe of the nations</u>. Edinburgh, Edinburgh City Press, 2011.
Book under editorship	# Saunders C, editor. <u>The Economics of reality</u>. Dublin, Shamrock Press, 2006.
Chapter in a book	# Johannes B. *Functional Economics*. In: Edouard, M. <u>The naked economy</u>. Cologne: Rhein Verlag; 2000.
Secondary referencing *	# Kay W. <u>The power of Europe</u>. Dover: Kentish Press; 2010.
Journal article	# Scott R. Informal integration: the case of the non-monitored economy. <u>Journal of European Integration Studies</u>. 2012; 2: 81–89.
Newspaper article	# Where the money moves. <u>Ferry Times</u>. 2011 April 12; 24.
Online resources	
Internet reference: e-books	# Dohmen W. Working for Europe. [book on the internet]. Brighton: Rock Press; 2011 [cited 2012 Apr 1]. Available from: http://www.brpress.org/dohmen/12/2011/
Internet reference: e-journal online only	# Hunter MM. Europe: a group of friends or rivals? J Ethical Enquiries 2010 [cited 2012 Oct 22]; 252 [about 10 screens]. Available from: http://www.ethicalenquiries.org/content/hunter/192784/
Journal article online in print and online	# Jenson TA. Europeans on the move. Migrant Working Association [Internet] 2010 August; [cited 2012 February 14]; 3(2): 199–208. Available from http://www.mwa.ac/vol3/issue2/199/
Video recording	# *Europeans going it alone*. [DVD] Bern: Alpine Productions; 2010.
Website	# Duncan SJ. Designing Europe. [Internet]. [Place unknown]: Transnational Co-operation Associates; 2009 [updated 2011 Dec. 14; cited January 2012]. Available from: www.tca.org

* Secondary referencing: where you have read information cited in a book you have read but which you have not been able to source in order to read it for yourself; in this case list the book you have read personally.

Note: Further detailed discussion and layouts can be found in McMillan, K. and Weyers, J., 2012. *How to cite, reference and avoid plagiarism at university*. Harlow: Pearson Education.

Table 35.5(a) Outline of the Chicago style (scientific) for citing references. This footnote style of referencing enables the reader to see the full bibliographical information on the first page the reference is made, but subsequent references to the same source do not give the same detail. If the full bibliographical information is not given in the footnote for some reason, a full bibliography is given at the end of the work. To save space here, this example has been laid out in single-line spacing. The *Chicago Manual of Style* (2010) stipulates double-space throughout – texts, notes and bibliography.

How to cite the reference in the text	Quotations in the text
The cause of European integration has been further hampered by the conflict between competing interests in a range of economic activities.[1] However, Hobart and Lyon[2] have argued that this is a symptom of a wider disharmony which has its roots in socio-economic divisions arising from differing cultural attitudes towards the concept of the market economy. Morrison *et al.*[3] have identified 'black market' economic activity in post-reunification Germany as one which exemplified this most markedly. Scott[4] suggests, however, that the black economy which existed prior to reunification operated on strong market economy principles, while Main[5] has supported the view that black market economies are not culture dependent. Statistics presented by Johannes[6] suggest that as many as 23 per cent of the population are engaged at any one time as part of the black economy. This does not support the findings of Hobart and Lyon,[7] but it has been suggested by Scott[8] that this is probably an exaggerated statistic which it is impossible to verify. Scott[9] estimates a more modest 10 per cent of people of working age are actively involved in the black economy. Brandt[10] has conducted research into the phenomenon of the black economies of Europe but has been unable to confirm such estimates.	The movement of money within the so-called black economy is regarded by Finance Ministers in Europe as "a success story they could emulate".[11] According to Saunders, "black economies build businesses".[12] [11] "Where the money moves." *Ferry Times*, (Edinburgh) 12 April 2011, 24. [12] C. Saunders, ed. *The Economics of Reality* (Dublin: Shamrock Press, 2006), 82.
[1] P. Roche, *European Economic Integration* (London: Amazon Press, 2009), 180. [2] K. Hobart, and A. Lyon, *Socio-economic Divisions: The Cultural Impact* (London: Thames Press, 2012), 101. [3] F. Morrison, et al. *Europe of the Nations* (Edinburgh: Lothian Press, 2011), 99. [4] R. Scott, "Informal Integration: the case of the non-monitored economy," Journal of European Integration Studies, 2 (2012): 81. [5] K. Main, *Power, Politics and People* (Plymouth: Maritime Press Co., 2008), 74, quoted in W. Kay, *The Power of Europe* (Dover: Kentish Press, 2010) 218. [6] B. Johannes, "Functional Economics" in *The Naked Economy*, ed. M. Edouard, 121 (Cologne: Rhein Verlag, 2010). [7] Hobart and Lyon *op. cit.,* 102. [8] Scott, *op. cit.,* 83. [9] *Ibid.* [10] K-H. Brandt, "Working the System." last modified Sep 30, 2010, http://www.hvn.ac.uk/econ/trickco.htm.	**How to lay out the reference list or bibliography (note that layout differs for the footnotes)** Brandt, K-H. "Working the System." Last modified September 30, 2010 http://www.hvn.ac.uk/econ/trickco.htm. Hobart, K. and Lyon, A. *Socio-economic Divisions: The Cultural Impact.* London: Thames Press, 2012. Johannes, B. "Functional Economics" in *The Naked Economy*, edited by M. Edouard Cologne: Rhein Verlag, 2010. Main, K. "*Power, Politics and People*". Plymouth: Maritime Press Co., 2008, quoted in W. Kay, *The Power of Europe.* Dover: Kentish Press, 2010, 218. Morrison, F., et al. *Europe of the Nations.* Edinburgh: Lothian Press, 2011. Roche, P. *European Economic Integration.* London: Amazon Press, 2009. Saunders, C., ed. *The Economics of Reality.* Dublin: Shamrock Press, 2006. Scott, R. 'Informal Integration: the case of the non-monitored economy,' *Journal of European Integration Studies* 2, No. 1 (2012), 81–9. 'Where the money moves,' *Ferry Times*, (Edinburgh) 12 April 2011, 24.

Table 35.5(b) How to list different types of source following the Chicago style (16th edition)

The Chicago style uses footnote style referencing. Below are the references as these would appear in the *footnotes*. Note that the layout differs for the presentation of the information in a *bibliography* using the Chicago style.

Hard copy resources # symbol denotes number of footnote	Basic Footnote format: # Author initial | author surname| title | (place of publication | publisher | date of publication) | page number | Listed in numerical order as marked in text.	Basic reference list format: author surname | author initial | date | title | place of publication | publisher | **Listed in alphabetical order by author surname.**
Book by one author	# P. Roche, *European Economic Integration* (London: Amazon Press, 2009), 180.	Roche, P. *European Economic Integration*. London: Amazon Press, 2009.
Book by two authors	# K. Hobart, and A. Lyon, *Socio-economic Divisions: the cultural impact* (London: Thames Press, 20‑2), 101.	Hobart, K. and A. Lyon. *Socio-economic Divisions: the cultural impact*. London: Thames Press, 2012.
Book with four or more authors	# F. Morrison et al., *Europe of the Nations* (Edinburgh: Lothian Press, 2011), 99.	Morrison, F.,* C. Drake, M. Brunswick, and V. Mackenzie. *Europe of the Nations*. Edinburgh: Lothian Press, 2011, 95–101.* alternatively: Morrison, F. et al.
Book under editorship	# C. Saunders, ed. *The Economics of Reality* (Dublin: Shamrock Press, 2006), 82.	Saunders, C, ed. *The Economics of Reality*. Dublin: Shamrock Press, 2006.
Chapter in a book	# B. Johannes, "Functional Economics," in *The Naked Economy* ed. Maurice Edouard 121 (Cologne: Rhein Verlag, 2000).	Johannes, B. "Functional Economics." In *The Naked Economy*, edited by Maurice Eduard. Cologne: Rhein Verlag, 2010.
Secondary referencing	# Main, K. "Power, Politics and People " (2008), quoted in W. Kay, *The Power of Europe* (Dover: Kentish Press, 2010), 218.	Main, K. "Power, Politics and People." (2008). Quoted in W. Kay *The Power of Europe*. Dover: Kentish Press, 2010, 218.
Journal article	# R. Scott, "Informal Integration: the case of the non-monitored economy," *Journal of European Integration Studies*, 2 No. 1 (2012): 81.	Scott, R. "Informal Integration: the case of the non-monitored economy." *Journal of European Integration Studies*. 2 No. 1 (2012): 81–96.
Newspaper article	# Craig L. Scott, "Where the money moves," *Ferry Times*, (Edinburgh) April 12, 2011, Financial section.	Scott, C.L. "Where the money moves." *Ferry Times*, (Edinburgh) April 12, 2011.

continued overleaf

Table 35.5(b) *(cont'd)*

Hard copy resources # symbol denotes number of footnote	The Chicago style uses footnote style referencing. Below are the references as these would appear in the *footnotes*. Note that the layout differs for the presentation of the information in a *bibliography* using the Chicago style.	
	Basic Footnote format: # Author initial | author surname| title | (place of publication | publisher | date of publication) | page number | *Listed in numerical order as marked in text.*	**Basic reference list format: author surname | author initial | date | title | place of publication | publisher |** *Listed in alphabetical order by author surname.*
Online resources		
Internet reference: including e-books	# Willi Dohmen, *Working for Europe* (Brighton: Rock Press; 2011), doi: 10-006/500878-010-0120-6	Dohmen, Willi. *Working for Europe.* Brighton: Rock Press, 2011. doi: 10-006/500878-010-0120-6
Internet reference: e-journal online only	# Moyna Hunter, "Europe: a group of friends or rivals?" J Ethical Enquiries, 24 No. 5, 276, accessed Oct 22, 2012, www.ethicalenquiries.org/contents/hunter/192784.	Hunter M.M. "Europe: a group of friends or rivals?" *J Ethical Enquiries* 24 No. 5 (2010): 252–77 Accessed Oct 22 2012. http://www.ethicalenquiries.org/content/hunter/192784/
Journal article online in print and online	# Thomas A. Jenson, "Europeans on the move." Migrant Working Association 3 no. 2 (2010): 199, accessed February 14, 2012, http://www.mwa.ac/Vol3/issue2/199/.	Jenson, T.A. "Europeans on the move." Migrant Working Association 3 No. 2 (2010): 199–210. Accessed February 14, 2012. http://www.mwa.ac/uk/Vol3/issue2/199.
Film, video or radio programme	# *Europeans going it alone,* Film, directed by Berndt Brenner Bern: Alpine Productions, 2010.	*Europeans going it alone.* Produced and directed by Berndt Brenner. Film. Bern: Alpine Productions, 2010.
Website	# "Designing Europe," Transnational Co-operation Associates Last modified December 14, 2011, http://www.tca.org.	"Designing Europe." Transnational Co-operation Associates Last modified December 14, 2011. http://tca.org.

Notes:

- Uses superscript numbers or full-size numbers within brackets in the text ordered consecutively. These relate to a footnote on the same page as the reference. Where references are repeated, then a new number is assigned each time it occurs in the text. Place the number **after a punctuation mark.**
- If you need to cite two (or more) pieces of work published within the same year by the same author, then refer to these texts as 2012a, 2012b and so on.
- Some abbreviations are used in this style. They are printed in italics, because these are Latin. The most commonly used are op. cit. (in the work already cited) and ibid.(in the same place – usually in the same place as the last fully cited reference.) Thus, in the example above [9] relates to [8] which, in turn, relates to [4].
- In the footnotes the author's first name or initial precedes the surname.
- Second or further lines in the Reference or Bibliography list should be indented five character spaces.
- For secondary referencing, when compiling the reference list cite both articles – the original source and the one that contained the reference (the source you read).
- Further detailed discussion, layouts and styles can be found in McMillan, K. and Weyers, J., 2012. *How to cite, reference and avoid plagiarism at university.* Harlow: Pearson Education.

36

PLAGIARISM AND COPYRIGHT INFRINGEMENT

How to avoid being accused of 'stealing' the ideas and work of others

Many students have only a vague understanding of plagiarism and copyright issues. However, failing to take account of these matters means you may risk serious disciplinary action.

Plagiarism and copyright are two related topics that are extremely important academically and legally, but which are often misunderstood by students. They have become more significant in recent years due to technological advances such as digital scanners, photocopiers and electronic file exchange, which make it simple to 'cut and paste' and copy materials. This means it is easier to commit the offence of plagiarism unknowingly. You need to be fully aware of the issues involved so you can acknowledge intellectual property appropriately and avoid losing marks or being involved in further disciplinary action.

WHAT IS PLAGIARISM?

Plagiarism can be defined as: 'the unacknowledged use of another's work as if it were one's own' (University of Dundee, 2005).

Alongside other forms of academic dishonesty, universities regard intentional plagiarism as a very serious offence. The regulations normally prescribe a range of penalties depending on the severity of the case, from a simple reduction in marks, to the ultimate sanctions of exclusion from the university or refusal to award a degree. You will find the exact penalties for your institution specified in departmental or school handbooks.

Plagiarism is thus something to be avoided, and it is assumed that no one would deliberately set out to cheat in this way. The problem is that it is easy to plagiarise unwittingly. Regarding such 'unintentional plagiarism', you should note the following:

- The concept of 'work' in the definition of plagiarism given above includes ideas, writing or inventions, and not simply words.
- The notion of 'use' in the definition does not only mean 'word for word' (an exact copy) but also 'in substance' (a paraphrase of the notions involved).
- Use of another's work *is* acceptable, *if* you acknowledge the source.

The first two of these aspects give an indication of the potential dangers for students, but the third provides a remedy. To avoid the risk of unintentional plagiarism, adopt the following advice: if you think a particular author has said something particularly well, quote them directly *and* provide a reference to the relevant article or book beside the quote (**Ch 35**).

Cutting and pasting

The practice of cutting (copying) and pasting electronically (for example, taking material from websites) and using this in an essay or other piece of work without citing it is regarded as plagiarism and will be punished if detected. Universities now have sophisticated electronic means of identifying where this has occurred.

Note that the convention in academic writing is to use inverted commas (and sometimes italics) to signify clearly that a quotation is being made. The reference or citation is generally given in one of several standard forms: some examples are given in Table 35.1.

Punishments for copying

Copying an essay or other piece of work by a fellow student (past or present) is cheating. The punishment is often an assessment mark of zero *for both parties*, and further disciplinary measures may be taken. If you let someone copy your work, you are regarded as just as culpable as the 'real' cheat – so consider the risk to your academic future if you misguidedly allow someone to copy your work.

STRATEGIES TO ENSURE THAT YOU AVOID PLAGIARISM

Once you have identified the source material that you wish to use in your assignment, you will need to identify the function that the citations related to this material will perform in your work. For example, you will need to ask yourself whether the text you wish to cite endorses an idea, contradicts it or is neutral. In some cases you will need to make a decision about how you will incorporate the ideas from your source material within your own text. There are essentially three options:

- Quoting
- Summarising
- Paraphrasing

Characteristics of these methods of using sources are shown in Table 36.1.

How much quotation is acceptable?

Too much quotation is regarded as plagiarism, even if all the source information is provided. Aim to limit use of quotation to 10 per cent of the total work as an absolute maximum. In many cases the proportion will be well below the threshold.

Table 36.1 Characteristics that typify quoting, summarising and paraphrasing

	Characteristics
For quotation (see **Ch 35**)	• 'short' quotes – include in the text • 'long quotes' (usually 30+ or 40+ words) in some style guides require to be indented; in others they may be italicised and indented. • Punctuation conventions – Single quotation marks (British English) – Double quotation marks (American English)
For summarising	• Broad overview, briefly stating the main points from the original • Less detailed than a paraphrase • Ideas expressed using your own words • Technical terms can be retained, but otherwise ideas are expressed using different sentence structure and vocabulary
For paraphrasing	• Broad theme condensed from the original • More detailed than a summary • Ideas expressed using your own words • Technical terms can be retained but otherwise ideas are expressed using different sentence structure and vocabulary

Regardless of which of these approaches you choose to adopt, within the layout conventions of the citation and referencing style you are expected to adopt (**Ch 35**), you will require the following information:

- Author
- Date
- Title
- Place of publication
- Publisher
- Page number(s).

HOW TO PARAPHRASE

1 Read the text to establish overall meaning; it may help to use the speed-reading strategy of reading *topic sentences* first of all to gain this overview (see **Ch 25**).

2 Turn over the text and note down key ideas.

3 Reread the text intensively for greater detail.

4 Turn over the text and, from memory, note points that support the key ideas. This encourages you to use your own words and makes you less dependent on words from the text.

5 Note how you intend to use these ideas in your work.

6 Record bibliographical details for your reference list (see **Ch 35**).

Sometimes it is helpful when constructing paraphrased text to begin with the concluding idea of the text and work through the key ideas from that perspective, rather than in the logic sequence of the original. In this way you are less likely to lapse into the pitfalls of word substitution or over-quotation.

EXAMPLES OF SUMMARISING AND PARAPHRASING

The excerpt of original text in Table 36.2 represents material that a student might wish to use in relation to an assignment on the relative merits of e-books and traditional bound volumes, demonstrating poor and good examples of summarising and paraphrasing technique.

Avoid a word substitution exercise when citing the work of others either in summarising or in paraphrasing: this is plagiarism. You need to show that you have engaged in a critical analysis of the material and demonstrate this by using the citation material to good effect in structuring your discussion. In the good models shown in Table 36.2, the writer has processed the ideas from the original text and presented them in a fresh manner, demonstrating engagement with the meaning of the original text and hence independent thinking.

Table 36.2 Examples of summarising and paraphrasing

Original text:		
E-books are a function of the internet era and make access to otherwise unattainable material possible to wide audiences. The globalisation of literature means that individual authors can present their work to a wider audience without incurring abortive publication costs. This facility constitutes a considerable threat to publishers of traditional books. *Source:* Watt, W. (2006) *The demise of the book.* Dundee: Riverside Press. (p. 13)		
Summarising		
Poor model of summarising	**Explanation**	**Good model of summarising**
It has been suggested that **'e-books are a function of the internet era'** and that **'globalisation of literature'** allows authors to **'present their work to a wider audience'** without having to incur **'abortive publication costs'**.	*In this example, direct quotation (shown in bold) comprises 60 per cent of the total word count – this is excessive and could be regarded as a form of plagiarism. This fault is compounded because the writer has failed to give the source of the quotations.*	With the advent of e-books, individual authors are faced with new approaches to publication of their work (Watt, 2006).
Paraphrasing		
Poor model	**Explanation**	**Good model**
E-books are part of the internet *age* and allow people from all over the *globe* to use them. This *means that writers show* their *writing* on the internet and so they *do not have such high publishing costs*. This *feature* means that *publishers of old-fashioned books* are *under threat* (Watt, 2006).	*In this example, use of synonyms (underlined) in a superficial manner constitutes another form of plagiarism. Despite correctly citing the source, the writer has simply 'stolen' the essential meaning without engaging in any analysis or original thinking.*	Watt (2006) notes that there is concern amongst publishers of hard-copy printed books that the advent of e-books marks the end of their monopoly of the literature market, since authors can publish directly on the internet, thus avoiding publishing costs.

WHAT IS COPYRIGHT INFRINGEMENT?

Copyright law 'allows you to protect your original material and stop others from using your work without your permission' (Intellectual Property Office, 2009). Copyright infringement is regarded as equivalent to stealing, and legal rights are sometimes jealously guarded by companies with the resources to prosecute.

In the UK, authors have literary copyright over their material for their life, and their estate has copyright for a further 70 years. Publishers have typographical copyright for 25 years. This is why the copyright symbol © is usually accompanied by a date and the owner's name. You'll find this information on the publication details page at the start of a book. See p. iv of this book for an example.

Use of the copyright logo

The © symbol indicates that someone is drawing your attention to the fact that something is copyright. However, even if © does not appear, the material may still be copyright.

You will be at risk of breaking the law if you copy (for example, photocopy, digitally scan or print out) material to which someone else owns the copyright, unless you have their express permission, or unless the amount you copy falls within the limits accepted for 'fair dealing'.

'Educational copying', *for non-commercial private study or research*, is sometimes allowed by publishers (they will state this on the material, and may allow multiple copies to be made). Otherwise, for single copies *for private study or research*, you should only copy what would fall under the 'fair dealing' provision, for which there is no precise definition in law.

Private study or research

This means what it says: the limits discussed here apply to that use and not to commercial or other uses, such as photocopying an amusing article for your friends. Copying of software and music CDs (including 'sharing' of MP3 files) is most often illegal, although you are usually permitted to make a *personal* back-up copy of a track or CD you already own.

Approved copyright exceptions

Some copying for academic purposes may be licensed by the Copyright Licensing Agency (CLA) on behalf of authors. Other electronically distributed material may be licensed through the HERON (Higher Education Resources On-Demand) scheme. In these cases you may be able to copy or print out more than the amounts listed opposite, including multiple copies. Your university may also 'buy in' to licensing schemes, such as those offered by the NLA (Newspaper Licensing Agency) and the Performing Rights Society. As these can refer to very specific sources, consult your library's staff if in doubt.

Established practice suggests that you should copy no more than 5 per cent of the work involved, or:

- one chapter of a book;
- one article per volume of an academic journal;
- 20 per cent (to a maximum of 20 pages) of a short book;
- one poem or short story (maximum of 10 pages) from an anthology;
- one separate illustration or map up to A4 size (note: illustrations that are parts of articles and chapters may be included in the allowances noted above);
- short excerpts of musical works – not whole works or movements (note: copying of any kind of public performance is not allowed without permission).

These limits apply to single copies – you can't take multiple copies of any of the above items, nor pass on a single copy for multiple copying to someone else, who may be in ignorance of the source or of specific or general copyright issues.

In legal terms, it doesn't matter whether you paid for the source or not: copyright is infringed when the whole or a substantial part is copied without permission – and 'substantial' here can mean a qualitatively significant section even if this is a small part of the whole.

The same rules apply to printing or copying material on the web unless the author gives explicit (that is, written) clearance. This applies to copying images as well as text from the internet, although a number of sites do offer copyright-free images. A statement on the author's position on copying may appear on the home page or a page linked directly from it.

---

i   Complexity of copyright law

Note that the material in this chapter is a summary of some basic aspects of a complex body of law, and much may depend on individual circumstances.

PRACTICAL TIPS FOR AVOIDING PLAGIARISM

Avoid copying material by electronic means. You may only do this if you are prepared to quote the source. If you use the material in your work, and fail to add an appropriate citation, this would be regarded as cheating.

When making notes, always write down your sources. You may risk plagiarising if you cannot recall or find the source of a piece of text. Avoid this by getting into the habit of making a careful note of the source on the same piece of paper that you used to summarise or copy it out. Always use quote marks ('. . .') when taking such notes verbatim from texts and other materials, to indicate that what you have written down is a *direct copy* of the words used, as you may forget this at a later time. You do not need to quote directly in the final version of your work, but if you paraphrase you should still cite the source.

Try not to paraphrase another person's work too closely. Taking key phrases and rearranging them, or merely substituting some words with synonyms is still regarded as plagiarism.

Follow the academic custom of quoting sources. You should do this even if you prefer to use your own wording rather than a direct copy of the original. The reference to the source signifies that you are making that statement on the basis of the ideas reported there. If you are unclear about the different methods of mentioning sources and constructing a reference list, consult Ch 35.

Avoid overuse of quotations. Plagiarism still occurs if a considerable percentage of your assignment is made up of quotations. In general, quotations should be used sparingly. In some referencing styles, the convention is that where more than 10% of the text is quotation, then plagiarism has occurred.

Double-check on your 'original' ideas. If you have what you think is a novel idea, do not simply accept that your brainwave is unique. It's common for people to forget the original source of an idea, which may resurface in their mind after many years and perhaps in a different context – this may have happened to you. Think carefully about possible sources that you may have forgotten about; ask others (such as your tutor or supervisor) whether they have come across the idea before; and consult relevant texts, encyclopaedias or the internet.

Read the documentation about photocopying often displayed by photocopiers in university libraries. This will provide detailed information about current legislation and local exceptions. Be aware also that libraries monitor usage/printing of online resources as part of their subscription obligations. If one person copies/prints over the permitted amount, then the library could have its very expensive subscription terminated. If you are unsure, then ask one of the librarians for advice.

37

ACADEMIC WRITING STYLE

How to adopt the appropriate language conventions

Writing for academic purposes is a vital skill, yet the stylistic codes you need to follow are rarely comprehensively defined. This chapter will help you understand what it means to write in an academic style and outlines some forms of language to avoid.

At university, you will be assessed in a number of ways, but this assessment will most commonly involve producing a piece of written work. This assignment could take several forms, such as an essay, a report, a project portfolio, a case study or a dissertation (**Ch 32, Ch 45**). One thing that is common to all these types of writing is that they need to follow academic style. While it is possible to identify differences between 'scientific' and 'humanities' styles in the finer detail, this chapter covers the common features of all types of academic writing.

WHAT IS ACADEMIC STYLE?

Academic style involves the use of precise and objective language to express ideas. It must be grammatically correct, and is more formal than the style used in novels, newspapers, informal correspondence and everyday conversation. This should mean that the language is clear and simple. It does not imply that it is complex, pompous and dry. Above all, academic style is *objective*, using language techniques that maintain an impersonal tone and a vocabulary that is more succinct, rather than involving personal, colloquial, or idiomatic expressions.

i British English (BE) versus American English (AE)

Academic writing in the UK nearly always adopts BE. The differences are most evident in spelling; for example, 'colour' (BE) and 'color' (AE). However, there are also differences in vocabulary, so that in AE people talk of 'professor' for 'lecturer'; and in language use, so that in AE someone might write 'we have gotten results', rather than 'we have obtained results'. In some disciplines, there is an attempt at standardisation, for example, in chemistry the spelling of 'sulphur' (BE) has become 'sulfur' (AE) as the international standard.

BEING OBJECTIVE

When writing academically, it is important that your personal involvement with your topic does not overshadow the importance of what you are commenting on or reporting. The main way of demonstrating this lack of bias is by using impersonal language. This means:

● Avoiding personal pronouns – try not to use the following words:

   I/me/one   you (singular and plural)   we/us.

● Using the passive rather than active voice – try to write about the action and not about the actor (the person who performed the action – see Information Box below).

Passive and active voice

This is best explained from examples:

■ Pressure was applied to the wound to stem bleeding. (passive)

■ We applied pressure to the wound to stem bleeding. (active)

Some would argue that the second example is clearer, but their opponents would counter-argue that the use of 'we' takes attention away from the action.

You may find that the grammar checkers in some word-processing packages suggest that passive expressions should be changed to active. However, if you follow this guidance, you will find yourself having to use a personal pronoun, which is inconsistent with impersonal academic style. If in doubt, ask your tutors for their preference.

You can use other strategies to maintain an impersonal style in your writing. For general statements, you could use a structure such as 'it is . . .', 'there is . . .' or 'there are . . .' to introduce sentences. However, beginning a paragraph with 'it' is not advised as, by definition, this word has to refer to a preceding word or idea; a new paragraph introduces a new point. To avoid the initial 'it' position, change the sentence around so that 'It is important to note . . .' becomes 'The important point to note is . . .'.

For more specific points relating to statements you have already made, you could use the structures 'this is . . .' or 'these are . . .'; 'that is . . .' or 'those are . . .' with appropriate tense changes according to the context. When you use words like 'it', 'this', 'these', 'that' or 'those', there should be no ambiguity over the word or phrase to which they refer. Hence, to ensure clarity, it is better to use this/these/that/those followed by a *noun* (often defining a generic group), for example, 'this *evidence* suggests . . .' or 'these *data* imply . . .' (see Table 39.2).

Another way in which you can maintain objectivity by writing impersonally is to change the verb in the sentence to a noun and then reframe the sentence in a less personal way. You can see how this works in the example below.

This kind of text-juggling will become second nature as you tackle more and more assignments.

Transformation into noun expression

   We **applied** pressure to the wound to stem bleeding. (verb in bold)

   The **application** of pressure stemmed bleeding. (noun in bold)

APPROPRIATE USE OF TENSE

The past tense is used in academic writing to describe or comment on things that have already happened. However, there are times when the present tense is appropriate. For example, in a report (**Ch 54**) you might write 'Figure 5 shows . . .', rather than 'Figure 5 showed . . .', when describing your results. A materials and methods section, on the other hand, will always be in the past tense, because it describes what you *did*.

In colloquial English, there is often a tendency to misuse tenses. This can creep into academic assignments, especially where the author is narrating a sequence of events. For example:

> Napoleon **orders** his troops to advance on Moscow. The severe winter **closes** in on them and they **come back** a ragbag of an army. (present tense in bold)

Instead of:

> Napoleon **ordered** his troops to advance on Moscow. The severe winter **closed** in on them and they **came back** a ragbag of an army. (simple past tense in bold)

While the first of these examples might work with the soundtrack of a documentary on Napoleon's Russian campaign, it is too colloquial for academic written formats.

---

i Plain English

There has been a growing movement in recent times that advocates the use of 'plain English', and it has been very successful in persuading government departments and large commercial organisations to simplify written material for public reference. This has been achieved by introducing a less formal style of language that uses simpler, more active sentence structures, and a simpler range of vocabulary avoiding jargon. This is an admirable development. However, academic writing style needs to be precise, professional and unambiguous, and the strategies of 'plain English' campaigners may not be entirely appropriate to the style expected of you as an academic author. For the same reasons, some of the suggestions offered by software packages may be inappropriate to your subject and academic conventions.

✓ Non-sexist language

The Council of Europe recommends that, where possible, gender-specific language is avoided. Thus: 'S/he will provide specimens for her/his exam'. This is rather clumsy, but, by transforming the sentence into the plural, this is avoided, thus, 'They will provide specimens for their exams'.

Alternatively, if appropriate, 'you/your' could be used.

USE OF APPROPRIATE VOCABULARY

The 'plain English' movement (see Information Box above) recommends that words of Latin origin should be replaced by their Anglo-Saxon, or spoken, alternatives. However, this does not always contribute to the style and precision appropriate to academic authorship. For example, compare:

If we **turn down** the volume, there will be no feedback.

and

If we **turn down** the offer from the World Bank, interest rates will rise.

Both sentences make sense, but they use the two-word verb 'turn down' in different senses. These verbs are properly called phrasal verbs and they often have more than a single meaning. Furthermore, they are also used more in speech than in formal writing. Therefore, it would be better to write:

If we **reduce** the volume, there will be no feedback.

and

If we **reject** the offer from the World Bank, interest rates will rise.

By using 'reduce' and 'reject' the respective meanings are clear, concise and unambiguous. If you are restricted to a word limit on your work, using the one-word verb has additional obvious advantages. Table 39.2 on page 255–6 gives you the chance to explore some further two-word verbs and their one-word equivalents. **Ch 42** examines other areas of vocabulary usage and development.

TRANSFORMING NON-ACADEMIC TO ACADEMIC LANGUAGE

Thinking about the style of your writing should be a feature of any review you make of drafts of your written work (**Ch 43**) Table 37.1 gives a specific example of text conversion from informal to formal style. Table 37.2 provides several pointers to help you achieve a more academic style.

Table 37.1 Example of converting a piece of 'non-academic' writing into academic style. Note that the conversion results in a slightly longer piece of text (47 versus 37 words); this emphasises the point that while you should aim for concise writing (**Ch 32**), precise wording may be more important.

Original text (non-academic style)	'Corrected' text (academic style)
In this country, we have changed the law so that the King or Queen is less powerful since the Great War. But he or she can still advise, encourage or warn the Prime Minister if they want.	In the United Kingdom, legislation has been a factor in the decline of the role of the monarchy in the period since the Great War. Nevertheless, the monarchy has survived and, thus, the monarch continues to exercise the right to advise, encourage and warn the Prime Minister.
Points needing correction	**Corrected points**
• Non-specific wording (*this country*)	• Specific wording (*in the United Kingdom*)
• Personal pronoun (*we*)	• Impersonal language (*legislation has*)
• Weak grammar (*but* is a connecting word and should not be used to start a sentence).	• Appropriate signpost word (*nevertheless*)
• Word with several meanings (*law*)	• Generic, yet well-defined term (*legislation*)
• Duplication of nouns (*king or queen*)	• Singular abstract term (*monarchy*)
• Inconsistent and potentially misleading pronoun use (*he or she, they*)	• Repeated subject (*monarchy*) and reconstructed sentence
• Informal style (*can still*)	• More formal style (*continues to exercise*)

Table 37.2 Fundamentals of academic writing. These elements of academic writing are typically problematic in student writing. They are laid out in alphabetical order. Being aware of these and training yourself to follow them will help you to develop as an academic author and will ensure that you don't lose marks by making some basic errors of usage or expression.

Abbreviations and acronyms
It is acceptable to use abbreviations in academic writing to express units, for example, SI units. Otherwise, abbreviations are generally reserved for note-taking. Thus, avoid: e.g. (for example), i.e. (that is), viz. (namely) in formal work.   Acronyms are a kind of abbreviation formed by taking the initial letters of a name of an organisation, a procedure or an apparatus, and then using these letters as words in their own right instead of writing out the title in full. Thus, World Health Organisation becomes WHO. The academic convention is that the first time that you use a title with an abbreviation or acronym alternative, then you should write it in full with the abbreviation in brackets immediately after the full title. Thereafter, within that document you can use the abbreviated form. For example: The European Free Trade Association (EFTA) has close links with the European Community (EC). Both EFTA and the EC require new members to have membership of the Council of Europe as a prerequisite for admission to their organisations.   In some forms of academic writing, for example formal reports, you may be expected to include a list of abbreviations in addition to these first-time-of-use explanations.

'Absolute' terms
In academic writing, it is important to be cautious about using absolute terms such as: **always** and **never**   **most** and **all**   **least** and **none**   This does not prevent you from using these words; it simply means that they should be used with caution, that is, when you are absolutely certain of your ground (see page 127).

Clichés
Living languages change and develop over time. This means that some expressions come into such frequent usage that they lose their meaning; indeed, they can often be replaced with a much less long-winded expression. For example: **first and foremost** (first)   **last but not least** (finally)   **at this point in time** (now)   This procedure is the **gold standard** of hip replacement methods. (This procedure is the best hip replacement method.)   In the second example, 'gold standard' is completely inappropriate; correctly used, it should refer to monetary units, but it has been misused by being introduced into other contexts.

Colloquial language
This term encompasses informal language that is common in speech. Colloquialisms and idiomatic language should not be used in academic writing. This example shows how colloquial language involving cliché and idiom has been misused: **Not to beat about the bush**, increasing income tax did the Chancellor **no good at the end of the day** and he **was ditched** at the next Cabinet reshuffle. (Increasing income tax did not help the Chancellor and he was replaced at the next Cabinet reshuffle.)

Table 37.2 (*cont'd*)

'Hedging' language

For academic purposes, it is often impossible to state categorically that something is or is not the case. There are verbs that allow you to 'hedge your bets' by not coming down on one side or another of an argument, or which allow you to present a variety of different scenarios without committing yourself to any single position:

    seems that   **looks as if**   **suggests that**   **appears that**

This involves using a language construction that leaves the reader with the sense that the evidence presented is simply supporting a hypothetical, or imaginary, case. To emphasise this sense of 'hedging', the use of a special kind of verb is introduced. These modal verbs are:

    can/cannot   **could/could not**   **may/may not**   **might/might not**

These can be used with a variety of other verbs to increase the sense of tentativeness. For example:

    These results **suggest** that there has been a decline in herring stocks in the North Sea.

Even more tentatively, this could be:

    These results **could suggest** that there has been a decline in herring stocks in the North Sea.

Jargon and specialist terms

Most subjects make use of language in a way that is exclusive to that discipline. It is important, therefore, to explain terms that a general reader might not understand. It is always good practice to define specialist terms or 'regular' words that are being used in a very specific way.

Rhetorical questions

Some writers use direct rhetorical questions as a stylistic vehicle to introduce the topic addressed by the question. This is a good strategy if you are making a speech and it can have some power in academic writing, although it should be used sparingly. Example:

    How do plants survive in dry weather?

becomes

    Understanding how plants survive in dry weather is important. (Note: no question mark needed.)

Split infinitives

The most commonly quoted split infinitive comes from the TV series *Star Trek* where Captain James T. Kirk states that the aim of the Star Ship Enterprise is 'to boldly go where no man has gone before'. This means that an adverb (boldly) has split the infinitive (to go). It should read as 'to go boldly'. Many traditionalists consider that the split infinitive is poor English, although modern usage increasingly ignores the rule. Nevertheless, it is probably better to avoid the split infinitive in academic writing, which tends to be particularly traditional.

Value judgements

These are defined as statements in which the author or speaker is imposing their views or values on to the reader. For example, a writer who states that 'Louis XIV was a rabid nationalist' without giving supporting evidence for this statement is not making an objective comment in a professional manner. Rewording this statement to: 'Louis XIV was regarded as a rabid nationalist. This is evident in the nature of his foreign policy where he . . .' offers the reader some evidence that explains the claim (see page 125).

Good academic writers think carefully about their use of language. Therefore, as you develop your writing skills, you will need to learn how to 'play' with language. This involves experimenting with each choice of word, each phrase, the order of words, the construction of sentences and the sequence within paragraphs. The ability to manipulate writing in this way is important for a number of reasons:

● it allows you to exploit the flexibility of the English language to express your meaning as clearly and as accurately as possible;

● it demonstrates your ability to group ideas in a logical way;

● it ensures that you maintain the reader's attention and interest.

Table 37.3 shows examples of how language can be manipulated to improve communication.

Table 37.3 Examples of how 'playing with language' can improve your writing. Writing can often be improved by rearranging the order of words or phrases, by choosing more suitable words or by separating out ideas into independent elements. Examples A–C below illustrate possible techniques that you might adopt.

A. Heads and tails
Sometimes a sentence works better if you experiment by shifting elements around within it. A phrase or clause that is at the tail end of the sentence might be more powerful, and emphasise your meaning more strongly, if it is positioned at the head of the sentence. For example:
Version A1: The practical application of 'duty to disclose' in relation to the onset of multiple sclerosis was deliberately entrusted to the discretion of the medical profession **because it was seen as impossible to define in policy**.
could become
Version A2: Since it was considered impossible to define 'duty to disclose' in policy in relation to the onset of multiple sclerosis, the practical application was deliberately entrusted to the medical profession.
Both instances have validity. However, as a writer, you might wish to place the emphasis on the reason for the failure to define a policy. In that case, Version A2 would be better. However, if you felt the emphasis should rest with the role of the medical profession, then Version A1 would be better. This shows the importance of considering your intention as you construct and review your writing, and it emphasises how important applying logic is to the whole process.

B. Better word, clearer meaning
Academic writing should, by definition, be both precise and concise. However, sometimes in the process of writing the need to record the ideas overtakes the accuracy and clarity that might be desirable. Consequently, it is good practice to review your work to identify ways in which you can use words more appropriately to achieve clarity. For example:
Version B1: The practical application of 'duty to disclose' in relation to the onset of multiple sclerosis was deliberately entrusted to **the decision-making process operating** in the medical profession because it was seen as impossible to define in policy.
could become
Version B2: The practical application of 'duty to disclose' in relation to the onset of multiple sclerosis was deliberately entrusted to the **discretion** of the medical profession because it was seen as impossible to define in policy.
Not only is Version B2 clearer than Version B1, but it expresses more aptly the leeway that the situation implies.

Table 37.3 (*cont'd*)

C. Long and short sentences
Sometimes it is better to split an overly long or complex sentence. For example:

Version C1: The practical application of 'duty to disclose' in relation to the onset of multiple sclerosis was deliberately entrusted to the discretion of the medical profession **because it was seen as impossible to define in policy**.

could become

Version C2: The practical application of 'duty to disclose' in relation to the onset of multiple sclerosis was deliberately entrusted to the discretion of the medical profession. **This decision was reached because it was seen as impossible to define in policy**.

Version C1 places the reason as a tag on the end of the main clause, whereas Version C2 emphasises the reason by stating it as a separate sentence.

PRACTICAL TIPS FOR ENSURING THAT YOU WRITE IN AN ACADEMIC STYLE

Think about your audience. Your readers should direct the style you adopt for any writing you do. For example, if you were writing to your bank manager asking for a loan, you would not use text-messaging or informal language. For academic writing, you should take into account that your reader(s) will probably be marking your work and, in addition to knowledge and content, they will be looking for evidence of awareness and correct use of specialist terms and structures.

Avoid contractions. In spoken English, shortened forms such as, don't, can't, isn't, it's, I'd and we'll are used all the time. However, in academic written English, they should not be used. Texting contractions are also inappropriate.

Avoid personal pronouns. Experiment with other language structures so that you avoid the personal pronouns, I/me/one, you and we/us, and their possessive forms, my, your and our.

Check your course handbook for guidance on use of the passive. This may appear in the section on referencing style. Some referencing styles prescribe the use of the active voice in preference to the passive voice and encourage the use of personal pronouns. One example of this is the American Psychological Association style (APA) (**Ch 35**).

38

SHAPING YOUR TEXT

How to create effective sentences and paragraphs

When is a sentence not a sentence? What makes a paragraph? These are questions that often arise for students as academic authors. Sentences can sometimes be too short, too long, or poorly structured – and the same can be said of paragraphs. If you are not sure why any of this is the case, this chapter explains what makes a good sentence and a paragraph that is well-proportioned and thoughtfully composed.

Knowing how sentences and paragraphs are structured and how you can produce good, clear sentences for yourself will help a great deal in shaping a piece of academic text, whether it is for an essay, a report, a dissertation or another kind of assignment. It's important to recognise that academic writing does not mean constructing long and involved sentences full of impressive-sounding 'big' words. Sometimes short sentences have more impact because they are brief and simple. If there is a rule to remember here, it is 'write to express, not to impress'.

✔ Writers' tip

Reading a sentence aloud can be a useful way of deciding whether a sentence you have written works well and is gramatically correct. Your ears will perhaps make more (non)sense out of it than your eyes.

There are many excellent grammar books available to give detailed explanations and exercises on the mechanics of academic writing. In this chapter we aim to give only some of the basic information on sentence and paragraph construction. Experience indicates that students want to know why what they have written is wrong and so, by providing a little background understanding and some models that show some typical problems, we hope to help you to be more sentence- and paragraph-aware when you write and then review your own writing.

SENTENCE STRUCTURE

A sentence must have a verb, that is, a 'doing' word (**Ch 39**). Each of the following is a sentence (verb in bold):

Help!

Students **work** in the holidays.

Universities **provide** tuition in a wide range of subjects.

What follows is a basic outline of different sentence types.

Simple sentences

These have at least a *subject* (the person or thing doing the action) and a **verb**, sometimes followed by a phrase of other information. Together these make sense as a unit. For example:

Criminal Law **differs** from Civil Law.

Plants **require** sunlight and water.

Divalent ions **carry** two charges.

Non-sentences

Phrases such as the following do not constitute sentences:

'Bringing the debate to an end.'

'Having been at war for 100 years.'

Although they each begin with a capital letter and end with a full stop, they use participles – the '-ing' words – rather than active verbs (see Table 39.2 and Figure 42.2). Just imagine that someone walked into a roomful of people and uttered either of these phrases. It is unlikely that anyone would understand what they meant. To make sense, each would need further information added, for example, 'The parties reached a compromise, bringing the debate to an end.' or 'Having been at war for 100 years, the states were impoverished and their war chests empty.' These types of non-sentences are common in student work, in part because we often use this strategy in speech to expand on a point made previously or to leave unsaid further development of a point. However, in written text they are not acceptable.

Compound sentences

These are two simple sentences joined by a word such as **and** or **but**. There will be two verbs in this combined sentence. For example:

Scots Law and English Law are fundamentally different, **but** there are some areas in which they are similar.

Compound sentences should contain two specific elements only. Thus, the following sentence is incorrect:

Scots Law and English Law are fundamentally different, but there are some areas in which they are similar, and this is taken into account in framing legislation but the Scottish legal system still defines aspects such as house purchase and matrimonial issues.

This sentence is also too long and should be written more appropriately as:

Scots Law and English Law are fundamentally different, but there are some areas in which they are similar. This difference is taken into account in framing legislation, but the Scottish legal system still defines aspects such as house purchase and matrimonial issues.

Avoid the common error of the 'comma splice'

This is where two sentences that should either be independent, or joined by 'and' or 'but', or another conjunction, are instead connected with a comma:

Fiona is a redhead, Beatrice is a blonde. (incorrect)

Fiona is a redhead. Beatrice is a blonde.
or
Fiona is a redhead, but Beatrice is a blonde.
(either could be used)

Complex sentences

These sentences consist of a main clause with additional subordinate clauses. A clause is a unit of meaning built round a verb. There are two categories of clause: principal (sometimes called independent or main clause, which is like a simple sentence) and subordinate clauses. The subordinate clause contains a verb, but would not make sense if it were to stand alone. It does the work of an adjective, adverb or noun. For example:

Gait analysis gives insights into the walking difficulties **that are experienced by people with cerebral palsy**.

Social work legislation protects the rights of the elderly **when they are no longer able to cope independently**.

Although Britain is regarded as a democracy, it has no written constitution **that can be cited as the basis of Constitutional Law**.

Complex sentences can be quite long and can contain more than one subordinate clause. Varying the length of your sentences enlivens your text and helps to keep your reader's interest. Shorter sentences containing a single idea generally have a stronger impact than longer complex sentences. If you want to balance two ideas, compound sentences are best.

PARAGRAPH STRUCTURE

A paragraph is a unit of text usually comprising several sentences. It has a topic that is outlined in the first sentence; the topic is developed further within the paragraph; and the paragraph concludes with a sentence that terminates that topic or, possibly, acts as a link to the topic of the following paragraph.

 Models for academic writing: what to avoid

Newspaper journalism and layout favours paragraphs of single sentences. These are not good models for academic writing. Similarly, adopting a flowery or pompous style is not appropriate to academic writing. There is a happy balance between these two extremes.

The building blocks of paragraphs are sentences, each performing a particular role: as detailed in Table 38.1, and seen in action within the example shown in Figure 38.1. This example is a very straightforward listing paragraph; Table 38.2 gives examples of signpost, or linking, words that you can use to join the component sentences within a paragraphs so that your text flows smoothly.

> ### The layout of paragraphs
>
> Paragraph layout can follow a 'blocked' style or an indented style. Examples of layout are given in **Ch 44**. The example in Figure 38.1 is laid out in blocked style.

Table 38.1 Some types of sentences that are used to make up a paragraph

Type of sentence	Role in the paragraph
Topic introducer sentence	Introduces the overall topic of the text (generally in the very first paragraph)
Topic sentence	Introduces a paragraph by identifying the topic of that paragraph (see also **Ch 24**)
Developer sentence	Expands the topic by giving additional information
Modulator sentence	Acts as linking sentence and is often introduced by a signpost word (see Table 38.2) moving to another aspect of the topic within the same paragraph
Terminator sentence	Concludes the discussion of a topic within a paragraph, but can also be used as a **transition sentence** where it provides a link to the topic of the next paragraph

If the building blocks of paragraphs are sentences, paragraphs themselves are the building blocks of text. Each paragraph performs a particular role in the structure of text. This means that the examples of paragraph formats shown in Table 38.3 can be used to construct extended written text. The example in Figure 38.2 shows how paragraphs flow within a piece of text.

Deductive and inductive paragraph models

These are alternative methods of laying out an argument:

- **Deductive model:** the writer moves from the key point and follows it with supporting information or evidence.
- **Inductive model:** the writer presents the supporting information and concludes with the key point.

You might choose one or other of these methods to suit your context and content of your topic. You may also find that one of these approaches is preferred over the other in your discipline.

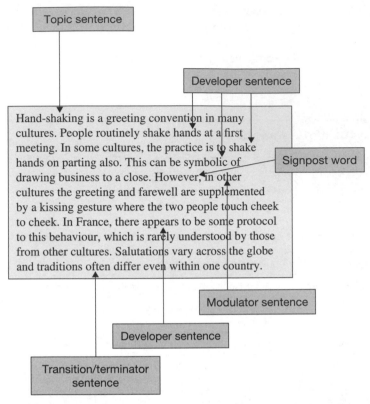

Figure 38.1 **How sentences make up a paragraph.** Part of a text on Anthropology, showing how different types of sentences are used to construct a paragraph.

Table 38.2 **Signpost words in text.** This table provides examples of words and phrases that can be used to improve the flow of your writing.

Type of link intended	Examples of signpost words
Addition	additionally; furthermore; in addition; moreover
Cause/reason	as a result of; because (mid-sentence)
Comparison	compared with; in the same way; in comparison with; likewise
Condition	if; on condition that; providing that; unless
Contrast	although; by contrast; conversely; despite; however; nevertheless; yet
Effect/result	as a result; hence; therefore; thus
Exemplification	for example; for instance; particularly; such as; thus
Reformulation	in other words; rather; to paraphrase
Summary	finally; hence; in all; in conclusion; in short; in summary
Time sequence	after; at first; at last; before; eventually; subsequently
Transition	as far as . . . is concerned; as for; to turn to

Table 38.3 Paragraph models. The construction of paragraph types is modelled under each heading. The numbers of intermediate sentences of each type is arbitrary – you could use more or fewer according to the need or context.

Describing: appearance/position	Describing: time sequence	Describing: process – how it works	Defining
• Topic introducer • Developer 1 • Developer 2 • Developer 3 • Terminator sentence Descriptive sequence examples: top to bottom; left to right; centre to perimeter	Either: • Event 1 • Event 2 • Event 3 Or: • By date order	• Topic introducer • Developer 1 • Developer 2 • Modulator • Developer 1 • Developer 2 • Topic sentence	• Topic sentence • Example 1 • Example 2 • Example 3 • Terminator sentence Note: Don't use a different form of the word being defined in order to define it

Classifying	Generalising	Giving examples	Listing
• Topic sentence • Example 1 • Example 2 • Terminator sentence identifying category	• Developer 1 • Developer 2 • Topic sentence; generalisation Or: • Generalisation • Developer 1 • Developer 2 • Restatement sentence	• Topic sentence • Example 1 • Example 2 • Restatement sentence or terminator sentence	• Topic sentence • Developer sentence • Modulator sentence • Developer sentence • Terminator sentence

Relating cause and effect: method 1	Relating cause and effect: method 2	Comparing	Contrasting
• Topic introducer • Topic sentence • Developer 1 • Developer 2 • Modulator • Developer 3 • Developer 4 • Terminator/restatement sentence	• Topic introducer • Topic sentence • Developer 1 Theme A • Developer 2 Theme A • Modulator (transfer to B) • Developer 1 Theme B • Developer 2 Theme B • Terminator/restatement sentence	• Topic introducer • Topic sentence • Developer 1 Theme A • Developer 2 Theme A • Modulator (transfer to B) • Developer 1 Theme B • Developer 2 Theme B • Restatement sentence	• Topic introducer • Topic sentence • Developer 1 Theme A • Developer 1 Theme B • Developer 2 Theme A • Developer 2 Theme B • Terminator • Restatement sentence

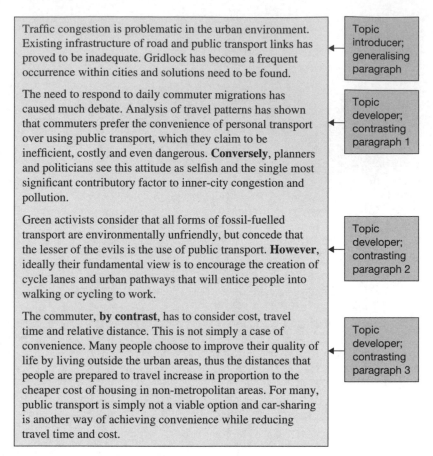

Figure 38.2 **How paragraphs make up a piece of text.** Part of an essay on town planning, showing how different paragraphs have been used to construct a flowing piece of text. Note how the bold signpost words (Table 38.2) have been used to bring cohension to the arguments.

PRACTICAL TIPS FOR CREATING GOOD SENTENCES AND PARAGRAPHS

How long should a sentence be? This is a 'how long is a piece of string?' type of question. A sentence can be long or short. There are two tests for good sentence structure. First, simply read it out aloud. Your ear will hear inconsistencies of logic or grammar. Second, if you feel a need to take a breath in mid-sentence, a comma is probably needed, or even a full stop followed by a new sentence.

Vary sentence length. A sentence 'mix' of short and long sentences is probably more reader-friendly than lines and lines of unbroken text. As a rule of thumb, if a sentence runs into three or four lines of typescript, consider restructuring it in some way or breaking it up into two smaller sentences.

How long should a paragraph be? The length of a paragraph depends on the content, but generally extra-long paragraphs will have some topic shift within them. If you find that your paragraph seems disproportionately long, again, read it aloud and listen for a 'natural' break point. This is probably a good place to start a new paragraph.

Use signpost words. These words are used to assist your reader by moving them through the logic of your text, for example in modulator sentences. Some words are most frequently used at the beginning of sentences: for example – however, moreover, furthermore, nevertheless. These are followed by a comma.

Follow the discussion style of your discipline. Study a paper or book chapter on a topic in your discipline area and analyse whether the writer has followed a deductive style of writing or an inductive one. If you look at a few more examples, you may find that there is some commonality of approach. You might then compare these with paragraphs of your own writing and so establish whether you follow the same 'pattern' as others in your field. If your approach to discussion differs from the pattern you have identified in the writing of others, then consider adjusting your style to follow the norm in your subject.

39

IMPROVING YOUR GRAMMAR

How to avoid some common errors

> Many people, not just students, state that they don't know much about the grammar of English – but what exactly do they mean? Spelling? Sentence structure? Parts of speech? Tense? Word order? The list seems to be endless. This chapter takes a quick look at some common mistakes and tries to give you enough in the way of grammatical terms to allow you to understand the guidance on electronic grammar checkers or in the feedback you receive on your assignments.

Grammar is the series of rules that governs the use of any language. It is a vast field and, although intuitively people know many of the 'rules' of grammar when speaking, it is often less easy to apply them in writing. This chapter cannot give you a complete set of rules, but gives you enough information to help you find what you need in a specialist grammar book or in a standard dictionary.

WHY GRAMMAR IS IMPORTANT

Grammar is important to you as a student because it is an integral and expected component of academic writing (**Ch 37**). Good grammar is essential, because without it your writing may be nonsensical, illogical or ambiguous. In the course of your university studies you will come across many aspects of language where you need to know exactly how the appropriate grammar rule needs to be applied.

In the past, there have been two approaches to teaching grammar. The traditional approach teaches the 'technical' terms, for example, 'clause', 'preposition' and 'tense', so that these can be used to explain the mechanics of language; the other, modern, approach encourages people to write freely and then provides them feedback with correct models. For the purposes of this book, we shall use elements of both techniques because we believe that some people do want to know the 'proper grammar', but, at the same time, they may learn best by seeing models of how this works in practice. So, we'll show you some of the more common grammatical errors and explain these as simply as possible, using the grammatical terms only where absolutely necessary.

If you are eager for more information, you may find it helpful to look at **Ch 37** on academic style, **Ch 40** on punctuation, **Ch 41** on spelling and **Ch 42** on vocabulary. These elements are all interdependent in the production of good style, structure and grammar in academic writing.

There are many common errors that occur in academic writing. In order to understand comments or corrections on your written work, it may be helpful to be able to identify some grammar terms. Table 39.1 defines and explains some of the terms you may come across. Table 39.2 gives some examples of errors and their corrections. Highlighting those that could be helpful to you in your writing will help you to create a personal checklist so you can avoid mistakes in future. Table 39.3 demonstrates how grammatical errors in a weak style of writing can be corrected to produce a more academic form of writing.

Table 39.1 Grammar toolkit: definitions to help you seek more information

Grammar term	Definition/model	Example
Adjective	Describes nouns or gerunds.	A **red** book; an **innovative** project.
Adverb	Adds information as to how something is done.	The student read **quickly**.
Articles	There are only three in English: a/an (indefinite); the (definite). You will find the particular rules about using these in a grammar book.	**A** shot in the dark. **An** empty house. **The** Highway Code.
Clause	Part of sentence containing a verb. If the verb and the words relating to it can stand alone, they make up the main clause. If the words cannot stand alone, the verb and the words that go with it form a subordinate clause.	**Cats eat mice** which are vermin. *Main clause Subordinate clause*
Conditional	Used to explain a future possible situation; note the comma after the condition.	If I had the time, **I would go out.** *Condition Consequence*
Conjunction	Word that joins two clauses in a sentence where the ideas are connected or equally balanced.	The book was on loan **and** the student had to reserve it.
Demonstrative	There are four in English: this, these, that, those (see Table 39.3).	**This** house supports the abolition of smoking in public.
Direct object	The noun or pronoun that is affected by the verb.	Foxes kill **sheep**. Foxes eat **them**.
Future tense	Explaining things that have not yet happened. There are two forms: will/shall, going to.	I **shall work** until I am 65. They **will** come early. He **is going to** work harder.
Gerund	Gerunds act as nouns and are formed with the part of the verb called the present participle: . . . -**ing**.	**Speaking** is easier than **writing** for most people.
Indirect object	The person or thing that benefits from the action of a verb.	Tutors give (to) **students** written work. They give (to) **them** essays.
Infinitive	Sometimes called the simple or root form of the verb. This form is usually listed in dictionaries, but without 'to'.	**To work.**
Noun	Term used to refer to things or people. There are different types: e.g. abstract (non-visible), concrete (visible) and proper nouns (names of people, places organisations, rivers, mountain ranges).	*Abstract noun*: thought. *Concrete nouns*: chair, table. *Proper nouns*: Caesar, Rome, the Post Office, the Rhine, the Andes (always begin with capitals).

continued overleaf ▶

Table 39.1 (*cont'd*)

Grammar term	Definition/model	Example
Passive voice	Used to describe things objectively, that is, placing the emphasis of the sentence on the action rather than the actor. Although some electronic grammar checkers imply that the passive is wrong, it is perfectly correct. Often used in academic writing (**Ch 37**).	**Essays are written** by students. *Action* *Actor*
Past participle	This is usually formed by adding **-ed** to the verb stem. However, in English there are many irregular verbs (see 'tense', below). You will find lists of these verbs in many dictionaries.	Work**ed**. Examples of irregular verbs: bent, drunk, eaten, seen, thought, understood, written.
Phrasal verb	These are two- or three-word verbs made up of a verb plus a particle (similar to a preposition). These verbs are generally regarded as being less formal in tone than single-word verbs.	**set down** (deposit) **pick up** (collect) **write down** (note) **look out for** (observe)
Present participle	This is formed by adding -**ing** to the simple verb form. It is used to form continuous verb tenses.	The sun is **setting**. We were **watching** the yachts.
Possessive	Word indicating ownership: my, mine, your, yours, his, her, its, our, ours, their, theirs.	**My** house and **his** are worth the same. **Mine** is larger, but **his** has more land.
Preposition	Word used as a link relating verbs to nouns, pronouns and noun phrases. Sometimes these are followed by an article, sometimes not: at, by, in, for, from, of, on, over, through, under, with.	Put money **in** the bank **for** a rainy day or save it **for** summer holidays **in** the sun.
Pronoun	Word used instead of nouns: I, me, you, he, him, she, her, it, we, us, they, them. Also words such as: each, everyone.	I have given **it** to **him**.
Relative pronoun	Words that link adjective (describing) clauses to the noun about which they give more information: that, which, who, whose, whom.	This is the house **that** Jack built. Jack, **who** owns it, lives there. Jack, **whose** wife sings, is a baker. Jack, **to whom** we sold the flour, used it to bake a loaf.
Sentence	A grouping of words, one of which must be a verb, that can stand together independently and make sense.	The people elect their leaders in a democracy.
Subject	The person or thing that performs the action in a sentence.	**Caesar** invaded Britain. **Caterpillars** eat leaves.
Tense	In English, to show past, present and future tense shifts, the verb changes. This often involves adding a word to show this. Some verbs behave irregularly from the standard rules. Here are three basic tenses; more can be found in a grammar book or language learner's dictionary.	*Simple* *past* *Present* *Future* I studied study shall study You studied study will study S/he studied studies will study We studied study shall study You studied study will study They studied study will study
Verb	The action or 'doing' word in a sentence. It changes form to indicate shifts in time (see tense).	I work, I am working, I will work, I worked, I was working, I have worked, I had worked.

Table 39.2 Twelve common grammatical errors

Error	Incorrect example (✗) and correction (✔)
1 Comparing Sometimes there is confusion with when to use a word ending in -er or -est rather than using 'more' or 'most'. For grammar book entries, look for **Comparatives** and **Superlatives** under **Adjectives** and **Adverbs**.	Comparing two things: ✗ The debit was more bigger than the credit. ✔ The debit was grea**ter** than the credit. Comparing three or more things: ✗ China has the most greatest population in the world. ✔ China has the grea**test** population in the world. Countable and non-countable: ✗ There were less cases of meningitis last year. ✔ There were fewer cases of meningitis last year. (Countable) ✗ There was fewer snow last year. ✔ There was less snow last year. (Non-countable)
2 Describing Commas can be vital to meaning – misuse can cause fundamental changes to meaning. For grammar book entry, look for **Relative clauses**.	✗ Toys, which are dangerous, should not be given to children. (Inference: all toys are dangerous – not what the author means) ✔ Toys which are dangerous should not be given to children. (Inference: only safe toys should be given to children – what the author means)
3 Encapsulating Using one word to represent a previous word or idea. For grammar book entry, look for **Demonstrative pronoun**.	✗ . . . impact of diesel use on air quality. **This** increases in rush hour. ✔ . . . impact of diesel use on air quality. **This impact** increases in rush hour.
4 Its/it's These two are often confused. For grammar book entry, look for **Possessives (its)** and **Apostrophes (it's)**.	✗ As it's aim, the book describes the whole problem. ✔ As its aim, the book describes the whole problem. (Possession) ✗ Its not a viable answer to the problem. ✔ It's not a viable answer to the problem (It is . . .) ✗ Its not had a good review. ✔ It's not had a good review. (It has . . .)
5 Joining Words such as 'because', 'but' and 'and' join two clauses; they never begin sentences. For grammar book entry, look for **Conjunctions**.	✗ Because the sample was too small, the results were invalid. ✔ Since the sample was too small, the results were invalid. ('Because' is a conjunction and is used to join two ideas.) ✗ But the UN failed to act. And the member states did nothing. ✔ The country was attacked, **but** the UN failed to act **and** the member states did nothing. ('But' and 'and' are conjunctions that join two separate ideas.)
6 Double negative Two negatives mean a positive. Sometimes using a double negative can cause confusion. For grammar book entry, look for **Double negatives**.	✗ They have not had no results from their experiments. ✔ They have not had any results from their experiments. ✗ The government had not done nothing to alleviate poverty. ✔ The government had done nothing to alleviate poverty.
7 Past participles These are sometimes misused, especially when the verbs are irregular. For grammar book entry, look for **Past participles**.	✗ The team had went to present their findings at the conference. ✔ The team had gone to present their findings at the conference.

continued overleaf

Table 39.2 (cont'd)

Error	Incorrect example (✗) and correction (✔)
8 Prepositions These should not come at the end of a sentence. For grammar book entry, look for **Prepositions**.	✗ These figures are the ones you will work with. ✓ These figures are the ones with which you will work.
9 Pronouns These are used to replace nouns. The singular pronouns often cause confusion because they need to agree with the verb. For grammar book entry, look for **Pronouns**.	**Singular pronouns:** anybody, anyone, anything, each, either, everybody, everyone, everything, neither, nobody, no one, nothing, somebody, someone, something – all take a singular verb. ✗ Each of the new measures are to be introduced separately. ✓ **Each** of the new measures **is** to be introduced separately. **Reflexive pronouns:** ✗ Although disappointed, they only have theirselves to blame. ✓ Although disappointed, **they** only have **themselves** to blame.
10 Specifying Words that are used to identify specific singular and plural items must match. For grammar book entry, look for **Demonstratives**.	✓ **This** kind of mistake **is** common. ✓ **These** kinds of mistakes **are** less common. ✓ **That** result **is** acceptable. ✓ **Those** results **are** not acceptable.
11 Subject–verb agreement Often singular subjects are matched with plural verbs and vice versa. For grammar book entry, look for **Subject–verb agreement**.	✗ The Principal, together with the Chancellor, were present. ✓ The Principal, together with the Chancellor, was present. ✗ It is the result of these overtures and influences that help to mould personal identity. ✓ It is the **result** of these overtures and influences that **helps** to mould personal identity.
12 There/their/they're These simply need to be remembered. For grammar book entry, look for **Words that are often confused**.	✗ They finished there work before noon. ✓ They finished their work before noon. ✗ We have six places at the conference. We'll go their. ✓ We have six places at the conference. We'll go there. ✗ Researchers are skilled but there not highly paid. ✓ Researchers are skilled but they're not highly paid.

HOW TO USE GRAMMAR CHECKERS TO BEST ADVANTAGE

Some software packages provide a grammar-checking facility. Although this can provide you with some helpful tips, it is important to recognise that it is not infallible. As an artificial intelligence device, it cannot always fully respond to more sophisticated grammatical logic. For example, in the following sentence, the words 'a lot of' were underlined as grammatically incorrect by an electronic grammar checker:

You get <u>a lot of</u> help for projects from the tutors.

The suggested adjustment was to reform the sentence as:

You get <u>many</u> help for projects from the tutors.

This is obviously grammatically incorrect.

Table 39.3 Comparison of weak and strong academic writing. This text is part of an answer to the question: 'Did Napoleon achieve most for France at home or abroad?' The original answer, written in a style that is essentially non-academic, is in the left column. The middle column points out some grammatical weaknesses in the use of language, and the right-hand column provides one possible example of how the same text could be written in a more academic style. The superscript numbers used in columns 1 and 3 refer to the numbered list in column 2.

1 Non-academic style (bold text indicates error)	2 Error and correction analysis	3 Academic style (bold text indicates correction/ addition)
Napolion[1] came up trumps[2] in both French domestic and foreign policies that were many and varied.[3] How you have to think about[4] the value of these achievements is the million dollar question,[5] while his domestic reforms survived after his collapse,[6] most of the affects[7] of his foreign policy necessarily perished with his imperial power. In addition to this,[8] the value of his achievements has to be considered in the light of whether they were achievements for France or achievements in consolidating his own position and popularity. In this essay I will talk about[9] his foreign and domestic policys.[10]	1 Misspelling of key name	Napoleon's[1] achievements[2] in both French domestic and foreign policies were significant.[3] However, the relative merit of these achievements must be considered[4,5] at two levels. First, although his domestic reforms survived his downfall,[6] most of the effects[7] of his foreign policy necessarily perished with his imperial power. Second, the extent to which his achievements were truly for the greater glory of France or were simply strategies for consolidating his own position and popularity has to be taken into account. The purpose of this essay[9] will be to evaluate these two dimensions within his foreign and domestic policies[10] in the longer term. Domestic and foreign policy in this period cannot easily be separated. In foreign policy,[11] Napoleon's primary achievement was the Peace of Lunéville (1801) with Austria and subsequent Treaty of Amiens with Britain in 1802. The significance of this achievement was that it gave both France and Napoleon, and their antagonists,[13] an interval[14] in which to collect their[15] resources and reorganise themselves for further hostilities. This initial accord[16] enabled Napoleon to survey[17] the domestic state of France after a decade of almost continuous fighting[18] preceded by a major internal political revolution. He applied the same methods to the affairs of state as he did to the tactics of the battlefield;[19] in both[20] he had to take into consideration the outlook and demands of the French people as a whole.[21] This approach he took because[22] 'I act only on the imagination of the nation. When this means fails me, I shall be reduced to nothing and another will succeed me' (Grant and Temperley, 1952).[23]
	2, 3 Clichés	
	4 Personal expression;	
	5 Cliché/inappropriate language	
	6 Ambiguous	
	7 Misspelling	
	8 Unnecessary words (phrase not used in corrected version)	
	9 Statement of intent: use of personal pronouns – and you cannot 'talk' on paper!	
In foreign policy, Napoleon's primary achievement was the Peace of Lunéville (1801) with Austria and subsequent Treaty of Amiens with Britain in 1802. This achievement was significant 'cos[12] it gave both France and Napoleon, not to mention[13] their antagonists, a breathing space[14] in which to collect there[15] resources and reorganise themselves for further hostilities. This initial bargain[16] enabled Napoleon to have a look at[17] the domestic state of France after a decade of almost continuous international squabbling[18] following a major internal political revolution. Applying the same methods to the affairs of state as he did to the tactics of the battlefield.[19] In both two[20] ways he had to take into consideration the outlook and demands of the French people as a hole.[21] This approach he took on the grounds that[22] 'I act only on the imagination of the nation. When this means fails me, I shall be reduced to nothing and another will succeed me.'[23]	10 Misspelling	
	11 Add transition sentence to new version to link topic sentence with preceding paragraph	
	12 Shortened word (not used in corrected version)	
	13 Unnecessary words	
	14 Informal language	
	15 Misspelling	
	16 More appropriate word required	
	17 Too informal	
	18 More appropriate word required	
	19 Incomplete sentence/phrase (hanging participle)	
	20 Tautology (same meaning twice)	
	21 Misspelling;	
	22 Wordy cliché	
	23 No reference cited: Harvard method citation added	

In another example using the passive voice:

The limitation of feedback from teaching staff was noted by other students to be frustrating.

was 'corrected' to:

Other students to be frustrating noted the limitation of feedback from teaching staff.

This clearly makes nonsense of the original text and meaning. The message is clear: you should not blindly accept all changes recommended by the grammar checker.

> ## ✔ Grammatical terms
>
> Grammar has its own particular terminology. This is used as a shorthand reference to allow discussion of more complex ideas. It's rather like the way that knowing the names of the main parts of a car engine helps you to understand the explanation of the mechanic who's fixing your car. If you can become familiar with some of the basic terms, this may help you to understand comments written on your assignments. This will also help you when looking up the relevant section in a good grammar book.

If you have had an error pointed out to you, but don't understand it fully, ask the person who made the correction to explain to you what is wrong. If you are unable to do this, check out some of the resources given below. You can do a little bit of detective work first by looking at your error in conjunction with the grammar definition list in Table 39.1. Once you have an idea of what the problem might be, then you could consult one of the many good grammar books available by looking for the key grammatical term in the index or contents. For example, you could have a look at *Longman's Advanced Learners' Grammar* (Foley and Hall, 2003), which has very useful diagnostic tests to help you identify difficulties. The book gives clear explanations of each grammar point with exercises for practice and an answer key. Another source is *Fowler's Modern English Usage* (Fowler and Winchester, 2004). More modern, user-friendly sources include the *Chambers Dictionary A–Z* (2012) or the *Longman Dictionary of Contemporary English* (2009), both of which give words, meanings and examples of correct usage.

🔧 PRACTICAL TIPS FOR UNDERSTANDING GRAMMAR

Identify and understand your errors. Markers of your assignments often indicate errors on written work, sometimes simply by underlining, sometimes by restructuring or inserting a correction. Spending time looking over your marked work to understand different points that the marker has identified will be time well spent. Some comments may be related to subject matter, some to grammar and some to punctuation. If you can isolate the latter two types, noting the errors and how these have been corrected, you are well on the way to avoiding them in the future. This could make a real difference to you in your marks on future assignments.

Make your own checklist. Once you have identified an error that you have made, make a note of it (you could keep a glossary notebook and isolate a few pages for grammar points). It's a good idea to write down the error, its correction and, if you can, a quick note of what is wrong and why.

40

BETTER PUNCTUATION

How to use punctuation marks appropriately

Punctuation is an important 'code' that helps the reader understand your message. If you misuse it, ignore it or abuse it, you will not be transmitting your ideas clearly and, indeed, may confuse your reader. This chapter lays out some of the principles of standard punctuation and gives you some tips on how to avoid punctuation errors.

Consider how people speak – they use gestures, intonation and pauses to indicate emphasis, astonishment, suspense and a whole range of other emotions and ideas. In writing, punctuation helps to send similar signals by splitting up or joining ideas – for example, by using the full-stop (.), exclamation mark (!), question mark (?), comma (,), colon (:), and semicolon (;).

Similarly, other signals are used to inform the reader of ideas that may not be those of the writer – for example, quotation marks ('. . .') to indicate what someone else said or wrote; or apostrophes (') to explain the idea of ownership (for example, 'the student's bursary').

If you look back at a piece of your own work, you will probably be more aware of your own punctuation 'style'. This will probably involve using particular sentence structures repeatedly and favouring certain punctuation marks over others. If you want to add variety to your writing, you can do this by consciously trying to use a variety of forms of punctuation, and thereby changing the structure of some of your sentences. Simplified rules for punctuation marks are provided in Table 40.1.

WHY PUNCTUATION IS IMPORTANT

Punctuation is essential and has evolved as an aid to the reader to help convey meaning, emphasis and style. It is a recognised code and learning how to use that code contributes to your skill as a writer.

The omission of a punctuation symbol can make a sentence ambiguous – that is, have more than one meaning. For example:

1 The inspector said the teacher is a fool.

2 'The inspector', said the teacher, 'is a fool'.

3 The inspector said, 'The teacher is a fool'.

These three sentences show that punctuation makes a critical difference to meaning. The first one *reports* what the inspector said; the second is *what the teacher actually said* about the inspector being a fool; the third is *what the inspector actually said* about the teacher being a fool.

Table 40.1 Simplified rules of punctuation

Punctuation	Mark	How the mark is used
Apostrophe	. . . '	• For possession: e.g. Napoleon's armies (singular owner); students' essays (plural owner) • For contraction: e.g. Don't cry; I'm hungry; it's late • But note: As **its** central theme, the book considered wind power (no apostrophe required at **its** – possessive of 'it')
Brackets (parenthesis)	[. . .] (. . .)	• Square brackets [. . .]: for adding words within a quote • Round brackets (. . .): to isolate explanatory information
Capital letter	ABC . . .	• Starts sentences, proper nouns, seasons, rivers, mountain ranges, places, Acts of Parliament, titles, organisations
Colon	:	• Leads from one clause to another: e.g. from introduction to main point, from statement to example, from cause to effect • Introduces lists (examples throughout this table) • Introduces a 'long quote' (**Ch 35**)
Comma	. . . ,	• Separates items in a list of three or more: e.g. tea, beer, juice and wine • Separates part of a sentence: e.g. He came home, ate and fell asleep • Separates additional information within a sentence: e.g. Rugby, in the main, is a contact sport • Marks adverbs: e.g. Certainly, the results have been positive
Dash	—	• Marks an aside/addition: e.g. Murder – regardless of reason – is a crime
Ellipsis	. . .	• Marks words omitted from a quotation: e.g. 'taxes . . . mean price rises'
Exclamation mark	!	• Shows shock, horror (rarely used in academic writing): e.g. Help!
Full stop	.	• Marks the end of a sentence: e.g. This is the end. • Marks an abbreviation where the last letter of the abbreviation is *not* the last letter of the complete word: e.g. Prof. etc., i.e., m.p.h., p.a.
Hyphen	-	• Joins a single letter to an existing word: e.g. x-ray • Separates prefixes: e.g. post-modern • Prevents repetition of certain letters: e.g. semi-independent • Joins a prefix to a proper noun: e.g. pro-British • Creates a noun from a phrasal verb: e.g. show-off • Joins numbers and fractions: e.g. twenty-three; three-quarters • Indicates a compound modifier where two adjectives or noun adjectives are used to describe something e.g. orange-red shirt; post-office counter
Italics	*italics*	• Differentiates text to show quotations, titles of publications in citations, species, works of art, foreign words: e.g. *déjà vu*; *et al.*
Question mark	?	• Ends sentences that ask a direct question: e.g. Who am I?
Quotation marks (inverted commas)	' . . . ' " . . . "	• 'Single quotation marks' mark exact words spoken/printed in a text • "Double quotation marks" place a quotation within a quotation (British English) • Note that in some word-processing packages it is possible to choose between 'smart quotes' (". . .") and 'straight quotes' (". . .")
Semicolon	;	• Separates two or more clauses of equal importance: e.g. They won the battle; the other side won the war. • Separates listed items, especially when description uses several words

Where punctuation is omitted entirely, then it is difficult to identify separate points. For example:

> The character of james bond created by ian fleming portrayed a fastliving but urbane spy whose coolness was apparently imperturbable he became a real screen hero.

Without punctuation, this text becomes simply a string of words rather than a meaningful set of statements. (The correct version is on page 265.)

Paragraph alignment

Although not strictly punctuation, this can greatly affect layout and readability of text. Paragraphs can be aligned in two ways: fully justified and indented. **Ch 43** and **Ch 44** give more detail on this.

PUNCTUATION GUIDELINES

In some respects, the way that punctuation rules are applied depends on the conventions of different genres, that is, the categories of writing. In fiction, for example, the rules are followed less rigidly, and sometimes do not follow the rules exactly as they would in a non-fiction book, such as an academic text.

For your purposes as a student, it is important that you follow the punctuation codes correctly as this will reflect on how others judge the quality of your work. In some disciplines, marks may be deducted for punctuation errors. Table 40.2 (on pages 263–4) gives examples of the more common errors.

Overuse of certain punctuation marks

Two punctuation marks that are commonly overused in some academic writing are parentheses and exclamation marks.

- Parentheses are sometimes a symptom of 'lazy' writing (or a feeling that you need to add more detail than you probably require). If you feel you have a tendency to use parentheses excessively, you can often replace these marks with commas.

- It is rare that an exclamation mark is appropriate in academic writing! (This can be seen in the example of the previous sentence, where the exclamation mark is unnecessary.) If you find you use exclamation marks a lot, these can often be simply replaced with a full stop with no great loss of effect.

Sentences

These begin with capital letters and finish with either a full stop, a question mark or an exclamation mark (**Ch 38**). In a sentence that ends with a quote, the full stop comes after the final quote mark 'like this'. If, however, the quotation looks as though it is probably a complete sentence, or if more than one sentence is quoted, the full stop precedes the final quote mark. (Similarly, a complete sentence within parentheses has the full stop inside the final bracket, as in this sentence.)

'Open' and 'closed' punctuation

'Open' in this context means using minimal punctuation. While this has gained some acceptance in letter-writing, it is not universally accepted within the academic world.

- Example of open punctuation:

    Dr Douglas M Kay the world famous projectile designer outlined his research to staff of the Ministry of Defence (MOD) and the Foreign Office (FO).

    Note that full stops are not generally used if the last letter of a contraction is also the last letter of the full word (Mr, Dr) or in abbreviations such as TV, BBC, USA, VCR, or in acronyms such as NATO, UNICEF, scuba, and so on.

- Example of closed punctuation:

    Dr. Douglas M. Kay, the world-famous projectile designer, outlined his research at the conference in St. Albans for staff of the Ministry of Defence (M.O.D.) and the Foreign Office (F.O.).

You may come across both these styles of punctuation in your reading. This arises from transatlantic differences in punctuation styles. However, since academic writing is often complex in its structure, generally, the academic world would favour the more traditional 'closed' punctuation style.

If in doubt, the guiding principle should be whether the addition of a punctuation symbol adds to the clarity.

Lists

Lists use a variety of bullet-point or numerical styles. You should use numbered lists when there is an inherent priority, hierarchy or sequence. Where the list is introduced by the beginning of a sentence, you should introduce the list with a colon (:). The follow-on words in the list should begin with lower-case letters and each item, except the last one, should be finished with a semicolon. By some conventions, 'and' is optional after the semi-colon for the second-last item on the lists. The final point finishes with a full stop. Where the list is not introduced by the beginning of a sentence, then each bullet point should begin with a capital letter.

Punctuation of bulleted and numbered lists

Minimal punctuation:

The causes of migration include:
- drought
- famine
- disease.

Famine relief agencies:
1 UN
2 OXFAM
3 Save the Children.

The list as a sentence:

Population decreases because:
- drought dries up pastures;
- people do not have food;
- lack of food lowers resistance to disease; and
- people either die or migrate.

To save your document:
1 click on File;
2 select Save As;
3 choose directory;
4 choose file name; and
5 click on Save.

Note that the use of lists in text is not favoured in some disciplines.

Table 40.2 Common punctuation errors and their corrections. The following common errors with their corrections should help you to find an answer to most punctuation dilemmas.

Punctuation mark	Error	Correction	Explanation
1.1 Apostrophes: singular	The **Principals'** Committee will meet at noon today.	Principal's	There is only one Principal, therefore the apostrophe goes immediately after the word 'Principal'. Then add the s to make it correctly possessive.
1.2 Apostrophes: plural	The **womens'** team beat the mens' team by 15 points and the **childrens'** team beat them both. The **boy's** team won the prize.	women's men's children's boys'	The words 'women', 'men' and 'children' are plural words. To make them possessive, just add an apostrophe after the plural word and add 's'. The word 'boys' is a plural and is a regularly formed plural, thus, the apostrophe comes after the 's'.
1.3 Apostrophes: contractions	**Its** not a good time to sell a property. **Its** been up for sale for ages. **Well** need to lower the price.	It's = it s It's = it has We'll = we shall	'It's' is a contracted form of the words 'it is' or 'it has'. In this case: 'It is not a good time to sell a property'; and 'It has been up for sale for ages'. 'Well' clearly has a different meaning to 'We' 'u'.
1.4 Apostrophes: not needed	The **tomatoes'** cost 60 pence a kilo.	tomatoes	The word 'tomatoes' is a plural. No apostrophe is needed to make words plural.
1.5 Apostrophes: not needed	The Charter includes human rights in **it's** terms.	its	No apostrophe needed to show possession. 'Its' is the exception to the general rule of adding apostrophes to indicate possession. You will see the potential conflict with the contraction for 'it is' (see above).
2.1 Capital letters: sentences	**the** first day of the term is tomorrow	The	The first letter of the first word of a sentence in English always needs a capital letter.
2.2 Capital letters: proper names	The **prime minister** is the first **lord** of the **treasury**. The **north atlantic treaty organisation** is a regional organisation. Pearls found in the **river tay** are of considerable value.	Prime Minister; First Lord of the Treasury North Atlantic Treaty Organisation River Tay	Proper nouns for roles, names of organisations, rivers, mountains, lochs, lakes and place names. These all require a capital for all parts of the name.
3 Colon	A number of aspects will be covered **including** • Energy conservation • Pollution limitation • Cost control	. . . including: • energy conservation; • pollution limitation; and • cost control.	A colon to introduce the list. Each item, except the last one, should be finished with a semicolon. No capital is necessary at each bullet if the list follows from an incomplete sentence introducing the list.

40 • Better punctuation   263

Table 40.2 (cont'd)

Punctuation mark	Error	Correction	Explanation
4.1 Commas	**The leader of the group Dr Joan Jones** was not available for comment.	The leader of the group, Dr Joan Jones, was not available for comment.	This is a common error. The name of the person gives more information about the leader; thus, the person's name needs to be inserted with commas before and after.
4.2 Commas	There are several member-states that do not support this view. They are **Britain France Germany Portugal and Greece.**	There are several member-states that do not support this view. They are Britain, France, Germany, Portugal, and Greece.	Strictly speaking, when making a list such as in the example, a comma should come before 'and'. This is called the 'Oxford comma' and its use has caused much debate. 'However', increasingly, the comma is being omitted before the word 'and' in lists such as this one.
4.3 Commas	**However** we have no evidence to support this statement.	However, we have no evidence to support this statement.	The 'signposting' words often used at the beginning of sentences are followed by a comma. Some of the more common of these words are: however, therefore, thus, hence, nevertheless, moreover, in addition.
4.4 Commas	**Although we have had significant rainfall** the reservoirs are low.	Although we have had significant rainfall, the reservoirs are low.	When a sentence begins with 'although', then the sentence has two parts. The part that gives the idea of concession in this sentence is 'Although we have had significant rainfall'. The second part gives us the impact of that concession, in this case, that 'the reservoirs are low'. A comma is used to divide these parts.
4.5 Commas	**To demonstrate competence** it is important to be able to face challenges.	To demonstrate competence, it is important to be able to face challenges.	Another way to write this sentence would be: 'It is important to be able to face challenges to demonstrate competence'. By putting the phrase 'to demonstrate competence' at the beginning of the sentence, it places emphasis on the idea of competence and, in order to make that word-order distinction, a comma is needed.
5 Ellipsis	There is a deficit in the budget . . . . . . brought on by mismanagement at the highest level.	There is a deficit in the budget . . . brought on by mismanagement at the highest level.	Ellipsis marks always consist of three dots, no more.

PRACTICAL TIPS FOR CLEAR PUNCTUATION

Check your punctuation is appropriate. Read your work aloud at a reasonable pace – imagine that you are a television newsreader who has to convey the item so that it makes sense. As you read, your ear will identify the pauses and inconsistencies in your text in a way that sometimes the most careful silent editing misses. For example, if you need to pause for breath, there is a chance that you need to insert a comma or start a new sentence.

Use symbols to help proof-read your work. It is helpful to print out a hard copy of your draft text and then to go through it methodically, marking it with the proof-reading symbols (**Ch 43**) in both the text and the margin. This will help you to go through your work systematically on-screen at a later point. The double-entry method helps to ensure that you don't miss out any of your corrections.

Use lists, bullet points and sub-headings. In some disciplines it is permissible to use sub-headings and bulleted or numbered lists. This strategy enables you to avoid some of the pitfalls of punctuation, but it is not universally accepted in academic writing. If you do use devices such as bullets and lists, you need to observe the punctuation conventions shown p. 262. Some people use sub-headings to help them focus on writing content and then, when they have finished writing, they replace the sub-headings with a topic sentence (**Ch 38**).

Check that your punctuation – or lack of it – does not create ambiguity. Go back to the example about James Bond on page 261 and insert punctuation so that the meaning of the text is clear. Your corrected version should read:

> The character of James Bond, created by Ian Fleming, portrayed a fast-living but urbane spy, whose coolness was apparently imperturbable. He became a real screen hero.

41

BETTER SPELLING

How to spell competently

Spellcheckers make life easy, but doing the checking takes time and you won't always necessarily be writing using a personal computer. Therefore it makes sense to brush up your spelling skills. This chapter looks at some of the basic rules of spelling and gives some examples of these rules. It also looks at 'irregular' words that are often used in academic contexts and at some words that are commonly misspelled.

Some people will have been routinely taught to spell at school, others may not. Whichever category applies to you, developing your spelling skill is an ongoing process. This chapter explains some important basic spelling rules and gives examples of how they work. Table 41.1 covers twenty basic spelling rules, including some for words more likely to be used in formal academic text than informal writing. If you are unfamiliar with some of the terms used to explain these rules, you might find it valuable to check these out by consulting a more specialist text.

WORDS TO WATCH

English is a language that has borrowed quite freely from other languages and this means that its spelling 'rules' are quite diverse. For many words, where there is a 'rule' more often than not there are exceptions to that rule. This means that you simply need to learn these exceptions. One way to carry out this rote learning is to memorise a few examples at a time. If you keep a note of words that cause you difficulty, you can return to this from time to time to test your progress.

Table 41.2 provides a listing of words that are often misspelled in academic written work. In addition, some words that are often confused with words that are either similar in meaning or have a similar 'word shape', and so people often transpose letters in the middle of a word: for example, 'goal' and 'gaol'. Both words are correctly spelt, but they are different in meaning. Some of the most commonly confused 'pairs' are given in Table 41.3.

Table 41.1 Twenty basic spelling rules. In English the 'rules' are difficult to define because frequently there are exceptions to them. Here are some of the fundamental rules, with some examples of exceptions where these occur.

Number	Rule	Examples, with exceptions as applicable
1	i comes before e (except after c)	belief, relief, chief *but* receive, perceive, deceive, ceiling
2	**Verbs**: where verbs end in -eed and -ede, then the -eed ending goes with suc-/ex-/pro-; -ede applies in all other cases	–eed: succeed, exceed, proceed –ede: precede, concede
3	**Verbs**: where verbs end with -ise, nouns end with -ice	practise (verb)/practice (noun) *but* exercise (both verb and noun)
4	**Double** final consonants before using -ing when the words are single syllable and end with b/d/g/m/n/p/r/t	robbing, ridding, bagging, summing, running, hopper, furred, fittest
	Double consonant when the stressed syllable is at the end of the word	occurred, beginning, forgettable
	Double l when words end in an l preceded by a short vowel	travelled, levelled
5	**Nouns** ending in -our drop the u in the adjective form	glamour/glamorous, humour/humorous
6	**Plurals** generally add -s, or -es after -ss/x/ch/sh/	boys, cats, dogs; crosses, fixes, churches, dishes
	Nouns ending in -y drop -y and add -ies	ally/allies, copy/copies *but* monkeys, donkeys
	Nouns ending in -o add -s for the plural	photos, pianos *but* tomatoes, volcanoes, heroes
	Nouns ending in -f and -fe: no consistent rule	Chief/chiefs *but* half/halves
	Some 'foreign' nouns follow the rules of their own language	medium/media, criterion/criteria, datum/data, bureau/bureaux
	Hyphenated words	brothers-in-law, commanders-in-chief (not brother-in-laws/commander-in-chiefs)
	Some nouns are the same format for singular and for plural	sheep, fish
7	**Prefixes** dis- and mis- plus noun or verb (no double 's'); but where such words begin with an 's', insert prefix (do not drop 's')	dis + agree, mis + manage, *note* dis + satisfaction, mis + spell
8	**Suffixes** -ful, -fully, -al, -ally: adjectives formed with the suffix -ful and -al have only one l	careful, hopeful *but* carefully, hopefully
	When forming adverbs, add -ly	skilfully, marginally
	Adjectives ending in -ic form their adverbs with -ally	basic/basically
9	**Compound words**: where there is a 'double l' in one of the words, one l may be dropped	Well + fare = welfare; un + till = until *but* well + being = wellbeing; ill + ness = illness

continued overleaf

Table 41.1 (*cont'd*)

Number	Rule	Examples, with exceptions as applicable
10	**Silent** e: usually keep –e when adding the suffix	hope + full = hopeful
	If suffix begins with a vowel, drop final –e	come + ing = coming
	After words ending in –ce or –ge, keep –e to keep sounds soft when suffix is added	noticeable, courageous, etc.
11	For words ending in –y that are preceded by a consonant, change –y to –i before any suffix except –ing, –ist, –ish, –ism	dry/driest *but* drying, copyist, dryish cronyism
12	For words ending in –ic or –ac, add –k before –ing, –ed or –er	trafficking, mimic/mimicked, picnic/picnicker
13	For 'joins' within word, do not add or subtract letters at 'join'	meanness
14	**Silent** letters. In certain cases, the letters b, g, k, l, p and w are silent	debt, gnat, knot, palm, psychiatrist, wrong
15	**Latin** words in English ending in –ix or –ex in the singular, end in –ices in the plural	appendix/appendices, index/indices
16	**Latin** words in English ending in –um in the singular, generally end in –a in the plural	datum/data, medium/media, stratum/strata
17	**Latin** words in English ending in –us in the singular, generally end in –i in the plural	radius/radii
18	**Latin** words in English ending in –a in the singular, end in –ae in the plural	agenda/agendae, formula/formulae
19	**Greek** words in English ending in –ion in the singular, end in –ia in the plural	criterion/criteria
20	**Greek** words in English ending in –sis in the singular, end in –ses in the plural	analysis/analyses, hypothesis/hypotheses

USING SPELLCHECKERS

The commonly used word-processing packages have a spellchecking facility. This will alert you to possible misspellings by underlining a word that the package does not recognise. That allows you to go back and check the word in a standard dictionary if the error is not a simple 'typo'.

Some systems will allow you to add words to the package dictionary so that a common error will automatically be changed as you mistype it. You can add words of your own choice to the dictionary part of the software package. In Word, this facility is found under Tools/Autocorrect.

However, despite all these aids, you should still be very conscientious about proof-reading your work. The spellchecker will accept any word that is in its dictionary so that, for example, if you type 'bear wires', the spellchecker will accept this as both words are correctly spelled, although what you really meant was 'bare wires'. At the same time, the word-processing dictionary will not always have a word that you are looking for. In that case, you will need to check the spelling in a dictionary – off the shelf or online.

Table 41.2 Some words that are often misspelled in academic work

Incorrect spelling examples	Correct spelling examples	Incorrect spelling examples	Correct spelling examples
alotof (or alot of)	a lot of	knowlege	knowledge
arguement	argument	maintainance	maintenance
begining	beginning	neccessary	necessary
behavior	behaviour	occassion	occasion
beleive	believe	occured	occurred
Britian	Britain	paralel	parallel
buletin	bulletin	parlament	parliament
campane	campaign	priviledge	privilege
comitee (or comittee)	committee	procede	proceed
comitment	commitment	recieve	receive
could of	could have	sissors	scissors
definatly	definitly	soperate	soparate
developement	development	should of	should have
embaras	embarrass	temprary	temporary
enviroment	environment	tomorow	tomorrow
Febuary	February	Wedensday	Wednesday
goverment	government	wereas	whereas
imediate	immediate	wether	whether
jepardy	jeopardy	witch	which

SPELLING DICTIONARIES

If you find that spelling is a particular difficulty for you, consider buying a spelling dictionary. Some of these dictionaries not only give the correct spelling but also list typical misspelled formats with the correct format alongside. **Ch 42** gives some further information about spelling and other types of dictionary.

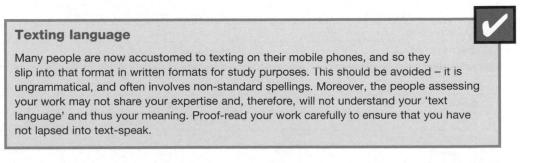

Texting language

Many people are now accustomed to texting on their mobile phones, and so they slip into that format in written formats for study purposes. This should be avoided – it is ungrammatical, and often involves non-standard spellings. Moreover, the people assessing your work may not share your expertise and, therefore, will not understand your 'text language' and thus your meaning. Proof-read your work carefully to ensure that you have not lapsed into text-speak.

Table 41.3 Some word pairs that are commonly confused. The sense is given in parentheses. These pairs are similar in pronunciation. This can cause confusion and means that they are more likely to the written incorrectly.

accent (speech)	**ascent** (climb)
aerial (antenna)	**arial** (font)
affect (change – verb)	**effect** (change – noun)
aisle (passage)	**isle** (small island)
aloud (audible)	**allowed** (permitted)
ascend (climb – verb)	**ascent** (climb – noun)
bare (uncovered)	**bear** (animal/to carry)
blew (past form: blow)	**blue** (colour)
board (strip of timber)	**bored** (wearied of)
born (birth)	**borne** (endure)
canvas (strong fabric)	**canvass** (get opinion)
cereal (grain)	**serial** (in a row)
choose (present form: select)	**chose** (past form: select)
complement (enhance)	**compliment** (praise)
constituency (electoral area)	**consistency** (texture of liquid)
council (committee)	**counsel** (advice/adviser)
currant (dried grape)	**current** (present/flow)
desert (sand)	**dessert** (pudding)
discreet (tactful)	**discrete** (stand-alone)
draft (first copy)	**draught** (wind)
forward (toward front)	**foreword** (book preface)
heal (to make whole)	**heel** (part of foot)
hear (to listen)	**here** (at this place)
holy (sacred)	**wholly** (completely)
loan (money)	**lone** (single)
lose (misplace)	**loose** (slack)
lose (misplace – verb)	**loss** (item lost – noun)
mail (post)	**male** (gender)
peace (tranquillity)	**piece** (portion)
plaice (fish)	**place** (location)
plain (ordinary)	**plane** (tree/aircraft)
practice (noun) (similarly, 'advice')	**practise** (verb) (similarly, 'advise')
principal (main idea/person)	**principle** (fundamental)
root (part of plant)	**route** (journey)
scene (part of a play)	**seen** (past form: saw)
seize (grab)	**cease** (stop)
sight (sense of seeing)	**site** (location)
stationary (not moving)	**stationery** (pens, etc.)
weather (climate)	**whether** (as alternative)
were (past tense: are)	**where** (place)

Avoid using alternatives to standard spelling. It is not advisable to use slang and short word forms such as text-messaging language because examination scripts have to be written in standard English. In any case, the fact that the marker may not be as 'fluent' in the use of text-speak could mean that your point may not be understood.

Learn the correct spelling of the key words in your discipline. Specialist terms need to be accurately spelled. For example, if you are studying politics, it is advisable to learn how to spell 'parliament' correctly. Likewise, if you are studying a scientific subject, it is important to know that the plural of 'formula' is 'formulae' and that 'data' is a plural word with a singular 'datum'. In some disciplines American English is used as the international standard: for example, in chemistry 'sulfur' is used rather than the British English 'sulphur'.

Check on the correct form of a word. If you look up the root form of the word in a good dictionary (which probably means a big dictionary), you will find the different forms of the word, including its plural; if it is deviant from the rules in any way, it will be shown under the headword (see Figure 42.1, page 273). The very act of looking the word up in the dictionary will help to 'seal' it in your memory.

Get into the habit of checking spelling – it often feels better to carry on writing rather than check the spelling of a word, especially when you don't want to disrupt your flow of thought. However, if you make sure that you check the spelling in a dictionary as soon as you can, and write down your common mistakes for reference, this will help you to improve through time.

Spelling does matter! Often, people assert that 'spelling doesn't matter' – in the professional world, however, it really does matter and employers expect graduates to meet appropriate standards of writing, including spelling. People have failed to gain job interviews because their letter of application was sprinkled with grammatical, spelling and punctuation errors. Sometimes a spelling error can radically alter the meaning of a sentence or create nonsense phrases such that a reader would struggle to understand – not a good idea when your work is being assessed. To convince yourself of the potential for this, go back to Table 41.1 and particularly to item 4 on doubled letters, and consider the difference to meaning if an error of spelling was made and some of the letters were not doubled. The list yields several words which exist in their own right but which might not state what the writer intended: robing (robbing); riding (ridding), hoper (hopper). In these instances, the errors could produce nonsense sentences: 'Robing the bank was an act of fraud'; 'riding the world of childhood measles is an international aim'; 'putting the grain into the hoper at a steady speed is an important part of the process'.

42

ENHANCING YOUR VOCABULARY

How to develop your word power

> Whatever your discipline, you will find that, as a university student, you increasingly meet new words. These can be jargon terms that are special to your subject as well as words that are used to explain and discuss topics within your study areas. This chapter suggests some strategies to help you expand your vocabulary gradually, so that you can develop your powers of expression in discussion and in written work.

Expanding your vocabulary is something that you will find is essential, particularly as you start out on your studies. Many disciplines have their own terminology, sometimes called jargon, and you may need to master this before understanding higher-level concepts. Also, the expectation in academic writing (**Ch 37**) is that you use words effectively and correctly, and this implies having a wide vocabulary and expressions to use in the appropriate contexts. Access to a good dictionary – in hard copy or online – will be essential to help you build this up, to check on precise meanings, and to help you avoid using slang expressions or words that are too informal (**Ch 37**).

✔ Twin elements of expanding your vocabulary

1 Use a dictionary to check on the meaning of new words you come across.

2 Use a thesaurus to find new words of similar meaning (synonyms) to ones you already know.

If unsure, you should check words found in a thesaurus for their *precise* meaning, as this may differ subtly from what you intend.

GLOSSARIES

Textbooks in many subject areas now provide fairly comprehensive glossaries at the beginning or end of the book to help you to confirm the meaning of a term quickly. Sometimes textbooks provide a list of key words at the beginning of each chapter to identify new or specialist use of terminology.

Dictionaries vary in size and complexity. For example, some give words, pronunciation and meanings, while others also give examples of correct usage. Your university library will hold a number of different types of dictionary in the reference section and may also provide access to an online dictionary as part of its e-resource bank.

Figure 42.1 shows a typical dictionary entry. From this entry you will be able to identify the form of the word as it is used in your text, or, if you are writing, it will help you choose the correct form for your own work. Each entry is introduced by a headword and this is followed by information about its different forms, for example noun, verb, adjective, and so on. Terms are explained in Figure 42.2 and Tables 42.2 and 42.3. Table 42.1 describes some features of dictionaries and thesauri that can be accessed in hard copy and electronically.

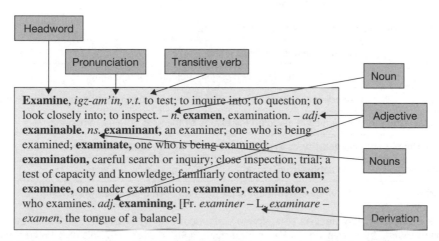

Figure 42.1 A standard dictionary entry, showing different parts and abbreviations

Source: The Chambers Dictionary, 2003. Edinburgh: Chambers Harrap Publishers Ltd.

Digital dictionaries: two types

- **Online dictionaries.** Your university library will normally have access to online dictionaries. These dictionaries offer pronunciations, meanings, different forms of the word, information about the origin of the word and examples of how to use the word. The *Oxford English Dictionary* (*OED*) is a commonly available resource giving British English words; American English can be accessed through the *Merriam–Webster Dictionary*.

- **Electronic dictionaries.** Often available as hand-held devices, part of a word-processing package or on CD-ROM, these vary considerably in price. It is probably best to opt for one that has a word database from a recognised dictionary publisher. Look for one that provides meanings, plus antonyms or synonyms, often provided in a thesaurus function.

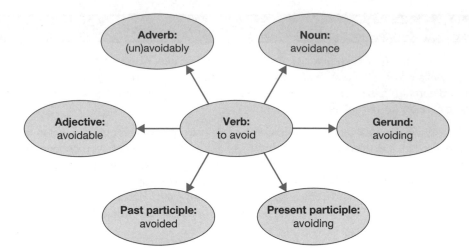

Examples of how to use these types of words in sentences:

Verb	Countries **avoid** war at all costs.
Noun	The **avoidance** of war is a primary objective of diplomats.
Gerund	**Avoiding** conscription in time of war is something many people strive to do.
Present participle	Students are **avoiding** the exams by trying to obtain exemptions.
Past participle	Students have **avoided** the topics that they found most difficult.
Adjective	**Avoidable** errors should be identified quickly by the writer.
Adverb	The judge stated that the plaintiff had been **unavoidably** delayed.

Figure 42.2 Word families. As you expand your vocabulary you will find that you know the word you want to use, but it may not look or sound quite 'right' in your text. This may be because you have not used the word in its correct form. This diagram explains some of the key grammatical terms with examples. If you would like to find definitions of these terms look at Table 39.1. Table 42.2 shows some of the more common word beginnings (prefixes) and Table 42.3 shows endings (suffixes) that identify the different forms of words in English.

i   Keep your writing as intelligible as possible

Each discipline has its own language, which is comprehensible to insiders; remember that one person's professional vocabulary or jargon can exclude others from understanding. Try to keep 'jargon' words to a minimum when you are writing. You can do this by using dictionaries and thesauri to help you find words that are close in meaning to the word(s) that were your first choice. This will enable you to be precise and professional in your use of language, while keeping your text clear and to the point.

SPECIALIST DICTIONARIES

- **Subject dictionary:** gives meanings of specialist terms within a discipline. Provides a quick reference to explanations of specialist terms that are not found in general dictionaries (see Table 42.1).

- **Spelling dictionary:** gives correct spellings as well as frequently misspelt versions with the correct spelling alongside (**Ch 41**).

- **Etymological dictionary:** gives the linguistic origins of words and developing meaning.

- **Collocation dictionary:** gives words that are often positioned together. This is useful when you find yourself searching for one word usually used alongside another.

- **Rhyming dictionary:** gives words with similar end sounds; useful for poetry.

- **Pronunciation dictionary:** gives a phonetic version of the headword. Work out the phonetic code from the symbols that are usually given at the front of the dictionary.

- **Bilingual dictionary:** gives equivalent words from two languages, often arranged in two sections, translating from one language to the other, and vice versa.

- **English learner's dictionary:** primarily intended for those learning English as a second language, but very useful for all because they normally include examples of use, including idioms and a pronunciation guide.

USING A THESAURUS

A thesaurus (plural thesauri) aims to provide words that are similar in meaning – synonyms – in groups. Opposites – antonyms – are sometimes included alongside. *Roget's Thesaurus*, originally published in 1852, was created as the first analysis of the English language structured in this thematic way. To use this type of thesaurus, you look up your original word in an index at the back, which provides a series of numbered sub-groupings with different allied meanings and word types (chiefly nouns, adjectives, adverbs and verbs). Choose the most appropriate, and then look up the numbered group within the main text, to find a listing of synonyms and antonyms. The principles of the original thesaurus have been continued in modern versions, but several publishers now produce A–Z versions. These types are generally more user-friendly than the original Roget-style thesaurus. Figure 42.3 illustrates an example of a thesaurus entry.

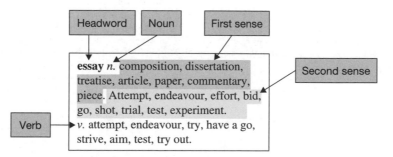

Figure 42.3 Example of a thesaurus entry

Source: The Penguin A–Z Thesaurus, 2001. Harmondsworth: Penguin Books.

Table 42.1 Different types of dictionaries and thesauri

Standard dictionary Dictionaries vary widely in size of content and in price; buying a good one is a sound investment	Subject dictionary Most libraries will stock at least one subject dictionary in your discipline
Features • Arranged in alphabetical order • At the most basic, gives pronunciations, meanings and different forms of the word • Some give examples of how the word is used in a sentence • May provide information about the origin of the word **Comments** • Some provide lists of foreign words used in English • May also include additional miscellany section giving, for example, information about weights and measures, acronyms and abbreviations	**Features** • Quick reference to explanations of specialist terms that you will not find in general dictionaries • Often provides guidance on pronunciation of terms and examples of usage • May give guidance on how to use a term in a sentence **Comments** • If you can afford it, a subject dictionary is a good investment: it will be something you will use throughout your student career and possibly beyond
Online dictionary Usually available via the university library website, but only when on a campus-based machine because of licensing agreements	**Hand-held electronic dictionary** Wide price range. You may be allowed to use these in exams if you are a registered dyslexic student
Features • Gives pronunciations, meanings, different forms of the word, information about the origin of the word and examples of how to use the word **Comments** • Immediately accessible • The *Oxford English Dictionary* (*OED*) provides British-English spelling and usage • The *Merriam–Webster Dictionary* provides American-English spelling and usage	**Features** • Type letters of word on keypad • Provides alternative meanings and word forms • May also give antonyms and synonyms • Some may give pronunciation information **Comments** • It is probably better to opt for one that has a word database from a recognised dictionary publisher
Thesaurus	**Computer software package dictionary and thesaurus functions**
Features • Provides synonyms (sometimes also antonyms) **Comments** • Principles of the original thesaurus have been continued in some modern versions but some publishers favour A–Z formats; these types are generally more user-friendly than the traditional Roget-style thesaurus	**Features** • Place the cursor on the word you want to look up; click on the thesaurus function on the toolbar and this will present options to expand your search **Comments** • A software thesaurus does not usually explain the meaning of the word; it simply gives you synonyms and antonyms

Table 42.2 Prefixes: word beginnings. This table shows how, by adding a letter or letters at the beginning of a word, the meaning can be changed. These beginnings are called prefixes.

Prefix	Meaning	Example
a-	on	aboard
a-, ab-, abs-	away from	avert, abuse, abstain
ad-, ac-, ar-	to	adventure, access, arrange
ante-	before	antenatal
anti-	against	antihistamine
bi-	two	biped
circum-	around	circumscribe, circumnavigate
com-, con-	together	communicate, convene
contra-	against	contrast, contradiction
de-	down	depose
dif-, dis-	apart, not	differ, discredit
ex-	out of	exit
fore-	before	foreknowledge
il-	not	illegible
im-, in-	in, into	implode, intrude
im-, in-	not	immature, inescapable
inter-	between	interact
ir-	not	irregular
mis-	wrong	misplace
ob-	against	obscure
post-	after	post-modern
pre-	before	prerequisite
pro-	forth	progress
re-	back	regress
sub-	under	subtract
trans-	across	transmit
un-	not	unpopular
vice-	instead	vice-president

Table 42.3(a) Suffixes: word endings. This table shows the endings (suffixes) that can be added to the root verb to change the form of the word. Thus, taking the example in Figure 42.2, the root verb is 'avoid' and, to make the noun, the noun ending '-ance' is added. To make the adjective, add '-able'.

Verbs	Nouns		Adjectives		Adverbs
-ain	-aint	-ing	-able	-ic	-ly
-ave	-al	-iour	-al	-ing	
-el	-ance	-ment	-ar	-ious	
-en	-cy	-ness	-ate	-ish	
-ify	-dom	-sion	-ent	-ite	
-ise	-ence	-son	-eous	-ive	
-ive	-ery	-th	-esque	-less	
-ise	-ice	-tion	-ful	-ous	
-uce	-ief	-y	-ial		

Table 42.3(b) Suffix meanings. Some suffixes have particular meanings and this can help to decode the meaning of the word.

Suffix	Meaning	Example
-able, -ible	capable of	readable, legible
-ain, -an	one connected	chaplain, artisan
-ance, -ence	state of	hesitance, difference
-ant	one who	applicant
-el, -et, -ette	little	parcel, pocket, statuette
-er, -eer, -ier	one who	butcher, auctioneer, collier
-ess	female	actress, princess
-fy	to make	pacify
-icle, -sel	small	article, morsel
-less	without	hopeless
-ling	little	gosling
-ment	state of being	encouragement
-ock	little	hummock
-oon, -on	large	balloon
-ory	place for	repository
-ous	full of	curious

✔ 'Decoding' unfamiliar words

If you spend some time studying Tables 42.2, 42.3(a) and 42.3(b), you will be able to deconstruct new words and make a reasoned guess as to their meanings where prefixes or suffixes can be identified. This could be particularly useful in exams where you might come across a word or expression that is unfamiliar.

Table 42.4 Basic personal glossary. You can use this 'quick glossary' for recording meanings or simply as a spellchecking list. If you have a lot of specialist terms to learn, then you might want to create a quick glossary for each subject or even topic. This can then be filed along with the relevant notes. In a very short time, you will have expanded your vocabulary considerably and will be able to use your glossary words correctly in your academic writing. Being more familiar with some of the terms and their meanings will also help to speed up your reading. A blank copyright-free version is included in the Appendix for your use (page 447).

A	B	C	D	E	F
antonym: word opposite in meaning			**derivation**: origin, tracing, word root		
G	H	I	J	K	L
glossary: word list	**headword**: key word for a dictionary entry				
M	N	O	P	Q	R
			phonetic: by pronunciation **prefix**: put at the beginning		
S	T	U	V	W	X Y Z
suffix: put at the end **synonym**: word similar in meaning					

PRACTICAL TIPS FOR DEVELOPING YOUR USE OF ACADEMIC TERMS AND LANGUAGE

Find out what the abbreviations mean in your dictionary and thesaurus. You won't always have access to online dictionaries or thesauri so it is important to know and understand how these reference resources work in hard copy. Look for the section on 'how to use this reference book', as this will explain the symbols and abbreviations that have been used. Knowing these will save you time and will help you to get the most out of the reference source you are using. For example, you can find out more about grammar terms and the code used for the pronunciation guides.

Sign up for 'word of the day'. Some online dictionaries sites have a free sign-up feature that means you will receive a new word by email every day. While some of these words may be totally unusable as far as you are concerned, many will add to your working vocabulary. Two examples of sites that have this facility are:

http://dictionary.reference.com/wordoftheday
www.m-w.com/cgi-bin/mwwod.plv

Consult a dictionary and thesaurus while you are writing. The best time to pick up new words and check on their meanings is when you are writing. You should try to get into the habit of looking up either of these reference works any time you feel unsure about any word or its use.

43
REVIEWING, EDITING AND PROOF-READING

How to make sure that your writing makes sense

Looking critically at your own writing is essential if you want to produce work of the highest quality. These editing skills will allow you to improve the sense, grammar and syntax of your written assignments.

Writing is a process. It begins with a plan and it finishes with reviewing, editing and proof-reading. This means that you should read your text critically and edit it before submitting it for assessment. The effort you invest in this final stage will contribute to the quality of your work and to your assessed mark. Ideally, you should leave a gap of time between completing the writing and beginning the reviewing process, as this allows you to 'distance' yourself from the work and helps you look at it as a new reader would.

THE REVIEWING, EDITING AND PROOF-READING PROCESS

At this stage you are performing the role of editor. This means that you are looking critically at your text for content, relevance and sense, as well as for flaws in layout, grammar, punctuation and spelling. You should also check for consistency in all aspects, for example, in the use of terminology, in spelling, and in presentational features such as font and point size, layout of paragraphs, and labelling of tables and diagrams.

i

Definitions

Reviewing: appraising critically: that is, examining a task or project to ensure that it meets the requirements and objectives of the task and that the overall sense is conveyed as well.

Editing: revising and correcting later drafts of an essay, to arrive at a final version. Usually, this involves the smaller rather than the larger details, such as details of punctuation, spelling, grammar and layout.

Proof-reading: checking a printed copy for errors of any sort.

Clearly, there are a lot of aspects to cover, and some degree of overlap in different aspects of the process. Some people prefer to go through their text in one sweep, amending any flaws as they go; others, in particular professional writers, take a staged approach, reading through their text several times looking at a different aspect each time. Here are five aspects to consider in the reviewing process:

- content and relevance
- clarity, style and coherence
- grammatical correctness
- spelling and punctuation
- presentation.

Table 43.1 provides a quick checklist of key aspects to consider under each of these themes. This has been designed for photocopying so that you can, if you wish, use it as a checklist each time you complete a piece of work. Table 43.2 gives some strategies you can adopt when going through the editing process. Professional proof-readers have developed a system of symbols to speed up the editing and proof-reading process. You may wish to adopt some of these yourself, and you are certainly likely to see some of them, and other 'informal' marks, on work returned by tutors. Table 43.3 illustrates some of the more commonly used symbols.

REVIEWING YOUR ANSWERS IN EXAMS

In exams, the reviewing process has to be swift and efficient (**Ch 66**). Here, you will normally have time only to skim-read the text, making adjustments as you go. If you find you have missed something out, place an insert mark ($\wedge$ or $\curlywedge$) in the text and/or margin with the annotation 'see additional paragraph x'; then write this paragraph, clearly identified, at the end of the answer (where you will have left space for just this contingency). Similarly, if you have consistently made an error, for example, referred to Louis XIV throughout as Louis XVI, just put an asterisk beside the first occurrence of the error and a note at the end of your answer or in the margin 'Consistent error. Please read as "XIV"'. You will not lose any marks for correcting your work in these ways.

✔ **Technical notes**

The word processor has made the reviewing and editing task much easier. Here are some tips for using this software effectively:

- Use the word-count facility to check on length.
- Use the 'View' facility to check page breaks and general layout before you print out.
- Don't rely entirely on the spell- and grammar checker.
- Sometimes the grammar checker will announce that you have used the passive voice. This is often a standard academic usage and, therefore, is not an error.
- Sometimes staff add comments to students' work using 'Tools/Track Changes' on the Microsoft Word software. Depending on the version you are using, feedback information can usually be accepted or rejected by right-clicking on the word or punctuation point that has been marked for alteration. Alternatively, some staff prefer to use the *Comments* function.

Table 43.1 Proof-reading and editing checklists. Each heading represents a 'sweep' of your text, checking for the aspects shown. The text is assumed to be a piece of writing produced for assessment. This table is copyright-free for use when reviewing your work.

Content and relevance	Clarity, style and coherence	Grammatical correctness	Spelling and punctuation	Presentation
See also **Ch 32–Ch 37**	See also **Ch 37**	See also **Ch 38–Ch 39**	See also **Ch 40–Ch 41**	See also **Ch 44**
❑ The intent of the instruction word has been followed (**Ch 32**) ❑ The question or task has been completed: that is, you have answered all sections or required numbers of questions (**Ch 32, Ch 33**) ❑ The structure is appropriate (**Ch 33, Ch 34**) ❑ The text shows objectivity (**Ch 37**) ❑ The examples are relevant ❑ All sources are correctly cited (**Ch 35**) ❑ The facts presented are accurate	❑ The aims and objectives are clear ❑ What you wrote is what you meant to write ❑ The text is fluent, with appropriate use of signpost words (**Ch 38**) ❑ Any informal language (**Ch 37**) has been removed ❑ The style is academic and appropriate for the task (**Ch 37**) ❑ The content and style of each section is consistent (**Ch 37**) ❑ The tense used in each section is suited to the time-frame of your text and is consistent ❑ The lengths of the text sections are balanced appropriately (**Ch 33**)	❑ All sentences are complete ❑ All sentences make sense (**Ch 38**) ❑ Paragraphs have been correctly used (**Ch 38**) ❑ Suggestions made by grammar checker have been accepted/rejected (**Ch 39**) ❑ The text has been checked against your own checklist of recurrent grammatical errors (**Ch 39**) ❑ The text is consistent in adopting British or American English (**Ch 37**)	❑ Any blatant 'typos' have been corrected by reading for meaning ❑ The text has been spell-checked and looked at for your 'own' most often misspelled words ❑ A check has been made for spelling of subject-specific words and words from other languages ❑ Punctuation has been checked, if possible, by the 'reading aloud' method ❑ Proper names are correctly capitalised ❑ Overlong sentences have been divided	❑ The text length meets the word-count target – neither too short nor too long ❑ If no word-count target is given, the overall length is as might be expected for the time you were supposed to allocate to the task (ask a tutor if uncertain) ❑ Overall neatness checked ❑ The cover-sheet details and presentation aspects are as required by your department (**Ch 44**) ❑ The bibliography/reference list is correctly formatted (**Ch 35**) ❑ Page numbers have been included (in position stipulated, if given) ❑ The figures and tables are in appropriate format (**Ch 33**)

Table 43.2 Editing strategies. The reviewing/editing/proof-reading process can be done in a single 'sweep'. As you become more experienced, you will become adept at doing this. However, initially, it might help you to focus on each of these three broad aspects in a separate 'sweep' of the text. Note that the first two columns combine pairs of aspects considered in Table 43.1.

Content and relevance; clarity, style and coherence	Grammatical correctness, spelling and punctuation	Presentation
• Read text aloud – your ears will help you to identify errors that your eyes have missed.	• Check titles and subtitles are appropriate to the style of the work and stand out by using bold or underlining (not both).	• Check that you have made good use of white space: that is, not crammed the text into too tight a space, and that your text is neat and legible.
• Revisit the task or question. Check your interpretation against the task as set.	• Consider whether the different parts link together well – if not, introduce signpost words to guide the reader through the text.	• If word-processed, check that you have followed standard typing conventions **(Ch 44)**. Follow any 'house style' rules stipulated by your department.
• Work on a hard copy using editing symbols to correct errors (Table 43.3).	• Check for fluency in sentence and paragraph structure – remodel as required.	• Check that you have included a reference list, consistently following a recognised method
• Identify that the aims you set out in your introduction have been met.	• Check sentence length – remodel to shorter or longer sentences. Sometimes shorter sentences	**(Ch 35)**, and that all citations in the text are matched by an entry in the reference list and
• Read objectively and assess whether the text makes sense. Look for inconsistencies in argument.	are more effective than longer ones.	vice versa.
	• Ensure that you have been consistent in spelling conventions, for example following British-English rather than American-English spelling.	• Ensure all pages are numbered and are stapled or clipped, and, if appropriate, ensure that the cover page is included.
• Check that all your facts are correct.	• Spelling errors – use the spellchecker but be	• Check that your name, matriculation number and course number are included. You may wish to add
• Insert additional or overlooked evidence that strengthens the whole.	prepared to double-check in a standard dictionary if you are in doubt or cannot find a spelling within	this information as a footnote that appears on each page.
• Remove anything that is not relevant or alter the text so that it is clear and unambiguous. Reducing	the spellchecker facility **(Ch 41)**.	• Ensure question number and title are included.
text by 10–25 per cent can improve quality considerably.	• Check for cumbersome constructions – divide or restructure sentence(s); consider whether active or passive is more suitable. Consider using	• Check that labelling of diagrams, charts and other visual material is in sequence and consistently presented.
• Honestly and critically assess your material to ensure that you have attributed ideas to the sources: that is, check that you have not	vocabulary that might convey your point more eloquently **(Ch 42)**.	• Ensure that supporting material is added in sequence as appendices, footnotes, endnotes
committed plagiarism **(Ch 36)**.	• Check for use of 'absolute' terms to ensure that you maintain objectivity **(Ch 37)**.	or as a glossary as applicable.
• Remodel any expressions that are too informal for academic contexts.		
• Eliminate gendered or discriminatory language.		

Table 43.3 Common proof-reading symbols. University lecturers and tutors use a variety of symbols on students' assignments to Indicate errors, corrections or suggestions. These can apply to punctuation, spelling, presentation or grammar. The symbols provide a kind of 'shorthand' that acts as a code to help you see how you might be able to amend your text so that it reads correctly and fluently. In this table some of the more commonly used correction marks are shown alongside their meanings. The sample text shows how these symbols may be used either in the text or the margin to indicate where a change is recommended.

Correction mark	Meaning	Example
⌐ (np)	(new) paragraph	
≠	change CAPITALS to small letters (lower case)	
∼∼∼	change into **bold** type	
≡	change into CAPITALS	
⌒	close up (delete space)	
/ or ⌐ or ⊢	delete	
⋏	insert a word or letter	
⅄	insert space	
.... or (STET)	leave unchanged	
Insert punctuation symbol in a circle (P)	punctuation	
plag.	plagiarism	
⟶	run on (no new paragraph)	
Sp.	spelling	
⊔⊓	transpose text	
?	what do you mean?	
??	text does not seem to make sense	
✓	good point/correct	
×	error	

The Example column contains the following text and margin notes:

Text — *margin*

The correction marks that ⌒ tutors — ⌒

use in students' texts are generally — ⅄

made to help identify where there

have been errors of spllin or — ⋏e/⋏g

punctuation. They can often — (STET)

indicate where there is lack of

paragraphing or grammatical

accuracy. If you find that work is — (np)

returned to you with such

marks correction then it is — ⊔⊓

worthwhile spending some time

analysing the common errors as — ⟋

well as the comments, because this

will help you to improve the

quality of presentation and content

of your work this reviewing can — ⊙/≡

have a positive effect on your

assessed mark.

In the margin, the error symbols are separated by a slash (/), as in the third example down.

THE VALUE OF REVIEWING, EDITING AND PROOF-READING

Many students do not appreciate the potential complexity of the review process, and prefer to submit material as soon as they have written a first draft. However, a text that is not revised in this way will be unlikely to receive as favourable a reading – and possibly as high a mark – as one that has been fully reviewed, edited and proofed. It is the mix of style, content, structure and presentation that will gain you marks, and anything you can do to increase your 'mark-earning' power will be to your advantage. In the longer term, learning how to edit your work properly will help you to develop a skill of critical analysis that will stand you in good stead throughout your career.

PRACTICAL TIPS FOR REVIEWING, EDITING AND PROOF-READING YOUR WORK

Make time for checking. When planning the writing, ensure that you have allowed adequate time for reviewing and proof-reading. You don't want to spoil all your hard work by skimping on the final stage. Leave some time between finishing the final draft and returning to check the whole text, because you will return to your work with a fresh and possibly more critical eye.

Work from a hard copy. Reading through your work laid out on paper, which is the format in which your marker will probably see it, will help you identify errors and inconsistencies more readily than might be possible on the screen. A paper version is also easier to annotate (although this can also be done using the 'Track Changes' facility on your word processor). A printout also allows you to see the whole work in overview, and focus on the way the text 'flows'. If necessary, spread it out on the desk in front of you.

Follow the 'reading aloud' check. This is a tried and tested technique to ensure that what you have written actually makes sense. Simply read your text aloud to yourself. Your ears will hear the errors that your eyes might miss on a silent reading of the text. This will help you correct grammatical and spelling inconsistencies, as well as punctuation omissions. (Note: this method is not suitable for use in exams!)

Map your work to obtain an overview. 'Label' each paragraph with a topic heading and list these in a linear way on a separate paper. This will provide you with a 'snapshot' of your text and will allow you to appraise the order, check against any original plan, and adjust the position of parts as you feel necessary.

Check for relevance. Ensure from an early stage that you are interpreting the task, as set, sensibly and that your misinterpretation has not caused you to 'make up' another title for the task. Whatever you have written will be judged by the terms of the original task, not by the one you have created.

Check for consistency in the elements of your text. For example, ensure that your introduction and conclusion complement and do not contradict each other.

Check for factual accuracy. Ensure that all the facts are correct, for example, in a history essay that the date sequences are consistent, or in a scientific paper that a numerical answer you have reached is realistic. It is very easy to type a date erroneously or make a final slip in the transposition of an answer from one area of the page to the final answer and, thus, lose marks.

Stick to your word limits/targets. Remember that too few words can be just as bad as too many. The key point is that your writing must be clear to your reader. Sometimes this means giving a longer explanation; sometimes it means simplifying what you have written. However, at this stage, if you are over the word-count limit, check for ways in which you can reword the text to eliminate redundant words while maintaining the sense you intended to convey (see also **Ch 33**).

Check visual aspects. Diagrams, tables and figures should be drawn using a ruler, if you cannot create these electronically. Only in some subjects would freehand drawing be acceptable, for example, in the study of Architecture.

Create 'white space'. To help produce a more 'reader-friendly' document that will not deter the marker, try to create 'white space' by:

- leaving space (one 'return' space) between paragraphs;
- justifying only on the left side of the page;
- leaving space around diagrams, tables and other visual material;
- leaving reasonable spaces between headings, sub-headings and text.

Check that all the 'secretarial' aspects are in place. Neat presentation, punctuation and spelling all help your reader to access the information, ideas and argument of your writing. While this may not gain you marks, it will certainly ensure that you do not lose marks even indirectly by making the marker struggle to 'decode' your work.

44

PRESENTATION OF ASSIGNMENTS

How to follow the appropriate academic conventions

> **The presentation of your written work may be assessed directly and it may influence the way tutors mark the content. This chapter explains how to create a polished submission that follows the established standards of academic writing.**

Most marks for assignments are awarded for content, which depends on:

- activities that take place *before* you write, such as researching your sources, conducting experiments or analysing the literature;
- the way you express your ideas in writing (**Ch 32–Ch 43**).

However, some marks will always be directly or indirectly reserved for presentation, so the final 'production' phase can influence your overall grading.

Presentation involves more than layout and use of visual elements; it includes accuracy, consistency and attention to detail. For this reason it is often associated with editing and proof-reading (**Ch 43**). You'll need time to get these aspects right, so when you plan the writing-up process, you should include a final phase for tackling them. For an assignment such as a lengthy in-course essay, this could mean trying to complete the content phase at least a day ahead of the submission date.

? Why does good presentation matter?

- It may be an element of the assessment.
- It helps the marker understand what you have written.
- It shows you can adopt professional standards in your work.
- It demonstrates you have acquired important skills that will transfer to other subjects and, later, employment.

OVERALL LAYOUT

This will depend on the type of academic writing you have been asked to produce – an essay, report, summary, case study or a worked problem. An assignment like an essay could have a relatively simple structure: a cover page, the main essay text and a list of references. A lab report might be more complex, with a title page, abstract, introduction and sections for materials and methods, results, discussion/conclusion and references (Ch 54). Layouts for most types of assignment also vary slightly depending on discipline. You should research this carefully before you start to write up, by consulting the course handbook or other regulations.

COVER PAGE

This is important to get right because it will create a good first impression. Your department may specify a cover-page design that is required for all submissions. If this is the case, make sure that you follow the instructions closely, as the layout may have been constructed for a particular purpose. For example, it may aid anonymous marking or provide markers with a standard format for providing feedback (see Figure 44.1 for an example).

If detailed instructions for a cover page are not given, ensure that you provide your name and/or matriculation number at the head of your work. Where anonymous marking is applied, then your matriculation number only would be required. Add your course title and/or code. The tutor's name is also helpful. Give the question number and title of the question. The model layout in Figure 44.1 suggests one way to present the essential information neatly and clearly. Keep it simple: a cover sheet with fancy graphics will not add to your mark.

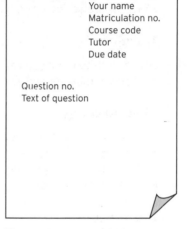

Figure 44.1 A model cover-page layout

MAIN TEXT

The majority of student assignments are word-processed, and this may be a submission requirement. You should always try to use a word processor and a good quality printer, if you can, because this makes the drafting and editing phases easier and gives a more professional result. However, if handwriting your submission, make sure you leave sufficient time to copy out your draft neatly and legibly. Write on only one side of the paper – this makes it easier to read, and if you make a significant error you only have to rewrite a single sheet.

Automatic wrapping of text ✔

A point to note for computing novices is that when typing text into a word processor the words will automatically follow on to the next line (wrap). This means that you don't need to press the return key at the end of every line.

Font

There are two main choices: serif types, with extra strokes at the end of the main strokes of each letter, and sans serif types, without these strokes (see Figure 44.2). The type to use is usually left to personal preference, but a serif font is said to be easier to read. More likely to be specified is the point size (pt) of the font, which will probably be 11 or 12 point for ease of reading.

You should avoid using elaborate font types as generally they will not help the reader to assimilate what you have written. For the same reason, you should not use too many forms of emphasis. Choose *italics* or **bold** and stick with one only. Symbols are often used in academic work and in Microsoft Word can be added using the 'Insert > Symbol' menu.

Serif font

Times roman 11 pt

Times roman 12 pt

Times roman 14 pt

Sans serif font

Arial 11 pt

Arial 12 pt

Arial 14 pt

Figure 44.2 Examples of the main types of font at different point sizes

Margins

Usually left-hand margins are 4 cm and the right-hand margins 2.5 cm. This allows space for the marker's comments and ensures that the text can be read if a left-hand binding is used.

Line spacing

It is easier to read text that is spaced at least at 1.5–2 lines apart. Some markers like to add comments as they read the text and this leaves them space to do so. The exception is where you wish to use long quotations. These should be indented and typed in single-line spacing (see **Ch 35**, page 215).

Paragraphs

The key thing to remember about layout is to make good use of the 'white space'. This means that you should lay out your paragraphs clearly and consistently. Some people prefer the indentation method, where the paragraph begins on the fourth character space from the left-hand margin (Figure 44.3a).

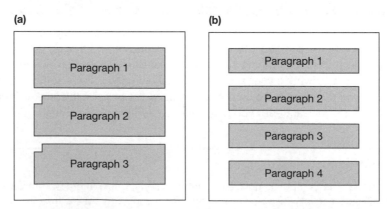

Figure 44.3 Types of paragraph layout. (a) indented and (b) blocked. Note in the representation of the indented model, that by convention, the first paragraph in any section is *not* indented.

Others prefer the blocked paragraph style, that is, where all paragraphs begin on the left-hand margin but are separated by a double-line space (Figure 44.3b). The space between paragraphs should be roughly equivalent to a missing line. In Microsoft Word these aspects can be controlled using the 'Format > Paragraph' menu.

Sub-headings

In some disciplines use of sub-headings is acceptable or even favoured, though in others these 'signpost' strategies are discouraged. It is best to consult your tutor or course handbook about this if you are uncertain. Sub-headings are usually in bold (**Ch 33**).

Punctuation

Standard punctuation applies to all types of academic writing and is dealt with in detail in **Ch 40**.

Word count

You may be asked to work to a word count and tips for doing this are provided in **Ch 43**. If you greatly exceed this limit, this will almost certainly impact on your presentation as you will confront the reader with too much information and will probably not be writing crisply and concisely (**Ch 32**).

CITATIONS AND REFERENCES

A citation is a mention of a source in the main body of your text – usually author surname(s) and date of publication and, in some styles, the relevant page(s). The associated reference consists of further details of the source that would, for example, allow the reader to find it in a library or online. Citing authors or sources is essential within your text when you refer to ideas or quotations that are not your own. This is an important academic convention that you must observe to avoid plagiarism (**Ch 36**). Providing a reference list is, therefore, standard practice and, for this reason, markers may deduct marks if you omit one.

There are several ways in which citations can be presented, and the more common methods are outlined in **Ch 35**. References are usually listed at the end of your text in a separate section, although in some systems they may be positioned at the bottom of the page where the citation occurs. You must be consistent in the referencing style you adopt, and some disciplines impose strict subject-specific conventions. If in doubt, consult your course handbook or your lecturer.

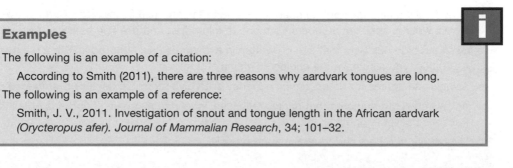

Examples

The following is an example of a citation:

    According to Smith (2011), there are three reasons why aardvark tongues are long.

The following is an example of a reference:

    Smith, J. V., 2011. Investigation of snout and tongue length in the African aardvark *(Orycteropus afer)*. *Journal of Mammalian Research*, 34; 101–32.

QUOTATIONS AND FORMULAE

Quotations and formulae can be integrated into the text when short, but are usually presented as a 'special' type of paragraph when long (**Ch 35**). In both cases, the source and date of publication are provided after the quotation.

- **Short quotations** are integrated within the sentence and are placed within single inverted commas. Quotations within the quote are in double inverted commas (Table 40.1 and Figure 44.4).

> The cultural values identifiable in one minority group create what has been called the 'invisible clamour' (Henze, 1990) as they conflict with those of the dominant culture.

Figure 44.4 How to present a short quotation in text form

- **Long quotations** are usually 40 or more words of prose (some propose 30) or more than two lines of poetry. They are indented by five character spaces from the left margin. No quotation marks are necessary unless there are quotation marks used in the text you are quoting (Figure 44.5). Usually long quotes are single-line spaced.

Paragraph A

Long quote

Source (date)

Paragraph B

Figure 44.5 How to present a long quote, shown in outline form (see also **Ch 35**, page 216)

Some disciplines, for example, English Literature and Law, have very specific rules for the way in which quotations are to be laid out and referenced. In such cases, consult your course handbook or ask for guidance from a tutor.

Short formulae or equations can be included in text, but they are probably better presented on a separate line and indented, thus

$$\alpha + 4\beta / \eta^2 \, \pi = 0 \qquad \text{(Eqn. 45.1)}$$

Where a large number of formulae are included, they can be numbered for ease of cross-reference, as shown above.

QUOTING NUMBERS IN TEXT

Adopt the following rules:

- In general writing, spell out numbers from one to ten and use figures for 11 and above; in formal writing, spell out numbers from one to a hundred and use figures above this.
- Spell out high numbers that can be written in two words ('six hundred'). With a number like 4,200,000, you also have the choice of writing '4.2 million'.
- Always use figures for dates, times, currency or to give technical details ('5-amp fuse').
- Always spell out numbers that begin sentences, indefinite numbers ('hundreds of soldiers') or fractions ('seven-eighths').
- Hyphenate numbers and fractions appropriately.

You may be expected to support your academic writing with visual material or data, and it is important that you do so in a fashion that best helps the reader to assimilate the information. You must also follow any specific presentational rules that apply in your subject area.

Figures

The academic convention is to include a wide range of visual material under the term 'Figure' ('Fig.' for short). This includes graphs, diagrams, charts, sketches, pictures and photographs, although in some disciplines and contexts photographs may be referred to as plates. There are quite strict rules regarding the way figures are used (see also **Ch 30**). Here's a set of guidelines to follow when including figures in an assignment:

- All figures should be referred to in the text. There are 'standard' formulations for doing this, such as 'Fig. 4 shows that . . .'; or '. . . results for one treatment were higher than for the other (see Fig. 2)'. Find what is appropriate from the literature or texts in your subject area.

- You should always number the figures in the order in which they are referred to in the text. If you are including the figures within the main body of text (usually more convenient for the reader) they should appear at the next suitable position in the text after the first time of mention. At the very least this will be after the paragraph that includes the first citation, but more normally will be at the top of the following page.

- Try to position your figures at the top or bottom of a page, rather than sandwiched between blocks of text. This looks neater and makes the text easier to read.

- Each figure should have a legend, which will include the figure number, a title and some text (often a key to the symbols and line styles used). The convention is for figure legends to appear below each figure. Your aim should be to make each figure self-contained. That is, a reader who knows the general subject area should be able to work out what your figure shows, without reference to other material.

Selecting what to put on each axis of a graph

The norm is to put the controlled variable or category of measurement on the x-axis (horizontal axis) and the measured variable on the y-axis (vertical axis).

y-axis

x-axis

i

Choosing the right *type* of figure to display information is an art in itself (see **Ch 30**). Although there are technical reasons why some forms of data should be presented in particular ways (for example, proportional data in a pie chart rather than a line chart), your main focus should always be on selecting a method that will best help the reader assimilate the information presented. Jones, Reed and Weyers (2012) or the 'Chart Wizard' in the Microsoft Office Excel spreadsheet program are possible starting points for exploring the range of possibilities.

When presenting individual figures, clarity should be your main aim – ensuring, for example, that the different slices of a pie chart or the lines and symbols in a graph are clearly distinguishable from one another. Consistency is also important, so you should use the same line or shading for the same entity in all your figures (for example, hollow symbols for 'controls'). The widespread availability of colour printers should help with this, but some departments may insist on the use of black and white, since this was the convention when colour printing was prohibitively expensive. If you are using colour, keep it 'tasteful' and remember that certain colour combinations are not easily differentiated by some readers. Take great care to ensure that the quantity plotted and its units are provided for all axes.

> ### ✔ Inserting figures in text
>
> Integrated suites of office-type software allow you to insert the graphs you produced using the spreadsheet program into text produced with the word-processing program. The two programs can even be linked so that changes on the spreadsheet data automatically appear in the graph within the word-processed file. Consult the manual or 'Help' facility to find out how to do this. In MS Word, digital photographs can be inserted using the 'Insert > Picture > From File' command.

Tables

These are used to summarise large amounts of information, especially where a reader might be interested in some of the detail of the data. Tables are especially useful for qualitative information (see **Ch 30** and examples in this text, such as Table 42.3 on page 278) but numerical data can also be presented, especially if they relate to a discontinuous qualitative variable (for example, the population sizes and occupation breakdown of various geographical regions).

Tables generally include a number of columns (vertical) and rows (horizontal). By analogy with figures, the convention is to put the controlled or measured variable on the column headers (horizontal) and to place the measured variable or categories of measurement in the rows (vertical). Do not forget to include the units of the information listed if this is relevant.

The rules for presenting tables are very similar to those for figures, with the important exception that a table legend should appear above the table. It is quite common to note exceptions and other information as footnotes to tables.

> ### ❓ Figure or table?
>
> In certain cases it may be possible to present the same data set as a figure or as a table. The first rule in such cases is never do both – choose the method that best suits your data and the target reader. An important criterion is to decide which will best help the reader assimilate the information. If the take-home message is best shown visually, a figure might be best; whereas, if details and numerical accuracy are important, a table might be more suitable.

PRACTICAL TIPS FOR PRESENTING YOUR WORK

Don't let grammatical and stylistic errors spoil your work. It is a waste of effort to concentrate on presentation without also ensuring that you have ironed out minor errors at the review and proof-reading stages (**Ch 43**).

Adopt standard word-processing layout conventions. Adopting the following guidelines will ensure a neat, well-spaced presentation:

- usually one character space after the following punctuation – full stop, comma, colon, semi-colon, closing inverted commas (double and single), question mark and exclamation mark (Note that, in some referencing style guides, the requirement is to leave 2 character spaces between sentences);
- no character space after apostrophes in a 'medial' position e.g. it's, men's, monkey's;
- no indentation of paragraphs (that is, blocked style);
- one standard line space between paragraphs;
- left-justified text;
- italicised letters for foreign words and titles of books, journals and papers (**Ch 35**);
- headings in same font size as text, but bold.

Adopt figure and table styles from the literature. If you have doubts about the precise style or arrangement of figures and tables, follow the model shown in texts or journal articles from your subject area. Also, check whether relevant instructions are published in the course handbook.

Don't automatically accept the graphical output from spreadsheets and other programs. These are not always in the 'correct' style. For example, the default output for many charts produced by some versions of the Microsoft Office Excel spreadsheet includes a grey background and horizontal gridlines, neither of which is generally used. It is not difficult to alter these parts of the chart, and you should learn how to do this from manuals or the 'Help' facility.

In numerical disciplines, take care in laying out your answer. Use plenty of space, working your way down the page in sequence. Don't work across the page, as this doesn't allow the flow of thinking to be apparent. Always give units, as this is a good way of trapping errors. Use a ruler for simple diagrams (for example, electrical circuits) as this will be much neater than freehand. Underline all answers and score out any rough work with a single diagonal line.

University assessment systems are complex and rather different from those used at school or college. This chapter clarifies the terminology involved and explains the rationale for different modes of assessment, while later chapters discuss how to tackle specific question types.

A university is an educational institution with a legal charter entitling it to award its own degrees. These degrees are granted on the basis of performance in assessments and exams, which may vary in character depending on subject and institution. As a result, each university has its own conventions regarding style of question, format of exams and marking criteria. No two universities are the same. It is essential that you take into account how the exam system operates in your own institution *before* you start revising.

Exam papers and diets may be structured in different ways, according to discipline. The design may reflect the different aspects of learning that your tutors wish to assess (**Ch 46** and **Ch 48**). For example, there may be a multiple-choice component that tests your surface knowledge across a wide range of topics, while an essay section may be included to test your deeper knowledge in fewer topics. Papers and questions may carry different weightings towards an aggregate mark.

Various levels of choice are given to reflect the nature of the field of study. In professional disciplines there may be a need to ensure you are knowledgeable in all areas, while in other subjects a certain amount of specialisation may be acceptable. Some exam papers are divided into sections, and you will be expected to answer one or more questions from the options within each of these. This format allows a limited amount of choice while ensuring that you have covered all major areas in your studies. It is vital that you take these aspects of exam paper design into account when arriving at a strategy for revision and exam-sitting (**Ch 66**).

FORMS OF ASSESSMENT

Each degree programme and every unit of teaching at university (usually called a 'module') will have a published set of aims and learning objectives or outcomes. Your performance in relation to these goals will be tested in various ways.

- **Formative assessments** are primarily designed to give you feedback on the quality of your answers. In some cases these are known as 'class exams'. They generally do not count towards your final module assessment, although sometimes a small proportion of marks will carry forward as an incentive to perform well.

- **Summative assessments** count directly towards a module or degree assessment. Many summative exams are held as formal invigilated tests where you work in isolation. These may be known as degree exams and, in the honours year, in some institutions, as 'finals'. These exams may comprise several sittings or papers, perhaps covering different aspects of the course, and often lasting for two or three hours each. The collective set of exams is sometimes known as an exam diet.

In some cases the assessment will be entirely based on in-course assignments. These may take the form of essays, projects and solutions to set problems (see Tip Box below). In most cases, however, the overall mark will consist of a mix of marks from such coursework and formal invigilated exams. The latter are favoured in later years, because the possibility of collaboration, plagiarism or impersonation is limited. You are expected to perform alone under a certain amount of time pressure.

Problem-based learning (PBL)

This is a form of learning where you are asked to investigate a specific problem, usually related to a real-life professional situation, which may be open-ended in nature (that is, not necessarily having a 'right answer'). You may be part of a small team asked to consider the problem, research the underlying theory and practice that might lead to a response, and arrive at a practical solution. Assessment of the exercise will focus not only on the solution you arrive at, but also on the way in which you arrive at it, so here process is often at least as important as the product. There may be group- and peer-assessment elements to your grade.

Exam papers and diets may be structured in different ways, according to discipline. The design may reflect the different aspects of learning that your tutors wish to assess (see **Ch 46–Ch 58**). For example, there may be a multiple-choice component that tests your surface knowledge across a wide range of topics, while an essay section may be included to test your deeper knowledge in fewer topics. Papers and questions may carry different weightings towards an aggregate mark.

Exam format

This should never come as a surprise to you as you should have checked up on it by looking at past papers and by confirming with lecturers that there have been no changes to the style of examination.

Various levels of choice are given to reflect the nature of the field of study. In professional disciplines there may be a need to ensure you are knowledgeable in all areas, while in other subjects a certain amount of specialisation may be acceptable. Some exam papers are divided into sections, and you will be expected to answer one or more questions from the options within each of these. This format allows a limited amount of choice while ensuring that you have covered all major areas in your studies. It is vital that you take these aspects of exam paper design into account when arriving at a strategy for revision and exam-sitting (**Ch 61, Ch 66**).

MARKING CRITERIA AND GRADING SCHEMES

Who marks your papers? How do they do it? Often students are unsure about this.

The norm is for papers to be graded by the person who delivered the lectures, tutorials or practical classes that are being assessed. However, due to large class sizes, alternative mechanisms may be employed:

- the marking may be spread out among several tutors;
- especially in multiple-choice papers, the marking may be automated;
- where teamwork is involved, peer assessment may take place (see Information Box below).

Each university, college or faculty will publish assessment reporting scales, usually in handbooks and/or websites. Some operate to a familiar system of banded percentages, often related to honours degree classifications, while others adopt a different form of qualitative band 'descriptors'. You should find out which system applies in your case and consult the general marking criteria used to assign work in each band. This will give you a better idea of the standard of work needed to produce a specific grade, and may help you to understand feedback from tutors (**Ch 58**).

To maintain standards and ensure fairness, several systems operate:

- marks may be determined according to an explicit marking scheme that allocates a proportion of the total to different aspects of your answer;
- double or triple marking may take place and if the grades awarded differ, the answer may be scrutinised more closely, possibly by a external examiner;
- papers are usually marked anonymously, so the marker does not know whose answer they are grading;
- the external marker will confirm the overall standard and may inspect some papers, particularly those falling at the division between honours grades or on the pass/fail boundary.

---

i | **Peer assessment**

This is where the members of a study team are asked to assign a mark to each other's performance. This might take account, for example, of the effort put in, the conduct in the assigned team role(s), and contribution to the final outcome. Clear guidance is always given about how you should assign marks.

---

i | **External examiners and assessors**

External examiners are appointed by the university to oversee marking in specific papers and to ensure standards are maintained and that the assessment is fair. They are usually noted academics in the field, with wide experience of examining. They will be asked to comment on the exam question papers in advance and will generally look closely at a representative selection of written papers and project work. For finals, they may interview students in an oral, to ensure that spoken responses meet the standard of the written answers, and to arrive at a judgement on borderline cases. Note that where papers are borderline pass/fail, they are often double-marked before being sent to the external examiner, who recommends the final mark. Papers are dealt with anonymously until a final mark has been agreed.

Accreditation bodies in the professions may be involved in the examination process, and some answer papers may be marked by external assessors appointed by these accrediting bodies rather than the university.

MODULES AND PROGRESSION

Modular systems of study at university have been developed for several reasons:

- they allow greater flexibility in subject choice;
- they can efficiently accommodate students studying different degree paths;
- they make it easier for students to transfer between courses and institutions;
- they break up studies into 'bite-sized' elements and allow exams to be spread more evenly over the academic year.

The modular system does have disadvantages, however, including the fact that it may tend to encourage students to avoid difficult subjects and to 'close the book' on a subject once it has been assessed. If you are studying in a modular system, you should be aware of these risks.

Modules may be assessed by a blend of formal exams and in-course assessment, as outlined above. If you fail the overall ('aggregated') assessment, you may be asked to return for a resit exam or resubmit new or revised coursework, while in some subjects, borderline cases are given an extra oral exam. Resit exams usually take place at the end of the summer vacation, with the result being based solely on your performance in that exam.

At the end of each academic year, and after any resits, you will be required to fulfil certain progression criteria that allow you to pass on to the next level of study. These criteria are normally published in course handbooks. If you fail to satisfy the criteria, you may need to resit the whole year or even to leave the university. Sometimes you may be asked to 'carry' specific modules: that is, study them again in addition to the normal quota for your next year of study. Some institutions may place a condition on your re-entry, for example, achieving a certain level of marks or passing a prescribed number of modules in order to progress. This would normally be discussed with your adviser/director of studies.

DEGREE CLASSIFICATIONS AND TRANSCRIPTS

Students with superior entry qualifications or experience may join university at different levels. There are also a range of exit awards – certificates, diplomas and ordinary degrees. However, the majority of students now enter at level 1, and study for an honours degree. At present, this encompasses three years of study in England, Wales and Northern Ireland, and four years in Scotland.

Sometimes entry into the final honours year is competitive, based on grades in earlier years. Some universities operate a junior honours year, which means you are accepted into an honours stream at an earlier stage and may have special module options.

Study abroad or within placements   ✔

Credit will normally be given for years of study carried out abroad or in work placement, according to specific schemes operated by your university. This includes participation in European Community schemes such as ERASMUS (see **http://ec.europa.eu/education/index_en.htm**).

Nearly all universities follow the same system for grading honours degrees. The grades are, in descending order:

- first class (a 'first')
- upper second class (a two-one or 2:1)
- lower second class (a two-two or 2:2)
- third class (a 'third')
- unclassified.

However, some universities may not differentiate between the second-class divisions.

In some institutions, these classifications will take into account all grades you have obtained during your university career; sometimes only those in junior and senior honours years; and in the majority, only grades obtained in the finals. This makes the finals critical, especially as there are no resits for them.

Once your degree classification has been decided by the examination committee or board, and moderated by the external examiner, it will be passed for ratification to the university's senate or equivalent body for academic legislation. During this period you will technically be a graduand, until your degree is conferred at the graduation ceremony. At this time you will receive a diploma certificate and be entitled to wear a colourful degree- and institution-specific 'hood' for your gown.

Employers will usually ask to see your diploma for confirmation of your degree and may contact the university to confirm your qualification and obtain a copy of your transcript (Ch 7). This document shows your performance in *all* assessments throughout your career at the university.

✔ **Job prospects with different degrees**

In a competitive job market, your chances of being considered for a position may depend on your degree classification, but employers also take into account other personal qualities and experience (Ch 71). Research positions that involve reading for a higher degree, such as an MSc or PhD, usually require a first or 2:1.

COMPLAINTS AND APPEALS

Because of the checks and balances outlined on page 298, the university examination system is usually robust. However, all universities have complaints and appeals procedures for situations where students feel they have been incorrectly or unfairly assessed. This will normally start with an appeal to the course leader, then the head of the school or department, and move progressively up the system if a student remains dissatisfied. Final recourse may be to an external ombudsman. Details of procedures will be published on your university's website.

Appeals against termination of studies

Your studies may be terminated for one of several reasons but most commonly failure to meet attendance or progression criteria. Occasionally, termination will be enforced due to disciplinary reasons, for example, in a case of plagiarism. In these circumstances, students will be offered a chance to appeal and will be expected to produce evidence of any extenuating circumstances, such as medical certificates, or notes from support service personnel. Such students may also wish to ask tutors to support their application where the tutor is aware of their personal situation.

PRACTICAL TIPS FOR UNDERSTANDING HOW YOU WILL BE ASSESSED

Ask senior students about the exam system. They may have useful tips and advice to pass on.

Find out where essential information is recorded. This could be in a combination of handbooks and web-based resources.

If you don't understand any aspect of the assessment system, ask course administrators or tutors. Knowing how the system works is important and can affect your performance.

Notify your institution of any disability. If you have a disability, you should make the institution aware of this. You may have special concessions in exams, for example, using the services of a scribe, being allowed extra time, or having exam question papers printed in large print for you. Appropriate entitlements take time to arrange and you must ensure that arrangements are in place well before the exam date. Contact your department and disability support service for guidance.

Be cautious when comparing exam systems. Particularly where students have come into university having completed school exams that are uniformly applied across areas of the United Kingdom, there is a tendency to think that the university syllabus in a given subject is the same in all institutions. This is not the case; as noted on page 296, universities operate as independent autonomous bodies with degree awarding powers. Therefore, they set their own exams; so there is no point in comparing notes with a friend studying the same discipline in another institution and then finding that one of you is panicking at exam time because your course of study has not covered an aspect that has been covered intensively in the other's institution. This is because the syllabus and its learning outcomes will differ and this will be reflected in the exams. Better to spend time looking at past papers in your own institution and thinking out a personal revision and exam-taking strategy on that basis.

46

MULTIPLE-CHOICE AND SHORT-ANSWER QUESTIONS

How to tackle short-answer formats

> Many university exams, especially at early stages, test your knowledge using 'objective' question types, which tend to be short and demand factual answers. This chapter explains how to adjust your revision and exam technique to suit these forms of assessment.

A multiple-choice question (MCQ) is one in which you are presented with alternative answers and asked to select one that is correct. In some cases, you may be asked to identify several correct answers rather than one. A short-answer question (SAQ) deals with topics of limited scope and you are generally expected to produce a mini-essay, bulleted points or a diagram in response.

Both MCQs and SAQs are used as alternatives to standard essay questions as a means of testing the breadth and detail of your knowledge across the whole syllabus. Generally, they are mixed with other forms of questions that are better for testing the depth of your knowledge and analytical capabilities.

Good technique and strategy with MCQs and SAQs can improve your marks and save time for answering other questions.

TACKLING MULTIPLE-CHOICE QUESTIONS

The most common form of MCQ provides some statement or question, then offers four possible answers. One of the answers is correct and the other three are known as distractors.

- If the question simply seeks a factual answer, such as a date, or the name of a person, the answers may simply present a series of alternatives to the true answer.

- Sometimes the question is devised to test your knowledge of technical terms or jargon, in which case the distractors may use similar-sounding terms to the correct answer.

- Some questions involve a quantitative problem and then give possible answers that you can only arrive at by doing the requisite calculation. The answers provided may include values that you will obtain if you carry out a faulty calculation.

- There may be a special way of identifying the answer, such as shading in a box or selecting an option with your mouse if it is an online test. Read the rubric (the instructions) carefully to make sure you do the right thing.

Example MCQ

The bone at the front of the leg below the knee is called:

A   The fibula
B   The tibia
C   The femur
D   The cruciate

B is the correct answer; A, C and D are distractors. You may know that all the potential answers are parts of a leg, but unless you know the anatomy well, you may not be able to identify the correct answer.

A good approach for approaching paper-based MCQ tests is as follows:

- **First sweep.** Read through the questions fairly rapidly, noting the 'correct' answer in those you can attempt immediately, perhaps on a separate sheet. Don't fill in or submit any answers properly yet.

- **Second sweep.** Go through the paper again, checking your original answers, and thinking for a longer time about uncertain answers. This time, mark up the answer sheet properly or submit answers online. Leave questions you are still uncertain about at this stage.

- **Third sweep.** Now tackle the difficult questions and those that require longer to answer (for example, those based on numerical problems). At this stage, whether you should guess answers depends on the marking regime being used (see 'Optimising marks' in the Practical tips section on page 306).

One reason for adopting this three-phase approach is that considering the full set of questions may prompt you to recall facts relevant to difficult questions. You can also spend more time per question on the difficult ones.

Increasingly, MCQs are presented via computers. This is usually termed computer-aided assessment (CAA) or online assessment (OA). Use of CAA means that the answers can be 'instantly' checked. Where such systems are used for formative assessments that are not part of your final assessment, the software may allow you to receive feedback on incorrect answers to help you learn more about aspects you evidently did not understand.

Alternative question formats

True/false questions, fill-in-the-missing-word and matching questions all attempt to test the same sort of knowledge as MCQs. Many of the tips given here also apply to these forms, but see also pages 305–6.

Getting used to software

If you are offered the option to practise CAA/OA, take it. Familiarity with the software and presentation may save you time in the real exam.

DEALING WITH SHORT-ANSWER QUESTIONS

The various styles that can be encompassed within the SAQ format (see Tip Box below) allow for more demanding questions than MCQs. For this form of question, few if any marks are given for writing style. Answers are often expected in note form or as a diagram. Think in 'bullet point' mode and list the crucial points only. The time for answering SAQ questions may be tight, so get down to work fast, starting with answers that demand remembered facts.

In SAQ papers, there is often a choice of questions. Choose carefully – it may be better to gain half marks for a correct answer to half a question than to provide a largely irrelevant answer or one that seems to cover the whole topic, but does so too superficially. Consider all sections of the question before you start answering, in case you cannot cope with secondary questions.

✔ **Time management for SAQs**

Divide the allocated time up appropriately, allowing some time for choosing questions and reviewing answers. Stick to your timetable by moving on to the next question as soon as possible. Strategically, it is probably better to get part marks for the full number of questions than good marks for only a few (**Ch 66**).

Always answer the question as requested – this is true for all questions, but especially important for SAQs. If the question asks for a diagram, make sure you provide one, and label it well; if it asks for *n* aspects of a topic, try to list this number of points; if there are two or more parts, provide appropriate answers to all aspects. This may seem obvious, but many marks are lost for not following instructions. Bear in mind that markers may award marks for correct use of key phrases – so try to use the terms and subject jargon normally used in the resources, lectures and discussions. Finally, remember to check through your answers at the end. You'll be able to correct obvious mistakes and possibly add points that come to mind when rereading.

ℹ **Examples of SAQs**

Here are three possible ways of asking a short-answer question about the knee:

■ Draw a labelled diagram of the knee.

■ Briefly explain the role of the meniscus, patella and cruciate and medial ligaments in the knee joint.

■ Give five common types of injury that affect the knee, and briefly indicate how they should be treated.

- **Multiple-response questions.** These are essentially MCQs in which more than one answer can be correct – and you may or may not be told how many. Marks are usually awarded for having the correct combination of answers, so you will really have to know the topic well to score highly. Guessing is not advised, especially if you do not know how many answers might be correct.

- **Fill-in-the-missing-word questions.** These can be tough options because you are not given prompts for the correct answer. However, you may be able to obtain clues from the surrounding text or other questions. When marked by software, allowance is often made for common misspellings, but it's worth taking special care over spelling in such cases: there is no guarantee that 'your' misspelling will be included and wrong answers may not be checked.

- **'Matching' questions.** You are asked to link a series of options to a series of answers or matching phrases. Start with the easy matches and see which questions and options remain. If you need to guess, remember that one incorrect answer will actually result in two lost marks, because you will have ruled out the correct answer to another question.

- **'Hot-spot' and other pictorial question formats.** These mainly apply to online assessment; the question may ask that you identify part of a diagram using the cursor – perhaps by clicking, dragging an arrow or symbol, or by dragging images to the correct spot. Alternatively, you may be asked to provide text for a labelled item. Make sure you are especially careful to identify the exact location where markers should be placed.

Gobbets, précis and other specialised assessments

Because of their subject-specific nature, it is not possible to give generalised advice on these. Consult the course handbook or lecturers to find out the recommended structure and content and the best way to approach them in exams.

PRACTICAL TIPS FOR ADDRESSING MCQS AND SAQS

Revise appropriately. If your paper includes MCQs or SAQs, keep this in mind as you study. Think how material might be assessed in these ways and make sure you learn potentially examinable definitions and facts. Also make sure you can draw and label relevant diagrams. You may find it useful to discuss potential questions with fellow class members (**Ch 64**).

Take a logical approach to MCQs. When unsure of an answer, the first stage is to rule out options that are clearly absurd or have obviously been placed there to distract you. Next, looking at the remaining options, can you judge between contrasting pairs with alternative answers? Logically, both cannot be correct, so you should see if you can rule one of the pair out. Watch out, however, in case *both* may be irrelevant to the answer.

Write down key information before looking at MCQ options. If you have key dates, facts or formulae to remember, write these down as soon as the exam starts. If you do this before looking at the options in the exam questions, you will be less likely to be confused or distracted by similar-sounding options.

Hints for numerical questions. If an MCQ involves a calculation, try to do this independently from the answers, so you are not influenced by them. Assuming you have done the appropriate revision, and have the required knowledge and skills, numerical questions in SAQ papers can be a valuable means of accumulating marks, because it is possible to score 100 per cent in them if your answer is correct and laid out appropriately.

Optimising marks. The best way of tackling MCQs depends on the marking regime. If there is a penalty for incorrect answers in a multiple-choice test (often referred to as 'negative marking'), the best strategy is *not* to answer questions when you know your answer is a guess. Depending on the penalty, it may be beneficial to guess, if you can narrow the choice down to two options, but beware false or irrelevant alternatives. If there are no such penalties, then you should provide an answer to all questions in the paper, even if this means guessing in some cases.

Guessing. If you have to do this to complete the paper (assuming negative marking doesn't apply), go with your first hunch for the answer rather than a second thought that might be influenced by the distractors. Your subconscious may have arrived at the correct answer, without your conscious mind understanding why.

47

NUMERICAL QUESTIONS

How to approach quantitative problems

> **Paying close attention to mathematical aspects of your course is worthwhile because, in exam situations, if you get the answers right, it is possible to obtain very high marks. Even if you don't consider yourself particularly numerate, tackling these topics head-on can repay the effort.**

Some students favour questions that require a numerical or statistical approach. Others struggle where maths is involved, or suffer from a lack of preparation. Whichever category applies to you, it is worth the effort of conquering mathematical assessments, because the payback can be excellent – answering this type of question correctly is one of the few ways in which you can obtain 100 per cent in a university exam.

WHY DO EXAMINERS ASK NUMERICAL QUESTIONS?

Quantitative problems allow examiners to test the following:

- your numeracy, mathematical skills and problem-solving abilities;
- your capacity to recall, understand and apply theoretical models within 'real-life' scenarios;
- your ability to think clearly and work quickly under pressure;
- your ability to follow a standard format for calculation, particularly where it may be related to professional competence, as in Engineering and Accountancy;
- your ability to present a logical sequence of operations clearly, such that another person can understand what you have done.

Numerical aspects of your course

Bear in mind that these elements, while tricky for some, are often essential for understanding material encountered later in your degree programme.

LEARNING KEY MATHEMATICAL SKILLS

You won't get very far without knowing the basic maths required for the types of problems you will encounter. This should be easy to find out by consulting the course handbook, examining past papers, reading textbooks or by speaking to lecturers or tutors.

A basic core of mathematical information and techniques valuable in many contexts is covered in **Ch 29–Ch 31**. If your course requires more advanced mathematics, it is likely that specialist modules or other forms of assistance will be available to you.

WHY PRACTICE IS ESSENTIAL

When it comes to numerical problems, there is simply no substitute for practice. If you have a block about numerical work, practice at problem-solving or standard forms of analysis will:

● demystify the procedures involved, which, in reality, may only involve elementary mathematical operations and just appear complex on the surface;

● allow you to gain confidence, so that you don't panic when confronted with an unfamiliar or apparently complex form of problem;

● help you to work faster, because the pattern of work will have become routine;

● help you to recognise the various forms a problem can take. This is useful because there are a limited number of ways lecturers can present questions and it is important to identify the relevant formulae or approach to adopt as soon as possible;

● help imprint the standard form of analysis and presentation, ensuring that you automatically adopt the correct procedure and presentation style.

> ### ✔ Revision tips for numerical questions
>
> Try as many examples from past papers and problems sheets as you can. A useful tactic is to invent your own problems, as this helps you understand the equations and mathematical models better.

TACKLING THE PROBLEM

A step-by-step approach is recommended. This may not always be the fastest method, but mistakes often occur when students miss out stages of a calculation, combine simple calculations, or do not make what they have done obvious to either themselves or the examiner. Error tracing (and, importantly, part-marking) is easier when all stages in a calculation are laid out sequentially.

> ### ✔ Have the right tools ready
>
> Calculators greatly simplify the numerical part of problem-solving. Make sure you know how to use all relevant functions on your model.

Approach the problem thoughtfully

If presented as a story or scenario, you may need to 'decode' the problem to decide which equations or rules need to be applied.

✔ Part-marking

This is where the examiner will give marks for the steps of a calculation even though the final result is incorrect due to a mathematical or copying error at some early stage. Part marks can only be given if the stages in a calculation are laid out clearly. Therefore, if you know you have ended up with an incorrect answer, perhaps because the scale of it is absurd, do not immediately scribble all over your working. Move on to another question and return to the earlier one at the end of the exam; even if you can't spot the error, you may receive part marks.

- Read the problem carefully – the text may give clues as to how it should be tackled. Be certain of what is required as an answer before starting.
- Analyse what kind of problem it is. Which equation(s) or approach will be applicable? If this is not obvious, consider the dimensions/units of the information available and think how they could be fitted to a relevant formula or form of analysis. In formula-based questions, a favourite ploy of examiners is to make you rearrange a familiar equation before you can work out the answer. Another is to make you use two or more equations in series. You may therefore need to revise the rules for rearranging formulae (**Ch 29**).

✔ Dimensional analysis

If you are uncertain of your recall of a particular equation, carry out a dimensional analysis. This involves substituting appropriate (usually SI) units for the symbols, then confirming that the units cancel out.

- Check that you have, or can derive, all the information required. It is unusual, but not unknown, for examiners to supply redundant information. So, if you decide not to use some of the information given, be confident about why you do not require it.
- Decide on the format and units in which to present the answer. This is sometimes suggested to you. If the problem requires many changes in the prefixes to units, it may be a good idea to convert all data to base SI units (pages 174–5) at the outset.
- If a problem appears complex, break it down into component parts.

Present your answer clearly

The way you present your answer obviously needs to fit the individual problem. In general, the final answer should be presented as a meaningful statement and any number given should carry appropriate significant figures and units. You should always show your working – most markers will only penalise a mistake once if the remaining operations are performed correctly, but they can only do this if you make those operations visible. Guidelines for presenting an answer include:

- Where appropriate, make your assumptions explicit – most mathematical models require that certain criteria are met before they can be legitimately applied, and some involve assumptions and approximations. In some cases you may be given credit for stating these clearly at the outset.

- Outline your strategy for answering briefly, perhaps explaining the applicable formula or definitions that suit the approach to be taken. Give details of what the symbols mean (and their units) at this point. If rearranging a formula, show how you have done this, using symbols first, then substituting relevant numerical values.

- Convert to the desired units step by step, i.e. taking each variable in turn. Try to get into the habit of writing all numbers with their units, unless they are truly dimensionless.

✔ Presentation tips

When you have obtained a numerical answer in the desired units, rewrite this in meaningful English and underline the answer. For example:

   The net profit in tax year 2012 was £334,091.

Make sure you use an appropriate number of significant figures (see **Ch 29**, pages 178–80).

Check your answer

Having written out your answer, you should check it methodically:

- Is the answer of the magnitude you might reasonably expect? You should be alerted to an error if an answer is absurdly large or small. If using a calculator, beware of absurd results that could arise from faulty key-pressing or logic. Double-check any result obviously standing out from others in a series of calculations.

- Do the units make sense and match up with the answer required?

- Do you get the same answer if you recalculate using a different method?

? What should I do if I know my answer is incorrect?

Be prepared to state that you know your answer is wrong, but cannot identify where the error has come – you may get a small amount of credit for showing this awareness. Also, if you know what to do to obtain an answer, but not *how* to do it, you may gain some credit for giving as much detail as you can.

Check your calculator. Before your exam date, ensure that you are allowed to use a calculator, and confirm that it is a model that is permitted for use if there are any restrictions. Make sure you understand how to carry out relevant functions. If your calculator is battery-operated, ensure a fresh battery is fitted or take a spare.

Analyse the question type. Make sure you understand which formula or formulae to use, or which approach to attempt before starting.

Work methodically and carefully. Double-check each step. Write neatly and add vital information such as units or assumptions.

Pay attention to presentation. Follow the tips given earlier in this chapter and always provide units or a written explanation with the answer.

Never give up. Even if you think you can't complete the answer, don't give up. Try to do the basics or a part answer, perhaps noting any points you can recall in a list. The part marks obtained could make the difference between grades or between a pass and a fail.

48

ESSAY-STYLE ASSESSMENTS
How to maximise your marks

> The essay is a traditional method of university assessment that allows you to discuss concepts and issues in depth. In coursework, it also allows you flexibility in the way you compose your answer and time to do this; while in exam situations you'll need to decide the format of your answer quickly. This chapter focuses on approaches you can take to deciding on content, organising this and producing an effective answer, moving from essay coursework to essays written under exam conditions.

Developing your writing skills is a gradual process, and one that is best done with time at your disposal. The coursework essay allows you opportunities to develop these skills. However, in most exams you will not have the luxury to spend a long time on constructing your response to the set task, and will be expected to perform under time pressure, without aids like dictionaries and thesauri and with very limited scope to review, edit and rewrite (**Ch 65**). This chapter provides tips for writing essay-style answers quickly and effectively so you can maximise your marks in exams.

WHAT LECTURERS EXPECT FOR ESSAY ANSWERS IN EXAMS

In both coursework and exams, essay-style questions are mainly used to elicit an in-depth answer to a complex issue. In many ways, the longer coursework essay is a preparation for the shorter essay-style exam question. Shorter essay forms (**Ch 46, Ch 47**) tend to be included in exams when examiners want you to address knowledge over a wide area. In exams, the essay format allows you to develop an argument, explain alternative views or provide a reasonable level of detail in your answer. There is often an element of choice in essay exam papers.

✔ Critical thinking

Essays are commonly used when tutors expect you to think more deeply. Often what you have to do is not framed as a question but an instruction. Typically, you will be expected to:

- **apply** knowledge and understanding;
- **analyse** information;
- **synthesise** new ideas or treatments of facts;
- **evaluate** issues, positions and arguments.

See Table 22.1 (page 122) for further explanation of what's expected under these headings, and watch out for instruction words that invite these approaches.

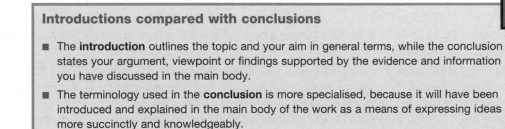

Writer's block

If you find you tend to get stuck at the start of an essay answer, try starting with a definition or simple statement of fact.

PLANNING ESSAY ANSWERS IN EXAMS

The main advice is to keep your writing simple. Working quickly, use a spider diagram or mind map to generate ideas relevant to the question (**Ch 26**). From this, decide on an outline structure. This approach helps you to think laterally as well as in a linear manner – important so that you generate all the points relevant to your answer.

Can I make notes and plans in exam books?

It is perfectly acceptable practice to make notes; however, you should always score through them before you submit the answer paper. A single diagonal line will suffice. Sometimes your plan may be used by the examiner to cross-check details of your answer (but do not count on this).

As discussed in **Ch 33**, you should probably think in terms of three basic components:

- **The introduction:** states briefly what your answer will say, sets its context and gives an insight as to how you intend to approach the topic.
- **The main body:** presents the information, the argument or key points of your response.
- **The conclusion:** sums up the answer as stated, reinforces the position outlined in the introduction, and puts the whole answer into a wider context.

Tips for writing these elements are provided in **Ch 33**, while potential ways of organising the main body of essay-style assignments are discussed in **Ch 34**.

Introductions compared with conclusions

- The **introduction** outlines the topic and your aim in general terms, while the conclusion states your argument, viewpoint or findings supported by the evidence and information you have discussed in the main body.
- The terminology used in the **conclusion** is more specialised, because it will have been introduced and explained in the main body of the work as a means of expressing ideas more succinctly and knowledgeably.

An important way in which marks can be lost is through poor structuring of exam answers (Table 65.1). You should allocate some time in your revision timetable to rehearse potential answers by drawing up rough plans based on potential questions from learning outcomes and previous coursework essay writing. This 'dress rehearsal' may assist when structuring an exam answer – but always be aware of the pitfalls of question spotting (p. 397). Thus, the exam essay title may not be exactly what you have rehearsed but your preparation may give you a head start so you don't have to think things through from first principles.

Where you have no coursework or revision rehearsal on which to draw, you need to be able to structure a plan quickly. Together with the thinking that will take place as the writing evolves, this will provide the shape and balance required in an essay-style exam answer. This initial outline plan should be seen as a flexible guideline that may change as you begin to think more deeply about the topic in the course of answering. If you ignore the planning phase, and only think about the structure as you write, then you could end up with a weakly structured essay (see Table 48.1).

✔ **Quotations and citations in exam answers**

Do not become bogged down in trying to remember direct quotes word for word (possible exceptions are in literature and law exams). Just give the sense of the quote, its relevance to your answer and its source.

THE IMPORTANCE OF ADDRESSING THE TASK AS SET

Another important way in which marks can be lost is when answers do not address the question (see Table 65.1). You can avoid this by:

- making sure you consider all aspects of the question. Brainstorming techniques (**Ch 34**) can help you achieve this;

- explaining what *you* understand by the question (perhaps in the introductory paragraph). This will make you think about the question and may clear up any doubt about how it can be interpreted. However, make sure you do not narrow the topic beyond what would be reasonable.

- focusing on the precise task you have been asked to do (**Ch 33**). Remember to tackle the question actually asked and not the one you would have liked to answer – this is a risk of question-spotting (**Ch 63**).

- ensuring your answer is planned. Creating a plan will make you think about the relevance and the logic of your argument (**Ch 33**).

- keeping to the point. Including irrelevant or repetitive content will not gain any marks and the time you spend writing it will be wasted, stopping you from gaining marks on other questions. Having said that, no marks are given for 'white space': even a few general points of principle may result in enough marks to help you pass, when added to those gained in other, better, answers.

- avoiding making unsupported value judgements. These are statements that impose the writer's views on the reader, often using subjective language, and which fail to provide sound evidence to support the position put forward (**Ch 22**). Make sure you write objectively and avoid using the personal pronouns 'I', 'you', 'we' and 'one' (**Ch 34**, **Ch 37**).

Table 48.1 Common faults in the structure of essay-style answers in coursework and exams. In these examples, attention to the planning phase would result in a better structure, and hence, better marks.

Symptom of weakness in structure	Analysis of the problem
The magical mystery tour. This type of answer rambles on, drifting from point to disconnected point with no real structure.	The essay may contain valuable content, but marks will be lost because this is not organised and parts are not connected appropriately to create a coherent response.
No introduction and/or no conclusion. The main body contains many useful points, but fails to introduce them and fails to draw conclusions based on them.	Facts, concepts and ideas alone are not enough – evidence must be provided of deeper-level analytical thinking (**Ch 22**). The introduction and conclusions are important parts where this can be achieved.
The overly detailed answer. The main body of the answer contains a wealth of information, some of which is relevant and some not. Despite the finely grained detail, little structure is evident and there is no discrimination between the important and the unimportant.	The writer has probably been preoccupied with showing how much has been memorised, without showing how much has been understood. Relevance of the material in relation to the instruction given has not been considered at the planning stage, nor as the essay-writing progresses.
The stream of consciousness. Often written as if it were a conversational monologue, this lacks internal organisation, few (or too many) signposting words, no (or few) paragraphs, and little apparent logic.	Academic writing style involves structural as well as linguistic components. Both are important elements of a good answer. Hence, the writing needs to guide the reader along a logical path to enable understanding.
The waffly, irrelevant answer. Unfocused, fails to get to grips with the question and may contain large amounts of irrelevant information, offered up seemingly without regard for the topic set.	Greater attention needs to be paid to analysis of the instruction given and converting these thoughts into a coherent answer plan. Irrelevant material should not be used as it will gain no marks.
The half-an-answer. Fails to appreciate that there were two (or more) parts to the question. Focuses solely on one part.	The essay should cover all aspects of the question as more marks may be allocated to the secondary part(s). This should be reflected in the essay plan and eventual structure.
Structure dominated by quotes. This might start with a hackneyed quote or be interspersed with extensive memorised quotes, with little effective use of these.	This type of structure leaves little room for evidence of original thought. Few marks are given for having a good memory – it's what is done with the information that counts.

Analysing the wording of each task as set

As discussed in **Ch 32**, you need to take a broader and more in-depth look at the task in the context of the whole question. To do this, you must consider:

- **The instruction word.** In what category does that place the task? For example, have you been asked to act, describe, analyse, argue, or do something else completely (**Ch 32**)?
- **The topic.** What is the core topic about?
- **The aspect(s).** What particular aspect of the topic has to be considered?
- **Any restriction(s).** What limits have been imposed on the discussion? Your answer must encompass each element of the task to ensure that it is a logical response to the task you were set. What you write must be relevant. Superfluous material or digressions will not earn you marks.

Mixing topics and multi-part questions in exam essay answers

Sometimes exam questions will blend two topics so that you may find that you can only answer half the question. This is one of the dangers of question-spotting (**Ch 63**).

Make sure you answer all parts in multi-part questions. These may not be worded in two or more sentences: phrases such as 'compare and contrast' and 'cause and effect' should alert you to this. Make sure that the weighting in marks given to questions is reflected in the length of the component parts of your answer.

It is important to consider the marking criteria in relation to your answer, and it may be worth reviewing these before starting to write. They should be published in the module handbook. Table 48.2 provides a checklist in relation to presentation (**Ch 44**), structure (**Ch 34**) and content (**Chs 22, 32** and **35**).

REVIEWING YOUR ANSWERS

This is an essential stage of creating a sound piece of academic writing, whether for an in-course assignment or exam. The key phases of reviewing are discussed in **Ch 43**, and tips for reviewing essay answers in an exam situation are provided in **Ch 65**.

Focus on providing evidence of deeper thinking. Especially at higher levels of study, this will help you gain better grades. On the assumption that you are able to include *basic* information and display an understanding of it, you can gain marks for:

● supplying additional and relevant detail at the expected depth;

● providing an analytical answer rather than a descriptive one – focusing on deeper aspects of a topic, rather than merely recounting facts;

● placing the problem in context, and demonstrating your wider understanding of the topic; however, make sure you don't overdo this, or you may risk not completing the task as set – remember that you cannot be expected to give the same amount of detail in an exam answer as you would in a piece of essay-style coursework;

● giving enough evidence of reading around the subject, by quoting relevant papers and reviews and mentioning author names and dates of publication;

● considering all sides of a topic/debate, and arriving at a clear conclusion – you may have to take into account *and explain* two or more viewpoints, and possibly weigh them up, according to the question set; where appropriate, your answer should demonstrate that you realise that the issue is complex and possibly unresolved.

Table 48.2 Checklist for essay writing in relation to typical marking criteria

Presentation	Structure	Content
☐ **Writing style:** should be • objective; • formal as appropriate to academic writing; and • clear, correct, standard English with no truncated text messaging or other inappropriate abbreviations.	☐ **Logic of writing:** your essay should be planned carefully so it has a logical structure. The construction of sentences and paragraphs should contribute to the overall cohesion of the text. Poorly constructed sentences will make the text difficult to understand and may hamper the reader's comprehension.	☐ **Quality of knowledge:** Your essay should reflect • an understanding of the range of module/course themes and your ability to make connections across topics; and • reading from source material in addition to that presented in lectures.
☐ **Printed format:** practice varies from institution to institution, but, generally, work is word-processed and printed. You need to follow standard typing conventions such as spacing, justification and punctuation. If work is handwritten, print neatly and never use capitals throughout. ☐ **Spellcheck:** word-processor spellchecking functions are not foolproof, so you also need to read your work over, paying particular attention, for example, to words that sound the same but have different spelling, or words that are specific to your subject and that may have been misspelled in the text.	☐ **Logic of discussion or argument:** evidence should be organised in support of viewpoint but expressed in ways that avoid making value judgements (p. 370). ☐ **Relationship to literature:** in many disciplines, the line of argument that you need to construct should relate to key works in existing literature. You will be given credit for making these connections within your text, being careful, of course, to avoid plagiarism. If you fail to make these links or fail to explain why you are making them, your work is weakened.	☐ **Relevance:** the text should relate to the aspect of the topic defined by the task brief. If you write too much general material and fail to tackle the deeper, more complex, issues, this will have a negative impact on your grade. ☐ **Critical thinking:** your essay must demonstrate an ability to analyse and synthesise complex ideas; and, at higher levels of study, demonstrate some ability to construct an original argument.
☐ **Grammar check:** your word-processor may indicate 'errors' of grammar (as well as misspelling) by underlining them. Check each of these, but note that often the diagnosed 'errors' are simply suggestions for you to consider in context. For example, use of the passive is often highlighted but is acceptable in academic writing and thus alteration may be unnecessary.	☐ **Use of tables, diagrams, graphs or figures:** some subjects routinely require evidence to be presented in a visual format. If you need to demonstrate evidence in this way, ensure that visuals are labelled appropriately and are integrated into the text in a logical manner close to the text that explains their content. This contributes to the cohesion of your argument and the structure of your text.	☐ **Use of primary sources:** in some subjects the ability to analyse and evaluate material from primary sources will set your work apart from that of others as significant and worthy of a higher grade.

Have potential answer formats in mind as you go into an exam. Ideally, your revision and pre-exam preparation (**Ch 61, Ch 63**) will have given you a good idea of the exam format and even potential exam questions. This will ensure you do not have to start answers completely from scratch.

Keep your writing simple. If you are to stick to your exam strategy, you must not lose valuable time creating an attention-grabbing piece of writing. You won't have time or space to refine your answer in the same way as you would with a piece of coursework. In particular, don't labour the introduction with fine phrases – get straight to the point of the question and give your response to it.

Balance your effort appropriately. For example, in exam answers your introduction need not be overly long. Most marks will be awarded for the main body and conclusions, so spend more time and brainpower on them.

Make sure you aren't losing marks due to poor presentation. Despite the time pressure, exam answers need to be legible and clearly laid out. If feedback indicates that tutors are having problems in reading your work, or consider it untidy, paying attention to this could be an easy way of gaining marks (**Ch 44**).

49

TUTORIAL ASSESSMENT

How to make your contribution count

This chapter explains what is expected of you in a tutorial and what might be taken into consideration when tutors or peers assess your engagement with the topic or problem.

The main purpose of a university tutorial is to learn interactively with others, either through discussion and debate of issues, or by considering problems you have been asked to address (Ch 21). Your output, such as a related essay or the answers to numerical questions, may be assessed, and, in some cases, your role as a participant may be evaluated. You need to understand exactly what is going to be considered so that you can make your contribution count.

ENGAGING FULLY WITH THE TOPIC

Preparation for tutorials was explained in broad terms in Ch 21. However, in the context of assessment you need to think in greater detail about how you go about tackling a set of problems or a topic. This will differ slightly depending on the type of tutorial.

Problem-solving tutorials

For problem-solving tutorials, you may be asked to work through problems beforehand or, conversely, you may be asked to review the problems in preparation for working through them as a group in the tutorial.

- Identify the area or theme being addressed.
- Read over the relevant sections in your textbook and lecture notes.
- Equip yourself with the skills to do the task. This might mean revising an area of maths or understanding relevant formulae.
- Look over the examples to see whether they are all of similar difficulty or whether they are ranged in ascending difficulty. This could, for instance, be a deliberate way of leading you through the process of developing a proof for a formula and then applying it to a more complex problem.

Presence and participation

Slipping into a lecture 10 minutes after the start may go unnoticed. The same will not be true of a late arrival in a tutorial. Show courtesy to your fellow students and the tutor by being on time and engaging actively with the intensive work designed to develop your understanding of the tutorial theme.

Discussion-based tutorials

For discussion-based tutorials, the topic will generally be given in advance.

- Analyse the topic in the same way that you would analyse a topic for a written assignment (**Ch 33**).
- Read over the relevant sections in your lecture notes and do the prescribed reading. Who are the key commentators on the topic? What are their perspectives on the topic?
- Make notes of key ideas and principles as appropriate, so that you can refer to these in the tutorials.
- You should be looking for aspects such as:
    - for and against positions;
    - cause-and-effect scenarios;
    - comparison of similar circumstances or attitudes;
    - contrasting viewpoints and the evidence in support and refutation;
    - inconsistencies and flaws in argument;
    - parallels and analogies used to illustrate points.

Student-led tutorials

Sometimes tutorials are organised so that each student is given an opportunity to lead the tutorial discussion, while the tutor observes the interplay of argument and debate. If you are required to participate in tutorials in this way, the tutorial 'characters' and the strategies to deal with them described in **Ch 21** will take on an added significance.

CRITERIA FOR ASSESSMENT OF TUTORIAL PARTICIPATION

Tutorial assessment may count for between 5 and 25 per cent of your total course assessment, with part or all of that mark being for 'participation', depending on the subject. Check the course handbook for details. Several generic aspects may be taken into account:

- your attendance over the series of tutorials;
- your active participation in the discussion or problem-solving aspects of the tutorial;
- evidence of reading and/or other preparation;
- your ability to think analytically and critically about points raised during the tutorial;
- your ability to present and defend a viewpoint, and the quality of your counter-arguments;
- your ability to relate the tutorial activity to other parts of the course and to the wider subject area;
- your ability to interact considerately and constructively with others;
- marks gained for any work handed in as part of the tutorial.

Tutorials linked to assessed course work

Sometimes the tutorial discussion is designed to help you to approach an assessed exercise such as an essay. In these cases, you should bear in mind the exact phrasing of the essay topic as you listen and contribute during the tutorial, and make notes that will help you to make full use of what you learn.

Relationships between tutorials and exams

Exams are not simply based on the lectures. They draw from the extended reading, exercises and tutorials that form part of your personal study. Tutorial topics and the preparatory work associated with them should be taken into account when you are planning your revision.

PRACTICAL TIPS FOR TUTORIAL ASSESSMENT

For problem-solving tutorials

Consider how the marks awarded for each tutorial will affect your assessment. Find out how many marks you will get for each element and how this fits into the overall marking scheme. Try your best to complete the full set of examples. This will help consolidate your learning and, if you are required to submit the worked examples, could contribute to your continuous assessment marks.

For discussion-based tutorials

Work out your position with regard to the topic. Reflect on what you have read and begin to evolve your personal position or viewpoint on the topic. Gather together evidence that supports your viewpoint and note down key points.

Consider the question from different angles. With regard to assessment, in particular, consider your viewpoint critically and anticipate what the counter-arguments might be. Build up your response to the counter-argument. If you hold an opposing view, what would be the strengths and weaknesses of your argument?

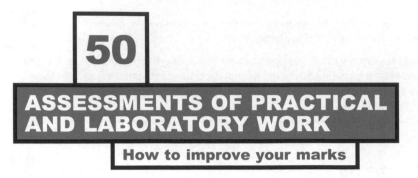

50

ASSESSMENTS OF PRACTICAL AND LABORATORY WORK

How to improve your marks

> The marks awarded to practical assessments can make up a relatively large proportion of the total for a module. Gaining better grades requires preparation beforehand, focused effort during the practical or practical exam, and care with writing up or answering.

Practical work is generally included in the syllabus to complement the theory covered in lectures and tutorials. Depending on your discipline, it gives you a chance to see specimens, develop skills and understand how research is conducted (**Ch 20**). However, it is worth noting that, in some courses, the theory may not have been covered at the time of the practical, so it is advisable to do a bit of background reading prior to the practical class.

The importance that lecturers attach to practical elements of the course can be seen from the proportion of your overall module grade that they assign to these aspects. This may be between 30 and 50 per cent, so you should devote a proportionate amount of study and revision time to related assessment activities.

FORMS OF PRACTICAL ASSESSMENT AND HOW TO APPROACH THEM

Consult your course handbook at an early stage to see how your practical work will be assessed. The main methods, including tips for tackling each one, are listed below.

Continuous assessment of lab work

This is a common way of assessing practical work, where grades are awarded for workbooks or lab reports completed during the course. As these marks may be relatively straightforward to achieve, this is a good way of building up a 'bank' of good grades so that it is easier to pass or do well in the overall module assessment.

To maximise your marks for completed lab workbooks you will need to ensure that:

- your work in the lab is neat and tidy;
- you have completed all that is required of you.

Because lab work often seems rushed, neither of these aims may be straightforward to achieve, but both will be easier if you have prepared well (**Ch 20**). During lab sessions, check with demonstrators and staff that each part is completed to their satisfaction and take heed of their tips and suggestions (see also **Ch 44**).

When preparing a formal report from a practical, adopt the format laid out in your handbook or the lab schedule (which may differ among subjects). If no format is specified, follow that given in Table 20.1 (on page 114). As marks are likely to be awarded for presentation, pay special attention to layout, print quality and order of sections. You may need to learn from lecturers' feedback how you can best approach writing style and the amount of detail required.

Practical exams

These 'summative' tests generally take place in laboratories during the main exam period. They usually involve:

- recall and understanding regarding specimens and techniques;
- tests of the observational and manual skills you have developed during the course;
- following procedures and using equipment;
- measurement and numerical analysis;
- interpretation or presentation of data.

Because of the 'unseen' and unpredictable nature of practical exams, there is less chance to prepare using standard revision techniques. You will need to be ready to think on your feet, adopting a logical approach. Make sure you read each question carefully (more than once) so you can carry out *exactly* what is required.

Past papers for practical exams are rarely available, and if they are, may make little sense in the absence of the real samples. To help your revising, you could look through the past practical schedules, highlighting parts that might be amenable to this form of examination. Some examples of types of practical questions in the sciences are provided in the Tip Box overleaf. Spot tests and oral forms of practical exam may involve moving around a 'circuit', examining specimens, or perhaps looking at slides through a microscope, then providing quick written answers or responding with spoken answers. Key tips for this type of exam are:

- Always take your time when answering.
- Always take a second detailed look at the specimen to check whether your first assumptions are correct.
- Consider all aspects of the question.
- Start with simple points, such as a straightforward description of the specimen (the markers may be using a checklist with some marks attached to these basic points).
- If you don't know an answer, don't waffle – move on to the next question quickly, if this is allowed.

Examples of practical exam questions

The following are examples of typical question styles (imagine the precise context yourself):

Draw a fully labelled diagram of specimen A.

Graph the following data and draw conclusions.

Examine specimen N and photograph M; and describe how the specimen relates to this environment.

Construct a calibration curve for a . . . test using the reagents and equipment provided. What value do you estimate for the unknown specimen X?

Comment on the syndrome evident in slide B.

Prepare a pure sample of . . . using the reagents and equipment provided.

Examine table Z (or picture A) and answer the following questions . . .

Given the data in Table F, calculate . . .

Compare specimens A and B, explaining . . .

Although you may think of the lab as an informal setting, formal practical exams will be subject to the same rules and regulations as written 'theory' exams (**Ch 45**). Some practical exams may be 'open book', where you are allowed to consult past schedules, for example as you tackle the questions. However, don't assume this is the case unless you have been specifically informed.

Practical questions within written/online assessments

Sometimes you will find that practical elements are assessed as a component of exams that you might assume would be solely about theory. For example, there may be questions in multiple-choice and short-answer papers that relate to work done in practicals. Look at the 'small print' in your course handbook to see if this might be the case, or ask lecturers, and adjust your revision accordingly. For example, this might imply that you rehearse simple calculations and learn relevant formulae.

✔

Don't think of practical work in isolation

You may be able to use information gained from practicals in essay-style answers, perhaps to provide relevant examples.

PRACTICAL TIPS FOR SITTING PRACTICAL EXAMS

Scan your practical schedules as an aid to revision. Try to see if you can predict possible question types, but avoid question-spotting (**Ch 63**). Memorise key procedures that might be tested, but bear in mind that there may be a limited time for each question on the paper. Think about the skills you may be asked to use and go through the instructions and tips you have been given about these.

Practise labelling diagrams. If you can identify a need to provide labels on diagrams of seen and unseen specimens, you may wish to test yourself by drawing up a schematic diagram, then labelling it without reference to supporting texts or schedules. This will give you feedback on how much you already know and what you need to learn.

Practise answering numerical questions. As recommended in **Ch 47**, this is the best way to ensure you perform well on the day in these types of assessments.

Take advantage of 'open door' revision sessions. In some subjects, the lab may be opened in the period prior to exams so you can have another look at key specimens. These sessions provide an opportunity to review the material and possibly ask questions of staff in attendance – very useful if you are unsure about some aspects, or think your memory will improve if you see the samples again, closer to the exam. These sessions are also an opportunity for collaboration with fellow students, as you can ask each other questions about the specimens to test your knowledge.

State the obvious, justify your conclusions. If you find that your mind has gone blank during a practical exam, start with the basics. For example, if asked to identify a specimen, do not give up because you can't immediately do this from memory. The question-setter may be trying to see if you can adopt a logical approach to the problem, and everyone in the class may be in the same situation. Start from first principles and basic observations ('the specimen has a yellow colour, therefore I conclude . . .') and move on from there. Similarly, when you do know an answer, state why you know it. There may be marks allocated to this aspect, which you will miss out on if you simply provide a bare answer.

Review good practice in graphing and tabulating. If constructing and interpreting data in graphs and tables might be a part of your exam, it makes sense to go over the basic principles and instructions for these forms of presentation beforehand (**Ch 30**).

Ensure that you have the correct equipment required for a practical exam. This will depend on the subject, but will be similar to the items taken to each practical (**Ch 20**). Remember to include a watch so that you can monitor time. Synchronise your watch with the clock in the exam hall so that you are working within the same time frame as invigilators and examiners. If you tend to use your mobile phone as a clock, remember that mobiles are not allowed to be taken into the exam room.

51

TACKLING A DISSERTATION OR PROJECT

How to make the best possible start

> **Dissertations and project reports are extensive exercises in writing and they usually contribute significantly to module and degree classification grades. It makes sense, therefore, to tackle them professionally and with energy. This chapter offers strategies that will help you to start off well and achieve your full potential.**

Looking proudly at the finished version of your dissertation or project report will probably be one of the highlights of your undergraduate academic career. In most cases, its production will be the result of many months of serious work. The final document will represent the pinnacle of your achievements at university and provide concrete evidence of your advanced academic skills in your discipline.

In carrying out the necessary research, thinking, writing and presentation, you will be delving deep into the subject material of your chosen discipline and stretching yourself in the production of a piece of original work. In some cases, the skills involved may be very closely allied to those you will use in the workplace: employers will be interested in seeing your work because it represents your full potential in the working environment. Your university tutors will demonstrate the perceived importance of dissertations and reports by allocating a high proportion of marks from them towards your final grade.

These are all good reasons for trying to produce the best possible product and to do well you will need to be focused from the start and disciplined in your effort.

✔ Taking account of the task you have been set

While there are many similarities in the production of dissertations and project reports, there are also some key differences. Throughout this book, we have tried to provide generic material wherever possible, but have also written chapters and sections that focus on tasks and outcomes relevant to specific types of document. You should select the material of relevance both to your personal needs and the approach required in your discipline.

STARTING OFF WELL

In this chapter, the emphasis is on starting as you mean to go on, and establishing good working habits. Many students drift aimlessly at the start of their project or research-based studies, so one of the most important things you can do is to become focused on the task right from the beginning. To ensure this happens, there are several things you should do:

- **Make sure you understand precisely what you are being asked to produce, and how.** You can do this by reading the supporting material in the course handbook or regulations (particularly the learning objectives or outcomes), or by speaking to your supervisor or a potential supervisor.

- **Try to make the initial connection with your research or source material.** Sometimes this will appear bewildering in its breadth, obscure in its jargon or genuinely difficult to master. The only way you will overcome this is to immerse yourself in the topic, read background material and ask questions. The sooner you take this step, the better.

- **Get an early grasp of the basic concepts.** You might do this by going back to a chapter from an introductory text or by revisiting relevant course notes.

- **Try not to luxuriate in the comfort of having a deadline many months away.** Graduates will tell you that every part of the process took longer than they estimated, and that, if they had to do it all again, they would try to organise themselves better. The time will quickly evaporate, and the earlier you start the task, the more likely you will be to avoid stress near to the end. Details of the component elements of any extensive writing task, and advice for good timetabling and project management, are provided in **Ch 8**.

- **Do something active.** Appropriate actions will depend on your subject, but will probably include taking notes of your background reading, or creating a plan of action or timetable. In some research projects it will involve making initial observations or setting up a pilot experiment; in others getting your hands on the right textbooks and references.

Starting off well also means understanding what constitutes good working practice and avoiding common pitfalls. There follows a quick summary of these aspects, as they apply to the research and writing phases of your dissertation or project.

How motivated are you?

Getting started and maintaining momentum depend on your motivation to succeed. It may be assumed by friends, family and tutors that you are highly motivated. If this is indeed true, use this feeling to energise your start to work, and tap into your motivation whenever things get difficult. If you feel that you lack motivation, you should speak to someone about this: some supervisors are excellent at motivating students; staff in support services such as counselling and the careers service will also be able to help. Sometimes all it takes to rekindle an interest in a subject is to immerse yourself in it. Recognise this fact and use it to push yourself over any initial barriers.

MAKING SURE YOU WORK EFFICIENTLY AND EFFECTIVELY

Efficient working means using your time well. If you can do this, it will mean you have more time available for thinking and relaxing, creating a virtuous cycle that will result in a better end product. The keys to working efficiently are:

- thinking and planning ahead for each day or part of a day;
- understanding what you are trying to achieve during each day or part of a day;
- getting down to work as quickly as possible;
- prioritising tasks appropriately;
- avoiding distractions;
- keeping your papers and workplace well organised; and
- taking breaks when you need to rest.

Efficient working in a nutshell

This means cutting out wasteful or unproductive effort, and focusing on using your time to maximise productivity.

Effective working is effort that results in meaningful results. It involves having a continual focus on the end product and making sure that for each subsidiary task undertaken you keep this in mind. The keys to working effectively are:

- getting started;
- focusing on the end product;
- minimising unproductive work;
- identifying things that are barriers to progress;
- finding ways to overcome obstacles to progress; and
- making sure you complete each component, even if this means some loss of quality.

Effective working in a nutshell

This involves smart working, rather than putting in extra effort. This means identifying **SMART** goals, that is, those that are:

Specific (What am I aiming to achieve in this work episode?)

Measurable (What milestones can I set myself for this period?)

Attainable (What can I achieve in the time available?)

Realistic (Have I created a goal that is achievable?)

Tangible (Will I be able to see the progress I'm making?)

AVOIDING THE COMMON PITFALLS

Your dissertation or project report will probably be the most extensive piece of writing you will have to complete on your course. In addition, it will require and test some demanding skills, in relation to both research and presentation. Because of this, you should be aware of potential risks, so that you can take steps to avoid them:

❑ you may underestimate the time it takes to carry out the research;

❑ your initial reading may be aimless;

❑ your writing skills may be rusty;

❑ you will need to organise large amounts of information;

❑ you will need to keep records of research sources so you can cite them properly;

❑ you may need to carry out advanced forms of data analysis;

❑ you may need to adopt a professional approach to data presentation;

❑ you may underestimate the time it takes to write, or suffer from writer's block;

❑ you will need to be aware of copyright infringement and plagiarism, and employ strategies to avoid them;

❑ you may need to allow time for your supervisor to provide feedback;

❑ you may need to allow time to take your supervisor's feedback into account; or

❑ for longer pieces of work, you will need to allow time for your dissertation or report to be typed, or, if you need this service, for graphics to be produced or printed, and for binding, if this is required by your department.

Suggestions on how to avoid most of the common problem areas are provided in subsequent chapters.

Try not to be a perfectionist

Many projects never get started, stall or fail to be completed because the people involved are aiming for perfection, when this is either impossible or impractical. Often, achieving perfection would be a waste of resources. If you identify this as a potential characteristic in yourself, try to accept that fact, and focus on minimising the larger flaws in your work and on completing the task despite any minor faults you believe are present.

Retaining bright ideas

As you become involved in your project you'll find that your thinking about the topic becomes a key focus in your life. Ideas will pop into your mind at the most unlikely times. Get into the habit of carrying a small notebook with you at all times so that you can note down these ideas as possible routes of research or for direct inclusion in your writing.

PRACTICAL TIPS FOR STARTING YOUR DISSERTATION OR REPORT

Engage with the subject as soon as possible. Read a basic text to gain background; create a personal glossary of specialist terms; ask questions of your supervisor or tutors; find out about current research in your area; explore online databases to begin your literature search.

Allocate a substantial period of time to carry out initial reading around your subject. Try to distance yourself from distractions and make sure you take notes as you go. Keep a meticulous record of all material you consult because you will need this for citations in your text and for compiling your reference list.

Clear the decks. Finish other tasks that are outstanding; tidy your work area; make it clear to others that you may not be available for socialising as frequently as before; make sure you have a good stock of all your stationery and other study requirements.

Start writing. Note-making is a form of writing that ensures that your reading has a purpose. Research into academic writing has shown that the act of writing is part of the thinking process, so creating isolated paragraphs on the basis of what you have read or on what you think about what you have read can help you to clarify your thoughts. These short pieces of writing can form the basis for further development once you have undertaken further reading and may fit within a structure that is decided later. However, even if you are unable to use what you have written, as an exercise it will probably have contributed to your understanding of your topic, so the effort will not have been wasted. There is the added advantage of providing you with the opportunity to find your own writing 'voice', that is, where you position yourself in relation to the topic, and this signals your development as an academic author.

Work through writer's block. Some days go well; some just do not. Accept that this is simply part of the process – a feature of the human condition. As an academic author, you'll find that sometimes the words will flow almost effortlessly. At other times, every paragraph, sentence or even word is a struggle. That's all part of the thinking process and will eventually contribute to a fresh stream of high-quality writing.

Make sure that you are keeping on track. Review each day as it passes. Ask yourself:

- What have I achieved?
- What went well?
- What could have gone better?
- Am I keeping up with my timetable?
- What do I need to do next?
- What do I need to do to ensure the next session is better?

52

CHOOSING A DISSERTATION OR RESEARCH TOPIC

How to decide on a theme for your investigation

The correct choice of dissertation topic or research project will improve the chances of a successful outcome. This chapter outlines the issues that you need to think about as you weigh up the possibilities.

The topic you choose to research has a great influence on how well you succeed in carrying out the investigation and in writing up your work. A crucial factor is whether you have a genuine interest in the subject matter, as this will motivate you to complete the task to the best possible standard. In addition, many practical matters need to be taken into account, such as the availability of relevant resources, or the feasibility of the intended investigation.

TAKING ACCOUNT OF THE OPTIONS OPEN TO YOU

In many cases, you may find that the dissertation or project topics are prescribed or restricted. The decision is not so much one of what you would like to research, but more which topic you will choose from a list of options provided by academic staff. A variation on this closed option list is the semi-closed list, where academics provide a list of broad topics but leave the student to choose the detailed perspective that they wish to pursue.

Constraints such as these may feel restrictive, especially at first when you do not know the details of the topics outlined. However, they are generally designed to provide you with a degree of freedom within parameters controlled by those who will need to supervise and assess the finished work, and who will have carefully considered the practicalities of each option and the chances of obtaining a successful outcome.

Putting forward your own topic

If you have a specific topic in mind that is not on a prescribed list of dissertation or research project options, you could try approaching a potential supervisor and asking whether it might be considered. If you do this, be prepared to answer searching questions about its viability as a research theme. You should, for example, have planned out your initial approach to the research and worked out what resources might be required.

A less restricted approach to the selection of dissertation topic or research project is also possible. In this case, no list is provided and you are asked to choose not only the topic but the specific research question to be addressed. In this open-choice case, you will be expected to make a selection largely on the basis of your personal interests within the discipline. These might have developed from your personal experience or from previous detailed consideration of related topics arising from your course of study, for example, from reading carried out when studying for coursework.

Where approval on the topic or perspective is required, you may need to present a written proposal that outlines the question and the method of approach to be adopted. This may involve presenting a reasoned argument justifying the research topic and approach. This then goes to the supervising academic or a panel of academics for consideration and approval.

✔ **Make your decisions with speed but not haste**

If a list of dissertation or research options is presented, find out about it as quickly as possible, as there may be competition for specific topics or for particular supervisors. However, make sure you take all relevant factors into account in a deliberate decision-making process, rather than hastily choosing under pressure. You should give the matter high priority and allocate time and attention to activities that may help you make a decision, such as library or internet searches and discussions with potential supervisors.

DECIDING ON YOUR PERSONAL RESEARCH INTERESTS

It is essential that you find your study area interesting and that there is enough about the topic that is novel and challenging for you. If this is the case, then your levels of motivation will be high and may sustain you through any problems you encounter. If not, you will be liable to become bored or disillusioned, and this will hinder your ability to complete and write up your work.

By the time that you're considering a potential research topic, you will almost certainly have an above-average interest in the broader field of study. However, you may never have thought rigorously about your true underlying interests. Now, when you are forced into making a decision, this will need to be considered quite deeply. For some, stating a primary interest might be easy, but for many, it will be quite difficult to commit their efforts to one highly focused subject, or to settle on which option on a list interests them most. There may be a range of possibilities, each with a balance of attractions and negative aspects.

✔ **Rewind your past experiences**

Remind yourself about the issues that arose in debate in the lectures, tutorials, seminars or practicals. Reflect on those areas of your course where you found your curiosity and interest being fired. This may give you some direction in selecting a topic.

What, then, is the best way to arrive at a decision? This may depend on your personality, the discipline and the degree of choice you have been given:

- If you have an open choice, one approach might be to brainstorm possible topics and sub-topics within your subject, then to rank these in order of your interest. You could do this in phases, moving sequentially from broader subject fields to more closely specified research areas, until a clear favourite emerges or you can narrow down the choices.

- If your choice is restricted or from a menu of options, consider each option in turn. Do not reject any possibility out of hand until you know more about it. Obtain background information where necessary and, if a reading list is offered, consult this. Rank the options according to how they appeal to you.

With luck, you will now have created a shortlist of potential topics. The next phase, potentially of equal importance, is to think further about the practical matters that should influence your decision.

A simple way of ranking your choices

Consider each option in turn, and award it a mark out of 10. When you have completed a scan of all the options, look again at the ones which scored highly and reject the ones that scored weakly. Try explaining the reasons for your scores to someone else. This may force you to put into words how you feel, and thereby become more confident in your decision.

OTHER FACTORS TO TAKE INTO ACCOUNT

Many factors will influence your ability to complete your studies to a high standard, and they should all be borne in mind as you arrive at a decision. You should also think about how useful the experience and end product might be. Again, it will be beneficial to score these aspects in relation to the specific topics in your shortlist. You may wish to take into account the following:

Potential research approaches

While you may have distinct preferences for specific areas of study, you should still consider the options at a finer level before making a final decision. Is it possible for you to identify the approach that might be required? Is there a question to be answered, a problem to be solved or an issue to be debated? How will you restrict the potential areas to cover? How exactly will you set about researching the topic? You may alter this 'research angle' through time, but refining your thoughts might aid the decision-making process. Also, bear in mind that if you have a distinct direction to your work from the start, this will increase your chances of success.

Finding out more about a research option

If the answers to questions about the practicalities or relevance of a topic are not immediately evident, ask around. Discuss options with a potential supervisor or other academic contact. Sometimes it is useful to get more than one perspective on the issue, so try to find several people who can give you an opinion.

Time aspects

In selecting a topic, it is particularly important to guard against being over-ambitious. Ensure that you will have enough time to be able to demonstrate, through your written work, that you have completed the task required. You need to factor in not only the time that you will need to read, analyse or present the material, but also the sometimes considerable period that it may take simply to obtain the material or data you need. You should also bear in mind that if you spend too much time on project work and/or writing, this may adversely affect your performance in other coursework.

In some cases, approval for your work will be required from an ethics committee, and this may also take time (see **Ch 53**). Remember too that the writing phase for a dissertation or a project report requires a lot of time. Where you can anticipate that simply identifying and obtaining the material, let alone reading and digesting it, is going to take an inordinate amount of time, then you may need to eliminate some of your first-choice possibilities.

Availability of resources or experimental material

Some dissertations or research projects run into difficulties because it is not possible to obtain the material required to carry out the work.

● **Obtaining printed material.** You will need to evidence your work by reference to the literature (**Ch 23**, **Ch 35**, **Ch 36** and **Ch 37**). Thus, access to printed material is critical to the research process. You need to review the materials relevant to each potential topic that:
  – are available locally in hard copy in book and journal format within your own institution's library;
  – can be accessed electronically through your library's subscription to online journals;
  – can be obtained through inter-library loan (taking into account any cost implications); and
  – may require you to visit another library site for on-site access.

> **? How can I find out about what sources are available?**
>
> The best people to consult are the subject librarians in your library. They will know about:
> ■ the resources already present in your library, including stored materials;
> ■ the main routes for obtaining information, including advanced online searches;
> ■ alternative approaches that you may not have thought about;
> ■ obscure resources and how to access these;
> ■ contacts at other institutions who can help; and
> ■ professional organisations that may have exclusive databanks that you might be able to access through your department.

● **Obtaining data.** You need to take into account the most realistic method of garnering data, recording and interpreting the findings within the time-frame that you have to do the work. If you need to analyse quantitative data, you should also consider what statistical analysis software packages you may need to master. Where your data are qualitative in nature, then you should also consider with your supervisor the most appropriate methods for gathering and interpreting the information. For example, an action research approach might require different techniques to a questionnaire-based approach.

Using new primary sources

Research topics may focus on contemporary events and you may have to use recently published primary sources as the basis for your study (see Table 24.1). For example, you might consult material such as a recently produced *Royal Commission Report*, a new piece of legislation, or a newly published item of literature. Since the novelty of the topic would make it likely that there would be very little, if any, critical appraisal of such things in the public domain, then your research task would be to place your own interpretation on this material. If you encounter difficulty, then seek advice from your supervisor.

Depth

Your dissertation or research topic will need to offer sufficient depth to allow you to show off your skills. These may depend on your discipline, but might include the ability to think critically through analysis and evaluation, or the ability to design an experiment or survey and report it professionally. Avoid choosing a well-worked area or even one that you feel is likely to provide easy results, if it will not allow you to demonstrate advanced skills.

Extent of support and supervision

At all levels of study, the writing of the dissertation or project report is a major task and you will not be expected to do this alone. Incorporated into the process will be a level of support provided by an assigned supervisor. However, you need to be clear at the outset about what you can expect in terms of this support. In some institutions, supervision is mapped onto the research/writing process with regular student–supervisor meetings. In others, arrangements are agreed by the partners for meetings as required. Generally, the supervision will enable you to ask questions, seek guidance and debate some key issues. Be sure, however, that you reach an understanding with your supervisor about the extent to which you can expect them to review and provide feedback on your written work. Often this will not extend to reading the whole dissertation, or to proof-reading the text, as this is regarded as being the responsibility of the student.

Choosing a supervisor

If you have a choice, bear in mind that this should be a member of staff you feel comfortable talking to, who you feel will offer support and guidance, and inspire you to work hard and complete on time. Ask past students if you want the 'insider information' on different tutors, and, where appropriate, the environment where you will be expected to work.

Impact on your CV and career options

Although this is rarely the primary aspect to consider, it is a factor to bear in mind. It may already be that your subject interests are very closely aligned to your ideas for your future career. You may also wish to take into account specific skills you might gain that will be of interest to an employer. If you are an undergraduate interested in further studies, your choice of topic may be valuable in giving you experience to take to a potential postgraduate supervisor.

Weigh up the pros and cons of your options

If you remain undecided after considering both your interest in potential topics and the practical aspects, try laying out your thoughts about the options in a set of simple tables with columns for advantages and disadvantages. This process may help order your thoughts and clarify the factors that are important to you.

PRACTICAL TIPS FOR CHOOSING YOUR DISSERTATION OR RESEARCH TOPIC

Make sure that you are making an informed choice. Do the necessary background reading. Discuss the topics with your course director or assigned supervisor so you avoid taking on a topic that is risky and understand fully the challenges of the topic area.

Speak to students who have already completed this kind of study. Postgraduates in your department might be useful contacts to ask. Discuss with them any aspects in the process that they felt were important to them when they were researching and writing their dissertations or project reports.

Look at past work. Dissertations and reports produced by students in previous years will help you gain a sense of the style and standard required. They will also enable you to look at a variety of approaches relevant to your discipline. However, don't be put off by apparently sophisticated structure and style in these completed examples. Remember that achieving this standard did not happen spontaneously. Your starting point may not be at this level, but the learning process will very likely result in a similarly high standard of report.

Plan out a dissertation or report as part of the decision-making process. Sketch out the structure at the macro-level and then, later, for selected options, think about a more detailed plan. In practice, you may not stick rigidly to the plan you create, but the process of planning will help you to sort out the ideas and decide how appealing and feasible they are.

Think for yourself. When choosing a topic, try not to be influenced by other students' opinions. This is, and should be, a highly personal decision. Some of your peers may have their own reasons for liking or disliking certain topics or supervisors; you will need to distance yourself from their thoughts when considering your own options.

Finding a topic for yourself. If you are given the option to choose your own topic, but have difficulty identifying a theme, you might find it stimulating to refer to some of the generic periodicals – such as *Nature*, *New Scientist*, *Time*, *The Economist*, or *The Spectator* – to identify emergent issues, new strands of research or possible controversies arising from contemporary developments in your field.

53

ETHICS IN RESEARCHING AND REPORTING

How to follow good research practice

For many research topics and methodologies, it is important to review the ethical position regarding your study. The precise details differ according to discipline and the nature of the investigation. This chapter outlines the principles and procedures that may apply.

The term 'ethics' in the research context refers to the principles, rules and standards of conduct that apply to investigations. Most disciplines have self-monitoring codes of ethical practice and your institution will operate its own internal research governance policy. The types of ethical requirements vary among disciplines and your study must comply with recognised practice in your field and your institution. It is imperative that you familiarise yourself with these codes and are able to bring that understanding to the initial discussion of the research project with your supervisor. He or she will be responsible for ensuring that your research proposal complies with ethical practice in your institution. Where necessary, your supervisor will help you prepare an application to conduct the research for submission to your institution's ethics committee. Note that there may be different committees and rules for clinical and non-clinical research.

ETHICAL PRINCIPLES

Any research project involving human beings should be characterised by protection of the human rights, dignity, health and safety of participants and researchers. This is achieved by observing three fundamental tenets:

- the research should **do no harm**;
- consent should be **voluntary**; and
- **confidentiality** should be respected throughout.

Ethical considerations may relate to non-human as well as human research activity. Controversial areas have included the use of animals in research, cloning, human embryo research, stem cell research, *in vitro* fertilisation, and nuclear research. In the UK, experiments involving animals are subject to Home Office approval. If this is required for your work, your supervisor will guide you through the procedures. Similarly, experiments involving genetic manipulation must comply with relevant legislation and you will be guided through relevant procedures if necessary.

SAFE RESEARCH

It is a fundamental of research activity in the spirit of international codes of practice that the health and safety of all those involved in research activity as participants or researchers should be a priority at all times.

All research approved by the appropriate ethics committee must follow passed protocols exactly. Any modification to the original proposal has to be referred back to the ethics committee. For the purposes of undergraduate research proposals, although the student is acting as the 'Principal Investigator', the actual Principal Investigator responsibility remains with the Supervisor.

CONSENT AND CONFIDENTIALITY

Participants may need to be informed in writing about certain aspects of your research. This is usually provided as a 'Participant Information Sheet'.

Key points in Participant Information Sheet:

❏ Outline of the purpose of the study

❏ Invitation and reason for being selected

❏ Explanation of the voluntary nature of participation and of the freedom of the subject to terminate participation at any time

- ❑ Explanation of the procedure to be followed in the research and the time commitment involved
- ❑ Advantages and disadvantages of participation
- ❑ Assurance of confidentiality and anonymity
- ❑ Information about outcomes
- ❑ Information about the funding source
- ❑ Names of lead researcher and assistants
- ❑ Information about any sponsorship or affiliation connected to the project
- ❑ Information about refunding of expenses, if applicable

Particularly in the clinical area, a 'template' is often adopted to frame the explanation for participants. However, in many instances, this is often unsatisfactory because the language used, and the format and layout are often unclear to the non-specialist. Every effort should be made to inform participants about the project as concisely as possible in 'plain' English, that is, in language that can be easily understood by participants.

In response to this information, participants are then requested to complete an 'Informed Consent Form' that requires their signature. In some instances, a debriefing form will also need to be completed once the data-gathering phase is concluded.

How ethical is your research?

Unethical approaches to research can be inadvertent and unintended. For example, vulnerable groups may feel pressured into participating although members of such groups may not express this to the researcher. Patients may feel that they will receive better treatment if they participate in a study and risk a poorer level of treatment if they don't. Consequently, your research design and consent forms must reflect your awareness of such potential perceptions. Cases of unethical research procedures are legion and, thus, the field of ethics is a complex one. If you have any doubts at all about the ethical dimension of your study, you should discuss these with your supervisor to ensure that neither you nor your subjects are compromised by the research activity.

Human participants must be assured that their identities will be protected by the promise of anonymity. This means that the confidentiality of any representation of data, whether in aggregated forms (for example, mean value) or as qualitative material that might be obtained from individuals (for example, through questionnaires, interviews or focus groups), is protected in any printed format. It is essential that written permission to quote informants be sought from them at the time of participation in the enquiry, with the proviso that identities will be protected when findings are reported.

Data protection

The storage and use of personal information is an ethical issue. In the UK, the Data Protection Act covers procedures that must be adopted. Consult your university's web pages for information and guidance on local procedures if you plan to store information either in paper files or electronically. Legislation apart, it is simply good practice to time-limit the period in which data will remain on your records – and to inform participants how their data will be stored, and when it will be deleted or destroyed.

OBTAINING ETHICAL APPROVAL

You should first read the guidance notes provided by your university's ethics committee or department. Once you have satisfied yourself that you have made arrangements to cover the ethical dimensions of your research project, you will be in a position to frame your proposal for ethical approval. Institutions will vary in the formats required. In general, you will need to provide information on:

- the title, purpose and duration of the project, and the location of the study;
- the methodological approach to be adopted, and information on how data will be stored securely;
- if appropriate, the way in which participants will be recruited, plus information as to age, gender and any inclusion/exclusion criteria;
- measures taken to ensure that all ethical dimensions are covered in compliance with the appropriate research code of practice in your institution, including confidentiality in reporting results; and
- if appropriate, identification of the involvement of any funding body.

In your research plan (**Ch 33**), you should make due allowance for the time taken to obtain ethical approval (your supervisor can advise on normal delays). Make sure that you carry out some relevant work, such as a literature review, while you are waiting.

PRACTICAL TIPS FOR ENSURING YOUR RESEARCH MEETS ETHICAL REQUIREMENTS

Consult your university's website for up-to-date and detailed information on approaches to research ethics. In addition to the ethical policy, there may be general guidance information, discipline-specific advice, and links to useful websites.

Consult appropriate texts related to ethics. Potential starting points are Sana (2002) and Shamoo and Resnick (2003), but either consult the library catalogue or ask at your library for holdings specific to your discipline.

Visit websites for learned societies in your discipline to obtain up-to-date information about ethical aspects that may impact on your research study. This may be important if you are required to take an oral exam on your research project and your external examiner may wish to explore the ethics of your study in the wider discipline with you.

Be alert to publicity that covers instances of unethical behaviour in any field of research. This may raise issues that subsequently you could have to address in other projects in the course of your studies.

Where possible, discuss ethical dimensions of research with peers and academic staff. This debate will raise your awareness of issues that can arise and may also provide you with some benchmarks against which to judge your own study.

54

REPORT WRITING

How to select and shape your content appropriately

> Writing reports of one kind or another is a part of many degree courses. These often have discipline-specific formats and it is important to follow these and select the correct information to put into the different sub-sections. This chapter considers common formats which may be suitable for the literature survey, the scientific report and the business report.

The purpose of any report is to convey information, usually on a well-defined topic. Conventions have evolved for the structure, style and content of reports in different subjects, and, while the scholarship underlying the report will always be foremost in markers' assessments, presentational aspects are also judged as important, so you should follow the appropriate format very carefully. You can find out about aspects of the research that precedes the writing of experimental and business reports in **Ch 20**, **Ch 22–Ch 24**. Methods of conducting literature reviews are discussed in **Ch 55**. Presentation is covered in **Ch 44**.

Why write reports at university?

Report writing is regarded as important because it:

- compels you to complete your work and present it in a neatly organised form for assessment;
- helps you to develop important professional skills;
- provides a record for replication or development of results for future research.

COMMON FEATURES OF REPORT WRITING

Writing a report is often a drawn-out task and may follow a lengthy period of research in the library, on the internet or in the laboratory. However, you should not consider the research and writing phases as separate. Your research must take into account the style and format of the report, while elements of writing up can and should be carried out as you continue to explore your topic.

Keep your focus tight

Students often fall into the trap of being overambitious in their goals. In general, it is better to cover a limited topic well than to write a shallow report covering a wide area.

The following stages are likely to be involved in most exercises culminating in a report:

1 **'Scoping'.** Here, you will be deciding on a topic or a specific aspect of a subject on which to concentrate. Sometimes the topic is decided for you, but in other cases it may emerge as you research. Even in the second situation, having a notional goal when you start is important: this will give you impetus, even though you may change the precise focus later.

2 **Research.** This consists of finding and selecting relevant information. Research may be experimental, as in many science subjects, or it may be desk-based, analysing and evaluating reports, texts and other sources (**Ch 23–24, Ch 55**).

3 **Writing.** This involves communicating your work using appropriate language. It's important that your writing provides evidence that you have been thinking at the appropriate level (see tip box below and **Ch 22**).

4 **Presentation.** You will be expected to present your work to a high professional standard and some marks will normally be awarded for this aspect.

Aspects of report writing

Description: reporting your experiments or summarising facts you have gathered.

Visual summaries: making diagrams, flow charts, graphs or tables to demonstrate your points more clearly.

Analysis: looking at results or facts and possibly working out descriptive or hypothesis-testing statistics.

Discussion: weighing up the pros and cons of a position.

Solution(s): explaining different options to solve an issue or problem being addressed.

Evaluation: deciding what's important and why.

Recommendation: identifying the best solution and giving evidence to support that choice.

Arriving at a conclusion: stating a position on the basis of your research.

REPRESENTATIVE FORMATS FOR REPORTS

Table 54.1 summarises the general components of reports and what they should contain. Reports for different purposes and in different subjects follow different designs and include various components, not always in the same order. Table 54.2 provides some examples, but you should follow closely the guidelines published by your faculty or department.

Table 54.1 Typical components of reports, and notes on the expected content of each part. These are arranged alphabetically and would not appear in this order in any report. For representative examples of report formats, see Table 54.2). *Always adopt the precise format specified in your course handbook.*

Section or part	Expected content
Abbreviations	A list of any abbreviations for technical terms used within the text (for example, 'DNA: deoxyribonucleic acid'). These are also given within the text at the first point of use, for example 'deoxyribonucleic acid (DNA)'.
Abstract	A brief summary of the aims of the experiment or series of observations, the main outcomes (in words) and conclusions. This should allow someone to understand your main findings and what you think they mean. This is normally written last, but is usually positioned at the beginning of the report.
Acknowledgements	A list of people who helped you, sometimes with a brief description of how.
Appendix (pl: appendices)	Includes tabular information, usually, that only an expert would want or need to consult; a section where you can put items such as a questionnaire template, and data or results that would otherwise disrupt the flow of the report or make the results section too lengthy.
Bibliography/references/ literature cited	An alphabetical list of sources cited in the text, following one of the standard referencing styles (**Ch 35**).

Discussion (or conclusions)	• **Scientific-style reports.** A commentary on the results and an outline of the main conclusions. This could include any or all of the following:
	  – comments on the methods used;
	  – mention of sources of errors;
	  – conclusions from any statistical analysis;
	  – comparison with other findings or the 'ideal' result;
	  – what the result means;
	  – how you might improve the experiment;
	  – how you might implement the findings;
	  – where you would go from here, given more time and resources.
	Sometimes you might combine the results and discussions sections to allow a narrative to develop – to explain, for example, why one result led to the next experiment or approach. Bear in mind that a large proportion of marks may be given for your original thoughts in this section.
	• **Non-scientific-style reports.** In this section you might restate the problem or issue to be addressed, outline the key 'solutions' or responses to the problem, and explain the reason for favouring one over another by providing evidence to support that choice. In some, but not all, instances, a set of recommendations might be appropriate and an indication of how they could be implemented.

Executive summary	Takes the place of an abstract in a business report. Gives the key points of the report, usually no more than one A4 page long. It should start with a brief statement of the aims of the report, a summary of the main findings and/or conclusions, perhaps given as bullet points, and a summary of the main conclusions and/or recommendations. You would normally write this part last.
Experimental	A description of apparatus and method, similar to materials and methods.
Glossary	A list of terms that might be unfamiliar to the reader, with definitions.
Introduction	• **Scientific-style reports.** An outline of the background to the experiments, the aims of the experiments and brief discussion of the techniques to be used. Your goal is to orient the reader and explain what you have done and why. • **Non-scientific-style reports.** The context of the study and an outline of the problem or issue to be addressed, in other words, the aim of the report. This may require reference to the literature or other resource material to be used.

continued overleaf

Table 54.1 (*cont'd*)

Section or part	Expected content
Main body of text	Your appraisal of the topic. It should systematically address solutions or issues in response to the report's purpose and provide an analysis of all pertinent matters. It may be subdivided into sections reflecting different aspects (**Ch 34**). In a scientific literature review, the approach is often to give a chronological account of developments in the field, quoting key authors, their ideas and findings. This section may include tables comparing different approaches or results in different studies. Figures tend to be rare, but may be used to summarise concepts or illustrate key findings.
Materials and methods	A description of what was done. You should provide sufficient detail to allow a competent person to repeat the work.
Results	A description of the experiments carried out and the results obtained, usually presented in either tabular or graphic form (never both for the same data). You should point out meaningful aspects of the data, which need not be presented in the same order in which the work was done.
Table of contents	Effectively an index to allow the reader to find parts in which they are interested. May also include a table of diagrams. More likely to be included in a lengthy report.
Title page	The full names of the author or authors, the module title or code and the date. In a business report this may also include the company logo, client details and classification (for example, 'confidential'). • **Scientific-style reports.** A descriptive title that indicates what was done, indicates any restrictions, and sometimes describes the 'headline' finding. • **Non-scientific-style reports.** A concise but comprehensive title that defines the topic.

Literature surveys

These follow the relatively uncomplicated format shown in Table 54.2(a). Two important formatting aspects to consider are citation of literature references and presenting quotes from your sources (**Ch 35**). Aspects of finding and analysing the literature are discussed in **Ch 55**.

Scientific reports

Representative formats are shown in Table 54.2(b), (c) and (d). These tend to mirror the format of journal articles in the primary literature for each subject area (**Ch 24**). Aspects you should bear in mind are that:

- anyone reading your report should be able to assimilate your findings quickly, and should be able to find relevant information in the expected place;
- your text should be objective and balanced, considering all possible interpretations of your results;
- appropriate statistical analysis should be included (**Ch 30**);
- you should provide enough information to allow another competent scientist to understand and repeat your work.

Reports for non-scientific subjects

Increasingly report writing is becoming a feature in non-scientific subjects. A report-style response could be required for a case study, project or group problem-solving exercise, for

Table 54.2 Designs of different sorts of report. The literature review (a) has a simple structure. The main body is the largest part, and may be subdivided into sections. The general scientific report (b) has a focus on materials and methods, but in some disciplines the components may be presented in a different order, as shown in the model for the report in chemistry (c). An undergraduate lab report (d) will probably be a stripped-down and shorter version of (b). A non-scientific style of report (e) would not focus on materials and methods, but might have a main body of text dealing with the topic being considered. A typical business report (f) includes the conclusions or recommendations as part of the main body and provides an executive summary for quick reading. It often has appendices and a glossary for the non-specialist. See Table 54.1 for details of content for each section.

(a) Literature review	(b) General scientific report	(c) Scientific report in chemistry	(d) Laboratory report in the sciences	(e) Non-scientific report	(f) Typical business report
Title page	Title page	Title page	Title page	Title page	Title page
Abstract	Abstract	Abstract	Introduction	Introduction	Executive summary
Introduction	Abbreviations	Abbreviations	Materials and methods	Main body of text	Acknowledgements
Main body of text	Introduction	Introduction	Results (brief)	Conclusion	Table of contents
Conclusions	Materials and methods	Results	Discussion/conclusions		Main body of text
References or literature cited	Results	Discussion			Recommendations
	Discussion	Materials and methods			
	Acknowledgements	Acknowledgements			Bibliography/references
	References	References			Appendices
					Glossary

example. Table 54.2(e) shows a representative structure. A good approach for the main body of text in these report-style tasks is to follow the situation–problem–solution–evaluation + (optional) recommendation (SPSER) model (**Ch 34**). This provides a basic skeleton. You may wish to tailor the headings and sub-headings to fit the context of the topic or problem that you are addressing, but the essence of the SPSER model remains intact 'below the surface' of these headings.

Business-style reports

The main aim of a business report is to provide information that helps decision-making. These reports differ greatly in their style and formality and the chief factor to consider is your audience. Table 54.2(f) illustrates one possible format. Possible variations might include:

- A report aimed solely at a shop-floor manager: relatively short and informal, focusing on production statistics and limitations.
- A business plan aimed at an investor or bank manager: fairly brief, focusing on financial projections given in charts and tables.
- An academic analysis of a business sector: relatively lengthy and formal, quoting many sources and views.

Structurally, a business report is unlike an essay in that you should use headings and sub-headings so that your reader can find relevant information quickly.

PRACTICAL TIPS FOR SELECTING AND SHAPING REPORT CONTENT

Find a model for the layout you need to adopt. This might be given in your course handbook or could be adopted from an example that you feel is well organised. If you are unsure, then you should follow one of the models in Table 54.2.

Be ruthless in rejecting irrelevant information. You must keep your report as short and to the point as you can. Especially if you have spent a long time obtaining information or conducting an analysis, you may be tempted to include it for this reason alone. Don't. Relevance must be your sole criterion.

Consider your writing style. Reports can be dense and difficult to read. Try to keep your sentences relatively simple and your paragraphs short. In reports you can use sub-headings and bullet points to break up the text. All these devices can make the content easier for your reader to assimilate.

Choose appropriate chart types. If you wish to present diagrams and graphs, keep these simple and use the title and legend to explain what you want to show in each case (**Ch 30**). Use a variety of types of chart if you can.

Think about your likely conclusions from an early stage. This may shape both the research you do and the content. However, make sure you keep an open mind if the evidence points you in another direction.

55

LITERATURE SURVEYS

How to research and shape a survey of facts and viewpoints

A review of literature is a specialised form of academic writing that requires a specific research approach and writing style. This chapter outlines ways of finding and selecting relevant literature and writing about the work of others in an appropriate way.

Conducting a literature survey is similar in many ways to writing a dissertation (**Ch 51**) in that it involves reading about a topic and summarising what different authors have said about it. You may wish to compare and contrast different viewpoints or research themes, or describe the development of an academic field through time. However, the product should be more than that, as the alternative name – the literature review – implies: you will need to carry out an *analysis* and *evaluation* of the literature, rather than merely describing what others have written (see **Ch 22** for an explanation of these terms).

> **i**
>
> **Definition: literature survey**
>
> A literature survey reviews comprehensively all the available publications related to a specific academic topic. It documents this literature; identifies the schools of thought within it; categorises viewpoints; explores the origins and development of authors' standpoints; analyses and evaluates the relevance and meaning of the facts and viewpoints encountered.

SELECTING A TOPIC

The first stage in a literature survey is choosing a specific area to research. If you are allowed a choice, you may be asked to choose from a list, or you may be expected to find a topic yourself within a broad area. In either case, you will find it useful to do a little reading before selecting.

Possible criteria for selecting a subject include:

- a topic that you find interesting;
- a research field with a reasonable amount of literature to discuss – not too small, with only a few papers available, nor too large, with too many;
- a subject where the literature is accessible – for example, published in English, or in journals available from your library;

- a field where there are different views or approaches that you can compare;
- a controversial area, or a topical subject;
- a field where a recent breakthrough has been made.

Narrow down your topic if you can and choose a working title. The wording of this is important, because readers' and markers' expectations of content will be influenced by your title. You should be prepared to alter the title or add a secondary element to it as your research develops and you decide on the precise 'angle' or viewpoint you will adopt.

HOW TO FIND THE LITERATURE ON YOUR SUBJECT

Your review will take into account information provided by various forms of written source:

- **Textbooks:** good for gaining an overview of a field.
- **Monographs:** books on a single, often narrow, subject.
- **Reviews:** analysis of a research area, often detailed and more up to date than books.
- **Reference works:** useful for obtaining facts and definitions, and a concise overview of a subject.
- **Research papers:** very detailed 'articles' published in journals, covering specific subject areas.
- **Websites:** not always wholly reliable as sources, but may be useful for comparing viewpoints and sourcing other information.

See also **Ch 23** regarding library resources.

Using more than one source

You should always consult a number of sources on any given issue (where this is possible). These may corroborate each other, or you may find that they take different views or support different interpretations. This is sometimes referred to as 'reading around' a subject.

If your work is supervised, your supervisor may be able to provide some articles to start you off, or some references may be given in handouts supporting the exercise. The majority of the papers you will consult will be in the primary literature (Table 24.1), and when you start will seem to be jargon-ridden and written in impenetrable English. However, as you become familiar with the terms of your subject, this will become less of a problem (see **Ch 42** for tips).

If you are unfamiliar with library research methods, it is a good idea to consult a subject librarian. Not only will they be able to teach you basic techniques, but they can also show you how to access databases and other tools to search for relevant material. Your library's website may also carry useful tips and online access routes to databases and e-journals (**Ch 23**).

There is a constant stream of academic work feeding into the primary literature. So long as you have one paper as a starting point, you can work *backwards* in the literature relatively easily by looking for other relevant references in the text, especially within the introduction and discussion of the paper. Use the context and article title as a guide to relevance. Each paper you then read will refer to others, and before long you will accumulate a body of references and have a feel for the important papers in your field.

Working *forwards* in the literature from a relevant paper is a little less easy. In some fields there are citation index journals that indicate which papers have been cited by others. This can let you see where a chosen reference has been mentioned recently – and sometimes the citing article will be of interest to you. Another approach is to put key words or authors into a database or search engine and see what turns up. You can also scan current journals for related material, though this is much less likely to turn up relevant material.

KEEPING TRACK OF REFERENCES AND THEIR RELEVANCE

As you read each article and review, you should be taking notes of key points (**Ch 26**), either in a notebook, or on index cards (see below). The matrix format of note-taking (Figure 26.6 on page 158) is a valuable way of summarising different aspects of sources and lets you see the whole picture more easily.

You may also wish to file papers so that you can find them when required. The simplest method is alphabetically by author, and then by date, as in a bibliography. An alternative, which is valuable if you expect to gather many papers, is to give each paper an accession number and note this on your index system or database. Papers are then filed in numerical order. This avoids the need to reorganise papers if your files become full.

One thing you will have to do is cite your sources in your text and prepare a bibliography or reference list. This is standard academic practice and helps avoid accusations of plagiarism (**Ch 36**). You will need to follow departmental guidance notes for the precise format or take an example from the discipline literature. **Ch 35** provides further information about methods of citing and quoting, and selected referencing styles.

Using index cards

Some people like to keep the reference details of their sources on index cards, along with any notes they make about them. This serves two purposes:

- When writing up, you can put the cards into piles representing different topics or viewpoints and then organise these appropriately, for example, by date. This makes it easier to include every reference in its 'right' place.
- The cards can be organised alphabetically to create your bibliography/reference list. If your review involves many papers, however, you may wish to spread the task of typing these by entering them into a word-processor file as you go along.

WRITING IN A BALANCED, OBJECTIVE STYLE AND ARRIVING AT A CONCLUSION

Although you may have, or develop, strong views about your topic and the issues and controversies that you discuss, it is vital that you write in a balanced way that gives a fair summary of the reasons for opposing viewpoints. This is one reason why an impersonal, passive style is favoured in academic writing (**Ch 37**).

However, it is important that you try to arrive at a conclusion. In doing so, you should give reasons why you have arrived at a particular viewpoint. Do not be afraid of being critical, so long as you can back up your position with supporting evidence.

PRACTICAL TIPS FOR WRITING A LITERATURE SURVEY

Try not to read aimlessly and passively. Taking notes is one way you can avoid this. Just as in revising, it will help you memorise key points. See **Ch 26** for advice and tips.

Start writing as soon as you can. Word processors allow text fragments to be moved around with ease. This means that you can write up some parts of your survey (especially descriptive parts) as you go along, and reorganise these when you have a better picture of the whole subject.

Discuss drafts with your supervisor or a friend. Your supervisor may not ask to see your drafts, but you will probably gain valuable advice if you can persuade them to comment. A friend, even one who doesn't know your subject, will also be able to point out where your explanations are obscure or your view seems biased.

Organise your references from an early stage. It can be very time-consuming searching for details and writing your bibliography and it is best not to do this at the last moment, when you should be focusing on higher-level aspects.

Review and edit what you have written. If at all possible, aim to finish your writing a week or so ahead of the submission date. Then, leave your work for a day to two and return to it, reading it in one sweep. This will help you take a more critical look at what you have written (**Ch 43**).

POSTER PRESENTATIONS

How to display your work effectively

In certain disciplines you may be asked to prepare a poster to summarise research you have done, often as part of a teamwork exercise. The main aim is to develop your communication skills, including how you select and present the content and are able to discuss your work with others.

The idea behind a poster display is to present a summary of research or scholarship in an easily assimilated format. Poster sessions are common at academic conferences, particularly in the sciences – they allow many participants to report findings or ideas within a single session and help people with similar interests to meet and discuss detailed information.

The concept has been adapted for undergraduate work for several reasons.

- It allows you to present the results of your work to tutors and fellow students.
- It provides a good end point for teamwork (**Ch 19**).
- It makes you focus on the essence of the topic.
- It develops your presentational skills.
- It allows tutors to observe your verbal communication skills.

Any or all of these aspects may be assessed as part of the exercise. Look into the way marks are allocated before you start so that you can balance your efforts appropriately. If peer assessment is involved, you may wish to discuss this openly at an initial team meeting.

The advice presented here will assume that your poster is part of a team exercise where you have been asked to look into a specific aspect of the subject you are studying. The same principles will apply if it is a solo effort, for example if you are reporting the results of a research project.

> **Definition: peer assessment**
>
> This is where members of a class assess each other's work. For a poster presentation, members of a group may assess each other's contribution as part of the team, and/or members of the class may judge each other's posters.

RESEARCHING AND DECIDING ON CONTENT

In team presentations, each member should do a little independent study in the first instance, so that everyone can gain a general picture of the whole topic. At some point you will want to meet up to decide on the exact focus of your poster, and perhaps allocate specific research tasks for each member. At this stage you should only be thinking about the specific aspects of the topic you feel you need to cover, rather than precise wording. Even seemingly narrow subjects will have scope for different approaches. Although a striking 'take-home message' is important, you should also bear in mind the need for visual impact in your poster when making your choices. There are certain components included in most posters, however, as detailed below.

You will normally be allocated a space to set up your poster (typically 1.5 metre wide and 1 metre high) and, although this may initially seem a large area to cover, you will probably have to select carefully what to include. This is because your poster will need to be legible from a distance of 1 metre or so, and the large font size required for this inevitably means fewer words than you might otherwise prefer. When thinking about content, therefore, it is best to assume that space will be limited.

> ✔ **Typical components of a poster – a checklist**
>
> ❑ **Title:** phrased in a way that will attract readers' attention
> ❑ **Author information:** names, and in the formal academic type of poster, their affiliation
> ❑ **Abstract or summary:** stating the approach taken and the main conclusions
> ❑ **Introduction:** providing brief background information essential for understanding the poster
> ❑ **Materials and methods:** describing experimental or field research, background theory or historical overview
> ❑ **Results:** key findings or examples
> ❑ **Conclusion:** giving the 'take-home messages' of your study or project
> ❑ **Acknowledgements:** stating who has helped you
> ❑ **References and sources**

DESIGNING YOUR POSTER

The key design principle for your poster is to generate visual impact. It needs to stand out among the others in the session and provide a visual 'hook' to draw a spectator towards the more academic content. This can be achieved in several ways:

● a striking overall design concept related to the topic;

● effective use of colour or a prominent colour contrast between the background and the poster elements;

● a large image, either attractive or horrific, at the centre of the poster;

● an amusing or punning title;

● some form of visual aid attached to the poster, such as a large model related to the topic.

Examples of imaginative poster design

- A poster about forest ecology where the text elements are presented as 'leaves' on a model tree.
- A study of urban geography where the poster has the appearance of a street map with aspects written within each building.
- A physiology poster where an organ like the liver is drawn at the centre, with elements attached to it via arteries and veins.

For convenience, most undergraduate posters are composed of A4 or A3 sheets, or shapes derived from them. These 'panels' will be attached to the main poster board, usually by drawing pins or Velcro pads, and their size or shape may place a constraint on your overall design – check the overall dimensions as soon as you can, to work out your options for arranging these sheets.

The next important aspect to decide is how your readers will work their way through the material you present. Each panel will be read left to right in the usual way, but the route through the panels may not follow this rule. Various options are shown in Figure 56.1. Whichever you choose, it is important to let your readers know which path to take, either by prominent numbering or by incorporating arrows or guidelines into the design.

The ideal text size for your poster title will be about 25–40 mm high (100–170 point size) for the title, 15–25 mm for subtitles (60–100 point) and 5–10 mm (25–40 point) for the main material. If you only have an A4 printer at your disposal, bear in mind that you can enlarge to A3 on most photocopiers, although this may restrict you to black-and-white text. Linear dimensions will increase by 1.41 times if you do this. Once point size and panel dimensions are known, you can work out a rough word limit for each component. When members of the team are working on the content, they will need to bear this limit in mind. Besides being succinct, your writing style should make it easy to assimilate the material, for example, by using bullet points and sub-headings.

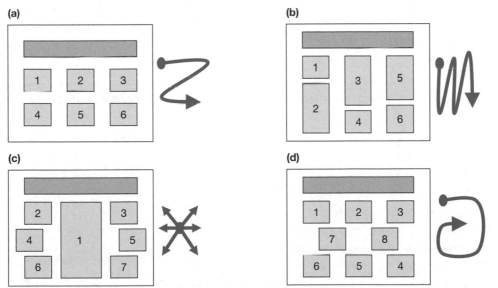

Figure 56.1 Options for laying out a poster. The numbers and arrows indicate the route taken by the reader, while the deeper-coloured bar at the top would contain the title and author details.

Group style

We all have our own styles of writing and it is important that you bear this in mind when composing the text, so that idiosyncrasies are ironed out and the overall style is consistent (see (**Chs 38, 39** and **40**).

CONSTRUCTING AND SETTING UP A POSTER

At an early stage, you should draw a diagram of your poster, mapping out the main components to scale. You may also wish to create a mock poster to the exact dimensions to gain a better idea of what the final version will look like.

Each part will need to be printed or copied according to your design brief. Using panels as described above makes it easier to construct the poster as a series of independent components and to bring these to the poster session for final assembly. They can be attached to your board directly or pasted on to card first. You may also wish to laminate each component, or cover it in clear plastic film. A photocopying specialist (see *Yellow Pages* under 'Copying and duplicating services') may be able to carry this out for a charge.

DEFENDING YOUR POSTER

The poster 'defence' for undergraduate work mimics the poster session at a conference where delegates mill around the posters, quizzing the authors about their work. These sessions can be very stimulating for all involved, and collaborations and job offers may result.

If your poster exercise involves an element of defence, it will probably take the form of a 5–10-minute question-and-answer session with your tutors. Expect probing questions to find out how much knowledge and understanding lies behind your presentation, not just what you have selected to display.

? Questions about your poster that you should be ready to answer

- Why did you select this topic?
- Who did which part of the research?
- Who thought of the design?
- Who made up the components?
- Can you give me further information on . . . ?
- How does this finding relate to . . . ?
- What does this graph or image mean?
- Where next for this topic or research area?
- How might you improve your poster?

You could have a rehearsal session when the team works out how these questions could be answered in the context of your poster presentation.

Use the poster title effectively. A two-part title can be used to draw the reader in – the first part being a 'hook' and the second giving more detail. The chapter titles in this book are examples of this approach, but there will be scope for more humour in your poster title, perhaps through a pun on the subject material.

Check out the font sizes you plan to use. Print out a specimen sheet and stand 1–1.5 metres away. You should be able to read the material easily from this distance. Copy some random text (for example, from a website) on to a sheet at the same font size and carry out a word count to gain an idea of what your word limit will be for each component.

Make sure that your poster is able to 'travel well'. You should think about how you take it from the point of construction to the display venue. The components should be portable and packaged in a weather-proof way.

Make sure you take a variety of 'fixings' with you. Sometimes organisers fail to provide sufficient plus stickers or tape to display posters, so it is useful if you go prepared with a variety of options – don't forget the scissors!

Remember that 'white space' is important in design. An overly fussy presentation with many elements covering the entire area will be difficult to assimilate. In this case, 'less can be more' if it helps you to get your central message across.

Consider colour combinations carefully. Certain colours are difficult to see against others and some pairings may be difficult to distinguish for those who are colour-blind (for example, red and green). Bold, primary colours will attract the eye.

Use imaginative materials. A visit to a craft shop or a do-it-yourself store might give you some ideas. For example, you might see a piece of fabric or single roll of wallpaper at a cheap price that could provide an interesting background.

Use language to draw the reader in. For example, if the titles and sub-headings are given as a series of rhetorical questions, a casual viewer will naturally want to read the text to find out the answer.

Don't provide too much detail. Keep the wording sparse, and be prepared to talk further about matters raised in the text during the poster defence.

Use a handout, if you have too much detail to cover. If you've done lots of research but have to cut some interesting parts out of the final design because of space constraints, consider giving readers a short handout to cover these aspects. This should contain the poster title, author names and contact details.

State your 'take-home message' clearly. Leave your reader in no doubt about your conclusions. You could, for example, list them as a series of bullet points at the end.

Work as a team when answering questions. Be ready to support each other, filling in if someone dries up. However, all members should know the fundamentals of the topic, as any group member may be expected to respond.

57

SPOKEN PRESENTATIONS

How to give a talk or seminar with confidence

Giving a presentation can be a rewarding experience. By following simple guidelines, you can prepare yourself well, gain in confidence and communicate your message effectively.

You may be expected to give a spoken presentation in several different situations – from a brief oral summary at a tutorial to a lengthy seminar on a final-year project. Your talk may be relatively casual or it may be supported by high-tech visual aids. This chapter will focus on more formal types of presentation, although similar principles apply elsewhere.

PLANNING AND PREPARING YOUR SCRIPT

Whatever the occasion, it is important to be well prepared. Having a well-thought-out plan, good supporting material and a clear picture of your main conclusions will boost your confidence and improve your audience's experience. However, over-rehearsal can lead to a dull and monotonous delivery and you should try to avoid this.

Experienced speakers know that being slightly nervous is important, because this creates energy and sparkle when delivering the material. Their view is that if the adrenalin isn't flowing, their presentation will probably lack vitality. Turn any anxiety you may have to your advantage by thinking of it as something that will work for you rather than against you.

✔ **Keep your introduction positive**

Never start a talk by being apologetic or putting yourself down. For example, you may be tempted to say that you are unprepared or lack expertise. This will lower your audience's expectations, probably unnecessarily, and get you off to a weak start.

✔ **Start your presentation with the basics**

Don't forget to begin with the seemingly obvious, such as definitions of key terms. Not all your audience may have the same background in the subject as you. If they aren't on the same wavelength, or don't understand key terms, you may lose them at the very beginning.

Structure

Every substantive presentation should have a beginning, a middle and an end. The old maxim 'say what you are going to say, say it, and then say what you have said' conforms directly to this structure and you need search no further for an outline plan.

- **Introduction.** Your task here is to introduce yourself, state the aim of your presentation, say how you intend to approach the topic and provide relevant background information.
- **Main content.** This will depend on the nature of the talk. For a talk about a project in the Sciences or Engineering, you might start with methods, and then move on to results, perhaps displayed as a series of graphs that you will lead your audience through. For a seminar in the Arts, you might discuss various aspects of your topic, giving examples or quotes as you go.
- **Conclusions.** Here your aim is to draw the talk together, explaining how all your points fit together and giving ideas of where things might develop in the future – for example, suggestions for further research or different angles to approach the subject. Finally, you should recap your whole talk in a series of 'take-home statements' and then thank your audience for their attention.

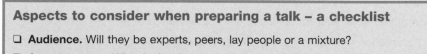

Aspects to consider when preparing a talk – a checklist

- ☐ **Audience.** Will they be experts, peers, lay people or a mixture?
- ☐ **Arrangements.** What is the date, start time and period allocated for your talk?
- ☐ **Venue.** How might the location and nature of its layout affect your delivery?
- ☐ **Facilities.** What equipment and AV aids are available?
- ☐ **Context.** Who will be preceding or following you? What introduction to you and your topic might be given?
- ☐ **Presentation style.** Do you want to use 'chalk and talk', overhead transparencies or PowerPoint?
- ☐ **Delivery.** Will you use a detailed script, prompts or simply improvise?
- ☐ **Requirements.** What might you need to bring? What equipment might you need to practise with?
- ☐ **Liaison.** Who should you contact to confirm details or make special requests?

Creating a script or series of prompts

Presentations begin as pieces of writing that evolve through several stages:

1 Creating a brainstorm or concept map of what you need to cover.
2 Laying out themes or headings with brief explanatory notes.
3 Producing a script – more or less the full text of your talk with stage directions and an indication of timing.
4 Reducing the script to a set of key words and bullet points – your prompts.

As you become more experienced, you will find you can move directly from stage 2 to stage 4, perhaps thinking through appropriate phrasing in your head rather than writing the exact words down.

Working from prompts, sometimes called 'cues', is recommended, whether they are produced as headings on cards or as bullet points in a PowerPoint slideshow (or similar). These basic headings provide the structure of your talk, so that you don't ramble or lose your place. They also help to promote an air of informality that will draw in your audience. All you need to remember is roughly what you intend to say around each point.

Reading your talk from a written script is probably a bad idea, even though you may feel more confident if you know in advance every word you are going to say. This kind of delivery always seems dry; not only because it results in an unnatural way of speaking, but also because you will be so busy looking at your script that you will almost certainly fail to make eye contact with your audience.

For similar reasons, you should probably not memorise your presentation, as this will take a lot of effort and may result in the same flat or stilted delivery, as if you had scripted it word for word. There is a happy medium where a presentation has been practised enough for the speaker to be confident, yet still convey an air of spontaneity.

- Practice will help you become more confident in the material.
- You can identify any complex parts that you cannot easily put into words, and practise these independently.
- You can find out whether your presentation will fit the allotted time.
- Make the presentation to a friend. Ask them to comment on your audibility and clarity, presentation style (including gestures) and use of visual aids.

EFFECTIVE SPEAKING

This is more than speaking loudly enough to be heard and pronouncing your words clearly so that the audience can make them out. These skills are fundamental – although you will already realise that many speakers fail even at this hurdle. Ask a friend to check and comment on your diction to make sure you meet these basic criteria.

Good speaking not only ensures that information is transmitted, but also engages the audience. You can do this in two main ways – through your actions and body language, and through the approach you take.

✔ Developing your own speaking style

Every speaker has their own idiosyncrasies but some elements of style can be learned. Consider the different ways your lecturers present their material. Some will be good and some not so good (see Table 16.1). Adopt techniques you admire and try to work these into your personal style.

First, don't just stand still and speak robotically. Aim for an element of variety to keep interest levels high:

- Move around a little – but make sure you face the audience so that you will be heard, and do not pace up and down excessively.

- Use moderate hand gestures to emphasise your points – but don't wave your hands around like a windmill.

- Ensure you make eye contact with the audience – but don't stare at one person or area all the time.

- Liven your talk by shifting between modes of presentation, for example, by drawing a diagram on the board or presenting a visual aid – but don't overdo this or the audience may be distracted from your theme.

Second, try to involve your audience. Use rhetorical questions to make them think, even though you will be supplying the answers. Ask them direct questions, such as 'How many of you have read this article?' then follow up with '. . . for the benefit of those who haven't, I'll just recap on the main points'. If it would be relevant, ask them to do an activity as part of the presentation. This takes confidence to handle, but it can work well and is especially valuable to break up a longer talk where attention may wander.

Pace your talk

When you practise your talk, watch the clock and note down timing points during it. When it comes to the real thing, check how you are doing and speed up or slow down as necessary. In some cases, the real talk will take longer than you anticipated. This will either be because the initial business of getting set up has eaten up some of your allotted time, or because you have relaxed during the presentation and said more than you thought you would. In other cases, you may find that slight nervousness means you have spoken faster than intended.

USING PRESENTATION SOFTWARE SUCH AS POWERPOINT

The standard methods of supporting a presentation with images and information used to be either overhead slides or 35 mm photographic slides. Overhead transparencies have the advantage over 'chalk and talk' of letting you see the same thing as your audience, while still facing them, but if filled with text they can seem dull. Slides are valuable where ultra-high-quality images are required, but an important disadvantage is that they require complex equipment and procedures to produce.

Nowadays, both these media have largely been replaced with virtual 'slides' produced via software such as Microsoft PowerPoint. These systems provide flexibility and allow you to incorporate digital images with ease. A significant disadvantage is that a computer and (expensive) digital projector is required to show them. If you are planning to use this type of software, check whether appropriate facilities will be available in the room or can be borrowed or booked.

You can select from a variety of designs for each PowerPoint slide, most of which help you to structure your talk around a series of bullet points and to mix text with images or graphs (see Figure 57.1). This may help you to organise your prompts, but you should make sure you don't simply read them word for word from the slide. Few things are more boring than a speaker reading out what you can already see on a screen.

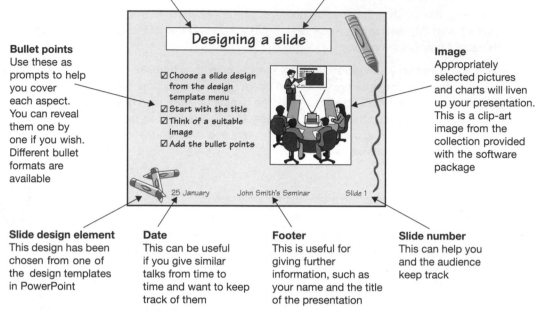

Slide title
You can use this to help your audience keep track of the topics you are covering

Slide background
You can alter this and the colour of text if you wish, even when using one of the design templates

Bullet points
Use these as prompts to help you cover each aspect. You can reveal them one by one if you wish. Different bullet formats are available

Image
Appropriately selected pictures and charts will liven up your presentation. This is a clip-art image from the collection provided with the software package

Designing a slide

☑ Choose a slide design from the design template menu
☑ Start with the title
☑ Think of a suitable image
☑ Add the bullet points

25 January   John Smith's Seminar   Slide 1

Slide design element
This design has been chosen from one of the design templates in PowerPoint

Date
This can be useful if you give similar talks from time to time and want to keep track of them

Footer
This is useful for giving further information, such as your name and the title of the presentation

Slide number
This can help you and the audience keep track

Figure 57.1 Elements of a typical PowerPoint slide. Similar features are available using other software.

> ✔ **Use PowerPoint to create professional overheads**
>
> If you wish to use overhead transparencies, it might be a good idea to create them first as PowerPoint slides. These can be printed as 'Slides' then copied on to special photocopy acetates or printed directly on to special material. They will be much neater and more legible than handwritten overheads. If you intend to incorporate coloured text, backgrounds or images, run tests first, however, as the projected results can be disappointing.

If you doubt your ability to speak freely around the bullet points, you can use the notes facility within PowerPoint to write down information you might not remember. You can then print out each slide and associated notes together on a single A4 page to act as a support during the presentation. Use the 'Print > Print What: > Notes Pages' command, but select 'Pure Black and White' under 'Color/grayscale' or your printout (including slide backgrounds) may appear in colour, wasting precious printer ink.

A step-by-step tutorial for setting up a PowerPoint presentation is beyond the scope of this book, but once the basics have been learned, for instance, from a handbook or online self-help tutorial, the tips shown in Table 57.1 may be useful. Always check that your version of PowerPoint is compatible with the computer system you will be using for the presentation.

Allow plenty of time for preparing presentation slides

The technology is helpful but, especially with complex material, each slide can take a lot of effort to set up. However, because of the flexibility of this system, you can save some time by merging the planning and writing phases of your talk into one session. For instance, once PowerPoint slides are constructed it is relatively easy to change their order or to alter formatting through the 'View > Master > Slide Master' function.

Table 57.1 Tips for constructing slides with presentation software such as PowerPoint

Aspect	Comment
Background and text colouring	Choose a background or slide design template with care. A lighter background with dark text will attract attention, but may be hard to concentrate on over the long term, whereas a darker background with light writing may be more restful on the eye.
Slide design	The standard PowerPoint designs are tried and tested, and are especially useful if you have little time to prepare for a talk, but many of your audience will have seen them before. You can easily be more original, for instance, by incorporating an image into the background, but be aware that this will take time to set up.
Text size and font	The standard PowerPoint text size defaults to values that mean that it is difficult to get much information on each slide. You can override this feature, but there is a good reason for it: cramming too much on to each slide is bad practice. A point size of 28 is probably the lowest text size you should use. Sans serif fonts, such as Arial, are said to be easiest to read on-screen.
Use of images	If you can, try to include an image in at least half of your slides. Even if these are only partially relevant, they help to maintain audience interest. A text-only presentation consisting of nothing more than bullet points will seem very dry. Use clip-art or images from copyright-free web resources if you don't have any images of your own.
Revealing your points one by one	Use the 'animation' feature to build up your slide line by line as you wish. This will help you pace your talk and ensure that the audience is listening to you, rather than reading ahead on the slide. To keep the audience on track, you may find it advantageous to use a slide giving sub-headings and reintroduce this as you move on to each new sub-topic on your list.
Use of special features	You can use special features for introducing each new slide and, within each slide, you can make text enter from different directions in different ways and even accompanied with noises. You can also link to websites (if your computer is appropriately connected) and run digital video clips. Resist the temptation to go overboard with these 'bells and whistles', because although such features can make a talk livelier, they tend to distract from your main message.
Handouts	Think about providing your audience with a handout of the slides. In PowerPoint you can use the 'File > Print > Print What: > Handouts > 6 slides per page' option to do this. When printing, it is best to select 'Pure Black and White' from the 'Color/grayscale' options, or all of the slides may print in colour, including the background. Numbering your slides (see Figure 57.1) will help your audience keep track with the handout.

ANSWERING QUESTIONS

This is a part of a talk that many people worry about, as they have no control over what may be asked, and feel they might look stupid if they don't know an answer. Tips for dealing with this element include:

- **Prepare for likely questions.** Try to anticipate what people might ask and have an answer ready.

- **Ask for clarification if you don't understand a question fully.** You could also ask the questioner or chair to repeat the question if a part of it was indistinct or didn't seem to make sense to you.

- **Repeat the question for the benefit of those who might not have heard it.** The questioner will be facing you, not the audience, and their voice may be indistinct. This will also buy you some time for composing an answer.

- **Think before you answer.** Rather than blurting out the first thing that comes to mind, take time to weigh up the different aspects. You may feel the necessary pause is long, but this will not be how the audience perceives it.

- **If you don't know an answer, say so.** Everyone will see through a speaker who is waffling. Try saying 'I don't know the answer at the moment, but I'll find out and get back to you' if you want to say something rather than leaving a pause.

PRACTICAL TIPS FOR DELIVERING A PRESENTATION

Dress appropriately for the occasion. You should look smart, but should feel comfortable in what you wear. Turning up in informal clothes may be interpreted as showing a lack of respect to your audience and may lead to the expectation of a sloppy presentation.

To reduce tension, take deep breaths. This can be done both before you address the audience and during pauses in your presentation.

Make sure you can be heard. At the start of your talk, ask the audience if they can hear at the back. Alternatively, when practising, try to use the room where the presentation will take place and ask a friend if they can hear you. If you know someone in the audience, you could ask them to signal to you if you are talking too quietly (or too loudly).

Make sure your audio-visual aids can be seen. If you are using some kind of projection system, make sure that you – or your shadow – don't block out the projected image. It's a good idea to ask your audience if they can see clearly before you start.

Engage the audience. Speak directly to them, not to the floor, your notes, the screen or a distant wall. Look at their faces and take cues from their reactions. If they don't seem to understand what you've said, repeat it in a different way. If they look bored, speed up, or ask a rhetorical question to engage their thoughts. Imagine the audience are your friends – speak to them with enthusiasm, warmth and genuine feeling. They will respond in kind.

Don't speak too quickly. This is a common response to nerves. Make a determined effort to slow yourself down and speak clearly.

Have a 'plan B' if your talk overruns or the projection system fails. Plan things so that you can miss something out from the main section of the talk if you are under time pressure (for example, by skipping over a few PowerPoint slides). This is preferable to being unable to complete your conclusions – people may be more interested in those than in the detail of your presentation, and they can always ask about the skipped material at the end. Print out the PowerPoint slides, perhaps in handout or note form, so that you can still use these if the projection system fails.

Try to enjoy the occasion. If you seem to be taking pleasure from speaking, your audience will also enjoy the session. Conversely, if you don't seem to be interested, why should they be?

58

EXPLOITING FEEDBACK

How to understand and learn from what lecturers write on your work and exam scripts

When you receive back assessed work and exam scripts, these are usually annotated by the marker. It is essential that you learn from these comments if you want to improve, but sometimes they can be difficult to understand. This chapter outlines some common annotations and describes how you should react to them.

There are two principal types of assessment at university: formative and summative. Formative assessments are those in which the grade received does not contribute to your end-of-module mark, or contributes relatively little, but which gives you an indication of the standard of your work. It is often accompanied by a feedback sheet or comments written on the script. Summative assessments contribute directly to your final module mark and include things such as end-of-term/semester exams, project reports or essay submissions.

TYPES OF FEEDBACK

The simplest pointer you will receive from any type of assessment is the grade you receive; if good, you know that you have reached the expected standard; if poor, you know that you should try to improve.

If you feel unsure about the grading system or what standard is expected at each grading level, your course or faculty handbooks will probably include a description of marking or assessment criteria that explain this (see **Ch 63**, page 396).

✔ Obtaining informal (preliminary) feedback

Your fellow students or family members can help by reading through your work and commenting. Even though they may lack subject knowledge, they will be able to comment on the clarity of your writing or the logic of your argument.

How well are you performing?

The answer, of course, depends on your goals and expectations, but also on your understanding of degree classifications and their significance. Even in early levels of study, it may be worth relating percentage marks or other forms of grades (descriptors) to the standard degree classes – first, upper second, lower second, third and unclassified. Certain career and advanced degree opportunities will only be open to those with higher-level qualifications, and you should try to gain an understanding of how this operates in your field of study and likely career destination.

Written feedback may be provided on your scripts and other work. This will often take the form of handwritten comments over your text, and a summary commenting on your work or justifying why it received the mark it did. Sometimes the feedback will be provided separately from your script so that other markers are not influenced by it.

Always read your feedback

The comments in your feedback should give you constructive direction for later efforts and are designed to help you to develop the structure and style of your work, as well as encourage you to develop a deeper understanding of the topic. Where students ignore points, especially those about presentation or structure, then they may find themselves heavily penalised in later submissions.

Some feedback may be verbal and informal, for example a demonstrator's comment given as you work in a practical, or an observation on your contribution during a tutorial. If you feel uncertain about why your work has received the grade it did, or why a particular comment was provided, you may be able to arrange a meeting with the person who marked your work. Normally they will be happy to provide further verbal explanations. However, do not attempt to haggle over your marks, other than to point out politely if part of your work does not appear to have been marked at all, or part marks appear to have been added up wrongly.

EXAMPLES OF FEEDBACK COMMENTS AND WHAT THEY MEAN

Different lecturers use different terms to express similar meanings, and because they mark quickly, their handwritten comments are sometimes untidy and may be difficult to interpret. This means that you may need help in deciphering their meaning. Table 58.1 illustrates feedback comments that are frequently made and explains how you should react to obtain better grades in future. This should be viewed with Table 43.3 (page 285) which explains some proof-reading symbols that lecturers may use. If a particular comment or mark does not make sense to you after reading these tables, you may wish to approach the marker for an explanation.

Table 58.1 Common types of feedback annotation and how to act in response. Comments in the margin may be accompanied by underlining of word(s), circling of phrases, sentences or paragraphs. Relevant chapters to consult are noted in brackets in the right-hand column.

Types of comment and typical examples	Meaning and potential remedial action
Regarding content	
Relevance *Relevance?* *Importance?* *Value of example?* *So?*	An example or quotation may not be apt, or you may not have explained its relevance. Think about the logic of your narrative or argument and whether there is a mismatch as implied, or whether you could add further explanation; choose a more appropriate example or quote. **(Ch 32)**
Detail *Give more information* *Example?* *Too much detail/waffle/padding*	You are expected to flesh out your answer with more detail or an example to illustrate your point; or, conversely, you may have provided too much information. It may be that your work lacks substance and you appear to have compensated by putting in too much description rather than analysis. **(Ch 22, Ch 32)**
Specific factual comment or comment on your approach *You could have included . . .* *What about . . . ?* *Why didn't you . . . ?*	Depends on context, but it should be obvious what is required to accommodate the comment.
Expressions of approval *Good!* *Excellent!* ✓ *(may be repeated)*	You got this right or chose a good example. Keep up the good work!
Expressions of disapproval *Poor* *Weak* *No!* ✗ *(may be repeated)*	Sometimes obvious, but may not be clear. The implication is that your examples, logic etc. could be improved.
Regarding structure	
Fault in logic or argument *Logic?* *Non sequitur (does not follow)*	Your argument or line of logic is faulty. This may require quite radical changes to your approach to the topic. **(Ch 33, Ch 34)**
Failure to introduce topic clearly *Where are you going with this?* *Unclear*	What is your understanding of the task? What parameters will confine your response? How do you intend to tackle the subject? **(Ch 33)**
Failure to construct a logical discussion *Imbalanced discussion* *Weak on pros and cons*	When you have to compare and contrast in any way, then it is important that you give each element in your discussion similar coverage. **(Ch 34)**
Failure to conclude essay clearly *So what?* *Conclusion?*	You have to leave a 'take-home message' that sums up the most salient features of your writing and should not include new material in this section. This is to demonstrate your ability to think critically and define the key aspects. **(Ch 33)**

Table 58.1 (*cont'd*)

Types of comment and typical examples	Meaning and potential remedial action
Regarding structure (*cont'd*)	
Heavy dependency on quotations *Watch out for over-quotation* *Too many quotations*	There is a real danger of plagiarism if you include too many direct quotations from text. You have to demonstrate that you can synthesise the information from sources as evidence of your understanding. However, in a subject like English literature or law, quotation may be a key characteristic of writing. In this case, quotation is permitted, provided that it is supported by critical comment. (**Ch 35**)
Move text *Loops and arrows*	Suggestion for changing order of text, usually to enhance the flow or logic. (**Ch 37, Ch 38**)
Regarding presentation	
Minor proofing errors *sp.* (usually in margin – spelling) *⋏* (insert material here) *⌐* (break paragraph here) *ᑒ* (delete this material) *P* (punctuation error)	A (minor) correction is required. Table 43.3 provides more detail of likely proof-reading symbols. (**Ch 43**)
Citations *Reference (required)* *Ref?* *Reference list omitted*	You have not supported evidence, argument or quotation with a reference to the original source. This is important in academic work and if you fail to do it, you may be considered guilty of plagiarism (**Ch 36**). If you omit to attach a reference list, this will lose you marks as it implies a totally unsourced piece of writing, that is, you have done no specialist reading. (**Ch 35**)
Tidiness *Illegible!* *Untidy* *Can't read*	Your handwriting may be difficult to decipher. Allocate more time to writing out your work neatly, or use a word processor if allowed. (**Ch 44**)
Failure to follow recommended format *Please follow departmental template for reports* *Order!*	If the department or school provides a template for the submission of reports, you must follow it. There are good reasons, such as the need to follow professional conventions, especially in sciences; you must conform. If you don't, you may lose marks. (**Ch 20, Ch 50**)

Applying feedback to exam performance

Look at the comments and advice given on written coursework and identify ways in which you can use the feedback constructively in the answers you give in exams. For example, if structure is identified as a weakness, then practise speed-planning answers so that your answers become focused and succinct.

PRACTICAL TIPS FOR DEALING WITH FEEDBACK

Be mentally prepared to learn from the views of your tutors. You may initially feel that feedback is unfair, harsh or that it misunderstands the approach you were trying to take to the question. A natural reaction might be to dismiss many of the comments. However, you should recognise that tutors probably have a much deeper understanding of the topic than you, and concede that if you want to do well in a subject then you need to gain a better understanding of what makes a good answer from the academic's point of view.

Always make sure you understand the feedback. Check with fellow students or with the lecturers involved if you cannot read the comment or do not understand why it has been made.

Respond to feedback. Make a note of common or repeated errors, even in peripheral topics, so that you can avoid them in later assignments. In particular, if grammar, spelling or punctuation are frequently mentioned, then look at **Chs 39–42** in this book for a 'refresher' on the relevant areas.

59

PHYSICAL AND MENTAL PREPARATION

How to gear up for exams

> To achieve your full potential in assessments and exams, your brain needs to be operating at its best. This also means that the rest of your body will need to be in good physical condition, as the health of body and mind are linked closely. This chapter explains how you can ensu re that you are in the best possible shape in the run-up to exams.

Good academic performance depends on your mind operating at or near to its peak ability, but we're all aware that our intellectual powers vary according to a range of influences, and are not always at their best. Having a better understanding of factors that influence your brain's function will help you prepare better for your forthcoming assessments or exams.

WELL-BEING, HEALTH AND NUTRITION

Most experts agree that that a healthy mind thrives in a healthy body. However, we don't always take care of our bodies or minds in the best possible way. For students, this condition may result from any of a number of factors related to university life. If you wish to take a professional approach to your exams, you may need to look for ways in which you can adapt your lifestyle to ensure that you are in the best possible physical and mental shape to face your exams. Table 59.1 provides a checklist of things to do, and things not to do, as you approach your exams. You may wish to focus on some of the following:

- **Regulating your sleep pattern.** Try to ensure that you have enough sleep and make sure that your pattern of waking coincides with the general working day, and in particular with your exam times.

- **Avoiding or cutting down chemical influences likely to interfere with your mental capacity.** The chief of these is likely to be alcohol, a known depressant. Others include nicotine, certain prescription drugs and most non-prescription drugs.

- **Avoiding overuse of stimulants.** Taking chemicals like caffeine (present in tea, coffee, 'Red Bull' and Coke-like drinks) may provide a temporary boost, but there is an inevitable downside after this, and your sleep pattern may be disrupted.

- **Keeping well hydrated.** Your water intake or lack of it has known effects on the ability to concentrate and learn.

Table 59.1 A quick checklist of things to do and things not to do to improve your preparation for exams

Positives (try to do these)	Negatives (try not to do these)
❑ Gain mental agility (puzzles, quizzes, sums, examples, reading)	❑ Abuse alcohol or other drugs that may impair your mental capacity
❑ Improve mental stamina (work for longer periods)	❑ Be distracted by less important things (e.g. TV programmes, socialising)
❑ Become fitter (a healthy mind in a healthy body)	❑ Study so much you do not sleep enough or distort your waking rhythm
❑ Eat well	
❑ Get your body clock in tune with 'exam time'	❑ Avoid key topics that you dislike
❑ Clean away clutter and start with a clear desk	❑ Read your notes rather than carry out appropriate active revision methods
❑ Sleep well (make sure you are physically as well as mentally tired)	❑ Carry out unfocused revision that fails to take account of learning objectives
❑ Carry out active revision that takes account of your learning style	

- **Knowing how and when to relax.** Exercise has an important role to play here, as does escapism, such as watching a film or playing games. Near to exams, these leisure and rest activities should not take up too much time, but they should remain a part of your timetable.

You should try to eat well when studying as your brain requires a good supply of energy and essential nutrients. A good breakfast is a good idea to kick-start your day, followed by light snacks to keep your energy levels up. Small, frequent snacks are best because after you eat large meals there are known hormonal responses that slow down metabolism and mental activity, leading to drowsiness and lethargy. If this effect is familiar to you, avoid fatty foods and note that more complex carbohydrates like starch provide a more slowly released supply of sugars.

i | **Vitamins and micronutrients and what they do**

Vitamin A: antioxidant. Important for vision; enhances immunity and helps prevent infections such as colds.

Vitamin B complex (there are at least twelve B vitamins): primary effects as enzyme cofactors, so important in ensuring that metabolism functions smoothly; also important for blood turnover. Many known effects on mental well-being. Certain B vitamins may need to be supplemented in athletes, alcohol drinkers and those taking the female oral contraceptive.

Vitamin C: antioxidant; important in fat metabolism and may boost immune system. Levels may be lowered by alcohol, painkillers or nicotine. Deficiency can result in depression.

Vitamin D: important in nutrient absorption and growth; beneficial effects on the immune system.

Vitamin E: antioxidant; important for blood function and circulation.

Micronutrients: most act as enzyme cofactors. Iron is essential for healthy blood function. Lack of magnesium and zinc have known effects on mental health.

(Sources: Rutherford, 2002; Graham, 2006)

Vitamins and micronutrients are known to enhance health and mental activity. Anyone who eats healthily should not be deficient in these dietary factors, but you may wish to consult a health professional if in doubt over the use of vitamin supplements.

If you feel unwell in the period prior to exams, you should visit your doctor or university health service, not only in hope of a diagnosis and treatment, but also to obtain necessary documentation that might explain a weak performance.

THE ROLE OF PHYSICAL EXERCISE

Aerobic exercise is an excellent way to relax mentally, reduce stress and improve sleep patterns. Carried out regularly over a long period, exercise improves your stamina, a valuable commodity for extended exam schedules, which can be physically exhausting as well as mentally draining. Non-aerobic and meditation workouts such as yoga, Pilates and T'ai Chi also have potential to help you in the run-up to exams by helping you to relax.

Exercise is also important in the short term because it stimulates brain activity by improving the blood supply to your brain, an organ that requires a surprising amount of oxygen and energy to function well. You should try to do some physical activity, even if it is as simple as a walk or swim, on most revision days. This basic exercise is probably the best quick fix to remove feelings of mental lethargy.

MENTAL EXERCISE, RELAXATION AND SLEEP

As an organ, your brain responds to being exercised. In a similar fashion to your muscles, the more it works, the better prepared it is for future effort. Unsurprisingly, revision itself is an excellent mental preparation for exams. This 'exercise' factor is independent from memorisation carried out during your revision; as you move through your revision timetable, your brain will become used to its daily mental workout and will be better prepared for the challenge of the exams.

> **Key facts about your brain**
>
> Your brain takes up only about 2 per cent of your body's mass, yet it receives some 15 per cent of your blood circulation. It consumes about a fifth of your total oxygen intake, and metabolises roughly a quarter of your body's glucose. Your brain absorbs approximately 50 per cent of the oxygen and 10 per cent of glucose circulating in your arterial bloodstream.
>
> (Source: Magistretti *et al.*, 2000)

Some ideas for exercising and relaxing your mind

Exercise:

❑ doing puzzles like crosswords and sudoku

❑ playing computer games (not in excess)

❑ taking part in TV and pub quizzes

❑ reading for leisure (in short bursts)

Relaxing:

❑ shutting your eyes and breathing slowly and deeply for 2–3 minutes

❑ watching films or TV soap operas

❑ taking a brief walk or swim

❑ having a bath, jacuzzi or sauna

These activities should be brief, relaxing and should not impinge on timetabled periods of study. Ideally, they should be incorporated into your revision timetable (**Ch 60**).

Equally, there will be times when your mind needs to relax. This can be accomplished by focusing your thoughts on a completely different matter. Physical activities and games can have this useful effect. A good sleep pattern is vital to rest your brain between intensive study sessions and before exams. Unfortunately, the anxiety many people feel immediately prior to exams is not conducive to sleep. If you have this as a persistent problem, you may wish to adopt some of the following tips, suggested by McKenna (2009):

● Get up earlier, consistently – this has the effect of making you more tired at the end of the day.

● Keep a consistent waking routine (even at weekends) – you can control this element, but not when you feel tired.

● Go to bed only when you feel ready to sleep.

● Keep bed for sleep – if you want to read, watch TV or eat, relax in a living space to do this.

● If you generally feel that afternoons are not your best time for studying, exercising in the afternoon can be helpful as a way of freshening you up for a study stint when you are more alert later in the day.

● Eat and drink (especially stimulants like caffeine and depressants like alcohol) well ahead of the time that you plan to go to bed.

● Rather than toss and turn when you cannot sleep, get up and do something useful until you feel tired.

● Drift off to sleep thinking about positives, rather than negatives.

● Tell yourself a story, preferably a boring one, as you attempt to fall asleep.

Maintaining a regular and appropriate sleep pattern

Your aim should be to align your waking times to the times of your exams. Some people like to rise early and others to rise late. Some people find that napping during the day is helpful as a means of giving them a second wind, while others find that this puts them off regular sleep patterns. Whichever type you are, remember that exams mostly fit into the working day and you must make sure that your regime has not turned night into day.

PREPARING THE GROUND

If you wish to revise effectively, it is crucial that you know what you are trying to accomplish. One way of gaining this understanding is to divide the revision and exam-sitting process into components and look at what you need to achieve at each stage. The process is essentially about managing information – the facts and understanding gained during your course – and can be separated into three main elements:

● information gathering;

● information processing; and

● information retrieval and delivery.

If you do the right things in each of these phases, you will greatly increase your chances of achieving excellent grades.

In the **information-gathering phase**, your aim is to ensure that you have copies of all that you require close to hand, and to make sure that it is well organised so that you can consult what you need, quickly:

❏ Check that you have all the lecture notes and make arrangements to download or copy them, if you do not have these things in place.

❏ File your notes in sequence.

❏ Buy or borrow the textbooks that support your course if you have not already done so (check the reading list in the course handbook). Alternatively, look these up in your library catalogue and place reservations on them if they are available only on limited access.

❏ Gather together all other materials that might be relevant, such as completed coursework with feedback.

❏ Bookmark any online resources that you might be expected to consult.

❏ Obtain copies of past papers and model answers, if available.

❏ Find out where the learning objectives or outcomes are published (for example, in the course handbook), and make a copy of them.

❏ Look in your course handbook for any special guidance notes on the exam and its format.

Key to managing time for information gathering

You must not let the information-gathering phase take up too much of your revision time – recognise that it can be a displacement activity and limit the time you allocate to it within your revision timetable (**Ch 60**).

The **information-processing phase** involves analysing and manipulating the material you have gathered, with the learning objectives and past exam papers in mind. The principle is not to study passively, for example, by reading through the written material, but to try to do something active, to help you to memorise it (**Ch 61** and **Ch 62**).

Thinking about thinking

It is important to recognise that university teaching is not solely about information transfer, where you just accumulate information and memorise a series of facts from lectures and other source material. You must be able to *use* information. In short, you must develop skills in critical thinking. The facts are still required, but it is what you do with them in response to the exam or assessment instruction that is important (**Ch 66**). When you analyse the instructions used in exam questions, you should take into account what type of thinking process the examiner has asked you to carry out, and try your best to reach the required level.

Thinking about learning

On coming to university, it may be useful to consider or reconsider the ways in which you learn best. People differ greatly in their preferences for processing and retrieving information. For some students, developing an understanding of this aspect of their character makes a huge difference to their levels of attainment. In **Ch 13** we discuss various types of learning personality, different methods of diagnosing your learning style, and the best ways of approaching study and revision once you know where your learning preferences lie.

Understanding the university exam system

Your department or school will provide plenty of helpful information about assessment. You can find it in course or programme handbooks, printed or online. Accessing this material will help you process the course material and your notes appropriately. You should look for:

● learning outcomes/objectives;
● design of exam papers, type of exam, style of questions and weighting of marks;
● marking criteria.

Chs 63 and **66** discuss these sources of information in greater detail.

Keys to successful information processing

As part of an approach based on active revision, you will probably wish to reduce or 'distil' the notes you have made (**Ch 61**). This can only be done effectively with a clear idea of the sorts of question that will be asked and an indication of the depth at which you will be expected to deal with the material. In part, this information can be obtained by studying the learning objectives or outcomes and past exam papers.

> ### ✔ Beware of changes to the syllabus or to the construction of exam papers
>
> It is worth remembering that courses may change over time, as can the staff teaching them. This can have a considerable impact on content and the course structure. These should be flagged to you within the course handbook, or by tutors, but it might be worth confirming with the course leader or departmental administrator if you see a mismatch between the syllabus as taught and the learning objectives or question papers. The same applies to checking whether you can assume that this year's exam papers will be constructed in the same way as in previous years.

The **information retrieval and delivery phase** will occur in the exam hall as you answer the specific questions as set. **Chs 65–Ch 67** provide tips for maximising your performance during this phase.

> ### ✔ Using feedback from past exams and assessment
>
> Feedback you have received about your previous exam and assessment performances (**Ch 58**) should affect how you carry out information processing during revision. For example, this might indicate that your answers have lacked relevance or sufficient depth. You should therefore adjust your approach to reflect any comments, perhaps by ensuring that you are applying higher-level thinking skills or have committed relevant facts to memory (**Ch 62**).

THINKING POSITIVELY

A key aspect of mental preparation for exams is to think positively. When you start to revise and are confronted by all your reading material, notes and seemingly endless facts and concepts, it is easy to become despondent and feel that there is too much to do in the time available. These sorts of thoughts can result in a negative spiral where you put off effective work and never actually get going.

These tips will help you adopt a positive frame of mind when revising:

- Get started on your studies, somehow. Don't put off this crucial moment. Once you become engaged with the material, your natural curiosity and interest in the subject will take over. Even if the topics have not seemed interesting in the past, once you begin to understand them in depth, they may become more so.
- Adopt an approach of breaking large topics into smaller chunks. That way each time you complete a section you will feel you have made progress.
- Make sure you mark off what you have completed in your revision timetable (**Ch 60**) as you cover the material. After a few sessions, this visual summary should give you a feeling of having made real inroads into the task.

- Link up with someone else studying the same subject and make a pact to try to encourage each other (Ch 64). Quizzing each other or working together on areas of the course that you both find difficult can help both parties feel more in control of the subject matter and, if you continue to have difficulty, you can go together to speak with your lecturer or tutor about your queries.

- Focus on the main goal (your degree, and the type of job you hope will come after it) and reflect on how each small study session is one small step on this important journey in your life.

- Recall positive experiences from your past exam-sitting history, focusing on how your hard work paid dividends in the end, despite any lack of confidence you may have felt at the time.

In the vital period just before you enter the exam hall, it is important to be completely focused and positive. Although there are benefits from meeting up with fellow students and sharing feelings and ideas about potential exam questions, these exchanges will almost certainly make you more nervous. If this is likely to be the case, find a spot nearby where you can gather your thoughts in peace and then time your entry to the exam hall to avoid meeting your friends. Things to concentrate on during this period are:

- your exam strategy – how you plan to tackle this particular paper (Ch 66);
- your approach to the questions – how you plan to structure your answers;
- key facts or formulae (you are unlikely to memorise them at this stage, but running over them may keep them fresh in your mind if you have already learnt them by heart: Ch 62);
- what you plan to do when all your exams are finished and how quickly this particular exam will be over;
- your determination to succeed and how you aim to squeeze every mark possible out of your brain in response to the instructions on the exam paper;
- how you plan to ensure your answers are relevant; and
- how you need to be working quickly and effectively for every second of the exam.

PRACTICAL TIPS TO HELP PREPARE YOURSELF FOR EXAMS

Ensure you eat healthily. This should include eating the right amount of calories (neither too many, nor too few) and plenty of fruit and vegetables.

Give 'you' some time. Studying without any let-up won't necessarily mean that you will do more. Taking some time out for you – listening to music, reading a novel, playing a game, pampering yourself with a favourite activity – will make you feel good about yourself and contribute to your sense of confidence and well-being. It will also help create a sense of revitalised motivation.

Go for a short walk. If you are feeling drowsy or lacking in concentration or focus when revising, go outside for a quick walk. A brisk ten-minute walk around the block will be sufficient to wake you up. You might use the route you take as one of your memory 'journeys' so that you could 'revise as you walk' (Ch 62).

60

CREATING A REVISION TIMETABLE

How to get yourself organised for exam study

Organising your activities in the run-up to exams is vital to ensure that you make the best use of the limited time available. Creating a revision timetable not only improves your time management but also helps you to balance your efforts among subjects and topics.

If your use of time is generally haphazard, a revision timetable will help to keep you on track with your studies. In addition, a timetable can help motivate you and provide confidence as you complete each topic. Used well, it can prevent you spending too much time on your favourite topics at the expense of others, and it can also ensure that you include relaxation activities to boost your energy and ability to concentrate.

SETTING UP AND USING A REVISION TIMETABLE

- Create a blank timetable. This will allow you to create an 'action plan' that gives details of the specific topics you intend to work on at any given time. The example illustrated in Table 60.1 and provided in blank form on page 448 is based on six subdivisions of the day, with two potential study periods in each morning, afternoon and evening. If you prefer to use shorter or longer units of work, modify the format appropriately, using a word processor or spreadsheet.

- Now fix your start and end dates: these are the points at which you wish to begin revising and the precise dates when your exams are to be held. Print or photocopy enough copies of the blank timetable to cover this period and write in these key dates.

- Start to fill in the timetable by noting your *essential* non-study commitments, such as employment, shopping, cooking, travelling, team sporting activities and important social or family duties. If at all possible, these responsibilities should be minimised when you are revising, especially as the exams draw closer. Contact employers and others as far as possible in advance so you can warn them of your needs.

> **Avoid over-elaborating your timetable** ✔
>
> Don't be tempted to procrastinate by taking too long pondering over your timetable or making it overly neat – it does not need to be a work of art.

Table 60.1 Sample revision plan for a student studying Environmental Sciences

Personal revision timetable
Sophie Pringle

Key to subjects/topics

Geography	Biomes + Diversity	Environmental Chemistry

Week: 12

	Monday	Tuesday	Wdenesday	Thursday	Friday	Saturday	Sunday
Morning	*Geog Lectures 1 & 2*	*Env Chem Topic B*	*Biomes + Div Week 3*	*Env Chem Topic C*	*Geog Lecture 8 & 9*	WORK	*Lie in*
	Env Chem Topic A	*Geog Lectures 3 & 4*	*Biomes + Div Week 4*	*Env Chem Topic C*	*Study buddy meeting Geog*	WORK	*Laundry*
Lunch							
Afternoon	*Env Chem Topic A*	*Geog tutorial*	*Geog Lectures 5 & 6*	*Biomes + Div Practicals*	*Env Chem Topic D*	WORK	*Biomes + Div Practicals*
	Prep for last Geog tutorial	*Break*	*HOCKEY*	*Biomes + Div Practicals*	*SPARE*	WORK	*Mock exam with Hilda*
Evening meal							
Evening	*Biomes + Div Week 1*	*Env Chem Topic B*	*EVENING OFF!*	*Library – look out past papers*	*SPARE (go out to union if up to speed)*	*Phil's birthday bash*	*Sunday tea with Mum and Dad*
	Biomes + Div Week 2	*SPARE*	*EVENING OFF!*	*Geog Lecture 7 (difficult)*	*SPARE*	*Phil's birthday bash*	

What's the ideal length of time for a study session?

Too long and you risk getting bored with the subject and losing concentration; too short and you won't be able to make decent progress. Table 60.1 proposes sessions of about $1\frac{1}{2}$ hours in length, but you may wish to subdivide or combine these according to your preference.

- Decide on the ideal number of 'sessions' you wish to study in each day and week, or are able to allocate due to your other commitments. Work out the total number of study sessions during the whole revision period and decide when they will be. For example, if you work best early in the day, you may wish to bias your studies to the morning slots that are available.

- The next stage is to allocate these revision sessions to the different subjects or topics you need to cover. You may wish to carry out this process in two stages – first in a coarse-grained manner (say, dividing the total time among three modules), then in a finer-grained way (dividing each module's allocated time among the individual topics that were covered). Be flexible – you may wish to spend a whole day on one topic to get deeper into the material, or break another day up to create variety. In allocating time slots for revision, work your way backwards from the exam date, as this will allow you to ensure that you cover each subject adequately just before the relevant paper.

  Try to balance the time appropriately among topics or subjects. Your aim should be to give more time to 'difficult' topics than to 'easier' ones, remembering that difficult or uninteresting material sometimes yields 'easy' marks when you have mastered it. As an incentive, you may wish to follow subjects you dislike with those you prefer.

  If you aren't happy with the time available to study each topic when this process is complete, you may need to increase the total time you have allocated and reconfigure the sheets.

- In allocating time, recognise that you cannot work continuously if you want to study effectively. If you spend lengthy hours revising without any rest, you may retain little because you aren't concentrating. Lack of focus and concentration will become worse if you tire yourself out.

  Break up your work with relaxation, preferably involving physical activity. You may wish to set up 'rewards' (for example, watching a favourite TV programme or meeting your friends) – but only take these if you achieve your goals; if you do not, use these periods to catch up.

- Include some empty slots in your timetable to allow for unforeseen problems or changes in your plans. Your timetable should be flexible – if you lose time somewhere due to unforeseen circumstances, you should try to make it up later using these slots or switching slots from recreation to study.

- If at all possible, try to ease back on your revision load near the exam. Your aim should be to plan your revision to avoid last-minute cramming and fatigue.

Are you a morning, afternoon or evening person?

Identify the best time of day for you to study (Ch 8). Focus your revision periods in these slots, and your routine tasks and recreation when you will feel less able to concentrate.

USING YOUR TIME EFFECTIVELY WHEN REVISING

Studying effectively is not simply a matter of giving over lots of time to the task: you must organise your activities well and use appropriate techniques to help you retain the material covered.

- Early in the revision period, focus on ensuring you have all the necessary materials to hand and that these are well organised – especially lecture notes and textbook information. Ask a friend for copies of their notes if you missed a lecture, or download copies of summaries, overheads or slideshows. Pay special attention to these topics when revising, as you will not have the same feel for the subject if you did not attend the lecture. Look out for your textbooks or visit the library as early as possible to ensure that you can reserve the books required. Avoid spending too long on this phase as a diversion from any real revision.

- Give your timetable the highest priority if conflicting demands are placed on you. If this means being a little selfish, explain to others why you need to focus on your studies. On the other hand, don't be a slave to your timetable. Be prepared to be flexible. If you feel you are really making progress with a topic, stick with it rather than changing topic. Make sure, however, that you make up the displaced work at a later point.

> ### ✔ Keeping tabs on your efforts
>
> When there's a lot to be done, marking off the studying you have completed on your timetable, perhaps with a brightly coloured highlighter, can provide a visual indication of how much you've covered and hence boost your confidence and morale.

- Recognise when your concentration powers are dwindling – take a short break when this happens and return to work refreshed and ready to learn. Remember that 20 minutes is often quoted as a typical limit to full concentration effort.

- Remember to have several short (5-minute) breaks during each hour of revision and a longer break every few hours. In any day, try to work for a maximum of three-quarters of the time.

- Use active learning techniques (Ch 61) so that your revision is as interesting as possible: *the least productive approach is simply to read and reread your lecture notes*.

> ### ✔ Avoid forgetting material you covered at the start of your revision
>
> Try to make sure you do *something* for each subject or topic in each week. A task as simple as revisiting your distilled notes (Ch 61) at intervals will keep facts and concepts fresh in your mind.

Make good use of your course handbook. This will help you find out about the structure of your exam and the content that will be covered. If learning objectives are published, refer to these to gain an insight into what lecturers will be expecting of you in the exam (Ch 63).

Use past papers as a guide. Past papers will give you an indication of the style of questions asked. Try to modify your revision to accommodate the question style (Ch 45–Ch 50). Note carefully the structure of the exam and, especially if it has sections, whether each part will require a different approach to revision, such as memorising particular facts or a requirement to synthesise answers from several sources.

Work out, as best you can, how the exam will be weighted towards different topics. Bias your revision time accordingly.

Use lists to keep track of progress. As you revise, make an inventory of topics you need to cover, definitions you need to learn, for example. Crossing out the jobs you have completed will give you a sense of accomplishment and, from this, a feeling of confidence.

Test yourself continuously. The only way you will know whether you have absorbed and memorised something is to test yourself, for example by trying to write what you think you have learned on a blank sheet of paper (see page 394). If you leave it until the exam to find out, it may be too late to do anything about it.

Try to keep your mind working. If you find you 'drift away' after a period studying the same topic, try adopting the notion that 'a change is as good as a rest': you may find you can keep your attention up by shifting between subjects at appropriate intervals.

61

REVISION TIPS

How to build understanding through active learning

Active learning is the key to understanding and remembering course material for recall during exams. It involves thinking through concepts, ideas and processes, as well as techniques for effective memorising.

Unless you are lucky enough to have a photographic memory, simply reading course material is a poor method for remembering and understanding it. Experience, backed up by research, indicates that you will remember things much better if you *do* something centred on the material (that is, 'actively' learn it). Moreover, this way of revising sometimes reveals flaws in your understanding that you may not appreciate when simply reading the material. There are many possible approaches to active learning and you should choose those that suit you and your circumstances.

BASIC ACTIVE LEARNING APPROACHES

You should probably use both the techniques outlined below for every exam.

'Distilling' or 'chunking' lecture notes

This involves taking your 'raw' lecture notes and reducing them to a series of headings and key points. This can be done in several 'sweeps', gradually reducing pages and pages of notes to just a few headings. An alternative approach to distilling is to reorganise your notes in grid format, as shown in Figure 61.1. The 'aspects' should be chosen to be relevant to likely exam questions. By creating this type of table you will force yourself to analyse the information you have been taught and hence understand it better.

The act of writing out the material when distilling or chunking your notes seems to help place it in a 'map' within your brain and aids recall. Another valuable aspect of these approaches is that they allow you to gain an overview of the topic – you can then appreciate where each aspect slots into the bigger picture. This may help you to memorise facts and place them in context within your exam answers. Finally, these methods are better than simply rewriting the material, because you need to *think* about the material as you transcribe into the new structure.

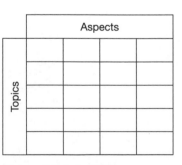

Figure 61.1 A grid for reorganising notes

Answering past papers and problems

Looking at past exam papers is important to let you see both the type and scope of questions normally asked. The depth of answer required may not be so obvious, however, and if this is in doubt, consult subject tutors. You can take a variety of active approaches thereafter, from thinking through an answer in your head (weak); writing out an answer plan rather than a full answer (good); and setting yourself a mock exam or timed exam question based on a particular paper (excellent). If possible, discuss your answers or plans with subject tutors and fellow students.

Particularly for subjects requiring numeracy, problem-solving and doing examples are acknowledged ways of testing understanding and reinforcing what you have learned. Try to recognise patterns in the types of calculations and problems usually asked. Consult with subject tutors if you do not understand how to answer any questions.

Benefits of mock exams

These help you practise writing against the clock. Although time-consuming, this gives you an idea of how quickly you will have to work and how much you will need to condense ideas to fit the time allowed. They also give you practice in writing quickly and neatly by hand, which is useful because this is a skill that may have eroded due to the widespread use of personal computers.

PREPARING TO LEARN AND MEMORISE

Understanding concepts and committing facts to memory can be hard, especially when you find a subject difficult or unattractive, or there are lots of obscure jargon to learn. To give yourself the best chance to absorb the material, you'll need to ensure that you have prepared mentally, and that your working environment is configured appropriately. Here are some principles that might help:

- **You need to be ready to learn.** Make sure you are not preoccupied by thoughts of anything else.

- **Make sure your desk space allows you to focus on the work in hand.** Declutter your desk. If necessary, take your papers to a library or a similar place, where there is plenty of space in which to lay them out.

- **Make sure you pace yourself.** You can only study effectively in short bursts, so take frequent breaks to keep your concentration at a peak.

- **You need to be determined to learn.** Avoid aimlessly reading material in the hope that it will 'sink in'. Convince yourself that you really want to learn. If you intensively focus on the material, fully intending and expecting to learn, you will.

Getting rid of distracting thoughts

If you can't concentrate because something is 'bugging' you, try this technique: write all your problems and issues down on a piece of paper, which you now put to one side. Promise yourself that you will deal with these matters later on, but meanwhile will focus on your studying. This may sound rather silly, but it works for some.

Remembering facts

In any subject there is a core of knowledge that you should be able to recall, but, in general, you should avoid rote learning and try to think more deeply about the subject material. The focus should be on using the facts you have learnt, not on the facts themselves. The module learning objectives may give you clues about the direction that these 'deeper' thoughts should take.

- **Gain an overview of what you have to learn.** Knowing the context helps you absorb and remember facts. If you see the bigger picture, it's easier to fit the component parts into it.
- **Limit the amount you have to learn.** Condense the material into lists or smaller chunks. Split large groups of information into smaller parts.
- **'Visualise' and 'associate' to learn.** At its most simple, this means knowing how many items you need to remember. It could also include recalling a doodle on the page of your notes beside the text. More complex methods include associating facts with a familiar journey or location (see **Ch 62**).
- **Check your recall.** Don't trust to chance that you have learned the material – test yourself continuously (page 394).

Keep your revision interesting

Try to use a variety of approaches to avoid boredom during your revision. Experiment to see which method suits you best.

PRACTICAL TIPS FOR ACTIVE LEARNING

Further information about some of these tips is provided in **Ch 62**, which includes a range of other methods to aid recall.

Make your notes memorable. Use coloured pens and highlighters, but beware of overuse of emphasis and 'absent-minded' or purposeless highlighting, that is, when you highlight almost everything or don't really think why you have highlighted something.

Use concept or mind maps. These help to condense your knowledge of a particular topic. If you include drawings you may find that such image-based notes make recall easier.

Test your recall of diagram labels. Draw up important diagrams without labels, copy these, and then use them to test yourself from time to time.

Try recitation as an alternative to written recall. Talk about your topic to another person, preferably someone in your class. Talk to yourself if necessary. Explaining something out loud is a good test of understanding.

Prepare a series of 'revision sheets'. Note details for each particular topic on a single piece of paper, perhaps arranged as a numbered checklist. If you have the room, make your sheets into a set of wall posters. Pinning these up on a wall may help you visualise the overall subject area. Some people like to use sticky notes for this purpose.

Share ideas and discuss topics with other students. The act of explaining can help imprint the knowledge in your brain, and it has the useful side effect of revealing things you don't really know, even if you thought you did (see **Ch 64** for further discussion).

Make up your own exam paper. Putting yourself in the examiner's mindset is very valuable. Inventing your own questions and thinking about how you would answer them requires a good understanding of the material.

Memorise definitions. These can be a useful starting point for many exam answers. Make up lists of key phrases and facts (for example, dates and events) associated with particular topics. Test yourself repeatedly on these, or get a friend to do this.

Adapt your revision methods to your preferred learning style, using information gained from Ch 13. For example, if you feel you are a 'visual learner' (Table 13.4), consider using diagrams and mind maps to summarise your notes; if your MBTI type is ESFP (Table 13.2), recall experiences and examples to help you remember facts (Table 13.3).

62

MEMORY TIPS AND TECHNIQUES

How to develop tools and strategies for remembering information and ideas

> **Having key facts at your fingertips is critical if you wish to approach exams with confidence. You will then be able to demonstrate higher-level skills in your answers, because you can focus on marshalling and analysing your knowledge, rather than struggling to recall details of your subject. This chapter outlines some ways in which you can train your memory to work for you in exams and in other situations.**

Being in a position to recall information under pressure is important, both in relation to the 'building blocks' of your answers – the essential facts and knowledge of your discipline – and in relation to concepts arising from the deeper thinking you have done about the subject. Moreover, in many cases the exam 'questions' will ask you to apply your knowledge in an unpredicted way. If you lack the crucial facts and theoretical framework to be able to do this, your marks will inevitably suffer. In some cases, being unable to recall details can lead to a feeling of panic in the exam that makes things even worse.

Few of us have natural 'photographic' memories and some struggle to retain information and ideas, especially in topics that we lack interest in or have difficulty understanding. Sometimes, also, it is the volume of material that has to be covered that makes remembering it difficult. However, you can gain in confidence, and also perform better under exam conditions if you learn some elementary memory 'tricks' that can kick into action in the exam hall.

WHERE MEMORY BEGINS IN LEARNING

While this chapter is about the memory tricks you can use in exams, it is important to recognise that the act of memorising begins at a much earlier stage in your revision – in essence, you need to be able to recognise what it is that you need to remember before you can adopt and adapt tricks to pull this information out in the exam. This involves the information-gathering and information-processing phases discussed in **Ch 59**.

The first step is to identify the content of your course, the key concepts of the subject within the themes that have been covered in lectures, tutorials, practicals and seminars as well as the topics that have been covered in assignments (information gathering). From this material, you then begin to synthesise organised revision notes that provide you with the facts and deeper understanding of the topics (information processing). For many people, this is an important preliminary stage to learning in that it provides a degree of reassurance that they have all the material required in a manageable form, but they would probably not yet claim 'ownership' of that knowledge. This point marks the transfer to the next stage of revision where you embark on active learning strategies to embed this understanding into your knowledge base, so that you are able to retrieve and deliver the information in an exam situation.

Memory and learning styles

Appropriate memory techniques are closely linked to your personal learning style (Ch 13). For example:

- **Sensory or visual learners** normally have a preference for practical approaches involving the use of images.
- **Active (extrovert or kinesthetic) learners** tend to prefer to learn by physical activity, such as manipulating materials.
- **Intuitive (introvert) or reflective learners** prefer theoretical and analytical approaches to derive the meaning that underpins what they need to learn.
- **Verbal (or read–write) learners** opt for word-based tactics.

The various approaches outlined in this chapter may resonate more with some learning styles than others, so it may be worthwhile analysing your learning preference as part of your preparation for revision.

STRATEGIES FOR ORGANISING NOTES INTO MEMORABLE FORMATS

For all students preparing for exams, there is a need to learn a considerable volume of facts – for example, dates of legislation, permutations of chemicals, stages in a procedure or sequences of events. However, it is important to recognise that university exams are not simply about information transfer from lecturer to student and then back to the lecturer. Thus, facts in themselves are not sufficient for most university exam formats. Instead, in your answers you need to demonstrate the understanding and analysis that distinguishes your ability to think critically (see Ch 22). A measured answer responding to the task is required, rather than one simply listing facts or providing a disorganised jumble of information on every aspect of the topic. This means that you need to create memorable revision notes that reflect your understanding of the way that the course – and hence the subject – fits together. Ways in which you can do this include the following:

Creating lists

This is the most basic technique of all. The idea is to distil your notes into a series of headings (see Ch 61). Doing this in several phases helps to imprint the knowledge and the end result provides an overview of your subject that allows you to place knowledge in its context. This method is particularly suited to those with verbal–linguistic or read–write learning preferences. Numbering your lists can be a useful memorising device (page 393).

Making time lines

You can use a time line (Figure 62.1) to plot the progress of events, a procedure or a development. Time lines can be drawn as vertical or horizontal. You might find these especially useful where a significant series of events have been referred to at different points in a lecture series.

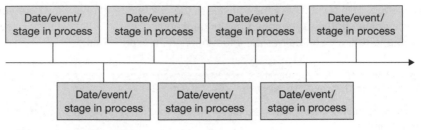

Figure 62.1 Example of a time line

Carrying out SWOT analyses

A **SWOT** analysis helps to analyse a situation, for example, as part of an appraisal of a case study or for a topic where a particular standpoint might be taken. It requires you to list aspects of the situation under one of four headings – **S**trengths, **W**eaknesses, **O**pportunities and **T**hreats. This analytical activity is an active learning technique that makes you think about the material more deeply. Noting bulleted points in a grid format, as shown in Figure 62.2, can be a useful memory aid that suits those with good visual recall.

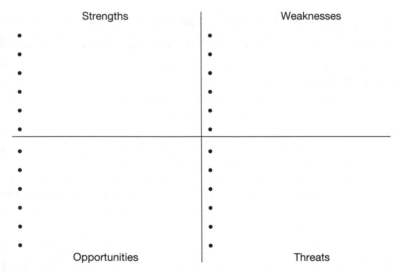

Figure 62.2 Example layout of a SWOT analysis. Each quadrant contains a series of bulleted points.

Creating 'contrast grids'

This technique adapts the 'Johari Windows' method developed by Joe Luft and Harry Ingham (Luft and Ingham, 1955), and called after the first letters of their names. The method looks at pairs of contrasting aspects of an issue or situation and organises information or viewpoints within a two-by-two grid. The original Johari technique was designed to aid self-assessment of personality, but the technique can be used for other contexts (see Figure 62.3).

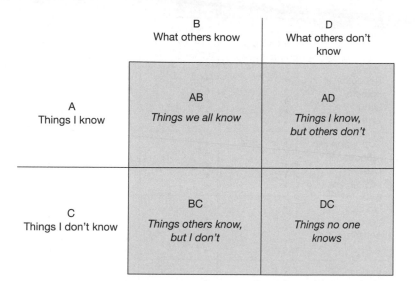

	B What others know	D What others don't know
A Things I know	AB *Things we all know*	AD *Things I know, but others don't*
C Things I don't know	BC *Things others know, but I don't*	DC *Things no one knows*

Figure 62.3 A 'contrast grid' used to analyse different viewpoints. This example could describe a student reflecting on their own learning in relation to others in a group. Note the letter coding to show how each combination is arrived at.

Organising complex information in grids

Tables and grids are good devices for helping to analyse systematically complex information that has been presented in a seemingly haphazard way, or that can be simplified by categorising the component parts. These grids or matrices can be particularly helpful in organising and remembering content for questions that require comparative and contrastive analysis. Figure 62.4 provides an example.

Sketching concept maps (mind maps)

Another form of organisational diagram (Figure 62.5) is variously called a concept map, scatter diagram, spray diagram or mind map. In their most refined form, these are extremely visual, relying on colour and shape to produce an image that is both memorable and attractive. Some practitioners are able to use concept maps to encapsulate an hour-long lecture or public speech. For practical purposes, in exam revision and in the exam itself, the use of concept mapping has to be quick, legible and coherent. If you are happy with the strategy, the concept map can be a useful revision device as well as providing an outline plan of a response to an exam question.

Drawing diagrams

Diagrams can be created to show hierarchies, processes or relationships, as illustrated in Figure 62.6. They can also be used in your exam to provide you with an outline for a potential answer. Sometimes they can be formal representations that might be used within your answer. Diagrams are extremely useful to those with a visual or visual–spatial type of learning preference. However, take care when your diagrams are simply personalised sketches that are meaningful to you but possibly not to others. Although they can act as a memory aid to give you cues in writing your exam answer, they may not add significant value to the content.

	Viewpoint of individual employees	Viewpoint of Trades Unions	Viewpoint of industrial companies	Viewpoint of Government
Reduction in hours of statuory working week	• • • • •	• • • • •	• • • • •	• • • • •
Corresponding reduction in pension entitlement	• • • • •	• • • • •	• • • • •	• • • • •
Reduction in holiday entitlement	• • • •	• • • •	• • • •	• • • •
Reduction in number of days per annum as sick leave	• • • • •	• • • • •	• • • • •	• • • • •

Figure 62.4 Example of a grid used to analyse viewpoints on an issue. In this case, the lattice of the grid allows the learner to note, in the relevant box, key points held by different stakeholders (listed along the top) on various aspects of a proposed policy (listed on the left).

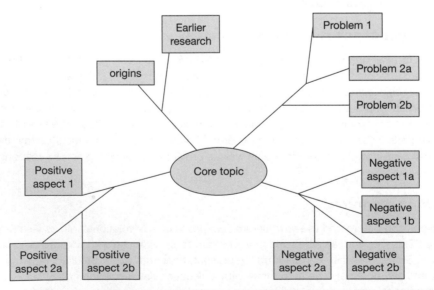

Figure 62.5 Example of a concept map. This generalised example does not include pictorial images, but adding colour, doodles and other visual links to the topics can help you to memorise the components.

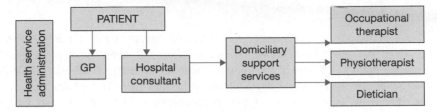

Figure 62.6 Example of the use of a diagram. This describes the organisation of health support.

Setting up posters or 'Post-it®' notes

This approach is useful for those who find that it helps their recall if they subliminally absorb information. It is a technique that particularly suits kinesthetic learners. The strategy is to construct a zone made up of posters or sticky 'Post-it®' notes on a wall in your hallway, bedroom, kitchen or bathroom to help embed the information into your memory, as part of your normal world. Thus, should your mind go blank in the exam, then you will be able to recall the missing information more easily simply by thinking back to the pattern of the notes in the context in which you have positioned them. This strategy relates to the 'pegging' of rooms described on page 392.

Using visual cues

In many of the models described here, the use of colour, different types of writing/printing, underlining, emboldening as well as use of layout, arrows and other symbols can influence your ability to remember the content. Some people go as far as to keep notes on different colours of paper or index cards to distinguish the level of their notes – for example, white sheets/cards for the longer, detailed version of notes on a topic pinned together with a coloured 'cover' sheet/card that contains topic headings and sub-headings for 'flash card' revision. In all of these strategies the aim is to capitalise on your visual memory as an aid to recall of concepts or written information.

TRICKS FOR RECALLING FACTS AND CUES

The final stage of revision is to ensure you memorise the material ready for information retrieval and processing. Some of the above strategies for organising information will contribute to your ability to recall knowledge under examination conditions. However, there are some additional memorising techniques that you might find useful. Some need a significant amount of practice beforehand to ensure that you can apply the strategy under the potentially stressful environment of the examination hall.

'Mnemonic' relates to the Greek word meaning 'of remembering'. This term encompasses a range of strategies that work on the principle of remembering by association. Some examples are provided below.

Nonsense words

Typical ways of using mnemonics are to create 'words' that are made up of the initial letters of lists of items you need to remember. These are called acronyms. Thus, some people find it easier to remember the first line of the Periodic Table as the acronym **HHeLiBeBCNOF**, whereas others can remember this more readily as: **H**ealthy **He**rbert **Li**ves **Be**side **B**oring **C**ountryside **N**ear **O**pen **F**ields (hydrogen, helium, lithium, beryllium, boron, carbon, nitrogen, oxygen and fluorine). Another nonsense word acronym describes the purpose of research: **SCADAC**: **S**ystematic **C**ollection and **A**nalysis of **D**ata for **A**ction and **C**hange.

Rhymes

From folklore, there are many established rhymes that can be used to aid recall. For example: 'Thirty days hath September, April, June and November . . .'. However, it is possible to make up your own rhymes either as a kind of doggerel verse or sung to some common 'nursery rhyme' type of tune.

Spelling tricks

Clearly, it does not represent your abilities very well if you misspell words that are key to your study. Therefore, it is important to devise strategies to help ensure that you use the correct form in your written work. For example, architects and designers might need to distinguish between the 'storeys' (levels of a building) or 'stories' (tales). It may be easier to remember the one that they usually want is 'storeys' because it contains the word 'store' and a store usually has different levels. Similarly, students of accountancy might find it difficult to remember how to spell 'debt' and 'debit' and they might find it helpful to remember that 'debit' rhymes with 'credit'. You will be able to design your own spelling tips if you keep a note of any rhymes or characteristics that you encounter.

Journey 'pegs'

In this approach you have to think of a fairly long journey with which you are reasonably familiar. The preliminary work that has to be done is to identify staging posts on the journey corresponding to the number of points that you need to remember. The strategy is then to 'map' the facts by relating each memory point to a staging post on the journey. This works from the principle of association where the different elements to be remembered are 'pegged' onto the known journey.

Special place 'pegs'

This is another strategy that relies on pegging the unfamiliar onto the familiar. You need to imagine a room, a picture or a view that is familiar to you and you select key items of furniture or features in the picture or view to associate with the factual elements that you need to recall. In the exam, you simply visualise the situation and then recall the items that you 'pegged' to them. A further refinement is to create a story around the image so, for example, you go into the room and switch on the lamp (West Germany), move over to the television (France) and switch that on also. You put your mug (Italy) onto the coffee table (Belgium) and place a cushion (Netherlands) on the sofa (Luxembourg) before you sit down. This 'story' could help you recall the six members of the original European Economic Community.

Story 'pegs'

Some people find that they can take the journey and special place pegs to a further level by creating a longer story that relates the events to the recall items. Here, people can base their story on a familiar tale, for example, 'The three little pigs' to remember Napoleon's path to taking over large tracts of mainland Europe – the house of straw (Iberian Peninsula), the house of wood (Italy) and the house of bricks (Russia). Alternatively, stories can be created by the individual and can be as innovative, ridiculous, violent or colourful as you wish. The object is to create a sequence of events that is meaningful to you and can easily be recalled along with the related associations.

Is the effort in 'pegging' worthwhile?

Some argue that the effort put into creating these scenarios might be better spent on just learning the material parrot fashion and it is also suggested that these pegging strategies introduce an additional series of stages in the memorisation process. However, the technique responds to the learning styles of some people – if it works for you, it is worth the time and effort, especially where more conventional memorising techniques have failed you in the past.

Numbered lists

Listing is a basic revision tool (page 387) and for people who like to learn in a linear fashion the use of numbered lists can be especially helpful. This is most valuable where there is a sequence inherent in the facts, and when knowing the total for the list can be useful in identifying whether you have recalled all the facts you originally collated. Breaking up larger lists into main points and sub-sections can be useful, particularly if the layout of the page 'staggers' the information by indentation and numbering of sub-sets. This can assist you to recall the image of the page and the list layout.

Logic rituals

For most of us, there are key things that we simply find difficult to remember time after time. However, if you can identify some ritual of logic that you can apply each time, you do have a way of unblocking that elusive piece of information. For example, the chemistry student who cannot remember how to calculate the density of liquid can recall the units of density, grams (mass) per millilitre (volume), which helps her to remember that density is calculated as mass over volume.

PRACTICAL TIPS FOR MEMORISING FOR EXAMS

Practise, practise, practise. There is simply no substitute for going over the material and/or your memory aids again and again.

Practise mnemonics. You should be able to rattle them off without difficulty – but of course you must be able to recollect what the mnemonic represents.

Practise using memory journey, special place and personal story 'peg' strategies. If these appeal, give yourself some practice in using this strategy before you go into the exam.

Practise recalling and writing quickly. As students increasingly type their assignments and work from pre-printed handouts in lectures, there are fewer opportunities to practise remembering and writing at speed, skills that are critical to answering questions against the clock in an exam. By rapidly scribbling down your memory cues, you can also work on developing the skill of writing quickly as part of your revision.

Review what you have learned. If anything is the key to memorising, this is it. Don't just rely on the vague hope that you will be able to recall something – check that you can, and check frequently. If these 'self-tests' indicate that you can't recall everything, go back and start again. This repeated activity works to imprint the knowledge – and if it works, you will *know* that you know the material. Here's a possible method to try:

1 Read the material and, as you do this, write it out in list form, focusing fully on each point, trying hard to remember it. Note the number of items on the list.

2 Turn over the list and remove all clues about it (for example, close your textbook).

3 Immediately, rewrite the list. If you can't remember everything, go back to point (1) and start again until you can rewrite the list completely.

4 Do something else for 5 minutes, then rewrite the list without clues. If you can't remember everything, go back to point (1) again.

5 Do something else for an hour, then rewrite the list. If you can't remember everything, go back to point (1) again.

6 After 24 hours, again try to rewrite the list. If you can't remember everything, go back to point (1) again.

This method also works well with diagrams.

63

FOCUSING YOUR REVISION

How to make full use of learning outcomes, past papers and other assessment information

> You can gain a deeper understanding of how you will be assessed from a range of sources. Studying these can help you to focus your revision and to enter the exam room better prepared.

Universities publish a great deal of useful information that can help you to improve your exam performance. The most important sources are likely to be: module learning outcomes or objectives, marking criteria, past exam papers and model answers. As part of your revision, you should find out what exists and make full use of it.

USING LEARNING OUTCOMES OR OBJECTIVES

You will normally find the learning outcomes in the module handbook alongside the detailed description of the curriculum (they are sometimes called learning objectives). These statements represent the 'take-home messages' of the teaching and they state what you are expected to accomplish in your learning. This is then tested in exams and other forms of assessment. Despite the obvious importance of learning outcomes, many students fail to look at them when studying.

Some departments lay out learning outcomes as a series of bullet points relating to individual lectures (for example, 'Following this lecture, you should be able to . . .').

Compatibility between content and assessment

In an ideal world, there should be an 'agreement' between the learning outcomes, the syllabus and the assessment methods. In other words, you should not be examined on something you didn't expect to have to learn.

In other cases, the outcome(s) may be framed in more general terms. Departments may also publish aims and goals for the entire module and it is also worth looking at these to place the course elements in context.

The relationship between exam questions and learning outcomes is generally easy to see if you look at past papers and match up the exam questions with the relevant learning outcomes and course material. However, you should be aware that the learning outcomes may have changed through time – ask the module organiser if in doubt.

If you do not feel able to achieve a particular learning outcome, it is worth checking with teaching staff. Perhaps you may have misunderstood the topic or the intention behind the outcome, in which case they may be able to provide you with further explanations. Also, a specific outcome might be redundant because a lecturer was unavailable or made a late modification to their teaching – check!

WHAT MARKING CRITERIA CAN TELL YOU

Marking or grading criteria provide an indication of what sort of answer would gain a particular percentage mark or grade in relation to a university's marking scheme. You'll probably find marking criteria in faculty or departmental handbooks or websites, because they tend to apply across many modules. However, they may also be published in each module handbook.

Typical marking criteria include the following elements:

- **Content:** covering the range of ideas or information discussed and their relevance to the question actually set.
- **Depth:** referring to such aspects as complexity, detail, intellectual insight and originality of argument.
- **Writing style:** relating to, for example, the logic, clarity and the quality of the English.
- **Presentation:** referring to the neatness and possibly also to the structure of your work.
- **Use of examples:** taking account of the relevance, accuracy and detail of those you quote.
- **Evidence of reading:** accounting for any reading around the subject you may be expected to do: this may come from the examples and sources you quote (not just those given in lectures).
- **Originality:** involving independent thinking (backed by supporting evidence and argument) or a new synthesis of ideas: these are dimensions that are highly valued, especially in later years of study.
- **Analysis:** including interpretation of raw data or information found in original (primary) sources.

Have a close look at your department's marking criteria. If you wish to gain high marks, these will tell you what standard your answers must be. Note, however, that although marking criteria provide a 'benchmark', the exact mark given will always depend on the topic and question and is a matter for the professional judgement of the academic and the external examiner.

Example of marking criteria

These are the marking criteria for a first-class answer (70–100 per cent) in a science subject at honours level:

- Contains all the information required with either no or very few errors.
- Shows evidence of having read relevant literature and uses this effectively in the answer.
- Addresses the question correctly, understanding all its nuances.
- Little or no irrelevant material.
- Demonstrates full understanding of the topic within a wider context.
- Shows good critical and analytical abilities.
- Contains evidence of sound independent thinking.
- Ideas expressed clearly and concisely.
- Written logically and with appropriate structure. Standard of English very high.
- Diagrams detailed and relevant.

EXPLOITING PAST PAPERS

Past papers or sample questions are a vital resource. They may be published electronically on websites or virtual learning environments, or in paper form within the library. If you can't find them in these locations, ask staff or senior students for help.

> ### Linking past papers and learning outcomes to enhance your revision ✔
>
> A possible approach is to photocopy past papers and then cut and paste all the questions into separate pages for each topic in the lecture course. By comparing the resulting groups of questions with the learning outcomes and the material as taught, you can gain a much better picture of how you will be assessed, what types of question might turn up, and what type of revision needs to be done.

Use past papers first to understand the structure of each of your exam papers, including:

- the format of answers expected (for example, essay, short-answer questions, multiple-choice questions);
- the number and style of questions you will be required to answer of each type;
- what the mark allocation is among sections or question types;
- the time allowed for answering;
- whether there is any choice allowed;
- whether the arrangement of sections forces you to answer on specific topics.

Second, use past papers or sample questions to understand the style being used. When looking at each paper, ask yourself the following questions:

- How much and what type of factual knowledge is required?
- How deep an understanding of the topic is required?
- How much extra reading might be required?
- How much or how little freedom will you have to express your opinion or understanding?
- Do lecturers have consistent styles of questions?

Use your answers to create both your revision and exam strategies and the content of your answers (**Ch 60, Ch 66**).

LEARNING FROM MODEL ANSWERS

If model answers are provided, spare time in your revision to read them carefully.

Consider each question thoroughly *before* you read the model answer. Jot down a few thoughts about the way you would tackle it. Identify the relevant learning outcomes that apply and think about the methods the lecturers are using to assess these.

Now read the model answer. This should be helpful in several ways, depending on how detailed it is:

- You should be able to grasp the language and style expected – for example, the type of introduction required, the use of headings and diagrams, what sort of things are in the conclusion.
- You should be able to evaluate the depth expected – for example, the balance between *description* and *analysis* that is present, the level of detail in any examples given, including use of dates, terminology and citation of authorities and authors. Especially at higher levels, university exams are more about using information to support a reasoned answer than simply regurgitating facts (**Ch 22**).
- You should be able to see how the different facets of the question have been addressed. Examine each part of the answer and identify what aspect it deals with, and how.

✔ Learning from poor answers

If your lecturers also provide a 'bad' model answer, see what you can learn by comparing this with the good answer. Are you guilty of any of the errors highlighted by the comparison?

SETTING YOUR OWN QUESTIONS AND EXAMS

After you have revised each section or topic, take the time to write out a few potential questions in the style of those seen in past papers. How would you set about answering your own questions? Write down plans as you would with an essay plan during the exam. This process helps you prepare mentally for sitting the exam. Consider it a bonus if any of the questions you predict come up in the real paper, but do not be tempted into question-spotting (see Tip Box below).

✔ Avoid question-spotting

At worst, this involves predicting (guessing) a limited number of exam questions in the hope that they come up and revising that material only. This risky strategy is rarely condoned:

- Most examiners pre-empt it by making sure that questions are not repeated between exam diets and that patterns do not occur among papers. The chances of 'your' question coming up are very low.
- If your predictions are false, you will probably be unable to answer on other topics because you have not prepared for them.
- If there are subtle elements to the wording of the question, you may be tempted to provide the answer to your predicted question, rather than the precise one asked. You will then lose marks due to lack of relevance.

A 'mock exam', where you attempt to answer questions or a paper under realistic exam conditions, can help you in the following important ways:

- Testing your subject knowledge – and giving you early feedback about what you do and do not know.

- Helping you get into exam-answering mode and 'voice' – so that you can get rid of your rustiness before the proper exams start, can get going quickly in the actual exam and can start writing quickly and appropriately.

- Timing your answers appropriately – so that you optimise marks and don't make the cardinal mistake of missing out questions through lack of time.

- Practising planning and laying out an answer quickly – so that you get used to the process of thinking rapidly through your answer before starting to write and, where appropriate, can check that you know the appropriate layout of your answer.

- Reducing the effect of nerves – rehearsing can help you perform better on the day. You should be less anxious if you are familiar with the act of answering.

PRACTICAL TIPS FOR FOCUSING YOUR REVISION

Keep the exam paper format in mind as you revise. Assess the style of questions at an early point and choose study methods appropriate to the style of questions you will encounter (Ch 45–Ch 50, Ch 61).

Use the learning outcomes to check your progress. Your revision should include reading the learning outcomes for each topic and ticking each off when you feel you know enough to be able to accomplish them.

Dealing with a lack of past papers. Your tutors may be reluctant to release past papers in cases where there is a limited pool of 'good' questions for them to use, as this might reward students who simply memorise answers. This is often the case where the paper is made up of multiple-choice questions. One way round this is to set your own questions, perhaps as part of a study group, and use these to test each other.

64

STUDY BUDDIES

How to work with fellow students to improve the revision experience

Teaming up with others as part of your revision effort is recognised as beneficial in many respects. This chapter explores some aspects of this 'study buddy' revision approach.

Revising for examinations is a positive experience in lots of ways. It heightens your understanding of your subject and allows you to make connections between different elements of the course. It needn't be a solitary activity and many people find that it improves their learning to work on revision with another person studying the same subject.

WHAT IS STUDY BUDDYING?

The study buddy concept is based on a mutual arrangement between two or more students studying the same or similar subjects, who agree to support each other in their learning by conducting joint study sessions within their revision timetable (**Ch 63**). Examples of suitable revision activities include:

- meeting together to work through tutorial questions, comparing answers and analysing the correct approach;
- studying a topic as individuals and then meeting at an agreed time to quiz each other on the topic;
- speaking to each other about a specific topic (even giving a 'mini lecture');
- sharing resources, such as missed lecture notes, handouts, website and textbook information;
- sharing advice about modules that one person may have passed but the other(s) not;
- working together on formulating answers to questions on past papers;
- providing psychological support when one of you needs motivating or prompting to study.

 How can you find a buddy?

The obvious starting points are friends from your class, members of a tutorial group or lab partners. You could also simply ask around before or after lectures or put up a request on an online discussion board. A lecturer might be willing to make an announcement on your behalf, asking anyone interested in forming a study group to come forward at the end of the lecture. You'll be surprised how many others will be interested in this activity.

This technique probably suits some personality types better than others (see tip below and Table 13.3). You'll need to decide for yourself whether it will be appropriate for you and, crucially, you'll need to find someone else who thinks the same way.

> ✔
>
> ### Personality types and learning styles most suited to study buddying
>
> The MBTI (Ch 13) divides people into either extrovert or introvert types, but individuals from both types can be suited to study-buddy learning strategies. If, having carried out the questionnaire in Tables 13.1–13.3, you identify yourself as one of the following types, then it might be worthwhile trying this approach: ENIJ, ENFP, ENTJ, ESFJ, ESFP, INFJ, INFP, ISFP, ISTJ.

THE ADVANTAGES OF STUDY BUDDYING

The study-buddy approach works very much on the principle that two or more heads are better than one and that the process of working together to tackle problems, key issues or difficult areas can assist all those involved to learn more effectively.

- You can play to your strengths by helping with areas where you are stronger; and you can receive help from others to strengthen your weaker areas.
- Explaining your understanding to someone else can help to clarify the issues, process or technique in your own mind. It can also help the other party, who may learn better when things are explained by a peer, because the language is less formal. They may also feel more comfortable about asking questions and seeking clarification or become less anxious about making mistakes.
- The pair or group dynamic can have a fun or competitive element that motivates some people; it can also generate confidence knowing that others feel the same.
- Arranging to meet with someone else to revise means you are more likely to do so.

Some advice worth remembering:

- Be sure that you don't spend too much time supporting others and thereby neglecting yourself.
- Make sure you and your study buddies focus on studying rather than chat.
- Don't assume that study buddying is an easy option to avoid the hard grind of studying alone – solo study may, in practice, be a part of the study-buddy process.

Some practical ideas for buddy activities

Different partnerships work in different ways; here are some tried and tested strategies that students have found useful.

■ Partners work on problems individually for a set amount of time and then reconvene to compare method and answers.

■ Student A uses a whiteboard or flipchart to explain a process to partner, Student B. Then they reverse roles for another topic.

■ Partners make up a 'bank' of short-answer topics by writing the question on one side of an index card and the answer on the other side. They test each other on random cards drawn from the pile.

PRACTICAL TIPS FOR WORKING WITH COLLEAGUES TO IMPROVE YOUR REVISION

Arranging meetings. Pick a mutually acceptable time and find a location that will allow you to sit and discuss your work without disturbing others. Ensure that you turn up with all the relevant notes, calculators, worked examples and resources like dictionaries as appropriate. It's best to aim for a neutral venue. Groupwork areas may be available in your library or you may find study rooms in the library, department, hall of residence or student association. You may be able to take over tutorial or small lecture rooms (check the booking system first): these have the advantage of having whiteboards and flipcharts, which you can use to note down points or give explanations to each other. Ask your tutors or the departmental secretary if you can't find anywhere suitable – they may be able to help.

Ground rules. Agree some basic rules, for example, start and stop times, and limiting coffee breaks to no longer than 15 minutes. Stick to what you all agreed. Make sure that it's clear that if anyone feels that the strategy is not working for them, they can walk away from it without fear of offending the others.

Tackling the revision. Decide on the areas of study for each session and stick to these. Draw up a 'wish list' of aims/topics at the beginning of each session and cross them off as you complete them.

Seeking help. If, between you, an answer is not found, go to your lecturer or tutor to ask for some guidance. Teaching staff are usually delighted when students show their interest in their topics by asking questions, so you shouldn't feel nervous about asking for some help. You may find that it is less embarrassing or daunting to do this as a pair or a group.

Short or long sessions? Working intensively for a shorter time is often better than a prolonged session where people end up chatting about other things. Keep focused.

65

IMPROVING YOUR EXAM PERFORMANCE

How to avoid common pitfalls

> **Why aren't you doing as well as you'd like to in your exams and tests? This chapter focuses on the main reasons why exam answers are marked down and provides a framework for assessing how you could improve.**

Poor exam performance is a relative term that depends on your expectations. There will probably be occasions when you can easily diagnose the reasons for weak marks. Lack of preparation, poor performance in the exam room, or revising the 'wrong' topics are common examples. In these instances, your expectations after the exam were probably low and you can accept that you deserved a low grade.

At other times, you may feel your marks were not as good as you thought they were going to be. You may have misunderstood the topic or failed to understand all the nuances of the question. Here, there is a gap between your expectation and the results of your efforts – one that is vitally important to understand if you wish to do better in future.

IDENTIFYING REASONS FOR WEAK PERFORMANCE AND AREAS FOR IMPROVEMENT

Where might you have gone wrong in the past, and how might you improve? To find out, you will need to:

- **Reflect carefully on past exams.** Look back and think about how things went, and whether you might have been guilty of any of faults shown in Table 65.1. You may find it beneficial to look at the original question papers to jog your memory. Also, refer to any feedback on coursework or comments on exam scripts if these are available to you. If you don't understand any of the comments, try to meet with the marker and ask for an explanation. Such discussions can often be very valuable, so it is worth making the effort required.

- **Try to do something about the faults you have identified.** Many of the causes of poor exam performance are simple to correct, once you have identified which might apply to you. If, after reading through this 'self-help' chapter, you still do not understand where you went wrong or what corrective action to take, you should ask to meet with your tutor(s) to seek their advice.

Table 65.1 Checklist of possible reasons for poor exam marks. Use the list to identify where you may have been at fault, and find possible routes for improving your performance.

Reason	Relevant for you?	Possible cure(s)
Not answering the exact question as set: • failing to recognise the specialist terms used in the question • failing to carry out the precise instruction in a question • failing to address all aspects of the question	❑	A range of solutions – discussed in detail within this chapter
Poor time management: • failing to match the extent of the answer(s) to the time allocated • spending too long on one question and not enough on the others	❑	A better exam strategy is required (**Ch 66**)
Failing to weight parts of the answer appropriately: not recognising that one aspect (perhaps involving more complex ideas) may carry more marks than another	❑	A better essay plan may be required (**Ch 34**)
Failing to provide evidence to support an answer: not including examples or not stating the 'obvious' – like basic facts or definitions	❑	Need to realise this material is required to gain marks (page 405); a better essay plan may be required (**Ch 34**)
Failing to illustrate an answer appropriately: • not including a relevant diagram • providing a diagram that does not aid communication	❑	Need to understand how diagrams should be used to support writing (**Ch 30** and **Ch 44**)
Incomplete or shallow answers: • failing to answer appropriately due to lack of knowledge • not considering the topic in sufficient depth	❑	Need a better revision plan (**Ch 60**), a better revision technique (**Ch 61**) or a better understanding of the thinking process demanded at university (**Ch 22**)
Providing irrelevant evidence to support an answer: 'waffling' to fill space	❑	See material on answering the question (**Ch 48**, page 314)
Illegible handwriting: if it can't be read, it can't be marked	❑	May need to consider type of pen being used; slow down writing speed or change writing style
Poor English: facts and ideas are not expressed clearly	❑	Need to address academic writing skills
Lack of logic or structure to the answer	❑	Need to plan your writing better (**Ch 34**)
Factual errors	❑	Poor note-taking (**Ch 17**), learning (**Ch 13**, **Ch 14**), revision (**Ch 61**, **Ch 63**) or recall
Failing to correct obvious mistakes	❑	Need to review and proof-read answers (page 406 and **Ch 43**)

HOW TO ENSURE YOU ANSWER THE QUESTION

Most lecturers agree that the number-one reason for a well-prepared student losing marks is because their answers *do not address the question*. This is especially true for essay-style questions (**Ch 48**) but also true for short-answer questions (**Ch 46**) and other assignments.

The main tips for answering questions directly and purposefully are covered in **Ch 48** and include:

- Making sure you consider all aspects of the question.
- Ensuring your work is well planned.
- Explaining what *you* understand by the question.
- Focusing on the precise task you have been asked to do.
- Keeping to the point.
- Making sure you answer all elements in multi-part questions.
- Avoiding making value judgements (**Ch 37**).

Include basic material in your answer, such as key terms and their definitions, and critical dates and names. Especially if a strict marking scheme is being used, tutors will be unable to award you marks if you do not provide this information. Draw on your understanding of the whole topic when creating an essay plan. Don't just focus on key phrases of the question in isolation, but consider their context. Be aware of the risk, if you have decided to 'question-spot' (**Ch 63**), of answering your own pre-prepared question, rather than the one that has actually been set.

Trouble-shooting poor performance

If 'nerves' affected your performance, then you might consider different methods of preparation or ways of settling yourself at the start of the exam (**Ch 66**).

If you ran out of time and some of your answers were incomplete, you probably need a better strategy for using time in your exams (**Ch 66**). This is a simple fault to rectify.

If you feel that your vocabulary is weak or your English style inappropriate, you might need a longer-term approach that would involve creating a glossary (**Ch 42**) or reading about text structuring or punctuation (**Ch 38, Ch 40**).

Reasons for loss of marks at advanced levels

The following are reasons why you might be marked down at higher levels of study:

- Not providing enough in-depth information.
- Providing a descriptive rather than an analytical answer – focusing on facts, rather than deeper aspects of a topic.
- Not setting a problem in context, or not demonstrating a wider understanding of the topic. However, make sure you don't overdo this, or you may risk not answering the question set.
- Not giving enough evidence of reading around the subject. This can be corrected by quoting relevant papers and reviews.
- Not considering both sides of a topic/debate, or not arriving at a conclusion if you have done so.

REVIEWING YOUR ANSWERS TO GAIN MARKS

Many students want to get out of the exam room as soon as possible, but you should not do this unless you are convinced you have squeezed every last mark out of the paper. Your exam strategy (**Ch 66**) should always include an allocation of time for reviewing. Trapping simple errors could mean the difference between a pass or a fail or between degree classifications. These are some of the things you could look for when reviewing your work (see also **Ch 43**):

- **Basics.** Make sure you have numbered your answers, answered the right number of questions, etc.

- **Spelling, grammar and sense.** Read through the answer critically (try to imagine it has been written by someone else) and correct any obvious errors that strike you. Does the text make sense? Do the sentences and paragraphs flow smoothly?

- **Structure and relevance.** Once again, ask yourself whether you have really answered the question that was set. Have you followed precisely the instruction(s) in the title? Is anything missed out? Are the different parts linked together well? Look for inconsistencies in argument. Add new material if necessary.

If required, 'small-scale' corrections like spelling errors and changes to punctuation marks can be made directly in your text using standard proof-reading symbols (**Ch 43**). If you want to add text because you find you have missed something out, place an insert mark ($\wedge$ or $\curlywedge$) in the text and/or margin, with the annotation 'see additional paragraph x'; then write this paragraph, clearly identified, at the end of the answer. You will not lose any marks for having to do this.

> ### i Try to to help staff to help you
>
> It's important to realise that the person who marks your work is not an adversary. Most lecturers are disappointed when giving students a poor grade, but they approach the marking process professionally and with ruthless objectivity. Tutors are often very frustrated when they see that simple changes in approach might have led to a better mark, and they cannot assume that you know things that you do not put down on paper.

PRACTICAL TIPS FOR IMPROVING YOUR EXAM PERFORMANCE

Go in well prepared. Of course, you'd expect any lecturer to say this, because in terms of gaining good marks, there is no substitute for effective revision. However, being well prepared means more than memorising facts and concepts. To do well you also need to arrive at the exam room in a good mental state, with a plan and a positive attitude and the determination to get down to work quickly and effectively.

Convert your brainstorm into a plan as quickly as possible. You can do this very quickly simply by numbering the headings in the brainstorm in the order you intend to write about them.

Have relevance as a mantra. As you create your answer plan, keep asking yourself the following questions. Am I really answering the question? Have I covered all the necessary material? Is all that I have included relevant to the question? Use these questions as a mental checklist before you finalise your plan and continue to refer to it as you construct your response to the task you have been set.

EXAM STRATEGIES

How to ensure you have the appropriate tactics

> **Assuming your revision has gone well, the main pressure point in an exam is time. Effective use of this resource through an appropriate strategy is vital to ensure the best possible performance.**

An exam strategy is effectively a plan for managing your time and effort during an exam. This is vital to optimise your marks, because rushing answers or failing to complete the paper are reasons why many students perform poorly (Ch 65). Having a clear strategy will also mean that you will be more confident going into the exam room and will address the questions in a more focused way.

KEY INFORMATION REQUIRED FOR A STRATEGY

Each exam will probably require a different strategy. For each one, you will need to do some research beforehand, by finding the answers to the following questions:

- How long is the exam?
- How is the paper subdivided into sections and questions?
- What is the nature of the questions?
- What proportion of the marks is allocated to each section/answer?
- What restrictions on answering are there?

You can find out these details from course handbooks or staff. Past papers are another source of information, but the rules may change, so confirm that the format is still the same.

Exam strategies do not need to be complex, but they do need to be planned with care, and ideally in advance as part of your revision effort. Table 66.1 illustrates some ways in which a strategic approach can help you avoid problems with exams.

---

i

Example: choosing a strategy

A common type of restriction in exam papers forces you to cover the full range of the syllabus by stating that you must answer one question from each of a number of sections, each covering a different subject area. As well as influencing your exam strategy, this type of restriction should also affect the way you revise (Ch 63).

Table 66.1 Types of approaches to exams and how to avoid similar problems

Approach	Experience	How to avoid this problem
The disorganised person	Dora has lost the scrap of paper that she used to note when and where her exam was. She plans to arrive at the time and place she vaguely remembers and see if she recognises anyone in the queue. Her bus is late, however, and everyone has already gone in. She arrives breathless at her seat, only to find she's forgotten her pen and it's an Atomic Physics paper rather than Edwardian history . . .	Dora could: • have checked the details the night before; • have planned to take the earlier bus to allow for hold-ups; • have used a checklist (Table 66.2) to make sure she has everything needed; • speak to the invigilator, who can give her correct information; • be allowed to sit part of the proper exam, if she can still get to the right place in time.
The nervous exam-sitter	Nadeem is totally consumed by nerves on the day of his big exam. He needs to visit the toilet immediately beforehand and then nearly throws up. In the exam, the words on the exam paper swim before his eyes and he can't make sense of the first question, nor any of the rest. The questions don't seem to relate to any of his course work. He rushes out of the exam hall, frustrated and anxious . . .	Nadeem could: • reflect ahead of time on his view of exams – why he feels nervous – and try not to allow a spiral of anxiety to develop; • try to exploit his energy rush positively, for example, by brainstorming key points as soon as he goes into the hall, thus giving him confidence; • use relaxation techniques within the exam hall.
The 'get-me-outa-here!' student	Graham would rather be anywhere else than in an exam hall. He rushes through his answers, then hands in his paper 30 minutes before the end and speeds over to the union bar to wait for his pals to come out. During post-exam discussions, he realises that one of his answers is incomplete and he hasn't even attempted section B . . .	Graham could: • familiarise himself with the format of the paper before the date; • plan his time in the exam so that he uses all of it profitably; • use spare time for checking answers to ensure he has done as instructed.
The perfectionist	Patsy has spent ages revising and knows the topics inside out. When she turns over the exam paper, she is delighted to find her ideal question and knows she can produce a brilliant answer. One-and-a-half hours later, it's nearly finished. Only problem is, she now has another two answers to complete in 30 minutes . . .	Patsy could: • do much the same as Graham, but also recognise that she will gain a better mark for doing reasonably well in all the questions, rather than extremely well in just one; • practise writing answers against the clock to improve her technique.
The mind-blocked writer	Mike has prepared for the exam well, but when he looks at the question, his mind has gone a complete blank. He can't remember anything to do with the subject material and feels like leaving the exam straight away . . .	Mike could: • begin by brainstorming a topic he knows well, from a nucleus of information that he can add to, and relate this to the questions asked; • ask a departmental representative for a clue; a note will be taken of this, but it's better than writing nothing and it will get him started.
The laid-back dreamer	Lin can't really be bothered with all the hassle of exams and the need for all that stress. At the start, she takes ages to choose a question and more time to think over her answer. In the middle, she finds herself dreaming of the summer vacation. Suddenly the exam is over, and she's only half way through her first answer . . .	Lin could: • focus on the exam and why it's important to her; • make a conscious decision to concentrate on the job in hand; • consider how much vacation time she will need to spend on revision if she fails.

The following is a straightforward method for an exam with a set of similar-length essay or short-answer questions:

- Translate the exam's total length into minutes.

- Allocate some time (say 5 per cent) to consider which questions to answer and in which order. Allocate another 5 per cent as a 'flexibility buffer'. Subtract these amounts (10 per cent) from the total time.

- Share the remainder of the time among the questions to arrive at an 'ideal' time for each answer.

- Think about how you intend to divide the time for each answer into planning, writing and review phases (see Tip Box below).

- Try to memorise roughly how long you intend to allocate to each section, question and phase, before going into the exam.

i

Example: exam timing

You have a 2-hour exam (120 minutes), in which you have to answer 10 short-answer questions from a list of 20. You might allocate 5 per cent of the time (6 minutes) to reading the paper, choosing questions and reviewing answers. That leaves 114 minutes, which means each question should be allocated 11 minutes, giving you 4 extra minutes for flexibility.

You might prefer a slightly different model where you would review all your answers towards the end of the exam, rather than reviewing each immediately after you have written it. If this would suit you better, you will need to deduct a further 5–10 per cent from the total before allocating planning and writing time to each answer.

Papers with mixtures of question types require more complex strategies. Much will rest on your estimate of the time each type of answer should take: base your estimate on previous experience (for example, in mid-term/semester exams) if you can, and take into account the proportion of marks allocated to each type of question or section. You may also need to decide on the order in which you do the different types of questions. For example, in the case of a paper with a multiple-choice component and an essay section, you may wish to do a sweep of the multiple-choice part first, then the essays, then return to complete the harder multiple-choice questions.

As part of study buddying (Ch 64), you could discuss ideas for appropriate strategies. This is a useful way of improving your focus before and during the exam.

In all cases your strategy should be flexible, in case things don't turn out the way you planned them – but only make changes during the exam if you are certain of what you are doing, and why.

> **? What if the exam paper is differently arranged from your expectation?**
>
> You will have to rethink your strategy quickly. It will still be worth doing this, as the penalties for running out of time could be severe.

WHAT TO DO DURING THE EXAM

- Quickly check the rubric at the top of the paper and that the questions are arranged as you expected.

- Look carefully at all the questions on the paper. You may wish to mark off the ones you feel you can answer well, or adopt some form of scoring system (for example, marks out of ten) for how well you think you can answer them.

- Thinking about your strategy, and the 'ideal' time for each question, decide which answers, if any, might require more time, or might provide a good return in marks for a little extra time invested, and which questions might require less time. A potentially good answer should be allocated only slightly more time than one you don't feel so happy about. If you concentrate too much on any one answer, the law of diminishing returns means that you will take time from other answers without gaining compensatory credit (see Figure 66.1).

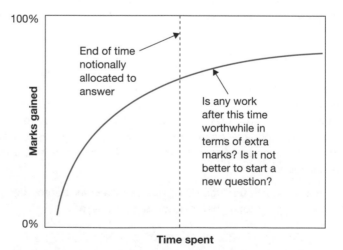

Figure 66.1 Why it does not pay to spend too long on any one exam answer. The marks you gain will tail off the longer you carry on writing. The extra return will simply not repay the investment of time. Ensure that you start answers to all questions to gain the 'easily obtained' marks, rather than wasting time perfecting one answer.

- Answer questions in a sensible order, which does *not* have to be the order they appear in the question paper. For example:
  - Some people prefer to answer 'fact-based' questions first, before they forget details memorised just before the exam.
  - Some people prefer to answer their 'best' question first, to get a good start to the paper. Others would prefer to do this second or even later, when they feel 'warmed up'.
  - Most people would agree that you should leave a question you feel unhappy about until the end: during the rest of the exam, ideas may come to you about it – note them down as you go along.

Example: benefits of answering all questions

Suppose you had a paper with four questions but only answered two, trying to do your very best in them. You might score, say, 75 per cent in each, but your total percentage mark would be (75 + 75 + 0 + 0) divided by 4, or 37.5 per cent (usually a fail).

On the other hand, if you answered all four questions, but perhaps less well, you might score 55 per cent in two and 45 per cent in the other two. Your overall percentage mark would be (55 + 55 + 45 + 45) divided by 4, or 50 per cent (usually a pass).

ARRIVING WELL PREPARED

Of course, the most important aspect of preparation is revision. No amount of exam technique will substitute for this. However, by ensuring that you also have the logistical aspects of exam-sitting under control, you can reduce the chance of making damaging mistakes and help to calm your nerves in advance of the event.

You may need to register and, in some cases, pay for certain exams – check this at an early stage. You should also confirm the date of the exam, where it will take place, when it will start and how long it will last. This information may be given in the course handbook, posted on noticeboards, published on a website or within a virtual learning environment module, or may also be provided by the exam office/registry by post. However, it is *your* duty to ensure that you arrive at the right place at the right time. Write down the information. Double-check, perhaps by asking a member of the class who has independently found out.

On the day, plan carefully so that you can arrive in good time – this will allow for unforeseen circumstances and will help to reduce the anxiety element at the start of the exam (**Ch 67**). Going over a checklist of items to bring to the exam (Table 66.2) may also act to calm you.

In the exam room, double-check on the rubric at the top of the paper. It is not unknown for students to sit the wrong exam by mistake.

Table 66.2 Checklist of items to bring with you to written exams

✓ Item
❑ Writing kit: pens and pencils (plus replacements), ruler, rubber, highlighter(s),correction fluid
❑ Student matriculation (ID) card (staff will use this to check your identity)
❑ Special equipment: calculators, protractor, compass, Walkman or similar for aural exams (check beforehand that you can use these aids properly), spare batteries
❑ Texts, where allowed for 'open book' exams
❑ Dictionary, if allowed (i.e. arranged beforehand with your department)
❑ Sweets and a drink, if allowed
❑ Clock or watch for timekeeping
❑ Mascot

PRACTICAL TIPS FOR TIME-SAVING IN EXAMS

Don't overelaborate your answer plans. Use simple forms of spider (pattern) diagrams or mind maps to brainstorm and plan your answer (**Ch 17**).

Use diagrams and tables in your answer. This saves time otherwise spent making difficult and lengthy explanations, but make sure they are worthwhile and that you refer to them in the text.

Use standard abbreviations. This will save time repeating text, but always explain the abbreviations at the first point of use. However, this is not necessary for 'standard' abbreviations such as e.g. (for example), i.e. (that is) and etc. (et cetera – and so forth).

Always keep your eye on the time. There is no point in having a strategy if you forget to stick to it. You may find it helps to take off your watch and put it where it can be easily seen on the desk. Some students find it helpful to work out the end times for each question beforehand as an aid to timekeeping. As the allotted period for each answer draws to a close, make sure your mind is on finishing your answer.

Consider speed of writing and neatness. Might you be wasting time by trying to write too neatly or using a type of pen that slows you down? Ballpoint and liquid gel pens are probably the fastest. Conversely, are you writing too quickly and making your script difficult to interpret? You can only gain marks if the examiner can read your script.

Keep your answer simple and to the point. It should have clear explanations of your reasoning. Even when working quickly, keep your eye on the task. You must answer the specific question that has been set (**Ch 65**).

Don't be tempted to waffle. Remember that time taken to write irrelevant material is time lost from another question. Don't waste time including irrelevant facts just because you memorised them during revision. This may do you more harm than good (**Ch 65**).

67

COMBATING EXAM NERVES

How to reduce anxiety and perform well under pressure

Turn exam anxiety to your advantage. Recognise that 'nerves' are your body's way of preparing you to perform at a higher level. Boost your confidence by having a 'game plan' ready.

Everyone worries about exams, even those at the top of the class, so if you get anxious you are not unusual. Nerves are best overcome through confidence generated by thorough preparation. Even if you've studied hard, it isn't possible to know 100 per cent of the coursework, nor to anticipate what exactly will be examined – and apprehension about the consequences of this is perfectly natural. Instead of fretting about it, turn it to your advantage, by recognising that being nervous helps provide both the motivation to study harder and a surge of adrenalin that is the body's way of helping you raise your game on the day.

Always try to think positively about your exams

Negativity can result in a spiral of gloom that reduces motivation. Time spent worrying is time wasted – instead, use it to your advantage by tackling the work. It's vitally important to believe that you can achieve something – and this carries through right to the very end of the exam. The last fact you learn and the last point you put down on paper might be the one that ensures you pass or takes you into a higher grade band.

PANIC DUE TO LACK OF PREPARATION

Feeling ill-prepared is probably the most common reason for being nervous about exams. Many a student has experienced the sensation of panic that comes when they realise that they have probably not done enough studying during the year – and that the time remaining for cramming has become very short. When this applies to you, make a resolution to space out your workload next time round, then determinedly try to maximise your return on the time remaining. If you apply yourself to the task with a positive attitude, and are willing to work hard, you will be able to achieve quite a lot in a short time. The following tips may help.

- When time is limited, effective use of it is vital. Create a revision timetable that helps you optimise your activities (**Ch 60**). Stick to it rigidly. Reduce all sporting and social events to a bare minimum and cut down on any employment you have taken on.

- Over brief periods, you can stretch your working hours – for example, setting an early alarm isn't something you might normally think of doing, but this can easily add an hour or two to each day.

✔ **Don't forget to exercise during the revision period**

Although you need to find as much time as possible for revision, don't reduce your exercise routine to zero. Besides being one of the best ways of reducing stress, exercise helps you maintain a good sleep pattern. Even a brisk walk can reinvigorate your mind.

- Spend some time with others in your class to exchange ideas about what's worth studying and to obtain quick answers to minor problems with coursework.

- Be strategic in your work and approach to the exam by following these steps:
  - Without taking 'question spotting' to extremes (see page 398), study so that you maximise the return on the time put in. Use a highlighter to pinpoint critical learning objectives from the course handbook.
  - Now make sure you have the framework and basic understanding to begin an answer on each of these topics.
  - Next, focus on the key facts you must remember.
  - Finally, and only if you have time, get into the detail and examples.

- Exploit the time remaining as much as possible, by adopting active revision techniques (**Ch 61**) and using normally 'redundant' time effectively. For example, try to do small chunks of revision when commuting or in the time between lectures – this all adds up.

✔ **Speed reading and skimming**

The tips presented in **Ch 25** can help you lift the essence from a text or set of notes in the minimum time.

PERFECTIONISM AS A SOURCE OF ANXIETY

Exams, with their tight time limits and tough marking criteria, are especially stressful for perfectionists. To counteract this tendency, focus on the following points before, during and after the exam:

- Don't go into an exam expecting to produce a perfect series of answers – recognise that this simply won't be possible in the limited time available.

- Don't spend too long planning your answer – for example, as soon as you have an outline essay plan, get started.

- Don't spend too much time on the initial parts of an answer, especially the first sentence, at the expense of the main message.

- Concentrate first on getting all the basics across – markers are looking for the main points first, before allocating extra marks for the detail. You may wish to rehearse these at the start of your answer as insurance against running out of time.

- Don't be obsessed with neatness, either in handwriting or in the diagrams you draw – but make sure your answers are legible.

- Don't worry if you've forgotten a particular detail or fact. You can't be expected to know everything. Most marking schemes give a first-class grade to work that misses out on up to 30 per cent of the marks available.

- After each exam in a series, avoid prolonged analyses with other students over the 'ideal' answers to the questions; after all, it is too late to change anything at this stage. Put all your mental energy into preparing for the next exam, so that you are ready to face that challenge with confidence.

PERFORMING UNDER PRESSURE

First, recognise that exams are to some extent a test of your ability to perform under pressure, and accept the challenge laid down by the system. To do this, you need to be well prepared and particularly to have practised. If you've done well in the past, draw confidence from this. Self-tests and mock exams (**Ch 61, 65**) are a good way of getting into the right frame of mind. They'll teach you much about the format and timing of the exam, and help you develop good habits.

Exams represent artificial situations contrived to ensure that large numbers of candidates can be assessed together with little risk of cheating. There is a lot to be said for treating them like a game. If you understand the rationale behind them, and adapt to their conventions and rules, this will aid your performance.

Mind gone a complete blank?

We all face this from time to time and also realise that the key to remembering a fact, date or name is often to think of something else. So, leave a blank space in your answer paper and come back to it later. Alternatively, if you can't see any way to answer a whole question, try one of the following:

- Brainstorm connections from things you *do* know about the subject.

- Work from basics, such as natural subdivisions of the topic (for example, hierarchical levels, such as parts of the body).

- As yourself 'Who? What? When? Where? Why? How?' in relation to the key subject matter (**Ch 32** on page 204).

- Think diagrammatically: base your brainstorm on doodles and images – this may open up different thought patterns.

- Search for associations: read through the other questions in the paper – they may trigger your memory.

- Get on with other questions if you can – the subject material might trigger your memory on others that are proving to be stumbling blocks.

PRACTICAL TIPS FOR COMBATING THE SYMPTOMS OF EXAM ANXIETY

Sleeplessness. This is commonplace and does little harm in the short term. Get up, have a snack, do some light reading or other work, then return to bed. Avoid caffeine (for example tea, coffee and cola) for several hours before going to bed.

Lack of appetite/upset tummy. Again, these symptoms are common. Eat what you can, but take sugary sweets into the exam (and/or drinks, if allowed) to keep your energy levels up. If allowed, take some water to avoid dehydration.

Fear of the unknown. Confirm dates and times of exams. Go through your pre-exam checklist (**Ch 66**). Check any paperwork you have been given regarding the format and timing of the exam. Take a mascot or lucky charm with you if this helps. In extreme cases, it might be a good idea to visit the exam room, so you can become familiar with the location.

Worries about timekeeping. Get a reliable alarm clock or a new battery for an old one. Arrange for an alarm phone call. Ask a friend or relative to make sure you are awake on time. Make reliable travel arrangements, so that you arrive early.

Blind panic during an exam. To reduce the symptoms, try doing some relaxation exercises (see below) and then return to your paper. If you still feel bad, explain how you feel to an invigilator. Ask to go for a supervised walk outside if this might help. If you have problems with the wording of a specific question, ask to speak to the departmental representative at the exam (if they have left the room, they can be phoned).

Feeling tense. Shut your eyes, take several deep breaths, do some stretching and relaxing muscle movements. During exams, it may be a good idea to do this between questions, and possibly to have a complete rest for a few seconds or so. Prior to exams, try some exercise activity, or escape temporarily from your worries by watching a movie.

Running out of time. Try not to panic when the invigilator says 'Five minutes left'. It is amazing how much you can write in that amount of time. Write note-style answers or state the areas you would have covered: you may get some credit. Keep writing until the invigilators insist that you stop.

Needing a toilet break. Don't become anxious or embarrassed about the need for a toilet break in the exam. Put up your hand and ask to go out. Your concentration will improve afterwards and the walk there and back will allow you to refocus your thoughts.

Think positively. You can do this!

68

PLANNING FOR A CAREER

How to focus on your future

> The sooner you start planning for your future career, the better. Finding out which occupations might suit your personality and anticipated qualifications will help you to focus your studies and choose appropriate vacation work, so that you can develop an effective curriculum vitae.

Thinking in detail about a future career is something most students may be tempted to put off for another day. Most careers advisers would say that this outlook is misguided.

If you are studying a subject that leads to a number of potential graduate careers, but no specific occupation, you may be tempted to delay your decision until you see exactly what qualification you obtain and what the job market looks like when you graduate. However, exploring possible career routes at an early stage will provide you with a better idea of the range of options you should be considering. It will also help you to make curriculum-related decisions that will place you in a better position to apply successfully for suitable jobs.

If you are studying for a degree that is a professional qualification, or your chosen discipline has a clear vocational aim, you may feel that you have made the most important decisions already. However, even for professional and vocational graduates, there are important choices to be made about which specialism you will target.

WHAT CAREER PLANNING INVOLVES

For an undergraduate student, this involves:

- clear thinking about your long-term goals and aspirations;
- looking at potential occupations and how they fit your personality and qualifications;
- researching your options, and finding out where the best opportunities lie.

You've then got to seek out suitable posts and apply successfully for one (**Ch 71**). Once on the first rung of a career, the process does not stop; then you need to gain experience and continue your professional development.

The first step in career planning is, therefore, to think about your goals and aspirations. Where would you like to be, both work-wise and in your private life, in 10 or 15 years? What would you like to have achieved? Some students will have a very firm view of this. Others, probably the majority, will be hazy about their future. If you are in this second group, the answers you give to the following questions might help you to narrow down your options.

● Would you like to earn a high salary, and are you comfortable with the commitment, work rate, competition and responsibility this might entail?

● Would you like to have lots of options within your career, either through possibilities for developing different career paths with your original employer, or by using your initial job as a springboard to different posts with other employers?

● Would you like your occupation to have a caring or ethical dimension, even if this might mean sacrifices in terms of pay and conditions?

● Would you rule out some work areas for ethical or other reasons?

● Would you like to work as part of a team, or would you relish having autonomy and freedom in your work?

● Would you like a career that eventually gives you power and influence?

● Would you like a long-lived, secure career that may offer lower reward, as opposed to taking a gamble on a shorter-lived, more highly rewarded position and trusting that things will work out in the end?

● Would you like your career to reflect the subjects you have studied at university?

● Would you like to continue your studies at a higher level, hoping to be appointed to a higher-level post, even though this may narrow your options and delay entry into the workplace?

The answers you give to these questions will reflect underlying aspects of your character that you may not have thought deeply about, but which you can investigate further through diagnostic careers-related personality tests. There are a number of these; your careers service may recommend a particular selection and you can find many online (see below). These tests generally aim to provide an objective analysis of your attitude to employment and then present a number of occupations for you to consider.

✔ **Online personality tests related to occupations**

There are many tests on the Web, some of which are paid-for services. Try two free examples before going further:

■ Career Planner: **www.careerplanner.com**

■ BBC careers test: **www.bbc.co.uk/science/humanbody/mind/surveys/careers/index.shtml**

You are advised to discuss the results with a careers adviser, who may be able to point you to other tests.

Another way of finding out about possible occupations is to explore the normal employment destinations for graduates in your subject. You may find that your department or university careers service is able to supply this information. If your degree leads to a professional qualification, you will probably find that the relevant professional body has a website that explains the options open to graduates.

You will need to bear in mind the supply and demand aspect of employment. For example, a scarcity of graduate applicants in one speciality can lead to enhanced pay and conditions, which then attracts students to the area, with consequent oversupply. Also, global and national economic conditions can have a profound effect on job availability. This means you should try not to pin all your hopes on one occupation, and should keep other possibilities in mind.

Some occupations may require further qualifications (for example, being a practising lawyer) and you may choose to continue with postgraduate studies before moving into a career. Your careers service is probably a good place to ask about options; in addition, ask your tutors, as they may be able to recommend courses and institutions for you to investigate. Studying for a higher degree normally requires that you achieve a certain standard of qualification (Ch 46), so you should probably explore this option alongside other possibilities so that you have a fall-back plan.

Studying for a higher degree **✔**

If you want to move without delay into a postgraduate course, you will need to explore possibilities well in advance of your expected graduation, since the closing dates for applications will typically be three to six months in advance of this.

What is 'Graduate Prospects'? **?**

Although this is technically a limited company, it is run for and on behalf of university careers services throughout the UK. It is therefore in a good position to offer impartial advice, and its websites and other resources are extremely useful. You may need to register online to gain access to some facilities.

Apart from salary scales, the following are aspects you should explore:

- Support for continuing professional development (CPD).
- Career progression – how you can move within the organisation, and how quickly you can expect to be promoted.
- Pension conditions.
- Location, and whether you will be expected to move around as part of your training.
- Relocation expenses.
- Security of position (for example, notice period).
- Perks, such as share ownership or profit-sharing schemes, company car, private medical care and health-club membership.
- The long-term prospects for the company and field of work.

FINDING OUT ABOUT DIFFERENT OCCUPATIONS

Having found some career routes that suit your personality, expected qualification and inclination, you should now find out more about each possibility. The first stage in this process is to carry out a general investigation, sifting through your options to find a shortlist to explore in more detail. This may involve:

- **Obtaining impartial information.** You can find this from, for example, the Graduate Prospects website. You will probably be interested in salary scales, options for progression and working conditions (see above). You should also try to find out precisely what minimum qualifications are expected and what skills and qualities will place you in a better position to succeed with an application. If you have a particular company or employment sector in mind, you can find out about its business and economic prospects from websites allied to share dealing and investment.

- **Reading companies' literature.** You can obtain this at your careers service, at careers fairs, or by writing to or emailing the personnel or human resources department of the firm. When you receive this information, always bear in mind that the company has an interest in presenting itself in the best light.

Having narrowed down your options, the next phase is to find out about specific jobs in reality. This is less easy to do, but your options include:

- **Speaking to someone already in the position.** This could be a friend of your parents, or someone you have met socially or at job fairs or on site visits.

- **Contacting a specific company.** You might, for example, write to or email the personnel or human resources department with any queries.

- **Gaining first-hand experience.** Try to obtain summer work or a job placement in a relevant position. Some companies offer internships and job-shadowing schemes designed for just this purpose, and they will be just as interested in finding out about you as you are in finding out about them.

CREATING AN ACTION PLAN

Having considered your long-term goals and aspirations, and looked into potential destinations, it's time to switch to the shorter-term picture. Here, you need to project forward to the application you could be making for a suitable job (**Ch 71**). Choices you make as an undergraduate can allow you to accumulate experience, skills and knowledge and enhance your employability. Relevant information can be presented in your CV and covering letter as appropriate to a position.

- **What sort of a degree will you need to bring about your ambition?** Assuming your programme of study allows you options, you may wish to consider:
  - your future module choices, so that the skills and knowledge you gain are well matched to your career aspirations;
  - the precise type of degree that you opt for (for example, joint honours or a particular named honours degree), if this might influence your chances;
  - the nature of project work or job placements you choose;
  - how hard you work to obtain the degree classification that may be required as a minimum qualification.
- **What experience might it be valuable to obtain in vacation or term-time employment?** This experience could be direct, if you are lucky enough to obtain a relevant internship, but it could also be indirect, such as a sales position that allows you to demonstrate that you can interact well with customers or clients.

Open or confidential references

Your vacation employer may be willing to act as one your referees (**Ch 71**) by providing a confidential reference; some are happy to provide an 'open' reference letter for you.

- **What skills and personal qualities will be relevant?** As well as your qualifications, employers will be interested in your personal qualities and in the examples or evidence you can provide to show that you have the skills and qualities they are looking for (**Ch 69**). You may wish to look into extra-curricular activities that could assist you to provide such evidence. Bear in mind that your experience and personal qualities can and should be supported by references from those who employ you. Before you leave any position, ask those who might be suitable whether they would be willing to act as one of your referees.

All these thoughts should put you in a good position to create an action plan. This should contain specific tasks (for example, contact the personnel department of Bloggs Plc to ask about vacation work; volunteer for a responsible position in your favourite sports club), and dates by which you hope to achieve them (end of the term or semester; at the annual general meeting).

> ✔ **Completing your career action plan**
>
> While the point of an action plan is indeed to be able to tick off the items on it, do not worry if you cannot achieve this in all cases. You should recognise that the process of thinking through and creating a plan can be just as important as carrying it out.

🔧 PRACTICAL TIPS FOR CAREER PLANNING

Investigate career options, even if you are studying for a vocational degree. Careers in professions like Law and Medicine offer many different options and specialities. If you are studying for a degree like these, you need to be just as clued up about these possibilities as if you were studying for a non-vocational degree and looking at a wide range of potential graduate occupations.

Use your personal development plan (PDP) process to help you map out your potential career. While the nature of PDP will differ depending on where you are studying, at its heart this process helps you analyse your goals and plan your future, so it overlaps greatly with the career planning process (**Ch 7**).

Keep your CV up to date. A professionally presented CV will always be required when you apply for a post, and it is time-consuming to produce this from scratch. Also, it is easy to forget the fine detail that you will need to include in it. While the advice given in **Ch 62** is to tailor your CV for every position you apply for, you will find this process easier if you have a generic version to hand that includes all relevant details. Drafting a CV will put you in a better position to view yourself as a potential employer would, which may help you plan activities to enhance your profile.

Seek opportunities to discuss possible occupations. As noted above, this can help you find out whether a particular occupation might be for you. However, you cannot expect people to come to you to talk about these matters; you will probably need to be proactive in obtaining contacts and asking for a word with them. Most will be willing to spare you a few minutes, but make sure you have some focused questions prepared, so you don't waste the opportunity.

69

ASSESSING YOURSELF

How to evaluate your skills, qualities, motivations and values

> Moving on from the university experience and fulfilling your professional ambitions are challenging and exciting steps. You need to think about what you have to offer to an employer. What skills do you bring with you? What marks you out as an individual? What makes you tick? You need to think about the abilities, traits, motivations and values that distinguish you as a person. In other words, you need to know yourself before you can hope to convince an employer that you are their ideal candidate.

When employers seek to fill a post by recruiting a university graduate, they tend to assume that applicants come with certain assets that distinguish them from non-graduates. Their main preoccupation lies with the job that needs to be done and appointing the candidate who is best suited to fulfil the role. Your degree is testimony to your academic ability; however, the knowledge base of your degree may be of less interest to employers than the personal qualities that you will bring to the job.

The experience of university will have influenced your personal development, especially the innate qualities and practical skills that make you unique. This is encompassed in the 'graduateness' that employers seek. In order to identify your graduate characteristics, your first challenge is to take a frank look at who you are, what your skills are and what qualities you possess.

The aim of this chapter is to help you to evaluate these qualities. Other parts of this book deal with:

- the transferability of skills and the notions of graduateness and employability (**Ch 6, Ch 68**);
- how you might record and reflect upon your developing qualities and skills as part of personal development planning (**Ch 7**);
- how qualities and skills can be communicated to an employer as part of your curriculum vitae and job application (**Ch 70, Ch 71**).

---

i

Definition: graduateness

Authorities disagree about this term and some even dispute whether there is value in defining it beyond 'having a university degree'. The concept certainly goes further than possessing transferable skills, and may involve having subject-related knowledge; the capability to manage tasks and solve problems; being able to communicate well; the ability to work with others; and having self-awareness.

ASSESSING YOUR SKILLS AND PERSONAL QUALITIES

Skills and qualities are often confused and the boundary between them can be imprecise.

- **Skills** are things you can do and are sometimes called competences. They can often be learned from scratch and improve as you become more experienced (**Ch 6**).
- **Personal qualities** are innate to you – traits that you are born with and are a reflection of your personality. These natural aptitudes adapt and develop as you gain experience. Your learning style (**Ch 13**) also reflects your personal qualities.

> ### Examples: skills and personal qualities
>
> **An example of a skill:** the ability to organise and deliver effective spoken presentations.
> **Examples of personal qualities:** integrity and patience.

To some extent, your individual traits set limits on the skills you can gain. For example, you may not be able to become technically proficient at any manual skill if you lack the personal quality of dexterity. It's easy to take your personal qualities and skills for granted. You may not regard some of your talents as anything remarkable if you see them only in one context – your studies or social life – and do not yet appreciate their potential relevance in the workplace.

Spending some time reflecting on your personal qualities and skills enables you to:

- identify examples of the skills employers may want;
- examine your strengths and weaknesses;
- reflect on what you have done to date – this will include your university career so far, as well as things you do outside university, for example part-time work or a leisure activity;
- think about and then rehearse how you might present and give examples of these traits and skills at interview;
- use this information to construct and develop your CV.

> ### Demonstrating your skills and personality traits
>
> - If you said that you were well skilled in giving spoken presentations, you might mention (and show) a PowerPoint presentation that you used to explain an honours project. Your referees might wish to describe the high quality of this presentation in any reference they were asked to provide.
> - If you describe yourself as trustworthy, an example to show this might come from acting as a treasurer of a voluntary organisation. Your referees may be able to confirm your honesty and trustworthiness.

No individual can be good at everything. Think about things that you know you are good at, for example working with others or your determination to do things as well as you can. Then, being honest with yourself, acknowledge those things that are your least strong traits and think about how you may need to work on those to make them less disadvantageous.

For example, if you are untidy or poor at organising your time or not particularly good at critical thinking, consider practical ways to improve. It's also valuable to remember that sometimes strengths have complementary weaknesses, and vice versa. This is evident, for example, in the parts people play in teams (Ch 19).

Complete Table 69.1 to evaluate your skills and Table 69.2 to assess your personal qualities. This will help you to think about what examples you could provide to demonstrate these dimensions of your personality, aptitudes and capabilities.

Table 69.1 Assessing your skills. Using the list below, draw an arrow on the appropriate side of the central column to indicate your personal rating of your skills. Ignore any categories that do not seem relevant to your degree, intended career or current stage of study, and add new categories where this would be relevant. If you aren't sure what something means, look it up in a dictionary – these terms might be valuable to understand for applications and interviews. Use different coloured arrows at a later time to see how your skills profile has changed.

Weaker ←	PERSONAL RATING	Stronger →
Could improve . . . . . . OK	**Skill and (relevant chapters)**	**Good . . . . . . Very competent**
	Analysing problems and tasks **Ch 33, Ch 34**	
	Career and entrepreneurial skills **Ch 9, Ch 68–Ch 71**	
	Critical thinking **Ch 22**	
	Contributing in meetings **Ch 18, Ch 19**	
	Communicating in a foreign language	
	Dealing with data **Ch 29, Ch 30**	
	Designing experiments/surveys **Ch 20**	
	Discussing and debating **Ch 18, Ch 19, Ch 21, Ch 49**	
	Exam-sitting **Ch 60–Ch 67**	
	Financial management **Ch 9**	
	ICT – general computing skills **Ch 27**	
	ICT – PowerPoint **Ch 27, Ch 57**	
	ICT – spreadsheets **Ch 27, Ch 30**	
	ICT – using the Web **Ch 24, Ch 27, Ch 28**	
	ICT – word-processing **Ch 27, Ch 33**	
	Information analysis **Ch 24, Ch 26**	
	Information retrieval **Ch 23, Ch 26**	
	Laboratory skills **Ch 20**	
	Listening to others **Ch 16, Ch 19, Ch 21, Ch 58**	

continued overleaf

Table 69.1 (*cont'd*)

Weaker ← Could improve . . . . . . OK	Skill and (relevant chapters)	Good . . . . . . Very competent → Stronger
	Logical approach to problems **Ch 7, Ch 22, Ch 34**	
	Negotiating skills **Ch 19**	
	Note-taking **Ch 17, Ch 26**	
	Numeracy – maths **Ch 29, Ch 31**	
	Numeracy – specific maths skills **Ch 29–Ch 31**	
	Numeracy – statistics **Ch 30**	
	Performance under assessment **Ch 45–Ch 50**	
	Performance under stress **Ch 67**	
	Planning your work **Ch 7, Ch 8, Ch 34, Ch 60**	
	Preparing a poster **Ch 56**	
	Project management	
	Reading for academic purposes **Ch 25, Ch 26**	
	Report writing **Ch 54**	
	Study and revision skills **Ch 14, Ch 17, Ch 26, Ch 60–Ch 64**	
	Social skills **Ch 11**	
	Speaking in public **Ch 54**	
	Teamwork **Ch 18, Ch 19**	
	Thesis or dissertation writing **Ch 55**	
	Time management **Ch 8, Ch 20, Ch 60**	
	Using library resources **Ch 23**	
	Writing – citing sources **Ch 35**	
	Writing essays and reports **Ch 48, Ch 54, Ch 55**	
	Writing letters, memos and emails **Ch 27, Ch 34**	
	Writing – organising and presenting **Ch 33–Ch 35, Ch 37, Ch 38, Ch 44**	
	Writing – use of English **Ch 38–Ch 43**	
	Other (specify)	

Table 69.2 Assessing your personal qualities. Using the list below, give yourself a mark out of five in the 'rating' column, being appropriately self-critical. You might like to ask a friend or a family member for their opinion too. Circle the relevant number, where 1 = not a strength, 3 = well developed and 5 = very highly developed. Ignore any categories that do not seem relevant to you and add new categories where this is relevant. If you aren't sure what something means, look it up – these terms might be valuable to understand for applications and interviews.

My personal qualities	Rating	My personal qualities	Rating
Adaptability	1 | 2 | 3 | 4 | 5	Personal fitness and health	1 | 2 | 3 | 4 | 5
Crisis management	1 | 2 | 3 | 4 | 5	Proactive approach	1 | 2 | 3 | 4 | 5
Determination	1 | 2 | 3 | 4 | 5	Seeing others' viewpoints	1 | 2 | 3 | 4 | 5
Energy	1 | 2 | 3 | 4 | 5	Self-discipline	1 | 2 | 3 | 4 | 5
Enthusiasm	1 | 2 | 3 | 4 | 5	Sense of purpose	1 | 2 | 3 | 4 | 5
Flexibility	1 | 2 | 3 | 4 | 5	Staying power/tenacity	1 | 2 | 3 | 4 | 5
Honesty	1 | 2 | 3 | 4 | 5	Taking the initiative	1 | 2 | 3 | 4 | 5
Innovation	1 | 2 | 3 | 4 | 5	Thoroughness	1 | 2 | 3 | 4 | 5
Integrity	1 | 2 | 3 | 4 | 5	Tolerance	1 | 2 | 3 | 4 | 5
Leadership	1 | 2 | 3 | 4 | 5	Rising to challenges	1 | 2 | 3 | 4 | 5
Motivation	1 | 2 | 3 | 4 | 5	Other (specify)	1 | 2 | 3 | 4 | 5
Patience	1 | 2 | 3 | 4 | 5	Other (specify)	1 | 2 | 3 | 4 | 5
Perseverance	1 | 2 | 3 | 4 | 5	Other (specify)	1 | 2 | 3 | 4 | 5

Your CV should reflect the fact that you recognise that you have particular qualities and skills. While the essential elements of your CV will probably not change for each job for which you apply, ideally, you should adjust your 'core version' CV in small ways to fit the requirements of the post, by highlighting appropriate traits and capabilities. Where space permits, you may wish to provide examples that demonstrate that you have been able to use these to good effect.

Table 69.3 shows how some of the academic skills that you develop on the way to your degree can transfer to professional situations.

Applying skills from university and beyond

If you are asked to conduct a critical review of a research paper as part of a study exercise, you will need to uncover the meaning of key words and trace other related work by the same author. In doing all this, you will have developed important information-gathering and critical-thinking skills that you will be able to apply elsewhere. However, extra-curricular activities, for example those gained through the Duke of Edinburgh's Award scheme, playing as a member of a sports team or performing supervisory responsibilities in your part-time job, can also be used to indicate your 'staying power', motivation, self-discipline, team-playing and leadership skills.

Table 69.3 How university academic skills transfer to the professional context. Note the emphasis on team and group activity in the work example. There are moves to include more groupwork activity at university, but it is harder for you to be assessed as an individual in these situations.

Nature of activity	Academic activity	Example of related professional activity	Nature of activity
Solo	Listening to lectures	Listening to professional presentations	Solo
Solo	Note-taking from lectures	Taking minutes of a meeting	Solo
Solo	Reading academic texts	Reading reports, professional papers and technical manuals	Solo
Solo	Note-making from texts	Synthesising information for dissemination to colleagues, often in collaboration with others	Solo/group/team
Solo/Group/Team	Researching material for assignments/presentations/examination	Researching material for company documentation/presentations	Solo/group/team
Solo	Planning writing assignments	Planning writing assignments and other duties	Solo/group/team
Solo	Writing assignments – essays, reports, case studies, projects and posters – following academic conventions	Writing briefing papers, publicity material, correspondence, reports for internal and external distribution – following the 'house' style	Solo/group/team
Group/Team	Preparing for, attending and participating in tutorials or laboratory practicals – following conventions of open discussion or safety regulations	Preparing for, attending and participating in meetings or briefings – following formal conventions of meetings and briefings, and using appropriate forms of speech	Group/team
Solo	Preparing for, attending and taking examinations, either on paper or orally	Preparing for interviews, and meetings with representatives of other organisations, clients and colleagues	Solo/team

SUMMARISING YOUR INTERESTS, MOTIVATIONS AND VALUES

One of the hardest things in life is to understand what your personal interests, motivations and values are. What drives or motivates you? What do you consider to be just and right? If you can assess your stance on these things, it can lead to satisfaction in both your private life and your career. University offers you 'space' to explore all sorts of ideas and activities. Some you will accept; others you will reject. These experiences will shape your interests, motivations and value systems.

Interests

In this context, these are the things that you enjoy doing outside your formal academic course (sometimes referred to as your 'extra-curricular activities'). Examples might include leisure pursuits such as playing or watching a team sport, listening to music, or some form of creative pastime such as oil painting. Interests may have guided your choice of degree. Someone who likes keeping pet animals might choose to study veterinary science or zoology, for example. Interests that have, or might have, a direct bearing on a potential career are known as occupational interests. You might discover both the talent and desire to become a journalist, for example, through helping to produce a student newspaper or community newsletter.

Categories of interests

It may help when summarising your interests to think of them under the main categories normally applied:

- artistic
- literary
- practical, conservationist and scientific
- social and interpersonal
- problem-solving
- enterprise-related.

Motivations

These involve a complex set of concepts that are closely tied to your personality. They include internal feelings that energise, direct and sustain your behaviour, and they contribute to the values that you embrace. Taken collectively, motivations are what 'make you tick' and make you behave in a particular way. When you feel motivated in your studies or work, you have the sense that what you are doing is something to which you are happy to devote time and effort.

Motivation and ambition

Employers often state that they wish to appoint a 'highly motivated individual' to a position. By this, they mean someone with energy and ambition. Such individuals will characteristically have a high work rate, be a dynamic colleague, and can channel or marry their personal drive to fit with the goals of the employer. Note that this aspect of motivation differs somewhat from the one discussed above.

Examples of factors that might motivate someone to choose a particular career path include: rewards – financial and material; altruism – the desire to help others; a wish to interact with people; and a need for security and stability.

Values

These reflect our sense of what is moral or ethical and are fundamental to many people. Thus, if you hold pacifist views you might not consider employment in the defence industry; if you have strong views on the environment, you may choose to take a lower-paid job that promotes conservation, rather than a higher-paid one where the core activity pollutes the environment or consumes excessive natural resources. You need to recognise your personal values so that you are aware of occasions where these may be compromised in your work, for example where, as a lawyer or social worker, you might be placed in the position of defending or supporting someone who has committed a serious crime.

Table 69.4 will help you to examine your interests, motivations and values.

✔ **Getting a second opinion**

To put your attributes and achievements in perspective, it is sometimes helpful to seek a second opinion, perhaps from a tutor or careers adviser. This can help you to achieve a balance between underestimating yourself and overselling yourself.

Table 69.4 A simple aid for recording your interests, motivations and values. In section A, use the categories as a prompt to help you think of different activities and pastimes that interest you and write these down in the spaces provided. In section B, make a personal assessment of your work-related motivations and values, rating them from 1 (not important to me), through 3 (I'm doubtful about this) to 5 (very important to me).

A My interests	B My motivations and values	
Artistic:	1 | 2 | 3 | 4 | 5	Prospects for advancement: promotion; career progression
	1 | 2 | 3 | 4 | 5	Environmental issues: work that enhances the environment
Literary:	1 | 2 | 3 | 4 | 5	Altruism: helping others; caring for the needy
	1 | 2 | 3 | 4 | 5	Independence: ability to make decisions; freedom of action
Practical – creative:	1 | 2 | 3 | 4 | 5	Desire to lead: wish for power and responsibility
	1 | 2 | 3 | 4 | 5	Material benefits: high salary; property; good standard of living
Practical – nature/conservation:		
Practical – scientific/technical:	1 | 2 | 3 | 4 | 5	Prestige: having achievements recognised; being influential
	1 | 2 | 3 | 4 | 5	Risk and excitement: need to take chances; opportunity to speculate
Social and interpersonal:	1 | 2 | 3 | 4 | 5	Security: continuity of employment; recognised structure of work
Problem-solving:	1 | 2 | 3 | 4 | 5	Team membership: stimulus from working with others
Enterprise-related:	1 | 2 | 3 | 4 | 5	Variety: change and diversity in tasks, people and places
	1 | 2 | 3 | 4 | 5	Other (specify):

PRACTICAL TIPS FOR EVALUATING SKILLS, QUALITIES, MOTIVATIONS AND VALUES

Recognise your strengths and play to them. Once you have a picture of your strengths, including those not measured in prizes and high marks but in 'softer' aspects such as patience, understanding and interpersonal skills, then explore ways to make the most of them, whether in curriculum choices, extra-curricular activities, or when researching possible occupations that might suit you.

Recognise your weak areas and develop strategies to counter them. Make a determined effort to overcome these frailties. For example, face up to your shyness by acknowledging that it's not the end of the world if you fluff a line in a presentation – just do your best and you may surprise yourself. Try to think positively rather than negatively about yourself, so that your concern about your weaknesses does not become a self-fulfilling prophecy.

Match your personality to occupations or branches of an occupation. If you are undecided about your career path, you may wish to explore the match between different types of work and your personal traits and likely qualification. This is best done with the expert advice of a careers specialist, and probably as soon as possible in your time at university. Even if you are studying for a vocational degree, it is worth researching the different branches of the job, to see if your degree choices, such as selection of an honours project or dissertation subject, vacation employment or extra-curricular activities, might assist you to make a decision or help you get on the first step of the career ladder.

Aim for progression. University is a unique experience and you will not leave higher education as the same person who started out. If you evaluate yourself using the information in Tables 69.1–69.3 at an early stage in your university career, you might like to list your characteristics on paper and put this away safely, perhaps with official certificates and papers. When you come to construct your CV for your first professional job application, you may find it valuable to look at this list again and analyse ways in which you have changed.

Think about examples and evidence. When you feel you possess a particular strength, and have recorded this in Tables 69.1–69.3, consider what example(s) or evidence you might show to a potential employer to demonstrate this.

70

YOUR CURRICULUM VITAE

How to describe yourself to potential employers

> A curriculum vitae (CV) is a standard mechanism for communicating to a potential employer who you are and what skills and qualities you have to offer. Your chances of reaching the interview stages of a job application may depend on its contents and presentation, so it is vital to construct it carefully so that you give a good impression.

The principal aim of a CV is to communicate, in brief, the qualifications, experience and skills you have that might suit you for a job. It's important to realise that your CV may be one of many that a potential employer will scan, and that you may only have a few moments of their attention to make a favourable impression. The quality of this document and of the accompanying application letter and personal statement are therefore vital for successful job-hunting.

Definition: curriculum vitae

Curriculum vitae is a Latin phrase meaning 'the course your life has taken' and is often shortened to CV (pronounced '*see vee*'). It is a written summary of your career history and achievements to date. Some sources, particularly, from North America, may refer to the term *résumé*. This is generally a shorter version of the UK CV, focusing on elements directly related to a specific position.

WHAT RECRUITERS ARE LOOKING FOR IN A CV

Typically, a recruiter will use the following criteria to evaluate your CV:

- **Good presentation.** They will want to see a clear layout that makes it easy to find the information they need, plus indications that you can express yourself fluently and have some design flair.
- **Relevance.** They will expect to see from the content that you would be a good fit to the job description. They'll need sufficient detail to determine this, but at the same time not too many facts of doubtful relevance that might waste their time and call into doubt your ability to evaluate and filter information.
- **Lack of obvious mistakes.** They will not think highly of CVs containing spelling errors or grammatical mistakes (**Ch 39–Ch 41**). They will think you may bring such sloppiness to their job.

Don't give employers an excuse for rejecting you

A busy employer simply does not have the time to look deeply at your CV, and may have hundreds of similar applications to deal with. If your CV is difficult to read, or fails to inform about crucial details, or is ambiguous in any way, it will be rejected immediately.

- **Honesty.** They will demand full information and frankness about personal qualities and skills. If there is an obvious mismatch between your CV claims and your references, university transcript or interview performance, this will count severely against you.

- **Character.** They will want to see evidence that you would make an interesting and stimulating colleague. They will *not* want to see yet another clichéd CV produced by one of the common templates.

- **Added value.** They will hope that you have qualities and skills additional to the ones in the job description. Since there may be many applicants with similar qualifications, this may mark you out from the crowd.

- **Evidence and examples.** They will want some means of confirming that the claims you make are valid. This may come from your referees or university transcript, but you should also mention reports, talks or other things you have done. They may ask you about these at interview.

- **Completeness.** They will expect your CV to be right up to date. Also, they will look for periods where you do not appear to have been doing anything – and ask you about these at interview.

How frequently should I update my CV?

You should update a generic CV roughly twice a year – for example, after each semester or term should be sufficient. Your CV should also be updated and adapted for each job for which you apply.

STRUCTURE AND CONTENTS

Seven basic elements of a typical UK-style CV are described in Table 70.1. Most CVs will include all these sections, but you may choose to use different titles for the headings and to include appropriate amounts of information, as suits the job specification. Of course, because you are a unique person, the precise details will be your own.

Your CV should be brief and to the point and appropriately balanced. Aim for about two to three A4 pages.

Sometimes you will be expected to fill in a form instead of supplying a CV. This aids the initial screening of applicants and is common where an employer regularly takes on large numbers of graduate recruits. Where a format is specified by an employer, make sure you comply with it.

Table 70.1 Elements of a typical CV

Element, with *alternative headings*	Usual contents
1 Personal details *Name and contact details*	Your full name, date of birth, contact address(es), contact phone numbers and email address. You don't have to include your sex, but may wish to, especially if your name could apply to a man or a woman.
2 Profile *Career aim* *Career objective* *Personal profile*	A summary of your career plans. Also aspects of your goals and aspirations on which you would like the employer to focus.
3 Education *Qualifications* *Education and qualifications*	The qualifications you have already achieved, including those that may be pending. Most people put current qualifications first, then work backwards. State educational institutions, years of attendance and the academic year in which each qualification or set of qualifications was gained. Include more detail if it is relevant, e.g. aspects of a subject covered in courses.
4 Work experience *Employment*	Details of past and current work (both paid and voluntary). These should be arranged in reverse time sequence – from present to past. Include dates, employer's name and your job title. You may also wish to add major duties if these are not obvious from the job title.
5 Skills and personal qualities *Skills and achievements* *Skills and competences*	An indication of the match between your abilities and the job description. You may wish to refer to examples and evidence here. **Ch 69** should help you assess your strengths and weaknesses.
6 Interests and activities *Interests* *Leisure activities*	This is a chance to show your character, and perhaps to indicate that you would make an interesting and enthusiastic colleague. Employers will use this section to build a picture of you as a person; however, they may be put off by someone who appears quirky or bizarre in their eyes. Also if this section is overemphasised, they may assume that you have placed greater emphasis on your social life than on your studies. Highlight interests that display potentially valuable traits, e.g. sports activities that indicate you are a good team member.
7 Referees *References*	This is where you provide the names and contact details for those who have agreed to provide a reference for you. Further details about what's involved in selecting and communicating with your referees is provided in **Ch 71**.

PRESENTATION

First impressions count. The presentation of your CV is the first thing a potential employer notices. Aspects such as quality of paper and print are important, but the document's design and the clarity of wording will be the most important influences. As these will be taken as an indication of your character, you should think about them very carefully. This does *not* mean you need to have a conspicuous or adventurous design. Most employers are traditional by nature and would prefer that you adopt a broadly conventional pattern by demonstrating 'controlled originality'.

The reader needs to be able to find the information they want quickly, so the 'signposting' from headings should be especially clear. To give you the best chance of being considered for a post, the language used in your CV should be clear and unambiguous. The layout should be unfussy (e.g. with a minimum of font types) and readable (in a clear font, such as Times Roman or Arial and in a reasonable size such as 12 point). If you submit your CV electronically, in the accompanying communication, state the software version used.

Tips for CV presentation

There are no hard and fast rules, but the following may help:

- Don't try to cram too much into your CV – the reader can only absorb the key points. They can always ask you more if they select you for interview.
- Avoid long paragraphs in favour of bullet points, as these are assimilated more readily.
- Use 'white space' to spread out the information so that it is easy to read and the design is pleasing to the eye.
- Use a single font throughout and avoid overuse of emphasis such as capitals, italics and bold.
- Limited use of colour can look attractive, for instance in headings, and might mark your CV out from the rest. However, do not overuse colour or it will lessen the impact and give an unfocused feel. Remember that colours may appear in greyscale or even disappear if your CV is photocopied for interview panel members – and may in fact dull down your document rather than brighten it.

TAILORING YOUR CV

When using your CV to make an application for a job, tailor it to the job specification, so that it reflects your qualifications, experience, skills and personality.

You will often find a brief job description within the job advert or associated web-based material, or this may be provided as part of an application pack. For each position you should carry out a mapping exercise between the key elements of the job description and your own CV. This should take into account the following:

- The minimum qualifications and skills required. If you don't have these, it will probably not be worth applying.
- The specific experience, competences and qualities required. It's important to be able to identify evidence that shows that you have these.
- Anything beneficial you might add if you were appointed to the job, such as an IT skill gained in a particular module.
- Anything not stated in the job description, but implied, such as numeracy, or the ability to write or edit copy.

DEVELOPING YOUR CV

Your CV is not a static document and should be reviewed and updated as you acquire new qualifications and skills. At intervals, you should think about additions to your CV and also your plans for developing it (**Ch 7, Ch 68**). Especially if you are in your early years at university, and have a clear idea of your career path, it should be possible to identify activities that might be useful to take part in. Also, thinking in this way may influence your choice of course modules and/or degree options.

PRACTICAL TIPS FOR CONSTRUCTING AND DEVELOPING YOUR CV

Use all your experience, qualifications, sports and leisure activities to your benefit. These can provide evidence about personal qualities, such as leadership or trustworthiness. Refer to them factually at the appropriate points in the CV (Table 70.1) and mention them again in relation to personal qualities and skills, either in the specific section on this or in your personal statement or application letter.

Get a second opinion on your CV and application letter. Ask a trusted and critical friend or family member to look through every version of your CV that you produce to check for errors and to help you bring out the best in your submission. Your careers service may offer assistance with this, or you may wish to seek the advice of an academic adviser.

71

KICK-STARTING YOUR CAREER

How to find suitable job vacancies and apply for them

Taking your first step on to the career ladder is a major event in your life and no one approaches it lightly. This chapter outlines how to search for suitable job openings, how to compose a letter of application and personal statement, and how to approach an interview. This information should also help you obtain term-time and vacation employment.

This chapter describes how to find out about job vacancies and how to apply for them. It assumes you know the *type* of job you want. If this is not yet the case, see **Ch 68**.

FINDING JOB OPENINGS

Different types of job require different job-finding strategies. First, you should find out what the common recruitment practice is for the type of work you are considering. You can find out about this from:

- the Graduate Prospects website (**www.prospects.ac.uk**) and, in particular, the occupational profiles in its Prospects Planner section (also available from your careers service);
- paper-based occupational files held by your university's careers service;
- word of mouth from careers advisers, tutors, professional associations, employers or fellow students.

Active job hunting

Successful job hunters are not always the people with the highest qualifications or the most relevant skills or experience. They are sometimes the people who have taken most care to find out where to look for jobs and who apply for them effectively.

Typical stages of recruitment

It might help your job applications if you understand the sequence of events that lead up to an appointment:

1 The need for a new position is identified.
2 A job description is constructed.
3 Funding for salary and added costs is agreed.
4 An advert is placed with a job description, giving a closing date for applications.
5 Applicants submit CVs and application letters.
6 Applications are sorted and a shortlist is selected for interview.
7 Interviews take place and the successful applicant is offered the post.
8 After the successful candidate accepts, others are informed.

Advertised vacancies

Jobs tend to be advertised in specialist national newspapers and magazines, or through particular recruitment agencies. Increasingly, vacancies are advertised online on company and agency websites. Most employers advertise specific vacancies only as needs arise. However, if a company has a graduate recruitment scheme, this may be advertised up to a year in advance. You may find information about these schemes on departmental noticeboards.

Speak to someone already working in your chosen field

Asking people doing the kind of job you are looking for how they found theirs should help you to identify strategies that will work for you. Opportunities to do this could arise during vacation jobs, through family contacts, or by writing a letter to the human resources department of a firm.

Unadvertised job openings

Advertising is expensive, and recruiters try to save money if they feel they can. Hence, many jobs are never advertised, especially those in small firms within the private sector. Many graduates find jobs through contacts they have made themselves. A contact may not get you a specific job, but may be able to help you obtain an interview or point you in the right direction. This networking approach does not mean sending out hundreds of speculative applications in the hope that one will hit the mark. Instead, you should:

● identify the organisations and the right people within them to contact;
● decide on the questions you wish to ask and make direct contact either by telephone or letter;
● try to arrange a face-to-face meeting to follow up your initial contact.

APPLYING FOR JOBS AND OTHER OPPORTUNITIES

Recruiters do not recruit to make life easier for job-seeking applicants: they recruit to meet needs and solve problems in their own organisations. They must be convinced that the expense of your salary is likely to prove a better investment than spending the same money in another way. For this, they need to believe:

- you have whatever formal qualifications and experience that the job requires;
- you have and will use the personal qualities and skills the job requires;
- you view the job as an important end in itself and not merely a means to obtain a salary or associated training opportunities and benefits.

Successful applications result, first, from applying for positions for which you are a genuinely suitable applicant and, then, from demonstrating your suitability in an effective way. This means that you need to be watching for and creating opportunities to put across important messages about yourself. The following are important ways of demonstrating your suitability for a post:

- Tailoring your CV so that it makes it clear that you have the necessary qualifications and aptitude.

- Providing evidence, both within a CV and covering letter or personal statement, that demonstrates this.
- Taking advantage of the interview, should you be selected to a shortlist of applicants.

If the job description indicates that you need a particular qualification or standard of qualification, then, in a competitive situation, all applicants who do not meet this criterion will be disregarded immediately. Perhaps surprisingly, overqualified applicants will also be looked at with caution. Employers will feel that they may not be satisfied with the challenges of a job, or may move on quickly to one more suited to their talents.

> **i** **Applying for postgraduate research positions**
>
> Many of the points noted in this chapter for industry jobs are equally relevant for these.

Application forms

When dealing with an application form, you should take every opportunity to demonstrate that there is a good fit between the job description and your qualifications, experience, qualities and skills, as well as your career enthusiasms. Make sure you fill in the form neatly.

Application letters

Your letter of application provides an additional chance to impress a potential employer. As with your CV, it should be well presented and error-free. Use the normal format and style that you would for a formal business letter.

Your application letter should not be lengthy, but it should include:

- both the name of the position for which you are applying and any reference number that is given;
- the key qualifications, skills and qualities you feel you can offer;
- if possible, specific links between your CV and the job description;
- reference to your commitment and enthusiasm for the job;
- your career objectives and what you hope to gain from the job;
- your contact details.

Personal statements

For some posts, you will be asked to provide a personal statement, which is a chance to expand on some of the points noted above for a standard application letter. As with your CV and covering letter, a personal statement should be closely linked to the job for which you are applying. This is your chance to stand out from other, similarly qualified candidates.

If a format or content is suggested, follow this carefully and, in particular, answer as directly as possible any questions that are asked. Keep to any word limit that is specified. Even if no limit is stated, write concisely and present things so that they can be easily assimilated, for example, by using short paragraphs, headings and/or bullet points.

Selecting referees

When you apply for any job, you will be expected to nominate at least two referees – people who know you and can comment on your character and suitability for the position. They may also be expected to confirm some details of your CV. This is known as providing a reference. A typical reference might cover the following information;

- how long the referee has known you and in what capacity;
- an outline of your qualities and skills, as they have observed them in your studies or present job;
- your qualities and skills in relation to the job description for the post for which you have applied;
- comments on aspects of your character, such as general health, timekeeping and motivation;
- an opinion as to your suitability for the post.

When choosing referees, select people who genuinely know you, and who can comment on different aspects of your CV. Typically, a recent graduate would pick one referee who knows about their academic history, and one who can comment on their work experience.

You should contact your referees in advance to ask politely whether they would be willing to provide you with a reference; and at that time you could tell them about a specific position for which you have applied, or give them details of the sort of jobs for which you intend applying.

It is in your interest to provide your referees with an up-to-date CV, as this will help them provide an effective reference. It is also good manners to let them know whether your application(s) were successful.

PREPARING FOR INTERVIEW

It is hard enough to be shortlisted for a post, but many people find the subsequent interview stage even more of a challenge. As well as the fact that you will be expected to answer difficult and unseen questions, you will be nervous, because your chances of getting a coveted post may depend on your performance. There are various ways in which you can prepare before an interview.

- Carry out some research on the company and organisation, and the key figures on the interview panel, if you know who they are.
- Look again at the job description and think through concrete ways in which you can demonstrate the ability to carry out the duties of the post.
- If the post is professional or technical, revise relevant theory, techniques, practice and law.
- Note down questions you may have about the organisation and post.
- Ensure you can answer some of the more common interview questions (see above) and, where these appear tricky, evolve strategies for providing a positive slant to your answer.
- Think carefully about appropriate dress for the interview (smart but comfortable).

? **What will they ask me at interview?**

These are typical questions in an interview, although they may be wrapped in subtly different phrasing, or specifically related to the organisation and job description:

☐ What attracted you to this post?

☐ What makes you think you are the right person for this job?

☐ How did your degree and/or work experience prepare you for the challenges of this job?

☐ Please tell me about your experience doing X . . .

☐ Tell me about your interest in [a hobby or pastime] . . .

☐ What are your strengths?

☐ What are your weaknesses?

☐ What would you do if you held this post and the following scenario occurred . . . ?

☐ How do you see your career here evolving?

☐ Could you tell me about . . . [techniques, procedures or legislation related to the role]?

☐ When would you be able to take up the post, if offered it?

☐ Seemingly 'off-the-wall' questions, such as: 'Do you keep a tidy or untidy desk?'

☐ Would you accept the post if offered and if so, what salary are you looking for?

☐ Do you have any questions for us?

At the interview itself, focus on the following:

● When you are introduced to the panel, make eye contact with each member and smile at them.

● Where appropriate, give a firm, confident handshake.

● Adopt confident and relaxed body language and try not to fidget.

● Listen carefully to each question, think about it carefully, then address it precisely.

● Give informative answers of appropriate length – neither too short, nor too long; neither too shallow, nor too detailed.

● Speak clearly and to the person who asked the question, making occasional eye contact around the panel.

● Try to be positive about all questions and take all opportunities you can to mention relevant experiences.

● Be genuine, truthful and never waffle.

● Remember that the interview is a two-way process: have one or two questions ready at the end of the interview, when applicants are traditionally asked whether they would like to ask any questions.

Good luck!

The STAR approach during interviews

This strategy helps when you are asked questions about your response to past scenarios. Before the interview, think through examples of your experiences that highlight aspects of your personal qualities or skills that fit well with the requirements of the job in question. During the interview, when presenting these as examples or in answer to a specific question, use the STAR approach when responding:

1 **Situation** – give relevant background information, moving from the general to the specific.
2 **Task** – describe more specifically what you or your team had to do, and give details of your role.
3 **Action** – Explain what you did and how this required you to use your personal qualities or skills.
4 **Result** – give details of the results achieved and demonstrate their connection with your decisions and actions.

You should spend relatively more time on the 'action' and 'result' elements and relatively little on the 'situation' and 'task' parts. For example, think through how you could use this approach to highlight your ability to communicate; cope with stress; project management; honesty, leadership, self discipline, and other relevant qualities and skills from Tables 69.1 and 69.2.

Job offers

It is rare for a job offer to be made at an interview. Normally, you will be informed by post. Reasons for this may be:

- There may be a further set of interviews.
- The appointment committee may wish to discuss all the candidates in detail.
- Clearance may be required to confirm a salary offer.
- An appointment may depend on confirmation of your qualifications.
- The appointment committee may wish to send for your references and/or to check on aspects of your references.
- Some posts, such as those involving security and working with young people, may require that a disclosure statement is obtained about you, stating criminal convictions, if any. You should, however, prepare for the situation in which you *are* offered a job on the spot: for example, what are your salary expectations? What other aspects do you require further information on, like relocation assistance? Are you in a position to accept the offer and when could you start?

PRACTICAL TIPS FOR MAKING EFFECTIVE JOB APPLICATIONS

Use adverts, contacts and other information sources creatively. Even if you are not qualified for a particular vacancy, don't just pass over it. If it looks interesting, can you find out more? Are there related jobs or assistant-level jobs that might be more promising? Can you use the information to gain a better picture of possible career paths? Is the position something to aim for in the future, perhaps by building up more experience?

Take care when filling in application forms. These will be scrutinised carefully. Make sure you fill in the form neatly and, if necessary, draft the content beforehand using a word processor. This will allow you to work through drafts and use the spell-checking facility. Jobs have been lost because of spelling and grammar errors!

Prepare thoroughly. You are much more likely to succeed if you know that what you have to offer will be of interest to the employer you approach. This implies that you have researched the company/organisation and the job area thoroughly and have a well-targeted CV (**Ch 70**) and covering letter.

Pay attention to detail. It can be the small things that make a difference, such as a spelling or grammatical error, an untidy or incorrectly formatted application or inappropriate dress. Employers are often faced with equally qualified candidates and may have to find some arbitrary reason to select or reject them.

Think past the question. At interview you need to go beyond simply answering each question directly. Without taking too much time, you should try to elaborate your answers so that you provide information that helps to show that you have not only the qualifications and experience but also the qualities, skills and career-related enthusiasms the recruiting organisation is seeking.

APPENDIX: STUDENT RESOURCES

The following pages have blank versions of tables for your own personal use. These are all copyright free, so you can photocopy them and use them as many times as you require.

Table Z.1 A budget for student expenditure. Depending on the item, it may be more convenient to fill in a yearly, monthly or weekly total and add a figure to the other columns by multiplying or dividing appropriately.

Budget period:

Predicted income Source	Yearly total (£)	Monthly total (£)	Weekly total (£)
Parental allowance/family income			
Term-time employment			
Child benefit/tax credits/other state benefits			
From savings (interest or capital)			
Scholarships and grants			
Loan			
Loan			
Other			
Other			
Total predicted income			

Predicted expenditure Source	Yearly total (£)	Monthly total (£)	Weekly total (£)
Tuition fees (if not deferred)			
Accommodation (rent, mortgage)			
Food			
Leisure and entertainment			
Annual memberships and fees (e.g. sports clubs, societies)			
Books, other course equipment, services and supplies			
Home and contents insurance			
Utilities (e.g. electricity, gas)			
Phone (mobile and landline)			
TV licence and satellite/cable fees			
Motor/transport costs including insurance			
Clothing and laundry			
Childcare			
Health (including optician, dentist, prescriptions)			
Credit-card/loan repayments			
Miscellaneous (e.g. haircuts)			
Presents			
Holidays			
Allowance for contingencies (e.g. unexpected car bill)			
Other			
Total predicted expenditure			
Predicted income minus predicted expenditure			

Table Z.2 Quick personal glossary

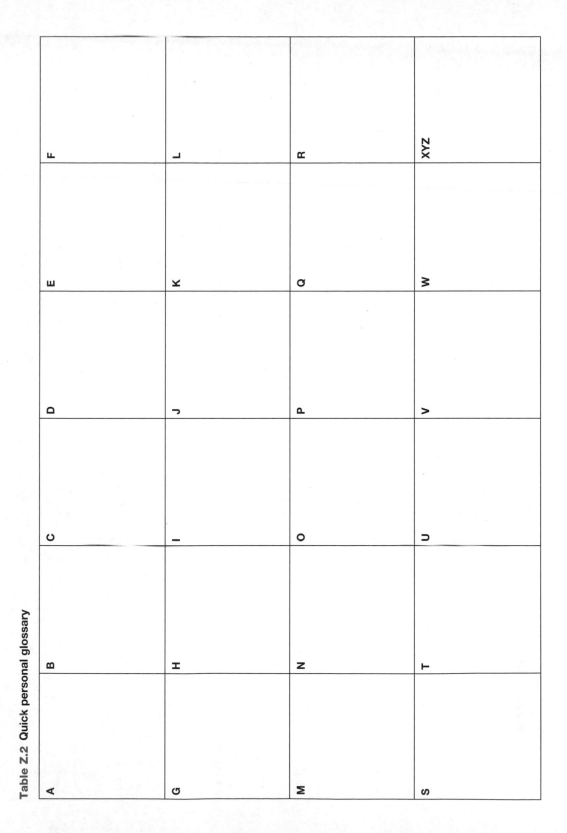

A	B	C	D	E	F

G	H	I	J	K	L

M	N	O	P	Q	R

S	T	U	V	W	XYZ

Table Z.3 Personal revision timetable

Week:

Key to subjects/topics:

	Monday	Tuesday	Wednesday	Thursday	Friday	Saturday	Sunday
Morning							
Lunch							
Afternoon							
Evening meal							
Evening							

REFERENCES AND FURTHER READING

Belbin Associates, 2006. *Belbin Team Roles* [online]. Available from:
www.belbin.com/belbin-team-roles.htm

Bloom, B. S., Englehart, M. D., Furst, E. J., Hill, W. H. and Krathwohl, D. R., 1956. *Taxonomy of Educational Objectives: Cognitive Domain*. New York: McKay.

Briggs Myers, I. and Myers, P. B., 1995. *Gifts Differing: Understanding Personality Types*. Palo Alto, California: Davis-Black Publishers.

Burchfield, R. W., *Fowler's Modern English Usage*. Oxford: Oxford University Press.

CILIP, 2012. Chartered Institute of Library and Information Professionals: Information literacy: definition. Available: http://www.cilip.org.uk/get-involved/advocacy/information-literacy/Pages/definition.aspx [Accessed 22 April 2012].

Chambers Dictionary, 2012. Edinburgh: Chambers Harrap Publishers Ltd.

Chicago Manual of Style, 16th edn, 2010. Chicago: University of Chicago Press.

Foley, M. and Hall, D., 2003. *Longman Advanced Learner's Grammar*. Harlow: Longman.

Graham, B., 2012. *The Role of Minerals and Vitamins in Mental Health*. Available at **www.nutritional-hoaling.com.au** [Accessed 22 April 2012].

Information Literacy Group, 2012. *Information literacy*. Available at: **www.informationliteracy.org.uk** [Accessed 22 April 2012].

Intellectual Property Office, 2012. Copyright. Available from: **www.ipo.gov.uk/types/copy.htm** [Accessed 29 February 2012].

Jones, A. M., Reed, R. and Weyers, J. D. B., 2012. *Practical Skills in Biology*, 5th edn. London: Pearson Education.

Krueger, R. A. and Casey, M. A. 2000. *Focus Groups: A Practical Guide for Applied Research*, 3rd edn. Thousand Oaks, California: Sage Publications.

Longman Dictionary of Contemporary English, 2009. Harlow: Longman.

Luft, J. and Ingham, H., 1955. 'The Johari window, a graphic model of interpersonal awareness', *Proceedings of the Western Training Laboratory in Group Development*. Los Angeles: University of California, LA.

Magistretti, P. J., Pellerin, L. and Martin, J.-L., 2000. 'Brain energy metabolism: an integrated cellular perspective', *Psychopharmacology: The Fourth Generation of Progress*. American college of Neuropsychopharmocology. Available at: **www.acnp.org/g4/gn401000064/ch064.html** [Accessed 12 April 2012].

Mckenna, P., 2009. *I Con Make You Sleep*. Bontam Press, Ealing.

McMillan, K. and Weyers, J., 2012. *Smarter Student Planner 2012/13*. Pearson UK: Harlow.

Morris, D., 2002. *Peoplewatching: The Desmond Morris Guide to Body Language*. Vintage: London.

Penguin A–Z Thesaurus, 2004. Harmondsworth: Penguin Books.

Ritter, R. M., 2005. *New Hart's Rules: The Handbook of Style for Writers and Editors*. Oxford: Oxford University Press.

Rutherford, D., 2011. *Vitamins: What Do They Do?* Available at: **www2.netdoctor.co.uk/health_advice/facts/vitamins_which.htm** [Accessed 16 March 2012].

Sana, L., 2002. *Textbook of Research Ethics: Theory and Practice.* New York: Kluwer Academic.

SCONUL, 2011. Society of College, National and University Libraries: The Seven Pillars of Information Literacy model. Available at: **http://ww.sconul.ac.uk/groups/information_literacy/sp/model.html** [Accessed 9 May 2009].

Shamoo, A. E. and Resnik, D. B., 2003. *Responsible Conduct of Research*. Oxford: Oxford University Press.

Trask, R. L., 2004. *Penguin Guide to Punctuation*. London: Penguin Books.

University of Dundee, 2006. *Code of Practice on Plagiarism and Academic Dishonesty* [online]. Available from: **www.dundee.ac.uk/academic/plagiarism.htm** [Accessed 31 March 2012].